A Novel Approach to Politics

Introducing Political Science through
Books, Movies, and Popular Culture

Douglas A. Van Belle
Victoria University of Wellington

Kenneth M. Mash
East Stroudsburg University

CQ PRESS

A Division of Congressional Quarterly Inc.
Washington, D.C.

CQ Press
1255 22nd Street, NW, Suite 400
Washington, DC 20037

Phone: 202-729-1900; toll-free, 1-866-4CQ-PRESS (1-866-427-7737)

Web: www.cqpress.com

Cover design: Matthew Simmons
Interior design and composition: Auburn Associates

Image Credits:
AllBlacks.com: 308
AP Images: 18 (background), 47, 70, 119, 169 (left and right), 174 (upper left), 195 (right), 264, 275
Columbia Pictures/PhotoFest: 143
Comedy Central/PhotoFest: 328
The Everett Collection: 93, 221, 249
Getty Images: 324
The Granger Collection, New York: 18 (inset images left to right)
Landov: 130
Library of Congress: 115, 195 (left)
Lucas Film/Twentieth Century Fox/The Kobal Collection: 1
Reuters: 174 (background and upper right)

⊚ The paper used in this publication exceeds the requirements of the American National Standard for Information Sciences—Permanence of Paper for Printed Library Materials, ANSI Z39.48-1992.

Printed and bound in the United States of America

10   09   08   07   06   1   2   3   4   5

Library of Congress Cataloging-in-Publication Data

Van Belle, Douglas A.
    A novel approach to politics : introducing political science through media and popular culture / Douglas A. Van Belle, Kenneth Mash.
        p. cm.
    ISBN-13: 978-1-56802-829-3 (alk. paper)
    ISBN-10: 1-56802-829-6 (alk. paper)
    1. Political science. 2. Popular culture—United States. 3. Politics and culture—United States. 4. Mass media—Political aspects—United States.   I. Mash, Kenneth M. (Kenneth Mitchell) II. Title.
JA66.V28 2007
320—dc22

                                                                    2006029254

Dedication

Ken would like to dedicate the book to his parents, Gary and Sandra Mash; thanks for all the fish.

Doug was going to dedicate the book to Ken's parents, but now that Ken has gone and already done that even though Doug told Ken whom he wanted to dedicate the book to a long time ago, Doug is going to have to dedicate the book to his own parents, Arch E. and Marilyn Van Belle. Doug is also going to dedicate it to his wife, Wendy Van Belle; thanks for not making me eat meatloaf very often.

Ken knows better than to not mention Christine now that Doug has gone and dedicated the book to Wendy, so he sees the wife dedication—Thanks, Christine Mash—and raises with the kids—Thanks, Peter, Mary, Katherine, and David.

Doug calls—Thank you, Tabitha, Jensen, and Samantha.

Ken would like to point out that that is only three, I raised with four.

Doug would like to remind his esteemed colleague and coauthor that his girls are free-range children, and that should count for extra.

Ken is pretty certain that free-range is a synonym for feral and should probably count for less.

Doug notes that that was kind of mean and that if Ken keeps it up, he is in danger of getting one of last year's after-Christmas-clearance Christmas cards this year.

Ken would like to calmly and soothingly suggest that Doug not do anything rash that he might regret later. After five years of working on this book, it is kind of silly to fight over the very last thing we have to write. There must be some dedication that we can both agree on. How about a generic, "To family and friends"?

Doug thinks that that is kind of a cop-out. Dedications are supposed to actually be to someone. How about, "To Penn and Teller"?

Ken has a better idea.

Dedicated to the Memory of

Jon Stewart

1962–2086

AUTHOR BIOS

DOUGLAS A. VAN BELLE

Sent to Earth shortly before Krypton exploded, Doug was raised by gorillas in Africa and then bitten by a radioactive spider while on a high school field trip. None of that helped much at all. He misspent his youth—and a bit more—trying to find a violent competitive sport that did not cause him serious harm, but the four times he broke his nose suggest that he is slow to learn. Somewhere in there, there were a bunch of degrees and some other learnin' stuff. He was awarded a full scholarship in chemical engineering, dropped out after the first year, went through seven other majors, failed a creative writing elective, took a semester off to work in the Alaskan commercial fishing industry, and somehow still managed to graduate on time. He is now a political science professor who writes science fiction and teaches in the media studies program at Victoria University of Wellington. He is the former president of both the Foreign Policy Analysis and International Communication Research sections of the International Studies Association, as well as the editor in chief of *Foreign Policy Analysis*. He has written extensively on theories of political decision making and the role of news media in international relations.

KENNETH M. MASH

Spurred on by the blatant discrimination inherent in the statement "Trix are for Kids," at age four Ken attempted to file a class-action lawsuit on behalf of the rabbit and other animals similarly situated. After three errors in one inning squashed his dreams of playing for the Mets, his overactive justice complex led him to pursue a career as a lawyer and politician. While earning his BA in political science he discovered what these jobs are really like. Thus, Ken's next degree was in mixology. Eighteen months later, his fiancée informed him that she was leaving town to do graduate work and that she would go either with him or without him. A couple of degrees later, he is currently a political science professor at East Stroudsburg University in Pennsylvania, where he is co-director of the honors program and the pre-law adviser. He has delivered numerous papers and talks on American politics, constitutional law, and civil liberties, and he is very active in the faculty association. He currently resides in Nanticoke, Pennsylvania, with his wife and four children, where he is now content in knowing that his parents were mistaken when, as a child, they told him that he was wasting his time watching TV and movies.

A Novel Approach to Politics

CONTENTS

A Novel Approach to Politics

PREFACE

This is not your grandparents' textbook. The fact that we use novels, films, television, and pop culture to introduce students to the study of politics might make that point seem obvious, but our use of fiction may well be the smallest of the differences between *A Novel Approach to Politics* and the other introduction to politics textbooks out there. When it came to writing this book we threw out the rules. Actually, with bratwursts in hand, we stood at the altar of Weber, the god of backyard barbeques, and ritually sacrificed the "suggested" content guidelines from the executive editorial committee of a big publishing house. We understood exactly why a collection of marketing managers, sales executives, and other risk-averse management types would demand that a textbook mimic the form and contents of all their competitors, but the last thing that political science needed was yet another mind-numbing, dreary slog—*not that there's anything wrong with that*—through what should be a dynamic, engaging, and challenging subject. To the credit of the folks at CQ Press, they understood exactly why we refused to write that textbook. They suggested we start from scratch, and they only objected a little bit when we took that as license to go far, far beyond just starting from scratch.

We could call this a rethinking or reconceptualization of the introduction to politics textbook, but in the same way that Tim Burton's radical rethinking of the *Planet of the Apes* led to a movie that is largely the same as the original, no matter how radical our rethinking, if we had started from the idea of an introduction to politics textbook, the end product would have been far too much like all those other texts that just do not work in the classroom. Instead of rethinking the textbook, we decided to examine the variety of ways that the people already using novels in the classroom had rethought teaching the subject and then write the textbook that was needed for that revised approach to the course. The result is a text that can be used just like a regular textbook. It has all of the necessary stuff. In fact, because our approach makes it easier to get across some relatively complex theoretical ideas, in many ways there is more of the important stuff in here than you would usually find in an intro textbook. An instructor can add a couple of lectures to reinforce the topics and add a few examples each week, and the semester will just fly merrily by. We have tried it with this material, and it works quite well. However, *A Novel Approach* can also be used as a starting point for exploring any of the huge number of films and novels that delve into the complexities of society and politics.

In the course of talking to our colleagues about the ways they used fiction in the classroom, the suggestions for novels and films were thrown at us like American Dodgeball Association of America regulation dodgeballs.* When confronted with the

---

*While it is true that if you can dodge a wrench, you can dodge a ball, books are a bit tougher. They open up and flop around in the air and don't fly straight.

challenge of including all of those ideas in the text, we decided that the only logical course was not to use any of them. Every single person had a different set of "absolutely, so totally must have" novels and films, and rather than trying to squeeze them all in, we decided to create a textbook that provided all of the background and information that students needed as a starting point for thoughtfully contrasting the religious and feminist stories in *The Handmaid's Tale* or any one of the hundreds of other suggestions that were flung at us.

With the marvels of modern technology, our master list of books, movies, and TV shows—our Fiction Appendix—can be continuously updated and appended by instructors and students alike. We have created a wikipedia just for this text, along with a companion Web site, that will give students plenty of opportunity to review, study, quiz, and banter to their hearts' content. Check out www.cqpress.com/cs/novel and contribute your two cents' worth.

We decided to write a textbook that students could read with little or no guidance from lectures; it is a book that students can and will read quickly so that two, or even three, chapters can be assigned per week, leaving half the semester or more for instructors to show or discuss any of the myriad of novels, films, and television programs of their choosing. In short, what we tried to do is create a textbook that reduces or eliminates most of the substantial barriers to using fiction in the classroom. However, the text also stands alone, and it can be assigned to students with the expectation that they can draw upon their own experiences to provide fodder for enlightened classroom banter. Regardless of the instructor's approach, when students finish the book, they should be both accustomed to thinking about the politics and social dynamics to be found in fiction and have the conceptual and theoretical background to actually think a few approximately profound thoughts.

The result is a textbook that focuses on the "why" rather than the "what," a textbook that builds upward from the underlying theories and dynamics, a textbook that has five chapters that come before the starting point of most introduction to politics textbooks. The result is a textbook with a conversational, albeit occasionally irreverent, tone. The result should be students who can explain how the tragedy of the commons can be applied to Marx's conceptualization of the pool of labor. Arrow's Theorem, the dynamics of power in anarchic environments, the role of ideologies in practical politics, Downs's spatial representation of the electorate, social contracts, the mediated construction of political reality, core and periphery in world systems theory, the differences between political structures and institutions—students should have these, and a whole lot of other conceptual weapons, in their arsenal, ready for attacking the complexity of social and political statements being made in fiction and, by extension, the world around them. It took five years to write *A Novel Approach,* but the end result looks like it just might justify that effort and persistence.

ACKNOWLEDGMENTS

Lance Bennett deserves at least a portion of the blame/credit for *A Novel Approach to Politics*. His use of novels in an introduction to politics class gave us the idea and made it clear that such a class needed a structure unlike that of a traditional textbook. Professionally, we also have to thank/blame those who formally and informally reviewed parts of the book: Robert Alexander, Ohio Northern University; Marijke Breuning, Truman State University; Stephen Eric Bronner, Rutgers University; Tom Doleys, Kennesaw State University; Nathalie Frensley, University of Texas at Austin; Doris Grant-Wisdom, University of Maryland; Deborah Johnson-Ross, McDaniel College; Steven Majstorovic, University of Wisconsin, Eau Claire; John Orman, Fairfield University; John Rapp, Beloit College; Mort Sipress, University of Wisconsin, Eau Claire; Sylvia Sipress, University of Wisconsin, Eau Claire; and Kevin Yenerall, Clarion University.

A few key people at CQ Press deserve mention—Charisse Kiino in particular, for both spotting the value in our idea and for steering it past all of the obstacles and insanity inherent in the publication process. Thanks, too, to Lorna Notsch, the production editor, who, through photo research for *A Novel Approach,* fulfilled a lifelong dream of sorting through ten thousand pictures of NASCAR wrecks to find exactly the right picture of an airborne Ford. And we must not forget Steve Glorioso's fantastic interior design. The red curtains provided a really nice accent to the flecks of color in the tile—he also did something or other with the way the book is put together or something. And Matthew Simmons's brilliant cover, even if it was the second choice. We liked his first suggestion better, but what can you do if your editors have a hang-up over the EPA forcing us to seal the book in a Mylar biohazard bag?

We would like to thank the Faculty Development and Research Committee at East Stroudsburg University of Pennsylvania for its early support of the project. We also would like to thank our colleagues, past and present, for all of their assistance and encouragement. We would especially like to thank Paul Lippert for his insights about film and politics, particularly his perspective on *Mr. Smith Goes to Washington*.

However, the contributions of all of those very, very important people pale in comparison to the critical role played by the crazy Russian barista of the Starbucks near the corner of 24th and M Streets in Washington, DC. Without her heroic and determined commitment to keeping our beleaguered copy editor, Anna Socrates, hovering right at the edge of human tolerance for caffeine, this text still would be just a bunch of scribbles and notes on California Pizza Kitchen napkins.

No animals were harmed during the making of this book.

Introduction/Warning/ Parental Advisory

This Book Contains Politically Explicit Material

This is a dangerous book. Even after the valiant struggles of CQ Press's legions of brave editors—none of whom will ever be the same—this book far exceeds the acceptable levels of collateral damage for a textbook. Somewhere along the line, something in this book will upset you, at least a little. We blame politics. Because of the very nature of politics as a subject of study, we do not even have to try to upset you. Don't get us wrong, as part of teaching about politics we will occasionally try to annoy or provoke you. We will do whatever is necessary to force you to consider ideas that are contrary to what you believe or want to believe, if only so you can recognize some of your unnoticed beliefs, presumptions, and cognitive frameworks that provide the foundation for what you hold dear. This is necessary to understand the dynamics of politics, and if we do not infuriate you at least once with a topic or pointed comment, then we have probably failed to get you to really think about politics, to look beneath the surface of the politics you see around you. We will blame you, the student, if we fail to inflict some minor mental trauma—we are professors after all—but given our ability to annoy just about everyone else in the world, it will be truly disappointing if we cannot manage to get you riled up about something as controversial and as personal as politics.

Politics is personal. It limits, defines, or enables even the most intimate aspects of your life. You cannot escape politics and you cannot help but have preexisting ideas about politics that we must disturb in order to expose the underlying dynamics of the subject. Take the nice, safe, and completely uncontroversial topic of teenage sex as an example. Politics intrudes into just about every aspect of this most intimate of topics. In 1996, a seventeen-year-old girl was arrested in Idaho because she was both unmarried and pregnant. It seems that in an effort to reduce teen pregnancies, officials in Gem County decided to enforce an old and disregarded law forbidding sex outside of marriage and police officers were, literally, told to arrest young women who appeared to be pregnant but were not wearing wedding rings. While this deserves an honorable mention in one of the E! Channel's "bizarre but true" lists, the truly scary part of the incident was that the girl in question was actually convicted. She was found guilty of the alleged crime of fornication, fined ten dollars, and sentenced to three years of probation.

Most would probably agree that pregnant at seventeen is unwise, but if unwise was criminal then we would be obligated to arrest the entire cast, crew, and audience of *Jackass: The Movie*.[1] And regardless of how socially conservative or liberal you may be, you almost have to think that there has got to be a better way to curb teen pregnancy than arresting girls for becoming pregnant. However, it is in that thought that we find the key to understanding why and how any political example we might use or any political subject we might discuss will find a way to upset someone. If you look through the letters to the editor related to this incident, it is clear that many people would be offended by our suggestion that everyone would believe there had to be a better policy than giving unwed mothers a criminal record to help them through the difficulties of single parenthood. In response to the letters criticizing the arrest and conviction of the girl, many people wrote scathing letters that savaged the critics and defended the policy as long overdue and a perfect way to change the thinking of the criminally promiscuous teens of the day.

If this political act of criminalizing pregnancy offends you, you might well suggest an alternative, such as education and contraception. Do realize, however, that what a social liberal might consider to be a far less offensive policy is going to be deeply offensive to others. For many religious conservatives, any policy regarding public support for a birth-control method other than abstinence is morally reprehensible. When it comes to a public policy regarding teen pregnancy and teen sexuality—forgive us for assuming they kind of go together—all options, including the option of having no policy on the subject, is going to offend or upset someone.

Perhaps sexuality, as a political subject, does not bother you. How about fairness and justice? After all, even if you are not a feminist, it is hard to deny that arresting just the girl is grossly unfair. We do not claim to be biologists but we are pretty sure there was an alleged father of the alleged child and there is no mention of a guy getting prosecuted. That is unquestionably unfair.

Or is it?

It turns out that the prosecution of the girl and not the boy for fornication is not the biggest gender inequity in the politics and resulting laws that meddle in the sex lives of Idaho's alleged population, and there was a very good reason the guy was not prosecuted. If convicted of fathering the child, the boy that we presume was involved would have faced a sentence of life in prison. Yes, life in prison. In the alleged state of Idaho, sexual intercourse with a woman under the age of eighteen is rape, period, full stop, end of sentence. There are no exceptions.[i] It does not matter how old the boy was or even if he was younger than the girl. The reverse, however, is not true. While there are Idaho statutes that a girl could be charged with for having sex with an underage boy, the punishments for women do not include anything close to a sentence of life in a maximum-security prison. And do remember that the fine people of Idaho are extremely serious about the "life" part of the life sentence. Clearly that is a disparity in the ways that boys

---

[i] It is not clear how that exceptionless law for statutory rape fits with the fact that you can marry at the age of sixteen in Idaho, or even younger if both sets of parents approve.

and girls are treated in Idaho and if gender equity, or even just plain old fairness, is important to you, that should upset you.

Have we raised any hackles yet?

The political meddling in your sex life goes well beyond this example. In Idaho, no matter how old the two parties are, any sex outside of marriage is defined as fornication and is punishable by a fine of up to $300 and six months in jail. If it is an extra-marital affair, it is even worse because adultery is punishable by a fine of up to $1,000 and three years in prison. We suspect these laws are the primary reason why no soap operas are set in Boise.

The intrusion of politics into your sex life is not limited to Idaho. In Indiana mustaches are illegal if you have a "tendency to habitually kiss other humans." Note that the statute specifies humans. Hmmm? However, in Minnesota, it is illegal for any man to have sexual intercourse with a live fish. It is a little more complex in Utah, where sex with an animal is illegal, *UNLESS* you are doing it for profit. Sex while standing in a walk-in meat freezer is specifically banned in New Castle, Wyoming, and in Washington, DC, anything other than the missionary position is still illegal. The penalty for masturbation in Indonesia is decapitation. Virgins are forbidden to marry in Guam, but that is balanced out by the fact that in Washington State it is illegal to have sex with a virgin, period, full stop, end of sentence, no exception even for a wedding night.

While these may seem to be amusingly misguided and forgotten laws that are left over from an ancient age, on September 17, 1998, police arrested two men for violating Texas sodomy laws. Entering the men's apartment and bursting into their bedroom in response to a prank burglary call, the police arrested the men. In 2003, when the U.S. Supreme Court struck down the Texas sodomy laws in *Lawrence v. Texas,* it made it extremely difficult for states to convict someone for breaking any of the myriad of U.S. state laws forbidding particular sexual acts between consenting adults. However, most of these laws are still on the books, and there is nothing to stop a future set of Supreme Court justices from deciding differently on a future case.

You might argue that government has no place interfering in what consenting adults do in the privacy of their bedroom. However, that socially liberal position is clearly not universal. Chances are there is a fellow student in your course who would argue that government must act to preserve what he or she considers to be the moral fabric of society. This kind of socially conservative perspective is likely to include the belief that it is necessary to outlaw anything related to immoral sexual acts, which can include school nurses distributing condoms, sex education, homosexuality, and pornography. These are all subjects tied to public policy issues involving politics in this most intimate aspect of young people's lives. All of these topics are controversial and pretty much any position that might be taken on any of these subjects or issues related to them is guaranteed to upset someone.

In this text we do not shy away from issues because they might provoke; we cannot. We try to keep it casual and lighthearted. We also try to spread it around and poke fun at just about everyone, especially if they are French or, to a lesser degree, Belgian. However, we make no apologies if a topic or a sarcastic comment hits a nerve or two—it should. Going back to where we started, politics is deeply personal. To make it easier to openly engage these very personal topics, we use a bit of sarcasm and some admittedly questionable humor, but that does not alter the fact that many of the topics and examples, even the fictional ones, are sensitive and likely to upset someone. The movie *A Clockwork Orange*[2] will probably offend your sensibilities, but just because it might offend we cannot hesitate to suggest it as an example of the complex interplay between the rights of criminals versus the rights of victims versus the role government needs to play in protecting society.[ii]

HOW TO READ THIS BOOK

Our unconventional style should not get in the way of our serious effort to delve into the complex concepts and theories that underlie politics as a subject of study. Just because an example is from the *Fairly OddParents*[3] or a beer commercial does not make the underlying point about politics any less relevant than if it were tied to an example we might pull from a discussion of comparative political institutions. It is just more fun. In fact, lightening it up a bit with a bit of sarcasm and using fiction and pop culture to help give you a different perspective on the subject enable us to include more of the good stuff. It makes it easier to get past what you think you already know, or the things you did not realize were hiding something about politics, and delve into the underlying dynamics.

There are a lot of ways to write a textbook on politics, and when you read this text you should keep in mind that when we designed it, we wanted to create a book that focused on the how and why of politics, rather than just the what. We also made a conscious decision to repeatedly target Jon Stewart with shamelessly unprovoked assaults of extreme flattery in hopes that in a moment of impaired judgment he might invite us to appear on the *Daily Show,* but you should pretend not to notice that and instead focus on our concerted effort to coax/cajole/coerce you into engaging the dynamics that underlie the politics that pervades every aspect of your lives.

As wizened and extremely brilliant professors, one of the things that strikes us about the stone tablets and papyrus scrolls that we used as introduction to politics texts way back in college is how many of the specifics in those old textbooks, how many of the details and facts we remembered being tested on, are no longer relevant. There were entire chapters on Politburo politics. The odds are pretty good that most students

---

[ii]Interestingly enough, when we cut out the discussion on balancing the rights of criminals with the needs of society we also ended up cutting this one from the chapter on law and politics.

reading this text have no idea what that could possibly refer to. That is the nature of the subject, and it is an important part of why new editions of textbooks are constantly being churned out. It also exposes the problem of focusing on the "what" of politics. For both the teacher and the student, it is horribly tempting to focus on the what. Different types of parliaments, different categories of executive, different legal foundations, the history of different ideologies, different systems for serving this function or that function—it is easy to write exams that test that sort of knowledge and it is easy for students to study categories and lists of things. The problem is that the world changes, and the what of politics changes.

In contrast, the parts of those old textbooks that delved into the hows or whys of politics still seem to be relevant. As an obvious example, our discussion of why some democratic governments have two parties and why some have dozens is not that different from the one that we were taught. The specific examples from our old textbooks are no longer all that relevant, but the explanation is as strong as ever. The basic theory is about a half-century old. Yet it has lost none of its value. Thus, throughout, we focus on hows and whys. All of the examples we use—whether they are real-world examples or fictional—are chosen to get at the underlying logic of politics. As we explain in the first chapter, fictional examples are excellent for this purpose. For the student, our pursuit of this goal should provide a hint of how to engage this text. You know, help us out a bit, and look for the reason, cause, process, or dynamic we are trying to get you to understand.

Actually, we expect a great deal from you when you are reading this textbook. We expect you to explore the material. We expect you to think about the examples. We expect you to look for the dynamics of politics in fiction. We expect you to consider the arguments of people who disagree with you. We expect you to realize that an introduction to political science is just that, an introduction, a starting place, and it is neither definitive nor complete. The one thing we most sincerely hope to provoke with this text is an interest in knowing more about politics.

---

[1] *Jackass: The Movie,* directed by Jeff Tremaine (Paramount Pictures, 2002).

[2] *A Clockwork Orange,* directed by Stanley Kubrick (Warner Brothers, 1971).

[3] *Fairly OddParents,* created by Butch Hartman (Nickelodeon, 2001).

CHAPTER 1

Introducing the Ancient Debate
The Ideal versus the Real

Long, long ago, in a movie theater that used to stand not too horribly far from your favorite multiplex, *Star Wars* introduced two very likable, but also very different heroes.[1] Young, energetic, and ambitious, Luke Skywalker is the idealist who wants to rescue the princess because it is the noble thing to do.* Luke embraces the Force, and longs to join the rebellion to fight for all that is good in the galaxy. The film depicts Luke in stark contrast to the oddly asthmatic villain, Darth Vader, who is the embodiment of the dark side of the Force. Darth is driven by the primal emotions of hate, fear, and a lust for power that have thrown the galaxy into the grip of an evil empire. Luke is told that he is gifted enough to become a Jedi Knight, a guardian of peace and justice in a galaxy dominated by this darker power, and so the Force and the quest to transform himself into a Jedi become the focus of Luke's entire existence. He is willing to sacrifice, even to die for the ideals this cause represents.

While also a heroic figure, Han Solo is a very different character. A gritty smuggler and a worldly realist, he deals with the universe as it is rather than dreaming of how it could be. He wants nothing to do with the Force, which he derides as naïve, preferring to focus on his own life and his own concerns, which revolve around the fact that he is in debt beyond hope of repayment and a scant step or two ahead of bounty hunters. Han is not at all interested in rescuing the princess until Luke points out that she is rich and will reward him well. Han has learned to deal with the harsh realities of a universe full of ruthless characters whose only motivations are money and their own self-interest. From his perspective, the most important thing is survival, and survival is best accomplished by looking after oneself and one's closest friends.

---

* Well, Luke also appears to be enamored with her, which is kind of cute until we find out she's his sister.

The contrast between realists and idealists is a popular fictional theme. How often does a good story turn on the relentless enthusiasm of the young idealist who reignites the drive of the jaded realist who has given up hope? How many movies feature a tough, salty older realist who comes to the rescue of a younger, more naïve idealist? Brian De Palma's *The Untouchables* provides a perfect example of this theme at work.[2] Kevin Costner plays Eliot Ness, the idealistic federal agent whose mission it is to bring the notorious Al Capone to justice. Ness believes that a law enforcement official should play by the rules—regardless of how bad the criminals may be, the police should not break any laws in the process of bringing them to justice. Along the way, Ness meets up with Sean Connery's character, a veteran police officer and a man of experience who teaches him that if he wants to get Al Capone he will have to play by a different set of rules, those created by the reality of the streets: "He pulls a knife, you pull a gun. He sends one of yours to the hospital, you send one of his to the morgue. That's the Chicago way. And that's how you get Capone."

In *Star Wars,* it is the idealist who brings out the best in the realist, as Han Solo ultimately embraces the rebellion and pursues the hope of a better galaxy instead of the potential monetary reward. In *The Untouchables,* it is the realist who gives the idealist what he needs to succeed, as the Ness character ultimately throws a criminal off of a rooftop on the way to bringing down Capone. Regardless of the specifics in the particular fictional scenario, the struggle between the ideal and the real is a theme that has always been attractive, dramatic, and dynamic. Shakespeare's works are filled with examples of the same motif. In *Julius Caesar,* the idealistic Brutus, who joins in the plot to assassinate his friend, Caesar, for the noble goal of preserving the republic, is contrasted with other characters such as Cassius, who participate in order to better their own personal positions. The idealism of Romeo and Juliet stands in sharp contrast to the "real-world" rivalry between the Capulets and the Montagues.

We can all identify with these idealists and realists—depending on the specific work, every one of us can probably even identify a little bit with both. This ambivalence is part of what makes the fictional contrast so engaging. The give-and-take between Luke and Han reflects a struggle within ourselves, between what we would like to do (**idealism**) and what we must do or what is possible (**realism**). The Luke Skywalker within us tends to be more hopeful, driving us to look at the world and envision a better place, to look at human beings and see creatures who may be capable of so much more than they have accomplished so far. The Han Solo in us is the realist who looks at the way human beings actually behave rather than focusing on their potential for doing good. This inner pragmatist argues that we must work with the unseemly, self-interested side of life in the here and now to make the best out of an inherently bad situation. Thus, like Eliot Ness, each of us constantly fights an internal battle between realism and idealism.

The theme of ideals clashing with reality makes fiction a useful tool for exploring the fundamentals of politics. In novels and films, it is both a common motive that drives the heroic characters and a frequent theme in the settings and contexts of interaction, the plots, and the story lines. In politics, the tension between the real and the ideal is prominent both in theory and in practice. Virtually all who engage in politics must balance the dreams of what they would like to accomplish if they could against the limitations imposed upon them by the real world. For example, a legislator with an idea for a law may have to change her or his concept in order to gain the support of other lawmakers. A dictator may not be able to achieve all that he or she wants because of concern about a possible revolt. A peace negotiator cannot go into talks without understanding that there will need to be some compromise and that some of those compromises—such as agreeing to stop trying to depose a hated leader—may be quite distasteful.

Perhaps the greatest articulation of the contrast between realism and idealism is in the work of the ancient Greek philosopher Plato.* In the *Republic*, a centerpiece of political theory, the characters of Thrasymachus and Socrates represent the two sides engaged in a discussion about the purpose of politics. Thrasymachus is a **sophist**: one who teaches promising young men the skills, such as rhetoric, that they need in order to be personally successful in public life but who does not focus on ethics or the good of the society. For Thrasymachus and his fellow sophists, success means attaining tangible wealth and power; they are realists. Socrates represents the idealist position: he believes that there is more to politics than merely skill at reaching goals or attaining rewards. Socrates believes that the true leader must have genuine knowledge about ethics and about how to govern in the best interest of the entire community. In a famous part of the *Republic*, Socrates argues that a good shoemaker's interest lies not in making money, but in making the best possible shoes; an able ship's captain is concerned not with profit, but with the crew; an excellent doctor is concerned with the health of patients, not with money. Similarly, a skilled governor's interests should be in the happiness of the governed, not in the personal power or fortune of the leader. The purpose of the state, the purpose of politics, according to Socrates, should be to ensure the happiness of the citizenry. Thrasymachus responds by asking Socrates about the role of the shepherd: the shepherd, he says, looks after the sheep and does everything possible to keep them healthy, but he does so in order to turn them into nice, tasty lamb chops that people will pay good money for. And so it is with the politician and the state.[3]

Clearly, Thrasymachus has a point. If we look at how the world operates, we must realize that there are people who view others only as sheep to be fattened up in order to turn a profit at the slaughterhouse. If we ignore the realities of this world, there is a good chance that some calculating tyrant or even just some self-interested politician will take advantage of us. However, Socrates also has a point. If all people were only

---

*Plato is not that brightly colored and funny-smelling modeling clay that your pediatrician was constantly digging out of your ears. Plato was a philosopher, which appears to be a person who has found a way to make a living by admitting that he listens to imaginary people talking to each other. It's a good gig if you can get it.

> **Politics is all about the ongoing struggle between the dreamer and the pragmatist, the pursuit of tomorrow's ideals within the context of today's reality.**

interested in dealing with the existing reality, then no one would try to make the world a better place. Yet people often do make efforts, both large and small, in pursuit of noble goals and in spite of profit or personal benefit. What kind of world would it be if nobody had ever questioned the practice of slavery, if no one had ever fought for women's suffrage, if no one had ever demanded religious freedom, if no one had ever dreamt of combining malted barley, hops, water, and yeast? If no one had ever imagined a better world and pursued it despite the realities of the day, where would we be?

In many ways, politics is all about the ongoing struggle between the dreamer and the pragmatist, the pursuit of tomorrow's ideals within the context of today's reality. Keeping in mind the contrast between the ideal and the real also makes it easier to write a textbook that discusses the many complicated aspects of political concepts and theories. We can discuss the simplified and idealized version of a concept while recognizing that reality demands compromises and imposes limitations on the application of that ideal or between competing ideals. For example, we can envision an idealized version of democracy where the majority always rules and everybody votes on everything, but we must also acknowledge that reality demands limits on what majorities can do to minorities. Reality puts limits on the number of issues that the entire population is informed enough to cast a vote on. At the very least, a functioning democracy must prevent a majority from undermining the future of democratic competition. If it is to remain a democracy, the majority cannot vote to limit speech or persecute peaceful political critics and opponents.

Considering politics in terms of a balance between ideals and reality also serves as a good transition to a discussion of some of the challenges to learning the fundamentals of politics. While we note and explore many of these challenges as we examine different subjects, from the very start of our effort, you, the reader, must realize that one of the very real problems inherent in introducing you to the study of politics is, quite frankly, you.*

YOUR OWN PRIVATE IDAHO

While you may not exactly be living in your own private Idaho—and chances are you are too young even to remember the B-52's song—the simple fact is that you bring with you a distinctive past, a unique set of experiences, beliefs, pains, hopes, and fears that shape your perceptions and expectations about what goes on in the world. People make sense of new things and make judgments about their political preferences by referring to what they already know. Thus, none of us approaches the study of politics as a blank slate. We all have our own preferences. Even if you do not realize it, you have been immersed in politics throughout your life. In fact, politics is the very definition of your never-opened SAT/ACT preparation guide's word of the day, *ubiquitous*. Politics is absolutely everywhere.

---

*Please note that this represents a legally binding assignment of responsibility for your D− on the first exam.

Think about all the efforts that we make to influence and persuade each other at school, work, home, and practically anywhere else we have to deal with one another. Complicating matters further, even though we are constantly aware of and affected by the political behavior around us, our day-to-day involvement in politics does not help us to understand many of the very basic things about politics, such as why people engage in political behavior. The context of a situation, past history, and culture can cloud our attempts to understand what exactly drives people to act politically. People respond to this muddy picture by organizing and simplifying their understanding of politics, using their own **conceptual frameworks**, which are drawn from the personal experiences, preferences, and expectations that we all use to make sense of the world (see "Framing: Tastes Like Chicken").

What we do in our effort to come to grips with everyday politics, we also do when interpreting politics on other levels. For example, a Democrat and a Republican watching the same presidential debate will notice different details about the questions asked and how the candidates respond. Each person uses a unique conceptual framework to organize details into a coherent, simple conclusion. As a result, although they watched the same event, different people are quite likely to come to drastically different understandings of what happened. Furthermore, neither the Democrat nor the Republican is going to agree with the conclusions drawn by a radical environmentalist, a white supremacist, a gangster rapper, or that guy who lives at the bus station. Our backgrounds and personalities determine our understandings of politics. As a result, every example we offer in this book and every political dynamic we discuss here will mean something different to every reader.

We have developed a strategy for working with this diversity of cognitive frameworks. As noted later, this is part of the reason we have built this text around fiction. Usually it is easier to separate your personal viewpoint from the characters, plots, and settings of books and films than it is to remain objective about real events. Even when this separation is not entirely possible, fiction allows you to recognize how your conceptual framework colors your appreciation of the work. Hopefully, this strategy will allow us to provide examples that we can all understand similarly, even if we do, ultimately, reach different conclusions. However, as professors always do, we are going to ask you to do most of the work.* As we move through subjects, we will often ask you to recognize, explore, and challenge your own perspectives and opinions and to be open to at least understanding other perspectives that you may have not considered or may oppose. It should come as no surprise that many aspects of politics are subjective, prompting normative questions about what should be or how things should work. While you may consider some of the answers to be disturbing, inhumane, or horrific, there will be those who disagree with your assertion that it would violate the Geneva Conventions to make anyone live in your mother's

---

*Again, legally binding.

FRAMING: TASTES LIKE CHICKEN

A wedding in Thibodaux (Tib-eh-dough, not Thigh-bo-dux), Louisiana, is an interesting event. In addition to a bridal march that is played on an accordion and wedding vows that are neither French nor English but some mysterious consonant-deficient language in between, there is also bound to be a reception buffet that features deep-fried alligator on a stick. It is kind of like a Cajun shish kebab, and if you are brave, or if you just eat one before you find out what it is, you will discover that it tastes pretty good. However, you will also run into a big problem if asked to describe that taste to someone less adventurous. How exactly do you describe the taste of fried alligator? How do you explain to someone how something else tastes? Well, you try to find a shared cognitive referent—some culinary experience that you both have had—and you use that shared experience to build a common understanding of how deep-fried 'gator-on-a-stick tastes.

It tastes like chicken.

Actually, it does not taste much like chicken at all. It has the texture of geoduck (a giant clam from the Seattle area), some of the flavor of rattlesnake, and the greasy patina of walrus. However, if you are dealing with the culinarily timid, chicken may be the only shared mental framework you can use to try to describe the taste, so you blather, "It tastes like chicken, but it's chewy and a little bit greasy, with a hint of fish taste . . . and it doesn't taste like chicken at all." That explanation of the flavor of 'gator-on-a-stick is wholly inadequate, but it is the best you are going to manage, and if you are trying to describe the taste to a vegetarian, you may as well not even bother.

The same difficulty arises in politics. Each political event may be unique, but to describe it to someone, you must work with shared referents and shared understandings. You inevitably offer an analogy to suggest how it is like something else. The problem with using analogies in politics, however, is that they come with a great deal of baggage. An analogy that invokes a historical event includes a whole host of mental frameworks beyond the simple description of the event.

The day after Iraq invaded Kuwait, for instance, the first President Bush invoked the Hitler analogy to describe Saddam Hussein, instantly conveying the idea of a ruthless leader bent on military conquest and world domination. Unfortunately, the Hitler analogy also defined Saddam as someone who could not be negotiated with—who had to be conquered and destroyed. Thus, by introducing that specific comparison and all of the cognitive frameworks that go with it, Bush effectively defined away a whole host of policy options that might have made it possible to avoid hundreds of thousands of war deaths. Whether the outcome would have been any different is an open question: Saddam may indeed have been enough like Hitler that the only real way to deal with him was by military force. But the point here is that the Hitler analogy was used and the policy options effectively defined before there was any chance to explore any of the non-Hitler options. The choice of that mental framework was, quite literally, a matter of life and death.

idea of a perfect world. As noted in the preface,* if you do not become annoyed or downright angry at some point along the way, you are missing part of the introduction to politics. Politics is a highly personal subject.

FICTION AS A TOOL FOR EXPLORING POLITICS

At first it may seem odd that we chose fiction as a means to introduce you to politics. But fiction, whether it is presented on film, in a novel, or even on Saturday morning chil-

---

*The preface is that part at the beginning of the book that you did not bother to read because you did not think it counted as a proper chapter or because it wasn't assigned.

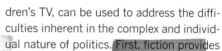

> **Fiction provides a window into an environment where our conceptual frameworks more easily give way to the author's creativity.**

dren's TV, can be used to address the difficulties inherent in the complex and individual nature of politics. First, fiction provides a window into an environment where our conceptual frameworks more easily give way to the author's creativity. By viewing events through the eyes of fictional characters, we find it easier to set aside our own personal preferences, ideologies, and experiences while, at the same time, still appreciating the adventures that the characters encounter. Thus, we can all share the characters' experiences and perspectives on a conflict, a struggle, or some other aspect of politics, and we can share that experience in a reasonably similar manner. Fiction, therefore, gives us an opportunity to transcend the individual, personal nature of politics.

Second, by living through the characters in novels, we can get a taste for political situations that we, as individuals, might never be able to experience in the real world. For example, George Orwell's novel, *Nineteen Eighty-Four*, shows us how government can be used to control every aspect of people's personal lives.[4] The narrative provides numerous extreme and obvious examples of how this might work, such as the government's placement of cameras in private homes and the use of children to spy on their parents. Most of us have never experienced such oppressive government, but through the eyes of the protagonist, we can see how it works and we get a feel for what it might be like to live in such horrible conditions. For those of us who would rather not have the government torture us by stuffing our heads into cages full of rats, there is the additional bonus that we can get a taste of such an experience without having to actually live it.

A third aspect of fiction that makes it valuable for learning about politics is that it is fiction—the characters and institutions are not subject to practical limitations. Authors and directors often exaggerate aspects of human interaction that in real life might remain hidden. They may do this for dramatic purposes, but these exaggerated social dynamics are often the very idea, influence, technique, or principle that we want you to recognize. Many of the books and films mentioned in this text are set in a speculative context, where the author extends some aspect of politics, government, or society out to its logical extreme. For example, to show the dangers of powerful governments, *Nineteen Eighty-Four* presents us with a government that is so extremely powerful and invasive as to be almost unimaginable. Fictional politicians, such as the chancellor in the *Star Wars* prequels, can be portrayed as far more calculating than any human being could possibly be in real life. These exaggerated contexts and personalities serve as magnifying glasses to highlight the forces that limit the characters' choices and motivate actions. It is much easier to recognize these forces in a speculative fictional context than in real life, which is comparatively complex, murky, and beige.

The characters and plotlines of fiction can also help us to develop insights into human motivation that lectures and textbooks could never hope to match. This is crucial for the study of politics because, unlike courses you may have taken in biology, mathematics, anatomy,* or some other straightforward subject that lends itself to multiple choice exams, politics requires an intuitive sense for how people interact. Thus, a fourth reason for using fiction as a window into politics is that it is an engaging and interesting way to help students develop that feel for the subject. Once you truly understand politics, you can read a newspaper story or watch a television news account and come away with a much richer understanding of what is going on because you have learned to read between the lines, to sense the reasons for action that might not be mentioned. You have to get used to uncovering the subtle aspects of politics in society—and it takes work. You must think critically. You must learn to be just as aware of the unspoken dimensions of how people, governments, and organizations behave as you are of what they say about themselves or what others say about them. It is the subtle details in William Golding's novel, *Lord of the Flies*—such as the shipwrecked boys' experiences of anarchy (a society without any hierarchy)—that prompt us to develop an intuitive feel for how that environment influences and drives the collective pursuit of security.[5] In the real world where you will almost certainly never have to deal with true anarchy, the fictional story may offer the only way for you to develop a feel for what the experience would be like. An instructor can explain anarchy and lecture about it until blue in the face, but until you investigate the issues and encounter the politics in a fictional yet realistic context, it will be difficult if not impossible to imagine the implications of the situation.

Last, the use of fiction can support and in some cases instigate an active approach to learning. In this text, we introduce a concept or dynamic of politics, then mention some† of the examples available from novels, films, and television. Some of it is literature, but we are quite happy to stoop to pulp fiction, commercials, or even children's cartoons to illustrate the point. Part of the goal is to entice you with fiction so that you personally engage the subject and resolve to explore politics on your own, thereby learning even more than you would otherwise. We believe that if you actively explore the subject, you can discover more about politics than a professor can ever teach. The more you work at discovering insights and examples in the books and films you enjoy, the more you are likely to learn about the study of politics.

Hopefully, the use of novels and films as a reference point will help you to appreciate not only how politics works but also what a dynamic and interesting subject it can be. How can you not? Even the definition of politics—or, rather, the lack thereof—is interesting.

WHAT IS POLITICS?

Writing a concurring opinion in a 1964 case involving pornography, U.S. Supreme Court justice Potter Stewart admitted his difficulty in defining specifically what types of adult films constitute pornography. Despite his trouble, he concluded, "I know it when I see

---

*We mean actual college anatomy courses, not playing doctor behind the bleachers.

†But obviously not all—we do not admit to watching that much cable.

it." [6] Students in introductory political science classes face the same dilemma. No, you do not have to define pornography, but like the justices watching dirty movies in the basement of the Supreme Court, you are unlikely to be able to offer a clear definition of the similarly indistinct concept called politics. However, more often than not, you will know politics when you see it. After thinking about it for a while, you can probably give examples of politics or political behavior, so the inability to define politics is not a sign of ignorance. Rather, the difficulty seems to arise because *politics* is a word that is so clouded with personal opinions and potentially conflicting examples that it defies a precise and complete description. You should also feel reassured by the simple fact that political scientists themselves disagree about how to define the term. In general, political scientists find it rather difficult to agree on anything,* but we all have to admit that to disagree about the very definition of the subject they study is truly bizarre.

What is politics? Well, you probably know it when you see it. Think about how you might have used the word in the past. Perhaps you were discussing office politics, and you were griping, whining, or laughing about something that someone did in the attempt to better his or her position within the company. You might remember a time when Pat, for example, spent weeks braving the boss's paint-peeling halitosis, flirting and laughing at all the bad jokes while pretending that your oblong, mentally defective boss was not the most offensive human on the planet. Pat, you may have thought, was "playing politics"—behaving in a calculating manner, trying to influence others in order to get something in return or attain a goal.

Politics does not end there. Those of you with a more critical eye for these sorts of things may have realized that "Pat" could be either a guy's name or a girl's name and that we did not identify the boss as a he or a she. You may be thinking that the authors have really gone to a lot of trouble to make this example gender-neutral and, hence, sexual-preference-neutral. That took some work, and there must be a reason for it. While we are not admitting anything, all the neutering in this example might well be a political effort to avoid the kind of typecasting that prolongs gender stereotypes. Or perhaps, we may simply realize that it would be politically unwise to upset professors who might otherwise assign this textbook to their students.

Behave politically? Who, us?

Another way to get to the meaning of the word *politics* would be to engage in word association. Think of the first synonyms that come to your mind when you hear the word "*Let's Get Ready to Rumble.*" Wait, sorry, we were thinking about something else, besides, that was five words. Try the word "*political.*" How many of them are positive? Do they include terms like greedy, disingenuous, manipulative, sleazy, and selfish? Do you think of someone who applies the ingenuity of Wile E. Coyote to construct elaborate

---

*An unfortunate exception is the unnatural tolerance all political scientists have for corduroy sport coats worn with pastel polyester pants.

plans for pursuing his or her own self-interest at the expense of others? Describing someone as "political" is not usually a compliment. Most people use the word in a derogatory sense. After all, the public seems to consider politicians to be somewhat less evolved than used car dealers.

It is easy to see how Pat's fawning attitude toward the boss fits in with the derogatory connotation of politics, and there are undoubtedly plenty of other examples that you might associate with the word *politics*. But, what exactly is Pat doing that is political? Pat is using a technique—in this case the art of flattery and perhaps even a bit of manipulative sexual flirtation—to try to get something from someone else. Pat is laughing at the boss's inane jokes in hopes of getting a better schedule, a raise, a promotion, a better work assignment, a new desk chair, or, perhaps Pat wants the coveted cubicle that is farthest from the desk of the amateur taxidermist who only showers on Thursdays. Clearly, behavior can be classified as *political* when it is aimed at getting something from others. We call Pat's behavior political in the same way that we would classify as political the behavior of a candidate who shakes hands with constituents or a member of Congress who tries to make a deal with a colleague in order to get a bill passed into a law. In each of these cases, someone is trying to get something from others, such as constituents' votes or colleagues' support for a bill. Whether the behavior is that of an individual, a group, or a government, this description seems to fit our popular understanding of the term.

Of course, the word *political* is an adjective, describing the everyday acts of persuasion or calculation that we all engage in. But here we are concerned with defining *politics*. There is one very clear difference between Pat's actions and those of the candidate and the legislator: Pat's behavior is unlikely to affect more than a small number of people. Normally, when we think of the word *politics,* we are referring to matters that directly or indirectly or potentially have an impact on a great number of people. Thus, we can state that **politics** consists of individual or combined actions of individuals, governments and/or groups, aimed at getting what they want accomplished, when those actions have public consequences.

Notice that this definition does not distinguish between what we might label "good" or "bad" behavior. We sort of did that on purpose. People, countries, and organizations can have lofty moral purposes or they can have very low, nasty goals when they are engaged in politics. Both Darth Vader and Princess Leia are involved in politics. Both Adolf Hitler and Winston Churchill were politicians. In fact, most of those striving for what you might consider good purposes are successful precisely because they are knowledgeable about politics. Politics can be engaged in by individuals or by groups of people. It can be aimed at achieving societal goals or personal ambitions. Politics can be the product of private individuals or government officials.

On its face, characterizing politics as *goal-oriented actions with public consequences* is not too different from one classic definition of politics offered by Harold

> **No matter how much the content of politics changes, it is always very much about action. It is about the things that people do or choose *not* to do.**

Lasswell: "who gets what, when, and how."[7] One major difference is that the definition we use places more stress on action—which means that the content of politics is never stagnant. New needs or desires arise. People are constantly coming up with new ideas about how to get what they want. Political entities are constantly changing. Advances in technology translate into new political strategies. The specifics about politics are always in flux. While this constant evolution of the specifics makes politics an interesting topic to study, it also means that the already difficult problem of definition is made all the more challenging by the fact that we are trying to hit a moving target.

Consider the fax machine. Nobody thought of a fax machine as a political tool until 1989, when the supporters of the political protesters occupying Tiananmen Square sidestepped the Chinese government's ban on press coverage by faxing copies of newspaper articles from other countries into China. This let the entire Chinese public know what was going on in Beijing even though the government-run news agencies tried not to report on it. By breaking the Chinese government's monopoly on information, the supporters of the political protesters made it a public event, and they drastically altered the context in which Chinese officials were making significant political choices. From that day on, the fax machine became a political tool as well as an office tool, and all governments now have to take this information-transmission method—and newer ones such as e-mail and blogs—into account before they act. No matter how much the content of politics changes, it is always very much about action. It is about the things that people do or choose not to do. And please remember that choosing not to do something is an action—that is often easy to forget.

This brings us to a very important point about politics. Many people are used to discussing politics as if they are the objects of others engaged in it—as in "they are raising my taxes," "they are starting a war," "they are letting too many immigrants into the country," or "they put the president's speech on all the good channels." But the very same people complaining about the political actions "they" are taking are also acting politically: even when actively avoiding political action, they are engaged in politics. Choosing not to participate leaves it to others to make decisions, and, just as surrender is a military option, inaction is a political option. If you have ever not voted in an election, you have taken a political action. In many cases, people choose not to participate in politics because they are happy enough with conditions as they exist and have more interesting ways to occupy their time, but there can also be insidious reasons, such as fear or surrender to a feeling of futility. Whatever the reason, not voting is a political action. Even in a brutal dictatorship, people's decision not to protest or not to rebel is a political choice.

Inaction may be something that is taught as a proper response to authority, it may be driven by religious faith, or it may be the result of ignorance. Inaction can also be a very carefully thought-out, rational choice. In the case of revolt, you can think of inaction as a calculation involving the potential gains versus the very high risks encountered in revolting against a stronger power—such as injury, torture, or death. Dictators are seldom very nice to participants in failed rebellions. Not all of the planets in *Star Wars* join in the rebellion against Darth Vader and the Emperor. This might be the wise or prudent decision—after all, most of us would like to stay alive and in one piece—but it is still a political choice.

The definition of politics we use also differs from another classic definition from David Easton, which holds that politics is the "authoritative allocation of values for society." [8] According to this definition, politics is about how governments determine who is entitled to have whatever lots of people want. However, we do not want to limit ourselves to the idea that government will be involved in all that is political. In fact, a number of important decisions with public consequences take place outside the control of the government.

One of the most fascinating things about studying political science is that the substance of politics is constantly changing. New political strategies are constantly being developed, new political actors arrive on the stage, and new political entities emerge. For example, faced with increasing globalization, whereby multinational corporations exert expanding power that cannot be checked by traditional governments, environmental and other interest groups searched for a new strategy for advancing their particular objectives. They reached back to the 1980s for a strategy that many had utilized to fight apartheid in South Africa: they began to try to influence corporate decisions from the inside. By purchasing stocks in corporations or acquiring proxy votes from willing corporate stockholders, groups such as the U.S. Public Interest Research Group, Greenpeace, and the World Wildlife Fund have introduced proposals designed to heighten corporate responsibility. At one time, corporations scorned the activities of these groups, but **socially responsible investing** (SRI) has had an increasing impact on these businesses. Even McDonald's, long the target of animal rights and environmental groups, has rethought its stance and now issues a report on its social responsibility. Despite the fact that there is no direct governmental activity, these organized actions are clearly political. [9]

A society's religion, its customs and traditions, its resources and its economy can all be part of its politics. People can even take actions with public consequences in their own homes. For years, feminists have argued that "the personal is the political." Private and personal actions, those that are not traditionally thought of as occurring in the public sphere, can have serious political consequences if, for example, they keep others from participating freely in the political process or from sharing proportionally in a country's resources. Thus, spouses who discourage their partners from participating in public debates or elections make decisions with political consequences and companies that frown on their employees participating in politics are acting politically. Furthermore, companies make decisions with public consequences all the time—when they close plant locations, hire workers, move their headquarters, or lop off the top of a mountain to get at the good stuff inside.

In *The Simpsons*, Mr. Burns's actions have clear political implications.[10] When you think about all the radiation that has leaked out of the nuclear power plant owned by Homer's boss, and the impact of these leaks on the citizens and environment of Springfield, the political consequences are quite obvious. Michael Moore's *Roger & Me* provides another good example, as Moore demonstrates the very public ramifications that the choices of the American automobile industry had on Detroit and the vicinity.[11] Those who are outside government commonly make decisions with political implications.

Politics is just one of many terms we will encounter that have disputed, complex, or unclear definitions. Power, legitimacy, authority, sovereignty, security, and a host of other essential political science concepts present similar challenges to our effort to explore the fundamentals of politics. To deal with this barrage of ambiguity, we sort of fudge it a little. We will give you simplified—sometimes extremely simplified—definitions that capture the basic elements of politics and political actions. We will try to remember to alert you to this deliberate oversimplification when we want you to be aware that there are nuances and complexities involved in a particular topic of discussion that you might encounter in another course or another context. As you progress, you will be able to build upon the definitions offered in the text. For now, we do not want you to lose sight of the hows and whys of politics because you are bogged down in debates over definitions. The use of simplified definitions for some complex terms is meant to keep a focus on the dynamics.

WHAT IS POLITICAL SCIENCE?

If politics is about goal-oriented actions or choices that have public consequences, what, then, is **political science**? Strange as it may seem, political scientists do not agree on a definition of this term either. In fact, the disagreement can often become heated, and the scholarly debate often escalates to the point at which, even though food is seldom thrown, you would still have to call it an argument. For political scientists, the stakes can be substantial. How the discipline defines the *science* part of political science can influence which approaches to research will be published in journals or scholarly books, and that determination has a tremendous effect on who can get jobs, promotions, and grants for research projects. Because of the stakes, the battle over the definition can be, well, political. For students, some aspects of how we define the science part of political science can be interesting and useful for understanding how researchers study political phenomenon.

When you hear the word *science*, chances are you do not think of politics. You probably think of people in white coats conducting experiments—the typical *Dexter's Laboratory* full of chemicals beakers and electric gadgets. However, over 2,000 years ago, Aristotle spoke of a "political science." [12] Could he possibly have meant science as we now think of the term? The answer is plainly no. When Aristotle used the term, he was referring to a body of knowledge regarding how to organize a state in order to obtain happiness. Perhaps it is unfortunate that he used the word *science* at all. When we mention science, we are thinking, instead, of the **scientific method**, a specific set of rules and processes for pursuing knowledge with observation, hypothesis building, experimentation, and replication. This is a way of finding factual information about what *is*, while Aristotle was clearly being normative when he used the term. He was offering opinions about what constituted the good life, and he sought to create a city-state capable of delivering that good life. Today, when we think of science, we try to separate it from discussion of what should be and try to concentrate on objectively gathered facts, sterilized as much as possible of opinions.

Much of the disagreement about the definition of political science stems from these fundamental differences. Some believe that political science should be a science in the same way that biology, chemistry, and physics are sciences—they believe that political scientists should employ a strictly defined scientific method. Of course there are many practical difficulties with this approach. Think about why it would be difficult to study politics in the same way that one could study a subject such as botany.*

Consider something straightforward—let us say, the effect of high-intensity halogen lights on the growth of plants that can *legally* be cultivated hydroponically in your grandmother's basement. You can take two healthy *and perfectly legal* plants into the basement and put one under a lamp and the other in a closet. You can then compare the growth of the two plants and draw conclusions about the effects that your independent variable, in this case the provision of light, has upon your subjects, the plants. This scientific study of plant cultivation can be repeated again and again, and again, and again, until you are caught. As you repeat this experiment, you can make changes to the environment or other factors that you think might influence the growth of these plants.†

In contrast, political scientists and other social scientists usually cannot isolate individuals, organizations, and groups in the laboratory or carefully manipulate the factors that might influence them. Instead, political scientists have come up with numerous ways of approximating the ideal of laboratory conditions, primarily through the use of statistics. Even so, some critics have argued that the use of statistics pushes researchers to examine whatever can easily be counted, cataloged, or quantified—money, votes, weapons—while other important concepts that cannot be counted—beliefs, expectations, hopes—are discounted or ignored entirely. For example, a researcher would have a much easier time studying *how* legislators vote than *why* they vote the way they do, although

---

*There is a bad pun about shopping that could be made here. Please note that we refrained.

†An additional benefit of this experiment is that when your flagrant disregard of our suggestion that you cultivate a legal plant leads to a handcuffed, shirtless, kicking and screaming involuntary guest appearance on an episode of *Cops*, instead of shouting something stupid, you can yell, "It was science, man!"

the latter question may be more important to understanding the political behavior of leg-islators. Nevertheless, despite the fact that statistical methods cannot perfectly replicate laboratory conditions, this approach to the study of politics has significantly increased our understanding and base of knowledge.

Other theorists believe that political scientists need not, and perhaps should not, try to force the study of politics to fit into the mold of other sciences. They argue that it is not possible to be objective about politics in the way one can be objective about biol-ogy, or chemistry, or the hydroponic cultivation of commercially lucrative plants. Political scientists making this argument have also significantly increased our under-standing of politics by offering insights into the influence of rhetoric, decision process, and culture on the behavior of individuals and governments.

As suggested earlier, Aristotle may have done future generations a disservice by using the term *science* at all. After all, he also referred to politics as "the master art."[13] Perhaps politics should be viewed as an art or, even more appropriately, as a craft?[14] Regardless, the best way for the student to approach the science part of political sci-ence may be to use a framework offered by social scientist Earl Babbie in his popular text on social science research methods.[15] Babbie argues that we all know two realities: **experiential reality** and **agreement reality**. This is a valuable concept for understand-ing the role of the news media in politics and we use it a lot in chapter 11, but it is also a good way to come to grips with the science part of political science. Experiential real-ity is composed of the things we directly experience—which, in fact, make up only a very small portion of our reality. Far more important is agreement reality, which con-sists of the things we believe are real even though we have never directly seen, touched, heard, smelled, or tasted them.

Agreement reality can be derived from interaction with parents, friends, authority figures, religious doctrines, celebrities, the media, and teachers. However, as Babbie argues, we can also think of science as a set of rules and processes that we use to gen-erate agreement reality. Every single scientist does not go out to replicate every single experiment conducted in his or her area of expertise. Instead, scientists agree on com-mon methods to be used in research. As long as they are convinced that other scien-tists have properly followed those methods, they accept their results as true, as part of reality. Thus, the science of political science is the effort to develop a greater under-standing of politics by conducting research openly and transparently, utilizing methods that will convince other political scientists to accept the results as accurate and cor-rect. The difficulty is that the personal, individual nature of politics extends to the study of politics. Just as there are a variety of reasonable perspectives on politics, there are a variety of reasonable and effective methods for pursuing an understanding of politics.

The intensity of the debate over the term *political science* centers around which set of research methodologies is best, and it probably has to be admitted that the dif-ferent perspectives in that debate are often driven by the self-interest of scholars. An academic scholar invests a great deal of effort—often several years of intense work—in learning one of these sets of research rules, processes, and procedures, and would be in serious professional jeopardy if his or her preferred methodology were to lose the debate. For beginning students, it is enough to know that all of these definitions of the science part of political science require that researchers always be honest about their methods, transparent about the steps they have taken, open with their findings and, ideally, receptive to criticism. In other words, in order to create agreement reality regarding politics, all researchers must carefully document their research, fully explain their findings, disclose any of their known biases, and acknowledge any known weaknesses in their research. They should do this not because they fear criticism, but because they wish to contribute to the development of knowledge and therefore welcome constructive criticism. It is through the accurate reporting of research and subsequent criticism that our knowledge of politics, or any discipline for that matter, increases.

Of course, this transparent research methodology does not mean that every study of politics is a good study or that all studies of politics equally contribute to our collective understanding. People engaged in political science must remain faithful to the rules of the methods they wish to utilize. For example, one who engages in statistical studies should follow the accepted norms of those engaged in statistical studies, and those who use case studies should follow the methods generally accepted by those who utilize this method. We encourage students to be open to any methodology that, when used properly, increases our understanding about politics. The amazingly profound academic research conducted by the authors of this text has benefited from research conducted employing a tremendous variety of methodologies, all of which have greatly influenced the content of this text. As we note in the following chapter, it is also true that the lines between political science, economics, history, philosophy, literature, geography, and even the natural sciences are not as clear as your university's course catalog makes them appear. They all play a part in the study of politics. We believe that is one reason why political science is such an interesting and rewarding subject to study. Finding such an argument in this book should not be too surprising—after all, we wrote this text with the assumption that some of the best ways you can learn about politics include reading literature, watching TV, and viewing movies.

KEY TERMS

agreement reality / **15**
conceptual frameworks / **5**
experiential reality / **15**
idealism / **2**
political science / **13**
politics / **10**

realism / **2**
scientific method / **14**
socially responsible investing (SRI) / **12**
sophist / **3**

CHAPTER SUMMARY

People's preconceptions affect the way they think about politics, which can make it very difficult to study politics systematically and to remain open to new concepts, different approaches, and alternative perspectives. Thus, it is important to find some mechanism that enables students of politics to take a step back from their biases, their own desires, their preference for realism or idealism, and so forth. The use of fictional examples can make it easier to set aside our predispositions and can help us to travel to places we typically could not visit and to share experiences that would ordinarily elude us. The difficulty people have when attempting to define the term itself, the changing nature of the subject matter, and disagreements about how to conduct research all further confound the study of politics. Students should learn two very important lessons from this first chapter. First, the study of politics is fascinating. Second, reading only the chapter summary will not adequately prepare you for class or for an exam.

STUDY QUESTIONS AND EXERCISES

1. What is it that makes *politics* a difficult term to define?

2. Why is fiction a good tool for the study of politics?

3. How is the study of politics different from the study of natural sciences (for example, biology and chemistry)?

4. Think of your own example to illustrate how a novel you've read or a television show, movie, or film that you saw demonstrates the difference between idealism and realism.

5. How have recent advances in technology changed politics, or how might they change politics in the future?

WEBSITES TO EXPLORE

www.apsanet.org. The American Political Science Association, the largest organization of American political scientists.

www.isanet.org. The International Studies Association, an organization of scholars and practitioners with an interest in international studies.

www.theonion.com. *The Onion*, weekly satire of the major news of the day.

www.lib.umich.edu/govdocs/polisci.html. The University of Michigan Library Documents Center's Political Science Resources on the Web, a great collection of Web resources for students engaged in political science.

Plato, an idealist; Machiavelli, a realist; Ghandi, an idealist who put his ideas into action to change the real world; and Jon Stewart, a guy with a TV show. Jon gets the big picture because you should always suck up to the guy with a TV show.

CHAPTER 2

Utopias, Theories, and Ideologies
Perfect Worlds and the Imperfections of Reality

Suppose you heard a disembodied voice that kept saying things like "Ease his pain," "Go the distance," and "If you build it, they will come." Some might seek the assistance of a mental health professional; those who understand the real truth would line all of their clothing with aluminum foil to keep out the alien mind rays. If you are anything like Ray Kinsella, however, you would run off to find an elderly writer, drive a Volkswagen van back in time, and then plow over your cornfield to build a baseball diamond on your farm so that some long-dead major league baseball players could drop by for a few innings. As you watch *Field of Dreams*, you see how this man's idealized vision of the game of baseball drives him to do whatever it takes to reach his **utopia**, his ideal world, and—if you can accept that Ray Kinsella does not know enough to go with the foil option—the preposterous seems believable.[1]

What makes Kinsella's actions relevant is that his dream colors his view of the world. He hears the Voice, and he knows how to interpret it. Most important for our purposes, as in the case of political dreams, he acts.

A baseball field of dreams, Eden, Shangri-La, Lake Wobegon, Grandma's house, an attic apartment above Willy Wonka's factory, Euro-Disneyland—some image of a perfect world is floating around in each of our heads. Imagining an ideal world seems to be common throughout history and across societies, as is the desire to attain it. Religions, myths, philosophies, ideologies, dogmas, and folklore all frequently involve some aspect of utopian thought, which consistently arises whenever people move from the tangible reality around them into the realm of hopes, dreams, beliefs, or faith. Utopias may conform to the ideal of the warrior or the pacifist, the prudish, or the denizen of fraternity row, but they always seem to depart conceptually from empirical reality.

Contrasting all these images of the ideal with reality makes a perfect theme for a textbook using fiction to explore politics, if only because the pursuit of utopia is a common theme of both fiction and politics. Novels, films, cartoons—even the amusingly dysfunctional families of television sitcoms—often make use of an idealized or utopian setting to explore an aspect of society, to provide a context for dramatic interaction, or to delve into human nature. Similarly, utopian visions, ideals, and ideologies shape not only how we think about politics, but also how we act politically as, like political Ray Kinsellas, we try to make the real world more like whatever it is that we imagine a perfect world to be.

Examining the utopian concept is also a useful place to begin our exploration of the fundamentals of politics, most obviously because utopian ideals help us to ruthlessly and recklessly exploit our central theme of idealism versus realism. Utopian literature offers a demonstration of how the critical examination of fiction can inform us about politics, political thought, and government, for it provides perhaps the clearest and simplest application of fiction to the study of politics. A discussion of utopias in literature is also a natural segue to consideration of their role in political theory and political ideology. The similarities in the use of ideal societies in these two realms are so extensive that it can, at times, be difficult to draw a clear line between literature and political theory. Indeed, Thomas More's *Utopia*—which is where the modern term originated—is just as likely to be assigned reading in college literature courses as it is in the study of politics or philosophy.[2]

UTOPIAS IN FICTION AND POLITICS

Although a utopia is a perfect world, that does not necessarily mean it will be perfectly wonderful. Believe it or not, frolicking on sunny beaches with singing llamas is not everyone's idea of utopia—some people may actually prefer skiing amid bartending St. Bernards. How about the utopia of a neo-Nazi, or one of those television preachers with plastic-looking hair, or a militant vegetarian, or your Aunt Daisy? How many of these perfect worlds would you find appealing or even tolerable? In fact, a utopia may be perfectly miserable, if only because one person's perfect world is quite likely to be another's nightmare.

The Subjectivity of Perfection

The subjective nature of a perfect world is often made quite clear in fiction that addresses the concept of utopia directly. In Ursula Le Guin's *The Lathe of Heaven,* the main character is a mental patient who can change reality through his dreams.[3] Once his psychologist realizes that this man is not insane but actually is changing the world, the doctor begins using hypnosis to direct the changes, and the story evolves toward a focus on how the effort to create a utopia pushes these two characters into conflict. The

THE ORIGINAL UTOPIA

First used as the title of Thomas More's 1516 book, the word *utopia* does not actually mean "the perfect place," as most people assume. The literal translation from Latin is "no place," or the place that does not exist. And, unlike the University of Washington, whose motto *Lux Sit* was supposed to signify "enlightenment" but actually means "light exists," it is quite clear that when Thomas More used the word *utopia*, he meant to signify "no place." Not only was the whole book written in Latin, but More was known for both his command of the language and his fondness for making up complex Latin puns. That last bit alone should tell you everything you need to know about both More and his book.

It is a good thing that More was talking about no place rather than the perfect place, because his utopia is dreadful. Everyone wears clothing of the same drab, natural-wool color. Children who wish to pursue a trade other than that practiced by one of their parents must go to live with another family. Similarly, should parents have too many children for the size of their house, some must be summarily shipped off to another dwelling where space is available. Colonialism, backed by military violence, is the solution to overpopulation problems, and slavery is practiced. One must have permission to travel outside of the boundaries of one's own city, and a second offense for wandering is punishable by enslavement. Premarital sex is severely punished, and adultery brings a sentence of a lifetime of hard labor, or death on a second offense. On the good side, the chances of getting killed for this particular transgression seem pretty low because there are no taverns, pubs, or anyplace else where people might "gather idly."

Although Thomas More does seem to have been the kind of dour prude who would have thought adultery merited capital punishment, many commentators have argued that *Utopia* is, in fact, a satire. And while it is hard to figure out what might be so funny about a place with no pubs, *Utopia* does fit the bill for a satire—a work that makes a social comment by ridiculing someone or something. More is clearly ridiculing nobility, excess accumulation of wealth, and the contemporary form of governance across Europe, and he is avoiding punishment by placing his social commentary in an imaginary place, using the name "nowhere" to emphasize that it does not exist. The degree to which he was successful is an interesting question. After he wrote *Utopia*, Thomas More was beheaded for treason, but he also served as one of the king's closest advisers—not necessarily in that order.

struggle between them repeatedly demonstrates just how different their perfect worlds are and just how miserable each of them becomes as the world moves closer to the other's utopia. A first step in understanding how utopias are used as tools for literature, political theorizing, and even practical politics is to drop the assumption that perfection implies a good or pleasant result. Because utopias are inherently subjective and human societies are so diverse, it is impossible to expect any one ideal context to be considered perfectly good by everyone.

Instead, a utopia might be better understood as an extreme version of an ideal, principle, or presumption about the nature of the world. The film *Logan's Run* is set in a world where the ideals of youth and beauty are taken to their logical extreme—the populace remains young and beautiful because the government kills off people on their thirtieth birthdays.[4] Even though Aldous Huxley wrote *Brave New World* in the 1930s, the novel might be described as a 1960s-style free-love, hippy commune pushed to the point of perfection.[5] The diabolically intrusive government in George Orwell's *Nineteen*

> **Whenever one takes an idea, social concept, or vision of the world to its conceptual extreme, otherwise unforeseen aspects of the idea—particularly its flaws—are exposed.**

Eighty-Four, which is sometimes referred to as a *dystopia,* might be instead a utopia in which government's control of society is perfected and pushed to an extreme.[6] Featuring shipwrecked children devolving into brutal savagery, William Golding's *Lord of the Flies* depicts the closest thing to perfect anarchy that might exist in the real world.[7] The list of examples ranges from the obscure libertarian/anarchic utopia of L. Neil Smith's *The Probability Broach,* where the idea of limited government sees the full light of day, to Captain Kirk and crew's exploration of some utopian planet on practically every third episode of *Star Trek.*[8] Besides teaching you never to wear a red shirt on any planet that looks like a bunch of sand and Styrofoam rocks tossed together on a soundstage,* the "perfect" societies of *Star Trek* and all fictional utopias demonstrate the concept of taking some idea and carrying it through so that it pervades every aspect of that world.

Although it is clearly impossible to get everyone to agree on one notion of perfection, and even if pretty much any image of perfect bliss is totally impractical, the idea of a utopia is still a valuable tool for political theory, political ideology, and even political action. Whenever one takes an idea, social concept, or vision of the world to its conceptual extreme, otherwise unforeseen aspects of the idea—particularly its flaws—are exposed. This effect is demonstrated in its simplest form when authors use the utopia to provoke reflection on our presumptions about society or to warn us against adopting seductively simple solutions to any one of the myriad of complex problems that challenge the real world. Theorists invoke utopian visions both to critique flaws in political ideologies and political processes and to envision a practical path to a better, though imperfect, future. Even political actors conjure utopias, whether by drawing mental pictures of where their policy ideas will lead or by establishing landmarks to guide their strategy for tackling the endless daily decisions they must make. Martin Luther had Ninety-Five Theses for a better church; Martin Luther King Jr. (no relation) had a dream about equality. Gandhi had both a unique fashion sense and a hope for peacefully attaining the freedom of India.

Utopias as Social Statement

The simplest and most obvious use of utopias occurs when an author of fiction makes a social statement by pushing an ideal, ideology, or political demand to its logical extreme in order to make it serve as a warning to society. For example, one can argue that Orwell wrote *Nineteen Eighty-Four* at the very beginning of the Cold War to demonstrate, among other things, what would happen if ardent anticommunists were actually to get what they were demanding. Zealously seeking to protect the capitalist way of life from what they perceived as a predatory political ideology, the anticommunists of the

---

*As any *Star Trek* groupie will tell you, it is the actor in the red shirt who is to die when our heroes visit Planet Doom.

postwar era aggressively sought to identify and remove from positions of power those who did not hold "proper" beliefs. Not only is mandating correct beliefs antithetical to the liberal ideology that underlies modern capitalist democracy, but also, the tactics used and the powers demanded by the leaders of this effort threatened the very freedoms and ideals they said they wished to protect.

To see how Orwell's novel could be intended as a warning to those who might support the communist hunt, compare the tactics and actions of Sen. Joseph McCarthy and the House Un-American Activities Committee as portrayed in the film *The Front* with those of the government in *Nineteen Eighty-Four*.[9] In the film, Woody Allen plays an average guy whose blacklisted screenwriter friends arrange to use his name on their scripts so that they can continue to work. Although it has a light edge, *The Front* bluntly depicts the United States at the height of the anticommunist frenzy, when a McCarthyite Congress spearheaded the persecution of "traitors" with "communist leanings" in the entertainment industry. From the presumption of guilt by association or innuendo, to the exercise of government coercion to compel individuals to testify against friends and colleagues in order to save themselves, the similarities between the real and fictional settings are all too obvious.

Nineteen Eighty-Four represents the extension of McCarthyism to the point at which the government regulates every aspect of life, from personal relationships to thoughts and language, so as to enforce the official ideology. In essence, one of many possible interpretations of Orwell's novel is that the anticommunist extremists, if successful, will impose the very dictatorship they claim to be fighting against. The novelist's dire warning eerily resonates with the real Senator McCarthy's later actions, as the imprisonment and torture of people for thought crimes depicted in *Nineteen Eighty-Four* found its perfect utopian parallel in the ability of the American anticommunists to ruin careers and lives in the name of defending freedom. When workers can be fired and generally shunned by employers for simply being named as communist sympathizers, you have to admit that sounds a lot like something a communist dictator would do to those accused of being sympathetic to capitalist pig dogs.* Regardless of the specifics, even the most pleasant of fictional utopias comes at a very high price to someone.

Just as novelists and filmmakers utilize utopias to analyze social or political phenomena, political theorists use them to evaluate aspects or dynamics of politics and political or social structures. **Karl Marx**, for example, applied utopian thought in his harsh and influential critique of capitalism.[10] We explore Marx's theories more fully when we discuss the economic dimensions of politics in chapter 5, but his work is notable here because of the way he extends capitalist ideals to their logical extreme for the purpose of exposing the social and political consequences of unfettered competi-

---

*We are not sure exactly what pig dogs are—whether you should barbecue them or pet them—but the communists in the movies talk about them a lot.

tion. Just as Orwell, the novelist, aimed to sound an alarm about the ramifications of giving the passionate communist hunters everything they wanted, Marx, the political theorist, envisioned a "perfect" capitalism in order to expose an aspect of its theoretical underpinnings that could be self-destructive if left unrestrained.

Utopias in Practical Use

More commonly, a political ideologist offers a utopian vision not only to conceptualize a better world, but also to suggest a means to achieve it. Again, Marx provides an example.* Having identified what he believed to be the fundamental flaw in capitalism, he proposed an alternative model—socialism—wherein society controls the economics of production. He projected socialism out to a communist utopia, a perfect socialist world, which he then used to prescribe specific instructions about how to get there from the starting point of a predominantly capitalist world. The fact that this road map to utopia included the revolutionary overthrow of capitalism and destruction of the governmental structures supporting that system is undoubtedly why Marx's theories continue to provoke a visceral response from capitalists and fearful political elites. Nevertheless, Marx's projection of a utopia as an orienting point for a political strategy is quite common for theorists, ideologists, and activists.

The evocation of utopias in theory, ideology, and practical politics probably reached its pinnacle in the wake of World War I. Sometimes referred to as the **idealist period**, at least in the study of international politics, the two decades between the world wars were marked by the effort to envision and attain a perfectly peaceful world. The attempt to pursue a utopian vision of global peace through world democracy, spearheaded by U.S. president Woodrow Wilson, was the most prominent example of this utopian thinking. The unbelievable carnage of World War I, which we describe in unpleasant if not gory detail in chapter 12, instigated a desperate search for an alternative to violence as a means of settling disputes in international politics. The liberal democratic political structures and institutions that operated in the countries that had managed to win the war appeared to allow for the reasoned resolution of political, economic, and social conflicts. Consequently, these institutions provided a seemingly natural basis for a worldwide system of peaceful politics, and the **League of Nations** was built upon this ideal.

Comprising an international court of justice, a legislative body, and lots of bureaucracy, the League of Nations appeared to be a substantial step toward a global democracy. However, like most paths toward perfection, it ran into the substantial imperfections of the real world. While the idea of a global government was tremendously appealing to the war-ravaged nations of Europe, that same vision of a path to world peace was frightening to the powerful and isolationist United States. The domestically oriented

---

*Marx went both ways. He was both a theorist and an ideologist.

U.S. Congress would neither submit to the democratic structure of the League of Nations nor risk entanglement in the European politics that had repeatedly lead to devastating wars. Some aspects of this resistance can still be seen, eight decades later, in public and political attitudes toward the United Nations and toward an international criminal court. The U.S. rejection weakened the League and made refusal to participate or to respect its role in world politics easier to justify by the fascist governments that arose in Japan, Germany, Italy, and Spain in the interwar period.

Whether it is depicted as utopian thinking in an imperfect world or as the gap between idealists and realists, the contrast between the real and the ideal is a constant throughout the practice, theory, and study of politics. It is also, incidentally, part of writing a textbook on politics. Ideally, the next section on political theorists would be a universally accepted, definitive listing of long-dead people with snappy blurbs on their importance. The reality, we are sorry to report, falls far short of the ideal.

THEORISTS AND THEORIES OF POLITICS

So what makes a simple list of the most important political theorists so problematic? After all, the local radio station seems to have no problem identifying the one hundred greatest rock-and-roll songs of all time—and in such precise order! The pervasiveness of politics, combined with the eclectic nature of political science, makes it difficult to settle on such a definitive set of "great names." Even when we do manage to put together a list of theorists, it becomes obvious that many of the critical conceptual contributions to the study of politics come from outside political science.

Several of the figures on a list of great political theorists would be hard to categorize within the modern notion of academic disciplines, and most of the others might be more accurately identified with disciplines or professions other than political science. Among them are political commentator Alexis de Tocqueville; philosophers Plato, Aristotle, and Hegel; economists Karl Marx and Kenneth Arrow; sociologists Lewis Coser and Seymour Martin Lipset; military officer Karl von Clausewitz; political leaders James Madison, Mao Tse-tung, and Vladimir Lenin; and political advisers Niccolò Machiavelli, Kautilya, and Confucius—all of whom might be considered among the key contributors to the conceptual history of political science as an academic discipline. If you focus on significant recent or contemporary contributions, this list might easily be expanded to include, among others, historians, essayists, psychologists, business professors, communications scholars, statisticians, mathematicians, geographers, anthropologists, and even linguists. The problem of the eclectic nature of political science is heightened by the fact that few of these key contributors focused their entire attention on developing a complete and systematic political theory.

Furthermore, it is hard to escape the fact that political science originated with and was refined by ancient Greek political theorists such as Socrates, Plato, and Aristotle, who practiced nothing close to the modern ideal of objective and scientific investigation of politics. Virtually all the Greeks agreed that the purpose of the **polis**, or state, was to obtain their version of a utopia—happiness for the community—and those who followed continued that tradition. Even the consummate realist, Machiavelli, who introduced the modern conceptualization of power as the primary variable in politics, wrote in order to promote his belief that Renaissance Italy needed to be united by a strong ruler. Anyone who truly wants to understand the development of the discipline and many of its major concepts should have some appreciation of political theory. However, we should also remember that the normative nature of classic political theory is in sharp contrast to the modern scientific ideal of dispassionate and objective study. Nonetheless, there are many modern political scientists who write normative political theory.

It is also useful to appreciate political theory because theorists ask different sorts of questions than do most political scientists. They conceive of politics on a grander scale. Rather than chronicling and hypothesizing about the little things we desire to make our lives better, they inquire into life's big questions. They do not dwell on how Social Security benefits are tied to shifting demographics, or relationship between political institutions and peace in the Middle East, or the stability of the government in Argentina, or how we can get all those lousy reality shows off the air. Rather, they concentrate on defining the true nature of human beings and distinguishing what is possible from what is impossible. They are concerned with dreams and reality, with what is and what should be—questions that are more commonly asked outside the narrow confines of our discipline. Modern political scientists tend to focus on problems in the real world. While these issues are important, it is worthwhile, at least every once in a while, to join the theorists in pondering the larger questions.

THE TOP SEVEN DEAD WHITE MALE POLITICAL THEORISTS

As a way of addressing the whole great-minds-of-political-science thing, we decided to put together a simple top-ten list of the most influential political theorists, but for several of the reasons just mentioned, that enterprise turned out to be impossible. The authors simply cannot agree on a list of ten. We tried asking other professors of political science to help, but that just made matters worse, since they usually added more names to the list we were trying to shorten. So, instead, we compromised on a list of seven who were frequently, but not always, mentioned when we surveyed colleagues and who are also particularly relevant to our theme of contrasting the real and ideal. Please do not ask us which of the seven is the *most* important—we are tired of arguing about it. While we believe that political theory is important, there is simply no way to do justice to these theorists and their theories in the space of a few pages. So what we offer here is a quick-and-dirty sample of theoretical delicacies to whet your appetite.

One interesting consistency across this list is that many of these theorists wrote in times of chaos or great change. For example, Plato wrote after the defeat of Athens in the Peloponnesian War, and Aristotle witnessed that city-state's further decline; Machiavelli wrote after violent invasions and changes of power in Renaissance Florence; Hobbes and Locke were both influenced by the English Civil War, Locke being further affected by the oncoming Glorious Revolution; Rousseau wrote amid the turbulence that provoked the French Revolution, and Marx amid the societal eruptions brought about by the Industrial Revolution. The changing world around these theorists prompted each of them to question the status quo and to criticize others' suggestions for changes to society. It also placed each of them in a position to imagine the structures of society giving way to those of different utopias.*

Plato—Commencing the Debate

There are those who claim that all of Western political theory is really only a response to **Plato** (427–347 B.C.). Indeed, it is difficult to read his works without being amazed by his ability to anticipate alternative political theories that would not be fully articulated by others until centuries later. Unfortunately, however, Plato was also an elitist snob. While many of his underlying premises are thought provoking and challenging, his antidemocratic ideas, beliefs, and arguments would be distinctly out of step with the liberal ideology that permeates modern, Western political theory.

It is generally agreed that Plato's greatest contributions to political theory can be found in the *Republic,* which, like all of Plato's works, is a dialogue.[11] In other words, it is written much like a play. The main character is Socrates, who was Plato's teacher, and a great political theorist in his own right. However, as in most of Plato's dialogues, the character Socrates is not the historical Socrates but a fictional persona that Plato uses to give voice to his own philosophy. In these dialogues, Socrates engages others in conversation as he makes philosophical points and demonstrates the flaws in the arguments they make. It should not be surprising that Socrates always wins the arguments—perhaps a world where he wins every argument is Plato's utopia.

While Plato envisions an ideal society in the *Republic,* that society is not in any sense democratic. He did not believe that the majority should have its way, and he especially did not believe that any decision should be accepted as correct simply because the masses favored it. After all, he had witnessed the democratic majority in Athens condemn his friend and mentor Socrates to death for corrupting the youth. Plato's disregard, if not contempt, for the average person derived from his understanding of the very ability of people to perceive the world around them.

Plato believed that one could not rely on his or her senses to discover what was real. He believed that what we see, touch, and taste are just imperfect representations of

---

*Oddly enough, we ourselves (the authors of this text) began studying and writing about politics during a similar time of great turmoil and upheaval: when real music returned to banish, but unfortunately not quite eradicate, the evil of disco. Clearly, therefore, we are destined for spots 8 and 9 in the next edition of this text.

another actual reality. Unlike the universe about which we are aware, the hidden "real world" is unchanging and perfect; it is a world of "forms." We may think we *know* what beauty is, but that is just our *opinion* of beauty. All we can have are opinions, because we do not know the true form of beauty. However, Plato would have us believe that there is such a thing as perfect beauty, which is real and unchanging. Similarly, he also believed that there was such a thing as perfect justice, or correct living, although this perfect form would correspond not with what a society commonly understood as just, but rather with a real, unchanging equity.

How does one learn about the perfect forms? According to Plato, one needs to begin at birth, because the ability to comprehend and appreciate the true world requires extensive training in logic and abstract thinking. And just in case you are thinking you want to get a glimpse of the true forms of truth and beauty, be advised that it involves a lot of math to become an expert in logic and abstract thinking. Here again, remember that Plato had little respect for the average person, and he did not believe that everyone could know the forms. In Plato's utopia it is only philosophers, like him, who have the ability to see the true forms. Only they can properly know truth, and they are the only ones who are in a position to share it with the general public.*

Key to Plato's theory is the belief that it is important for every person to do what he or she does well. On its face, this may seem like an innocuous statement. But Plato believed that people who are good at making shoes, for example, should stick to making shoes; that athletes should only concern themselves with athletics; and that those who can see the true forms (the philosophers) should be the ones to rule. Because of the importance of this governing class, much of the *Republic* is devoted to constructing a state that allows for the proper training of the elite ruling class of philosophers and to specifying the type of training that they should receive. Because Plato believed that there was an ideal world, and because he believed in creating a state with perfect justice, he is labeled an idealist. Rather than limiting his concerns to the way the world is, Plato focused on what could be. In reality, it is doubtful that Plato actually thought that his utopia would come to pass. Instead, he, like many who envision utopias, was using his ideal as a yardstick by which to measure the reality that only philosophers can see.

Aristotle—The Rebellious Student

Although he was Plato's student, **Aristotle** (384–322 B.C.) was more of a realist and, unlike our students, he was highly critical of his mentor. He neither believed that one should strive for a perfect world nor assumed that there is a perfect world of forms hidden in the shadows. Instead, he thought that we can learn far more by observing the

---

*If you think this sounds a lot like pretentious artists saying that only artists understand why throwing paint at something is worth billions of dollars, then you are clearly not philosophically sophisticated and you should immediately go do one of those philosophical things like visiting a Tibetan monastery or living in a mud hut in Java. Go. Now.

THE CAVE AND *THE MATRIX*

This is your last chance. After this, there is no turning back. You take the blue pill—the story ends, you wake up in your bed and believe whatever you want to believe. You take the red pill—you stay in Wonderland and I show you how deep the rabbit-hole goes.

—Morpheus to Neo in *The Matrix* (1999)

In his greatest political work, the *Republic,* Plato offers a famous allegory to explain what he means by the perfect world of forms. According to this story, there is a cave filled with prisoners, all of whom are chained together and facing a wall. Behind them is a fire that lights the space. The prisoners have never seen life outside the cave. Their only knowledge of the world is provided by their captors, who hold up puppets behind them, casting shadows on the wall in front of them.

Eventually, one of the prisoners breaks free and climbs out of the cave. At first blinded by the sunlight, the escapee manages, finally, to actually see the world as it is. Although he does not want to leave the world of the light, he descends back into the cave to share his discovery with his fellow prisoners. But they do not take it well—they mock the escapee as his eyes adjust again to the darkness, and they do not believe his version. Ultimately, they kill him.

If you feel bad for the escapee, think of how Socrates must have felt. This allegory is almost certainly the story of the life and death of Socrates. Plato believed that only the philosophers, who have spent a lifetime in pursuit of truth and knowledge (think Socrates), could see the forms—that is, the way things truly are. The rest of us, the prisoners in the cave, can see only the shadowy earthly representations of the true reality. This is why Plato believes that philosophers should rule: they can see the Truth.

This allegory was adapted by the makers of *The Matrix* to suggest that the vast majority of people are living in a computer-generated world, serving as batteries for their machine captors. When the film's protagonist, Neo, sees the world as it really is, he complains that his eyes hurt; his mentor, Morpheus, responds, "You've never used them before." Those who take the "red pill" can see the world as it truly is, but when they return to the world of the matrix, they, like Plato's escapee/philosopher, are treated as if they were crazy. Nobody will believe their stories about the real world. The world of shadows and illusion offers comfort and familiarity for its occupants, while the real world offers truth. For Plato, the quest for knowledge was the way out of the cave; it was the swallowing of the red pill. The world of the shadows was the blue pill, the world of ignorance.

In many ways, the quest for knowledge can be quite dangerous. It can cause you to question your long-held ideals and beliefs. It can make you stick out among your old friends and even your family as you question why things are done as they are. How seriously you want to take the quest for knowledge is up to you, but college does offer the possibility to climb out of the cave—to take the red pill. The choice is yours; which will it be? Do you take the red pill or the blue one?

world and drawing conclusions from what we see. He believed that we should study how things actually work and how people actually behave. As for states, he observed their functions and categorized them according to the type of rule exercised within each one. Thus, compared to Plato, Aristotle was pragmatic. He believed that people should do the best they can within the limits of the world as it exists around them.

Also, according to Aristotle, everything works toward a specific end, or *telos.* The *telos* for an apple seed is what it is to become eventually: an apple tree. The *telos* for a baby gorilla is a full-grown gorilla. The *telos* for human beings is happiness, and, therefore, people should create governing institutions with this human end in mind. Furthermore, Aristotle believed that it is natural for people to form associations because human beings are inherently social—that is, "man is a political animal." The polis is but an extension of these associations and is, consequently, something natural. This is a key point. To argue that the state is natural is to argue that people do not form states only because they are effective tools for meeting certain demands (such as protection from invaders or regulating trade), but because it is something human beings are innately inclined to do. In fact, Aristotle would argue, people move toward their telos through participation in the state.

Aristotle proceeded to demonstrate how it is that some types of government are better than others at helping people achieve the goal of happiness. He also pointed out that it is possible to take a bad form of government and improve it. Therefore, we must be concerned not only with the ideal world, but also with making improvements to the flawed world that we know. Aristotle was clearly more of a realist than Plato, but he is still considered to be an idealist because he believed that there is a goal toward which people should strive—happiness. The primary aim of government, in his theory, is to create happiness for the people; thus happiness is still the ideal.

Machiavelli—The Reality of Power

Many have heard the term "Machiavellian," which is usually used to describe someone with the cuddly warmth and humanity of a James Bond villain, but fewer know what **Niccolò Machiavelli** (1469–1527) actually wrote, or that he is often referred to as the father of the modern theoretical tradition known as realism. Machiavelli saw foreign powers and other Italian city-states constantly overrun his home city of Florence, where, consequently, the type of government frequently changed. He even worked in a short-lived republican government that ultimately lost power. Perhaps his realist perspective was shaped by the fact that he was tortured when the new government took power—after all, there is nothing like a few good turns on the rack to teach one that pain is real. A student of the past, he believed in applying the lessons of history to current reality in order to understand how one should govern. Even more so than Aristotle, Machiavelli worked under the assumption that theory should be based, not on ideals, but on the way that people actually live and the things that they actually do. However, unlike Aristotle, Machiavelli did not look to human potential, and, unlike Plato, he did not believe that it is possible to have leaders who can lead the state to true justice. All there is, instead, is stark reality: "For the gap between how people actually behave and how they ought to behave is so great that anyone who ignores everyday reality in order to live up to an ideal will soon discover he has been taught to bring about his own ruin." [12]

Key to understanding Machiavelli is to realize that, in his opinion, people "are ungrateful, fickle, deceptive and deceiving, avoiders of danger, eager to gain." [13] If it is

> **While politicians in democratic societies may not literally kill one another, they do often attempt to assassinate each other's reputations with scathing remarks, personal attacks, and negative campaign advertisements.**

true that people behave in this manner, then it must also be true that one who wishes to lead—one who would be capable of unifying Italy and stopping the political upheaval—must work with this basic understanding of human existence. The new type of leader that Machiavelli envisioned would be able to control human nature. Thus, he dedicated his most famous work, *The Prince,* to Lorenzo de Medici, hoping to convince this statesman to take on the task of unification (and probably also to convince Lorenzo to hire him as an adviser).

Because Machiavelli believed that it would be necessary to control the populace, he concentrated on the concept of power politics. The advice that he gives is often shocking even to the modern reader, making some view him as the Darth Vader of political theory:

> It is better to be feared than loved.
> A ruler should learn how not to be good.
> One should appear to be good.
> If it is necessary to use violence against people do it all at once.
> Never trust anyone more than you have to.
> If you will do favors for people, do them slowly and not all at once.

Furthermore, Machiavelli often based his dark politics on historical examples of horrible deeds, as when he advised his prince by citing the story of a leader who called his enemies into a room under the guise of a celebration and proceeded to have them killed.

If Machiavelli's advice seems archaic now, think about how it might work in a modern context. While politicians in democratic societies may not literally kill one another, they do often attempt to assassinate each other's reputations with scathing remarks, personal attacks, and negative campaign advertisements. In the presidential election of 2004, for example, think of how the opposing side characterized President George W. Bush's intelligence, or apparent lack thereof. Or how ruthlessly one conservative interest group disparaged Sen. John Kerry's military service.

Machiavelli's advice was cold, sometimes brutal, but it dealt with the realities of the politics he observed. If people in general are self-interested, and you want to achieve a political goal, you must do what is necessary to achieve that goal in the real world. Machiavelli's utopia was a simple one: he envisioned a government that was strong enough to secure peace and security. In contrast to *The Prince,* his later writings advocate a republican government—not because he regarded democracy as a fairer way of doing things (too idealistic), but because he had come to believe that a republic could supply peace and stability more effectively than a prince could.

Hobbes—The Purpose of Government

Influenced by the scientific revolution that occurred during his lifetime, the English philosopher **Thomas Hobbes** (1588–1679) rejected all information that was not acquired

empirically as he sought to craft a scientific theory of politics and government. In his most famous work, *Leviathan,* Hobbes sought to explain why government was necessary.[14] To accomplish this task, he asks us to engage in a thought experiment: imagine a time when there were no laws, no government, and no justice system at all, when individuals enjoyed perfect liberty to do whatever they pleased—sort of like a constant spring break in Florida or Mardi Gras in New Orleans. But what would life be like in this "state of nature"? Like Machiavelli, Hobbes considered human beings to be essentially egotistical and self-interested; in one of the most often quoted passages from political theory, he describes life in the state of nature as "solitary, poor, nasty, brutish, and short." It was a life of constant war and violence. It was *Lord of the Flies.*

Hobbes believed that people form governments because they are rational pleasure seekers, and peace and personal security are right at the top of their list. Thus, people are willing to trade some of their liberty in order to achieve tranquility. (Think of how many Americans are willing to trade away their personal liberty in the wake of the 9/11 tragedy—they, too, are willing to trade liberty for peace.) According to Hobbes, government begins when people join together to form a "social contract" with each other. Under the terms of the contract, they agree to trade their liberty for protection from the harshness of the state of nature. Their individual freedom is turned over to a sovereign—a person or a group of people with supreme authority—who is responsible for securing and maintaining the peace. Once the people consent to join into this social contract, they must follow the will of the sovereign. who has the power to do whatever is necessary to ensure domestic tranquility. They have surrendered all of their rights, including their right to disagree; there is no such thing as freedom of speech or freedom of religion. There is nothing except what is granted by the sovereign. Unlike Aristotle, Hobbes did not believe that the state is natural. It is merely a human creation that originated because it serves a useful purpose.

Thus, not only does Hobbes provide the reason for the origin of the state, but he also tells us about the obligations of the individual and the sovereign. The sovereign's responsibility is to provide for the safety of the populace. Consequently, Hobbes contrasts the perfect world of the state of nature with the positive utopia of a life of security. However, that original, negative utopia always lurks in the background as a justification for the sovereign's rule.

Locke—Civil Society

Like Hobbes, **John Locke** (1632–1704) was a Brit with a scary hairdo who also, in his *Second Treatise of Government,* begins with a state of nature.[15]* However, unlike Hobbes's vision, Locke's state of nature is not a bad place: in his conception, all have natural rights to "life, liberty, and property." People are social, and since they deal with

---

*It is rumored that John Locke never actually died, but was "Lost" on a tropical island and is now living with a French "woman" named Rousseau, polar bears, and a bunch of other survivors of a plane crash.

each other according to the rules of natural law, any social difference among them is due to how hard they work. However, the state of nature can suddenly turn into a state of war when a few people, acting like bullies at the playground, seek to violate natural laws and cause havoc for everyone. Furthermore, there are difficulties with meting out justice in the state of nature, such as preventing vengeance from leading to excessive punishment, and enabling the science-club members of the world to get some respect from the varsity football team.

Since Locke believed that the state of nature is not as nasty as Hobbes envisioned it, he argued that when people come together in a state of nature, they first form a "civil society," which then creates a government. Thus, civil society is superior to the government, and the government that is created is a limited one. People surrender only as much of their rights as is absolutely necessary for the government to carry out its primary function, which, according to Locke, is "the preservation of property." Hence Locke's utopia is one in which the government exists as a subcontractor to the civil society, and this subcontractor continues to work as long as it performs its responsibility to protect the natural rights of the populace. All are free to enjoy their rights (including life and liberty), property, and the fruits of their labor.

Perhaps what is most important in Locke's theory is what is left implied. If the government does not live up to its responsibility, can it be fired? Do the people have the right to cast off a government that fails to protect the rights and privileges of its citizenry or abuses its power? One answer can be found in the Declaration of Independence, which, building on Lockean theory, proclaims, "That whenever any form of government becomes destructive of these ends, it is the Right of the People to alter or to abolish it, and to institute new Government."

Rousseau—Why Can't We Be Friends?

Unlike Hobbes and Locke, **Jean-Jacques Rousseau** (1712–1778) was French. While that may seem an odd point to make, we insert it here to remind you of the normative nature of political theory. The answers to questions about what is right or wrong, what is better or worse, what should or should not be, are influenced not just by personal experience and history but also by the culture of the society from which you write. Just as you would not equate an English pub with a French bistro, you must recognize that the English and French political cultures are quite different, resulting in a profound divergence in the political theories produced by their philosophers. Thus, Rousseau's political theory does not stress individualism to the degree that the works of his British predecessors do. However, despite the jokes they make at each other's expense, the French and the English are part of a common Western, liberal tradition, and they share far more in the way of presumptions about the world and the nature of human society than is the case if you compare either of them to

Chinese, African, Native American, or other non-Western cultural traditions. If the difference between English and French perspectives goes all the way down to the level of whether the individual liberties are important, imagine how culture affects political theory when you look at political theorists from outside the club of dead white European male theorists.

Rousseau did not believe that civilized society is an improvement on the state of nature. In *On the Social Contract,* he writes, in his characteristic dramatic style, "Man is born free, and everywhere he is in chains." [16] Like Locke, Rousseau believed that life in the state of nature is not all that bad—the people may be primitive and simple-minded, but they retain their liberty. Rousseau believed that all of society, not just political society, is corrupt. It makes people focus on their individual desires, robbing them of their compassion and promoting inequality. Unlike Hobbes and Locke, who saw civilization as the answer, Rousseau thought it was the problem.

Rousseau believed that people need to reject societal inequality by placing the common good of all above their own personal interests. When the populace is prepared to make this commitment, it can form a new social contract that is unlike any of those previously discussed. Rousseau is not seeking democracy—at least not liberal democracy, wherein the voice of the majority is considered primary. Rousseau's new contract is formed by the "total alienation of each associate, together with all of his rights, to the entire community." [17] In exchange for the surrender of individual rights, each person gets to join in the solidarity of what he calls "the general will," which is the voice of the majority speaking for the common good of all. In essence, this is an experience in which participation is not just a means for reaching decisions, but a process that is itself enlightening as well. All who participate grow through their participation in the general will. Since the general will is comprised of equals with concern for everyone and since it is discounting private wills and personal stakes for the good of all, it can never be wrong.

Furthermore, the general will is the sovereign. Anyone who does not follow its rules will be "forced to be free." [18] The general will represents Rousseau's perfect world. It is a government that rules for everyone at nobody's expense. All who participate are enlightened by their participation, as the evils of society are cast aside. Obviously, Rousseau had a higher view of human nature and human potential than did either Hobbes or Locke. Casting aside Machiavelli's realism, Rousseau returned to idealistic views of what is possible.

Marx—You Will Wait!

Okay, so we promised you seven theorists. The reality is that Karl Marx gets a good chunk of chapter 5, where we introduce the connection between government and economics, where he made most of his theoretical impact. We did not want to leave him off the list, so here he is. If you absolutely cannot stand the wait, go ahead and peek at chapter 5.*

So that is our list of nearly ten. It is far from indisputable. Serious arguments can be offered for at least a dozen others, including Gandhi, Mao Tse-tung, Adam Smith, and Thomas Jefferson, and sarcastic but not completely ridiculous arguments might be offered for thinkers ranging from H.G. Wells to Walter Cronkite. In making such a list, one thing to avoid is an elitist, Platoian† attitude—dismissing political theories and thoughts because of the social status or intellectual pedigree of the person offering them. After all, *Bill and Ted's Excellent Adventure* contains some juvenile and simplistic but still mostly non-heinous political commentary.

Non-Western Political Theory

Non-Western is such a powerfully inelegant term. It is both humongous in scope and arrogantly dismissive to the point of belittling what it describes. The non-Western world encompasses half of the habitable continents—or more than half if you realize that Australia is not really all that habitable. *Non-Western* covers at least 85 percent of the non-alien sentient beings living on the earth, and it includes all of the oldest civilizations on the planet. However, the word also groups and defines all of those civilizations, religions, philosophies, and histories in terms of the one thing they lack—Westernness—while denying the myriad of qualities they possess.

We use the term anyway, but just to prove that we are not complete heathens, we also want to point out three of the largest and most coherent bodies of political theory that are not stuck in the long shadow of the lead-poisoned, wine-guzzling Greeks.

The longest history of serious excellence in theorizing in print award has to go to the Chinese. By some accounts, **Sun Tzu**'s *Art of War* is the oldest secular text still in existence and, more to the point, it is still widely read and incredibly influential.[19] While some might argue that Chinese political theory is a Confucian body of thought, and Confucius is a prominent intellectual figure in that body of literature, it should be noted that Sun Tsu is mentioned far more often than Confucius in reference to Chinese political thought. One of the key elements of Chinese political theory that stands in stark contrast to the Western models is its focus on the society first and the individual second. This is a gross overgeneralization, but we are good at gross overgeneralizations, so we stick with our strengths. This aspect of Chinese culture is also emphasized in every historical overview or reader that might be offered as an entry point into a discussion of Chinese political philosophy.

---

*You will be penalized 17 orange bonus points if you skip ahead, but that is the price you pay for impatience.

†As in reflecting the ideals of Plato. Not to be confused with platonic, which refers to some kind of dating without actually dating. It also has nothing to do with plutonium.

In many ways, Indian* political thought provides some even more interesting contrasts to the Greeks than that of the Chinese. Most obvious is the fact that Indian political theory is built upon the idea of innate human obligations rather than the Greek idea of innate rights. The resulting arguments about how leaders and those whom they lead should behave—such as those offered by Kautilya in his *Arthashastra*—create a remarkably different image of how a government and a society should function.[20]

Finally, in what may be the most important body of political theory for helping us to understand the modern world, there is a rich and extensive history of Islamic political thought. The Koran itself contains, explicitly, the foundations of Islamic political theory, but to say that an Islamic theoretical perspective conceptualizes politics as inseparable from religion oversimplifies and overlooks the complex social and historical dynamics that shape both Islam and the societies in which it significantly influences politics. Islam includes within it substantial space for what might be called tribal identities and other local adaptations. Those tribal identities and all of the local political dynamics associated with them and with the physical environs—such as the realities of living in the desert—shaped and continue to shape much of the expression of politics in the world's diverse array of predominantly Muslim societies. Islamic political thought is also the only major body of political theory that is not focused on the state, but on the idea of a nation that transcends borders and governments.

IDEOLOGIES

Karl Marx has already been named as one of our seven most notable political theorists, but as we already told you, his ideas can wait until we start talking about economics. For present purposes, however, he stands as a good example of the contrast between a **political theory** and **ideology**. In essence, the difference between these two bodies of thought centers on their basic dynamics: while theory is aimed at developing knowledge, ideology is about organizing and directing goal-oriented action. It is the difference between doing research on former ballplayers, as many popular authors do, and actually plowing over your cornfield in the hope that they will magically show up for a visit, as Ray Kinsella does in *Field of Dreams*. Marx explicitly wrote toward both ends. It is not difficult to interpret the meaning of *The Communist Manifesto*, which he wrote

---

*South Asian Indians, not Native American (or Cleveland) Indians. Although it would be interesting to examine the political thought of North American First Nations, there are some significant challenges. First, there were hundreds, if not thousands, of socially and politically distinct pre-Columbian societies spread across the continent, leaving little expectation of a common, shared philosophy. Second, most of what we have to work from is European transcriptions of oral histories, and there is no guarantee that European missionaries with limited fluency in local languages and a determination to spread Christianity got the nuances, or even the basic ideas, right. Third, the authenticity of even the best documents can be questioned. In a famous speech attributed to Chief Sealth (Chief Seattle) there is a passage about the loss of the buffalo—which is a very odd thing for the chief of an ocean-resource tribe to emphasize. It is particularly odd if you consider that the Seattle area is well outside the natural range of the buffalo, and so it is unlikely that Chief Sealth had ever actually seen a buffalo. Who, then, wrote this speech or added the passage referring to the buffalo?

with Friedrich Engels in 1848.[21] Its blistering, sharply written conclusion—urging, "Workers of the world, unite!"—is unquestionably the capstone of an argument that is intended to be put into action, to guide political struggle and change. This exhortation also stands in stark contrast to the theoretical and philosophical writings in which Marx makes use of utopias, idealized worlds, and perfect but impractical concepts. The motivations of the two kinds of writing are clearly different, but, because both make use of perfect worlds, political ideology and political theory are easily confused.

Distinguishing Ideologies from Theories

A crude way of distinguishing between theories and ideologies—though one with which Plato would undoubtedly have agreed—is to consider the intended audience. While political theories are written for elites who think intently about the details of the nature of the political world, ideologies are written for the masses. Ideologies are used to convey simple messages, much like the brief morals at the end of Aesop's fables. In terms of yet another grossly oversimplified analogy, political theories are to political ideologies what great works of literature are to their TV movie adaptations. Charles Dickens's *A Christmas Carol* is a complex narrative with layer upon layer of imagery, nuance, and subtle reference to religion, faith, society, and politics.[22] Scholars debate all manner of detail within its pages. In contrast, *Mr. Magoo's Christmas Carol* is an animated cartoon, made for mass consumption and intended to teach kids to share and be nice, and to ask if there really is such a thing as "razzleberry dressing." [23]

Political theories are usually very complex and logically robust, containing an epistemology (which is a theory of the nature of knowledge), and are written for a select audience. They are, in some ways, timeless—not because they have been around for a long time and you are likely to find several dog-eared copies at used bookstores, but because they raise questions and provide answers for problems that persist throughout the centuries.

An ideology, on the other hand, is created to convince large numbers of people to buy into a belief system. While political theorists often make use of utopian images in the development of their central points or in their critiques of the ideas of others, in the case of ideology, the image itself is the point. An ideology paints dramatic pictures of the utopia its proponents hope to achieve—doing so in simple enough terms to be convincing, and even offering how-to instructions for achieving that utopia. Interestingly, it is not uncommon for the tenets of an ideology to be logically inconsistent: the proponents of an ideology may dedicate themselves to war and power struggles as a means of attaining peace, or advocate imprisoning those who disagree with them as a means of preserving freedom and liberty. Having convinced its audience to be a believer, the ideology then provides a set of rules, a conceptual framework, to make sense of the complex world and to shape judgments about specific policy questions. Because ideologies must appeal to large numbers of people in specific countries at specific times, they are also usually malleable enough that they can be changed to meet the relevant conditions. This explains why there are often many different versions of similar ideologies.[24]

We think of an ideology as something someone else has, but we all adhere to or accept one or more belief systems ourselves. Whether these personal ideologies have been acquired through culture, religion, family, language, or conscious choice, we all view the world through lenses tinted by sets of beliefs that we share with others. It is important when studying politics to realize that we have these beliefs and to understand how our ideological lenses alter our vision, even if we cannot or do not wish to remove them. This reflection allows us not only to question why we hold a particular ideology, but also to more fully understand others' perspectives and to appreciate how our own beliefs control our perceptions of the complex world of political preferences.

Classifying Ideologies

There are several ways to discuss ideologies. Because they are temporal—they are born, they evolve, they die, and they spawn variants—it is possible simply to give a history of prominent or influential ideologies. We could organize them into family trees and discuss their intellectual roots and how they evolved. We could create a scheme for categorizing them, like the taxonomy of species that relates fossils and living animals. Because they are meant to be implemented, the proponents of ideologies are constantly looking for new followers to join their ranks. As such, ideologies are like television commercials for ideal worlds: just as a commercial is supposed to make you want to get up off the sofa and go buy something, an ideology is supposed to stir you to action. Therefore we decided to present to you our commercials for a few prominent ideologies. At first, we were just joking around while outlining this chapter and thought commercials for ideologies would be amusing. But then we realized that it worked. Fake commercials are a perfect metaphor to convey the idea that ideologies sell people the simplified image of an ideal as a way to enable groups or leaders to engage the realities of politics.

One more common thread characterizes ideologies. With the possible exception of classic conservatism, they all presume that human beings can make rational decisions and that people can mold their destinies. Although you may view this statement with something approaching the excitement of studying how paint dries,* it is a genuinely fascinating fact whose discovery was crucial to making modern political ideologies possible. Think about how many modern political ideologies could not have been imagined when people believed that kings ruled because God chose them. Think of how many ideologies remain inconceivable even now in countries where governments claim that they are ruling in God's name. This common thread also explains why the first great

---

*Those of you considering taking advantage of the entertainment value of watching paint dry, don't bother. It dries from the edges first and gradually gets lighter in color and tone.

WHAT IS THE DIFFERENCE BETWEEN LIBERALS AND CONSERVATIVES IN THE UNITED STATES?

When it comes to ideologies, Americans are flat-out boring. On an ideological continuum that ranges from socialism, on the one hand, to authoritarianism on the other, the vast majority of Americans fall right smack in the middle. Forget about the hyperbole you hear from politicians. Sure, the members of Congress like to call each other everything from communists to Nazis, but the simple truth is that most Americans are centrists—though they probably prefer to describe themselves as "moderates."

Most Americans believe that there are matters in which the government should not be involved—for example, personal economic decisions and choices about how one should raise one's children. On the other hand, most Americans also now believe that government should play at least some role in managing the economy. Thus, in the United States, the terms "left" and "right," "liberal" and "conservative" could be more accurately phrased as "left-of-center" and "right-of-center." Whereas in some countries—such as Italy—"the left" refers to real-life, honest-to-goodness, old-school communists, and "the right" includes some folks whose ideas would make Attila the Hun blush, partisans of either ilk are virtually nonexistent in the United States, and they are certainly without representation in the Congress.

In case you are wondering if politics really makes any difference when there is so little range among the politicians, relax: of course it does. Think of all the issues that are out there and the different solutions that have been offered for them. Whether the debate involves school prayer, the teaching of evolution, abortion rights, tax cuts, welfare programs, health care, environmental protection, the minimum wage, or just about anything else you can think of, it really does matter which side of the center a politician is on.

ideology really kicks in in 1776, when **Adam Smith** (1723–1790) published *The Wealth of Nations,* arguing that individual rational choices are the ideal way to foster efficient economic activity.[25]

Classic Liberalism: The Mother of All Ideologies

Although **classic liberalism** is rooted in the theories of freedom that were articulated by Hobbes and Locke and culminated in the American Revolution, Adam Smith added economic freedom as a key variable. He believed a nation could achieve economic success by keeping the government out of the economy and allowing the "invisible hand" of the market to work unfettered. While this economic aspect of the ideology is extremely important, classic liberalism also emphasizes the belief that people should be generally free from governmental constraints. As Thomas Jefferson wrote, "The government that governs best, governs least." Freedom of speech and freedom of religion owe their existence to adherents of classic liberalism. A classic liberal's utopia would be a country in which the government provides for maximum human freedom by staying out of the way.

The ideology closest to classic liberalism in existence today is Libertarianism. Libertarians believe that the government should provide military protection, a police force, and basic infrastructure (such as roads and bridges), but do little more. Should classic liberals be considered realists or idealists? Because they believe that government institutions are necessary to control the selfish nature of human beings—as is the

Thus far, however, we've managed to duck the question. What precisely is the difference between liberals and conservatives in the United States? Unfortunately, this difference is very difficult to define—it depends on geography, history, and the particular issue at hand. The matter is very much complicated by the fact that neither of the country's two major political parties is organized to promote an ideology; both are organized, instead, to win elections. In most democracies, the political parties try to present a coherent political philosophy. In the United States, however, the parties instead often try to obscure whatever differences do exist between them. It is much easier to win an election if you do not upset those who are clustered either just to the left or just to the right of center.

Here's our typically oversimplified but handy rule of thumb: the distinction boils down to neatly opposed attitudes toward issues of morality (such as abortion, school prayer, and physician-assisted suicide) and issues concerning the economy (such as tax cuts, minimum-wage increases, and government-supported health care). American liberals tend to believe that government should interfere in the economy—opposing tax cuts, supporting the minimum wage, backing government-supported health care—but should stay out of people's moral choices. American conservatives tend to believe that government should not interfere in the economy but should become involved in moral decisions—prohibiting abortions, authorizing school prayer, and proscribing physician-assisted suicide.

Unfortunately, if you cannot think of some exceptions to this simple rule, you are not really trying. In fact, if you really think about it hard enough, you will see that there are many politicians who cross over. It's all just one big muck in the middle.

case with the U.S. Constitution—they seem to be realists. However, some would argue that their faith in unregulated economic markets is just as idealistic as unbridled faith in human potential.

Classic Liberalism, the Commercial: Row after row of identical bureaucrats, in identical suits, with tons of papers on their identical desks, stretch off into the infinity of an impossibly vast office. Those same identical men are seen stapling a cease-and-desist order on a half-built tree house as they march children off in handcuffs. More government clones are shown out in a rainstorm, posting signs saying "Wetlands" at the edge of every puddle. A lemonade stand is suddenly crushed as a dump truck buries it under a mountain of papers printed with big red letters spelling out "GOVERNMENT REGULATIONS." A teenager in a fast-food uniform excitedly opens his first paycheck, just as one of the government clones pops up to snatch it away and then grabs all the others from the slots by the time clock. The Twisted Sister song, "We're Not Gonna Take It," stops blaring as the voice-over proclaims: "There are rights that no one can take away. You know what is best for you. You work hard and you're entitled to life, liberty, and the pursuit of happiness. You deserve the opportunity to make the most of yourself without government standing in your way or taking away your rewards with high taxes. Become a classic liberal and learn how to stand up for your rights."

Classic Conservatism

Generally associated with the eighteenth-century British parliamentarian Edmund Burke, **classic conservatism** developed as a reaction not to classic liberalism, but to the excesses resulting from the French Revolution. It is often said that conservatives do not like change, but, although this generalization originates with classic conservatives, it is not really accurate. What Burke objected to was the belief that unrestrained individual human reason could take the place of long-standing, traditional institutions. He believed that no group of people could possibly know all of the reasons why institutions such as the church and the aristocracy existed or why traditions evolved. These institutions served a purpose that had been carefully honed by centuries of experience, evolving through success and failure; they evolved and human knowledge grew. Thus, these institutions and traditions became shorthand for information that would be impossible for any group of human beings to possess. Classic conservatives believe that people should be very wary of changing things until they understand all the ramifications of those changes—lest they unleash unintended consequences, such as the havoc that followed the French Revolution. The perfect world envisioned by classic conservatives tends to be a negative one; it is a picture of the anarchy that might result from the careless elimination of treasured institutions.

> **Classic Conservatism, the Commercial:** Simon & Garfunkel's "Feelin' Groovy" plays in the background of a Norman Rockwell–ish small-town setting where beautiful children are sitting on their grandparents' laps and selling lemonade in front of their white-picket-fenced houses. The music screeches to a halt and is replaced by the Talking Heads' "Burning Down the House," while on the screen an unruly crowd pushes down a pillar, causing the town hall to come tumbling to the ground. Footage of hippies from the 1960s, carrying "Down with Marriage" signs, are followed by additional shots of the poster children of every unusual counterculture in existence, culminating in a scene of a crowd of them burning Bibles. The images conclude with a pan out to a vast desert where ruins are visible in the background. The voice-over announces: "They want to change the world. Do they really know what they are doing? What happens when they are done? What is to become of you and the way of life that you hold so dear? It's worked well for your great-grandparents, your grandparents, your parents, and you. But they want to change everything. Become a classic conservative and stand up for the good things that have lasted for generations."

Communism

For Karl Marx, the central problem with capitalism was the class division between the proletariat and the bourgeoisie. The bourgeoisie was comprised of the capitalists who controlled the entire machinery of the state and who benefited from the inequities created by the capitalistic system, while the proletariat was the working class, which was paid only a fraction of the worth of the goods it produced and the services it provided. Because the members of the proletariat did not make enough to purchase the goods they supplied, there was constant overproduction and, consequently, economic depressions. Marx saw the benefits of capitalism, including industrialization and modernization of feudal society, but he believed that there would come a day when the workers in advanced industrial nations would realize that they had more in common with other workers around the world than they did with the capitalists in their own countries. The workers of the world would revolt by casting off the rule of the capitalists and instituting **communism**, a classless society in which justice and fairness prevailed. In Marx's utopia, there would be no need for government as we know it because there would be enough material goods for all.

Marx's ideology has often been adapted to meet circumstances that were completely unlike the context he was describing. Most notably, Vladimir Lenin applied communist principles to the conditions of tsarist Russia in the early twentieth century. At the time, Russia was still a feudal land—a far cry from the industrial capitalist society that Marx confronted. In crafting what has become known as Marxist-Leninism, Lenin shifted the focus from the exploitation of the proletariat within capitalist societies to the exploitation and colonization of countries—**imperialism**—by advanced capitalist countries. Lenin also changed Marx's revolutionary vision to depend upon, instead of a spontaneous revolution by the proletariat, a central communist party that can organize the revolution.

Communism, the Commercial: Black-and-white image of an ornate carriage in which laughing people in tuxedos and lavish gowns sip champagne and nibble caviar. Their laughter fades as the carriage slows and stops, and the driver climbs down from his perch to inspect the bedraggled men and women who have been pulling the carriage. Stopping at one woman who has collapsed on an injured leg, he unhitches her and then throws her into a nearby dumpster before grabbing a random passerby off the sidewalk and hitching him to the cart. Suddenly, a man runs toward the team of harnessed humans. "This is their world," he yells, pointing to the people in the carriage as the police try to stop him. "It should be YOURS!" One of the harnessed draftees shimmers, changes from black-and-white to color, and says, "Ours." His harness falls away and he begins shaking the person next to him as the police close in. "It is ours!" he shouts gleefully, as a few others around him begin shimmering and gaining color. The police appear to panic as the color spreads to exhausted-looking factory workers, construction workers, teachers, coal miners, and sales clerks. The camera pans as color spreads to the grey of the background, where flowers begin to sprout in empty flowerboxes. Then, as it focuses in on a single flower, a voice-over intones: "Workers of the world unite! Join your fellow workers in throwing off the yoke of your capitalist oppressors. Create a world where those who do the work make the rules and reap the rewards for their labor."

Democratic Socialism

While there were socialists who preceded Karl Marx, it is certainly true that those who followed him were influenced by his view of communism. Like Marx, the democratic socialists who emerged in the early twentieth century believed that people are inherently social beings and that classic liberalism placed too great a stress on individualism. They, too, envisioned a society characterized by social, political, and economic equality. Their primary difference with Marx centered on the question of how to implement this utopia. While Marx believed in the violent overthrow of capitalist societies, the social democrats favored operating political parties in democratic countries in order to achieve their ends.

Although it may appear to be as confusing a point as the ludicrous debate between the Judean People's Front and the People's Front of Judea in the Monty Python film, *The Life of Brian,* there actually is a difference between democratic socialists and social democrats.[26] Democratic socialists believe that a socialist state can be achieved through democratic means, while social democrats aim merely to modify the harshness of capitalism by the infusion of some elements of socialism. A key advocate of **democratic socialism** was Eduard Bernstein (1850–1932), who was active in the German Social Democratic Party. While Bernstein believed that Marx's critique of capitalism was accurate, he advocated a more gradual or evolutionary approach to utopia.[27]

> **Democratic Socialism, the Commercial:** Over an image of Bill Gates posing in front of his mansion, the words "One Vote" are stamped across the screen. Next, an image of Donald Trump standing in the marble and gold lobby of the Trump Tower; again "One Vote" is stamped across the screen. Rupert Murdoch on his yacht—One Vote. Alex Rodriguez in front of his three Ferraris—One Vote. The image of an old coal miner—One Vote. Slow zoom out, and as the frame widens to include the images of various downtrodden people, the words, "One Vote" are stamped over each image, faster and faster until the screen becomes a blur. Voice-over: "We are equal in the voting booth; why not in life? Social democrats ask you to use your vote wisely." As the camera zooms back in to focus on the coal miner, REM's "Shiny Happy People" blares from a distance, and the still picture of the miner's face comes to life. Voice-over, gently: "Shouldn't everyone have a home before anyone gets two?" Zoom out as the miner walks into the front yard of a small, modest house and is hugged by a small child. "Everyone deserves the basic necessities."

Reform Liberalism

Motivated by the inequities of capitalism and the booms and busts of the economic cycles that occurred in the late nineteenth and twentieth centuries, several theorists—chief among them Thomas Hill Green (1832–1882)—began to think that classic liberalism needed to be modified. These advocates of **reform liberalism** began to argue that there was a role for government to play in regulating the economy and removing the major inequities inherent in the capitalist system. Government could both remove the obstacles that hindered people from pursuing their individual goals and guarantee opportunities for those who might not otherwise be able to take advantage of this type of freedom by providing education, job training, a safety net, and so forth. While classic liberals would agree with the first goal—which we call "negative liberty"—they would not agree with government's involvement in securing equal opportunity—which we call "positive liberty." While classic liberals believe that any governmental interference ultimately has a deleterious effect on the economy, the utopia envisioned by the reform liberals includes a government that ensures that no one is left behind. Adopting the ideal world of the classic liberals, reform liberalism hopes to spread it to all in society.

> **Reform Liberalism, the Commercial:** The camera zooms to a stadium where runners wait for the start of a race—although, in this race, it is clear that there is more than one starting line. Poised at the first starting line are contestants dressed in fancy tracksuits and running shoes. Behind them, at the second starting line, are people dressed in working clothes, including construction workers in heavy boots, postal employees carrying bags of mail, and a farmer pulling futilely on the rope-lead of a cow that seems interested in walking off in a different direction. Far behind them, at the last starting line, are others in tattered clothes and with bare feet; these entrants include children, the disabled, and the elderly. Jackson Browne's "Running on Empty" plays in the background as the camera pans across the faces of those on the last starting line, and the voice-over pronounces softly: "One of these people could be the fastest sprinter in the world, but we will never know if we never give them all a reasonable chance. Reward success, but give everyone a chance to succeed. We're the reform liberals."

Fascism

Fascism is a twentieth-century ideology that argues for the supremacy and purity of one group of people in a society. Fascists believe in strong military rule, headed by the charismatic dictator of a ruling party that exercises total control over all aspects of social life and molds it to suit the history and traditions of the superior group. In countries where fascism has taken control, such as Italy and Spain, the fascist party usually has risen to power during a severe economic depression. The leader promises to take control of the economy and works with business to plan recovery. Public spectacles are staged to reinforce traditions and to motivate the people to support the ruling party. Fascists tend to dislike democracy because it allows for the dilution of custom and tradition and because it undermines the dictator's ability to express the will of the people. Nationalism plays a strong role in fascism, as does a belief in constant vigilance against enemies at home and abroad. The fascist utopia is one in which people of the correct lineage return to the supposed greatness of their roots undistracted by enemies who would change or corrupt their way of life. Of course, the Nazis in Germany and the Italian and Spanish Fascists each had the opportunity to try out their utopias.

> **Fascism, the Commercial:** On the screen, soldiers are marching row after row. Patriotic tunes are playing in the background. Watching the parade are very Aryan-looking children waving flags and saluting. Voice-over: "Sick of all the political wrangling, the dirty deals, and the inability to cure our economic ills? We can have it all again and return to greatness. If you believe that REAL Americans should rule America, that someone who actually knows what REAL Americans want and need should make decisions that work—if you believe that the trains should run on time, even if that means running over some good for nothing un-American foreigners, then fascism's for you!"

Other Ideologies

Each of these ideologies has been rethought, remolded, and resold in different places at different times. It is not possible to characterize all ideologies in the space of one text chapter—which is why there are hefty textbooks and entire university courses dedicated to exploring ideologies. We should bear in mind that virtually any vision of a utopia can be transformed into an ideology simply by means of an argument expressing how and why people should take part in the pursuit of that utopia. Imagine the commercials for nationalists who hold that their own country is the best and that the rest of the world should emulate their way of doing things; for feminists (who can be divided further into several distinct ideologies) who look forward to a world in which women are empowered; for environmentalists, who envision a time when the Earth and all creatures are treated with respect and care; for technocrats, who eagerly anticipate a world in which people base decisions only on fact and not on belief; or for athleticists, who dream of a world in which everyone is devoted to a sport of their choosing.

Okay, we made that last one up. But it should be clear that virtually any belief system that includes a utopian vision of a perfect world can become an ideology if believers try to use it to shape political action. Where's your own private Idaho? What does the disembodied voice tell you? (Listen carefully: perhaps it is telling you to send lots of money to the authors of this textbook.) Regardless of what the voice is telling you, however, remember that it is reflecting your ideology. As you read the chapters that follow, you will be reminded to try to recognize your preconceived notions and how they may be shaping your insights as we further explore the real, the ideal, and the political.

KEY TERMS

CHAPTER SUMMARY

Fiction writers, political actors, political theorists, and ideologues commonly invoke images of utopia as a tool to communicate their views about politics. A utopia can be an effective device because, by pushing an idealized vision to its conceptual extreme, it can clearly project specific details of a better world—it may, in fact, expose the dangers of that world. Many people from many different professions have contributed to our understanding of politics. Those we can identify as political theorists use utopias to explore what is possible and what is impossible within the realm of politics. Some of these theorists are realists, and others are idealists. Political theories differ from ideologies in a number of ways. Those who promote an ideology advocate specific programs that are meant to achieve their utopia. Students should learn two very important lessons from this chapter. First, a general understanding of theory and ideology can help you to make sense of your own political opinions and to better understand other's views and political aims. Second, to be considered a great political theorist, you must have been dead for at least a century.

STUDY QUESTIONS AND EXERCISES

1. Why do political theorists and political actors use utopian themes? How can these themes help us to identify flaws in "perfect worlds"?

2. What are the differences between political theories and political ideologies?

3. Which of the political theorists introduced in the chapter would you classify as realists? Which are idealists? Why?

4. How does Thomas Hobbes's view of the state of nature differ from John Locke's?

5. Given the commercials for the political ideologies, what questions would you want answered before buying each product?

WEBSITES TO EXPLORE

www.political-theory.org/. Foundations of Political Theory, an organized section of the American Political Science Association that aims to promote the links between political theory and the discipline of political science.

plato.stanford.edu/contents.html. The Stanford Encyclopedia of Philosophy, encyclopedic entries on relevant authors, concepts, and terms.

www.gutenberg.org/. Project Gutenberg, free electronic versions of many classics, including the theory texts mentioned in this chapter.

www.library.vanderbilt.edu/romans/polsci/polthought.html. Vanderbilt University Library's Political Thought Page, a great collection of Web resources for students exploring an array of theories and ideologies.

www.etalkinghead.com/. eTALKINGHEAD's Political Blog Directory, an online magazine that has, among other things, a directory of political blogs covering an array of ideologies. Exploring these blogs is a great way to discover your own Field of Dreams.

www.cagle.com/politicalcartoons/. Daryl Cagle's Professional Cartoonists Index, an up-to-date collection of editorial cartoons. Cartoons can be powerful tools for promoting an ideology and critiquing others.

CHAPTER 3

Why Government?

Security, Anarchy, and Some Basic Group Dynamics

The ants appear to be doomed. Tormented by some seriously badass grasshoppers that are determined to steal the food that they have stored up for the winter, the colony of little blue cartoon insects will certainly die from starvation. Such is the gripping drama of *A Bug's Life*.[1]

Since it is a kids' flick, you can forgive the fact that the ants are cute, and you also know that since the ants are cute and the grasshoppers are mean-looking, the ants must prevail in the end. The ant hero, Flick, comes up with a plan, and the ants join forces with some circus bugs to fight off the stronger, but severely outnumbered, grasshoppers. While *A Bug's Life* may not be quite cute enough to convince you to welcome the next batch of creepy little critters that invades your home, it does teach us something about the need for security and the origins of government. It teaches us that, if properly organized and led, a group of individuals can accomplish things that are beyond the capacity of any single individual. This is important, because the idea of the many acting in concert to attain the otherwise unattainable is the key reason we have government in the first place.

Given the great joy we all experience when blessed with the chance to interact with government, it may seem unnecessary, if not absurd, to try to explain why we have it in the first place. Whether it is the hot summer hours we spent renewing our licenses at the Department of Motor Vehicles, or counting down the number of shopping days left before taxes are due, or getting a speeding ticket from Officer Bubba (who filled in half the ticket before you ever rolled through his speed trap), our every interaction with government reminds us of the lasting legacy of hope and determination left by those generations that struggled to build a better world. Hopefully, by this point, you have learned how to recognize our sarcasm?

Even people with an interest in politics are likely to describe their personal interactions with government as frustrating. We chafe at the restrictions government creates, we are annoyed by the taxes it imposes upon us, we fume over its inefficiencies, we gripe about its wastefulness, and we rage at its failures. Seldom does anyone praise government; yet, there it is. Except for passing moments of breakdown or revolutionary changes, government is always there. Whether in a communal tribe subsisting in an isolated jungle or in a virtual democracy emerging from a hyper-caffeinated suburban cybercafe, nearly every human being who has ever existed on the planet has lived in a governed society. Given its universality and its near-universal disfavor, we must wonder why people repeatedly create, sustain, and submit to government despite their dislike for it. Whims of fate or simple accidents can cause anything to happen once or even twice, but rational explanations are needed for phenomena that persist or occur frequently. There must be a reason why we all live in governed societies—and it is the business of this chapter to offer you a convincing one.

We all probably have some visceral reaction to this puzzle. The idealists among us are likely to believe that government exists to make humans happy—to argue, like Aristotle, that it is only through participation in politics that human beings can reach their full potential. They will point to government accomplishments that individuals acting without government could not possibly achieve. But there is another view that has its roots in the characterization of human nature promoted by Machiavelli and Hobbes: realists believe that human beings are essentially self-interested. It is this latter view that we would like you to consider when pondering the origins of government. We start with a ridiculously simple story, our own *Bug's Life* version of life in the state of nature and of how the first government was formed.

A MODEL FOR THE EMERGENCE OF COOPERATION: BOBSVILLE

One Thursday morning* tens of thousands of years ago, Bob the intrepid caveman wandered down to a swampy area near a stream. He hoped to make a breakfast out of some of the wild rice plants growing there, as he had done once every few weeks over his many years. However, on this particular morning, he tripped over his purebred hunting weasel and dropped the rice, scattering his handful of grain across the muddy ground. After the heartfelt use of whatever foul language Bob had at his disposal, he quit trying to pick up the rice, shrugged off the minor disaster, and went to look somewhere else for his meal.†

A week or so later, in his never-ending search for food, Bob decided to look in the swampy place again. While there, he noticed that the rice grains he had dropped were

---

*Things like this always happen on Thursdays.

†This is also when humans first decided to try domesticating dogs rather than weasels, but that is an entirely different story.

sprouting. A few weeks later, he saw that the sprouts had grown into rice plants. Then, checking back regularly, Bob watched that one handful of grain grow into plants capable of producing dozens of handfuls. Somewhere in the creaky and seldom-used depths of Bob's mind, it all came together—he could do this on purpose! Instead of eating whatever rice he found, he could spread the grain around on the damp ground and grow all the food he could ever eat.

Bob, in his primitive way, had discovered agriculture. He quickly began scattering rice across the mud, dreaming of the day when he would never have to worry about hunger again. Bob eventually realized, however, that his fantasy faced a very serious obstacle because he was not the only brute who would like to eat this rice. Others who had seen those plants knew what they were and where to find them. In fact, the sudden concentration of this food source attracted dozens of cavemen down from the hills to forage. All of Bob's effort and all the rice grains he had planted instead of eating were now feeding the marauders. In the end, outnumbered by the influx of hungry barbarians, Bob did not get much in return for his effort and sacrifice. In fact, he was lucky to get to eat any of his rice at all.

Bob, we can imagine, was not the first cave dweller to discover that he could grow food intentionally, and he was not the first to encounter difficulty in reaping the rewards of his labor. Over and over again, all around the world, this discovery was made, and, it seems likely, the same hard lesson was learned again and again as the experiment in agriculture failed. Growing food is relatively easy; keeping it is another thing entirely.

Somewhere along the way, one of the frustrated agricultural entrepreneurs had an inspiration, and—for the sake of our little story—let's assume it was Bob. What if several farmers working in close proximity were to join together to protect the grain? Even just a few cooperating farmers could defend the crops from the occasional barbarian wandering down from the hills. Coordinating their strength, several farmers could ward off more organized efforts to steal the food. Inspired, Bob searched for allies who could see the value of growing food, even looking for them among the horde of cavemen who had wandered down to take his first crop. After promising not to attack each other, they also agreed that they would coordinate their efforts to defend the rice they grew. Add a few huts for shelter, and Bob had created the first village and the first vestiges of government.

COLLECTIVE ACTION

In fact, Bob had achieved the essence of government—**collective action**, which is coordinated group activity designed to achieve a common goal that individuals acting on their own could not otherwise attain. Bob and his fellow farmers organized themselves to pursue a collective benefit, but what exactly was the specific goal that drew them together? Although raising food might be the first thing that pops to mind, farming was not the collective benefit this very first government was pursuing. Individually, each of the cavemen could raise plenty of food for himself, but as an individual he could not protect his crops from the other cavemen searching for food. The farmers needed the group first and foremost for the collective pursuit of **security**. Similarly, in *A Bug's Life,* the ants achieve collective security by working together to fight off the grasshoppers.

Our admittedly cartoonish story of Bob's transformation from wandering caveman to enterprising farmer demonstrates some of the fundamental reasons why we have government. Undoubtedly, historians and anthropologists who specialize in primitive governmental and social structures would offer valid criticisms of our "state of nature" story— mainly objecting to the omission of the role family structures played in the creation of Bobsville. The similarities between the organizational and power structures of extended families and the structures of primitive governments throughout history do provide evidence of a connection between family and early government. In fact, many of these family-derived governmental structures persist to this day in the form of hereditary dictatorships like that in North Korea, or in the relationship between the states and the U.S. federal government, which resembles the independent but connected relationships of an extended family. However, even a family-derived governmental structure would eventually face problems similar to Bob's. It would have to protect itself from others.

Thus, the story demonstrates that one essential element of government—if not its primary element—is collective action, which, in this case, is focused on the attainment of security. When Bob and his friends eventually realized that they could also be more productive by coordinating their efforts, they then became involved in a different sort of collective action. (The farming part of the story will be useful in discussing government's role in economics in chapter 5, and we return to Bobsville then.)

Collective action is the essence of government because there are certain things that only a group can accomplish. There are some things that simply cannot be attained by individuals. Consider the many things that government does—for example, building roads, protecting the environment, maintaining libraries, and constructing elaborate hoaxes about men landing on the moon. How many of those things would be difficult, if not impossible for even the wealthiest or most powerful of individuals? For now, however, the key element of this story is the connection between the purpose of government—people working together to achieve what they cannot do alone—and the quest for security.

SECURITY

What do we mean by the word *security*? Though we all have a sense of the concept, the term can be problematic, particularly for the study of politics. Security can involve anything from China pointing ballistic missiles at Taiwan to the blanket Snoopy is always trying to steal from Linus. Security can mean being able to walk from the classroom door to your car without fear of bodily harm, the assurance that you will have a paycheck arriving next week, or knowing that you can always drop by your parents' kitchen and walk away with a full stomach. Even if we limit the term to how it has been defined and used in the study of politics, it is still difficult to nail down—some scholars have even argued that the effort is futile. Moreover, when we attempt to define the term accurately, we wind up with so many nuances that even the clearest result tends to be overly complicated.

Rather than wrestling with the complexities, we offer a definition that cuts straight to the heart of the concept, much as we did with the term *politics* in the first chapter. Bob and his farmer friends attain security when they develop the ability to protect their crops. Thus, simply put, the quest for security is the effort to protect, preserve, or maintain control of something of value. Although this definition lacks the richness of some others, it nevertheless captures the basic idea.

Better yet, you do not even have to hope that we authors know what we are talking about. If you look at the way the term *security* is defined or applied in the research and commentary on politics, you can see that it is always a question of adding a specification of what is to be protected. For example, political scientist Brian L. Job lists four securities that are critical to understanding the political dynamics of developing nations.[2] Unlike the situation in the industrialized and developed countries of the world, the security that you know as national security but political scientists refer to as **state security**—the protection of borders and governmental structures from outside threats— is not the most important consideration in the international relations of developing nations. Instead, these countries' foreign policies are dominated by **regime security**, which is the leaders' ability to protect their hold on power. The pursuit of regime security is often complicated by issues related to what political scientists define as **national security**: the protection of the interests or survival of the ethnic groups that people identify with.* These ethnic groups often clash within countries, and they are often spread across the borders between countries, making their pursuit of security an international issue. Lost in the politics of state, regime, and national security is a fourth category, **individual security**. Notice that in this discussion of different securities, the key to understanding the politics is determining who is trying to protect what from whom.

In order to truly grasp the concept of security and to understand why the collective pursuit of security is such a central element for government, we have to define a few more closely related terms.

POWER

While *security* is a contested term, the debate over its meaning is nothing compared to the disagreements surrounding the concept of **power**. The manifestation of power can

---

*We know the world would be a better place if political scientists just defined national security as everyone else does, but if it were less confusing, there would be less need to teach this stuff to suffering university students and thus fewer jobs for political scientists so don't expect it to happen any time soon.

be as obvious as a tank rolling in to break up the protests in China's Tiananmen Square or as subtle as the student carrying bags of groceries stopping that tank by simply refusing to get out of its way. Power can be exercised through the brute physical force of a police officer's patrol stick or through an official's deft evocation of patriotism to provoke a desired response from a crowd. It is this wide range of applicability that makes the term so difficult to define with accuracy.

Again, we resort to a simple definition to capture the fundamentals of this concept. At its core, power is the ability to get something done. While this definition is so elementary that it borders on the tautological, it cuts right to the heart of the notion of power. We tend to regard any successful effort to accomplish a goal as an exercise of power. The tank had the power to disperse the protesters because it posed a threat to their lives. The student had the power to stop the tank by stepping in front of it because he could force the driver to choose between halting or accepting responsibility for running over an unarmed, non-threatening person. Brute force is power that surges toward a goal by means of a direct application of energy. The manipulation of language and imagery is power because it can channel the actions of a crowd. Whether direct or indirect—doing something yourself or getting others to do it for you—power is the ability to disturb the momentum of events. It is the ability to *influence*.

Power is widely believed to be the key variable in politics. Clearly, if politics is about acting to achieve a particular goal, then the ability to get it done is of the utmost importance. Power is so pervasive a concept that you likely take its role in your own life for granted. But think about all those people in your life who can get you to do certain things and how they go about getting you to do them. For example, your parents—how do they get you to do what they want? What about your boss? Your professors? Why, exactly, are you reading this book?

When we think of power, we are more inclined to picture the police officer's billy club, a tangible implement of the use of force, than the blue uniform and conspicuous patrol car, which make use of symbolism to alter people's behavior. However, the use of power can be, and usually is, conveyed in a form that is far more subtle. Think of the relationship between boss and employee—Mr. Spacely and George Jetson, Mr. Slate and Fred Flintstone, Mr. Krabs and SpongeBob SquarePants. Poor George is constantly taking abuse from Mr. Spacely. Mr. Slate is always firing, or threatening to fire, Fred. SpongeBob doesn't get it, but if he did, he would realize that Mr. Krabs exerts power to get him to use his skills as "fry cook to the gods." Why do George, Fred, and SpongeBob put up with it? Well, why does the supermarket clerk willingly clean up the baby's "accident" in Aisle 10? Why do millions of people comply with the wishes of their unarmed and physically unimpressive bosses? Is it because their kneecaps are in jeopardy? No, their acquiescence is probably due to the slightly subtler economic influence that all bosses have over their employees. At the extreme, bosses can fire their employees and deny them future paychecks, but they are more likely to exercise their power toward less drastic ends. After all, bosses also assign workloads, schedule vacations, distribute raises and promotions, and determine who gets the window office. In large corporations, the few sentences that a boss types into a performance review can facilitate or derail a worker's career. The diffuse power that the boss wields is probably why, in our androgynous workplace example way back in chapter 1, Pat was laughing at the boss's jokes—it was all about power.

Stretching the employment analogy far beyond the bounds of prudence or caution, we now suggest that power is to those active in politics what money is to the capitalist. The capitalist needs to accumulate money and then spend it carefully in the pursuit of profit and efficiency. The politician needs to amass power and then apply it carefully to gain the support of others, to win leadership positions, and to be effective in politics. In fact, we often apply the term **political capital** to indicate some official's reserve of power that can be called upon to achieve political goals. While it is not a tangible resource such as a stock option or a savings account, political capital can be stored or built up. Very often, political capital results from favors done for others in the hope that they will deliver their support at a future date. An individual might volunteer in an aspirant's campaign for office, vote for another representative's bill, give someone a job, or contribute money to a political action committee. For years, political parties in big cities provided jobs, food, and entertainment, and performed other favors for their constituents in order to ensure their support on Election Day.

Do note that there is a critical difference between power and **authority**. The easiest way to make the distinction is to think of authority as a subcategory of power—a type of power. A person has authority when the social structure or context leads others to accept that person's commands, direction, or control over their actions. We often talk about authority in terms of enforced legal systems for allocating aspects of social control to certain individuals, such as police patrolling the roads. However, authority can arise even where no formal coercion is involved in creating the leader-and-follower relationship. In the TV series *Lost,* Jack has some degree of authority on the island because the other survivors of the plane crash have chosen to give him (a doctor) the power to make certain decisions in the best interests of the group. Jack can then use that authority to get things done, such as moving to the caves.

The particular kind of power that is appropriate in a given situation is intimately related to the specific political and social context. Different social environments affect how power is used. For example, a president exercises a different type of power than a dictator does. A country with a nuclear arsenal exerts a different type of power than does one that is rich in petroleum reserves. However, there is one context, one structure of human interaction, that is fundamentally different from all others: anarchy. In order to comprehend how power works and why security is a fundamental reason for government—why the ants must work together, and why Bob and his cavemen-turned-farmers must cooperate to ward off the marauders—we must first understand anarchy.

ANARCHY

Unlike the concepts of security and power, the definition of anarchy is not something that political scientists argue about. However, in this case, it is the common usage of the term—as in the Sex Pistols image of punk rockers rioting in the streets—that is likely to create confusion. When political scientists speak of **anarchy**, they are referring not to chaos, but to an absence of any kind of overarching authority or hierarchy. In an anarchic situation, such as pre-cooperation Bobsville, there is no means for policing behavior or enforcing agreements. This absence can lead to chaos and violence, but there is no reason that it necessarily has to. In fact, many **anarchists** are ideologues who long for a lack of **hierarchy** not because they desire chaos, but because they believe that human beings are capable of peacefully intermingling and ordering society without broad, formalized governmental structures.*

Conversations in the classroom provide a good nonpolitical example of the difference between anarchy and hierarchy. Before the instructor arrives, there is no hierarchical structure in the room—no overarching authority—because none of the students has any control over the others. As a result, the conversation is reasonably anarchic. Any person can talk to any other person. The ability and desire to talk are the only things that really matter. Furthermore, as the relentless babbler next to you repeatedly demonstrates, it is not even necessary to find someone who agrees to listen before you start yapping. However, when the instructor arrives and starts class, the conversation becomes structured and hierarchical. There are rules for who can speak. The instructor directs the exchange, deciding who will speak and when, thus controlling both the content and the tone of the discussion.

Anarchy and Power

The classroom conversation example also demonstrates the connection between power and anarchy, suggesting why both are crucial concepts for the study of politics. Anarchy is important because of its relationship to power. Before the instructor arrives, your ability, or power, to speak is all that is necessary to allow you to do so. We could even think of the volume at which you can speak as the amount of power you have in this situation. The louder you can bellow, the more effective you can be at getting the words from your mouth to someone else's ears. In a hierarchical situation, however, the power of the individual is constrained. When the instructor is in the room and directing the conversation, the volume of your bellow is not the only factor relevant to your effort to get your words to someone else's ears. You must also consider the structure of the conversation. Your power to make yourself heard is tempered by the rewards and punishments that the authority in the room can direct toward you

---

*Oh don't act so surprised—we warned you that pretty much any preference can be pushed to the point of becoming an ideology.

FICTIONAL ANARCHIC ENVIRONMENTS

Most of the fictional anarchic environments we might mention are lawless, brutal, violent places. Furthermore, the *Lord of the Flies, Escape from New York* kinds of fight-for-your-life scenarios are one fundamental reason why people will accept some quite horrible forms of government rather than live in anarchy. However, there are more tolerable forms of fictional anarchic environments. One form celebrates extreme individualism, offering a perfect vision of enlightened cowboys in a utopic Wild West setting. L. Neil Smith's *The Probability Broach* depicts probably the best example of a world in which there is no overarching authority to govern the behavior of individuals. Everyone carries a gun, everyone knows how to use it, and that is enough to keep people from trying to take advantage of others. The resulting freedom from the restrictions and other burdens of government leaves everyone better off.

Surprisingly, the key to this National Rifle Association version of Disneyland is the same as the key to socialist versions of anarchic utopias. It is equality— the equal ability of all to defend themselves against the predations of others—that allows the anarchic environment in *The Probability Broach* to avoid the brutal orgy of violence that marks most other depictions of anarchic society. Those who would take advantage of others are either deterred from doing so or do not last long against well-armed victims who always fight back. In the socialist versions of anarchy,

such as the commune depicted in Kim Stanley Robinson's *Red Mars,* it is also equality that keeps things from getting ugly. In this communal-life version of an anarchic society, the descent into violence is forestalled by social and economic equality. Everyone gets what they need and no one is privileged, so there is nothing to fight over.

Additional parallels between these two idealized visions of pleasant anarchy can be found in the critical role of socialization and in the fact that neither can quite make it all the way to anarchy. In Smith's utopian novel, individualism has become such an intense social norm that it is tantamount to a religious sin to team up against another, even in self-defense. In the *Red Mars* commune, similarly intense socialization makes it possible to build an economy that contradicts the human instinct to be selfish. The guilt of not giving enough to others is a critical element of the gift economy that develops. Also, neither of these anarchies manages to avoid hierarchy altogether. In *The Probability Broach,* there is a council structure that can be invoked to enforce the code of pure individualism, and in Robinson's Mars series, there remain some informal but still important hierarchies of social status that allow the efforts of groups to be directed toward a common end, such as the group of scientists that acts to defend the planet against evil multinational corporations. None of that, however, explains why multinational corporations are always evil.

in response to your bellowing. By shutting out, quieting, disintegrating, or exiling the loudest voices, the classroom structure makes it possible for the soft-spoken to be heard. The structure and hierarchy of interaction both enable and constrain participation in the classroom conversation.

We spend so much of our lives in structured, hierarchical situations that it can actually be difficult to appreciate anarchy. As a result, this is a point at which fictional examples can be particularly valuable. *Lord of the Flies,* for instance, is a story about anarchy. The characters are boys who are stranded on a tropical island with no adults, no authority, and no rules.[3] The narrative's documentation of their descent into barbarity contributes a human face to the definition of anarchy and illustrates the ways in which people—even children—form groups and attempt to create governments. Post-apocalyptic stories and films also offer us a visceral brush with the true meaning of anarchy. In *The Road Warrior*,* Mel Gibson wins the all-time award for fewest lines spoken by a leading actor as his character becomes the reluctant savior of a small band of people trying to survive in a land without laws to protect them from the power of others.[4] Fans of classic westerns will recognize the theme in countless films in which a lone cowboy rides in to enforce order in a Wild West town; and devotees of *Lost* will identify it in the power struggles between alpha males over who will have authority on their anarchic island.[5]

The frequent brutality that is characteristic of post-apocalyptic stories demonstrates the connections between power, security, and anarchy. In an anarchic environment, power is the ultimate resource, because there is no overarching authority—no structure to prevent the strongest individuals from using their power to get whatever they want. The only way for those with less power to stop the bullies from acting as they wish is by mustering enough power to overcome their inherent advantage. In contrast, in a hierarchical situation, weaker individuals can use the coercive power of the authority structure to fight off their oppressors even though they personally lack the ability to oppose them directly. The only hope for survival of the band of desperate people in *The Road Warrior* is to find enough power to defend themselves against the roving bandits. It is important to emphasize here that hierarchy need not result from government, though governments do provide hierarchy. In an anarchic situation, even roving bands of thugs may constitute an authority structure. If the scenario of *The Road Warrior* seems far-fetched, think about how warlords who exercise power by virtue of the weaponry they acquire have, at various times, ruled countries such as Afghanistan and Somalia.

An Impetus for Government

Anarchy remains one of those ideal concepts that actually exists only rarely in the real world, yet it is crucial for understanding government. Although it may come as something of a surprise, anarchy can even be thought of as the *source* of government. Why? In an anarchic environment, the vast majority of people struggle to survive in a context of constant fear and constant threat. Everyone has to find ways to defend himself or herself from those who are more powerful. People need protection from bullies, and the bullies themselves sometimes need protection. After all, even a bully can be overcome by cooperating revenge-seekers armed with a boulder or two in the middle of the night. The collective pursuit of security—which is why Bob wants to form a village in the first place—provides an escape from this pervasive atmosphere of threat. People strive to protect themselves and those things they value from those who are more powerful.

---

*It must be noted that *The Road Warrior* is actually a sequel. Most of the world knows it as *Mad Max 2*, which should be a hint that there probably was a *Mad Max 1*.

We can make a reasonable sociopsychological argument that humans naturally tend to flee from anarchy toward hierarchical structures even when those structures are far from ideal. If you watch the way strangers herded together in a cafeteria seem to congregate in small groups, there does seem to be some aspect of human nature involved. Think about what happens when you meet and introduce yourself to people. The whole becoming-acquainted process is, in many ways, a method of establishing hierarchy based on information elicited by such polite questions as What do you do? and Where do you live? An extreme example can be found in Japan, where a round of introductions can make you feel like a Vegas table dealer as you swap business cards as fast as you can pull them out of your pocket. That exchange becomes a quick and direct means of establishing everyone's place in a social status hierarchy before the conversation can begin. Once the hierarchy is determined, the person at the top is then expected to initiate and shepherd the discussion. Japan's is one of the more formally hierarchical societies in the world, but, in general, all human societies are hierarchical. Every introduction establishes hierarchy.

However, we can also argue that the tendency to create and submit to hierarchies is a sign of the human ability to make rational decisions. Because anarchy is far worse than all but the most dysfunctional of hierarchical social and political structures, people consciously and consistently choose to flee in search of whatever order they can find. What makes anarchy so unpleasant? Why would Hobbes describe life in his anarchic state of nature as "solitary, poor, nasty, brutish, and short"? Simply put, it is because the lack of hierarchy means that life is filled with fear. Fear is not just a reaction to random scary stuff. It is an evolved human reaction that helps people to survive—and the fact that people fear anarchy should provide a strong clue to the reason for its scarcity in the real world. A hierarchical structure, with its rules and the means to enforce them, can keep the society under control and can remove many of the specific sources of fear that anarchy holds. Most important, hierarchy can protect us from the others around us.

A governed environment may also be appealing because anarchy is perhaps the most inefficient form of human organization, as can be seen in the story of Bobsville. Farming is, in essence, investing. Bob invests his time, his effort, and his food—the very thing that keeps him alive—in the belief that he will have a whole bunch to eat later. An investment such as this, or in any other form, is unlikely without some degree of security. There must be some reasonable expectation that the person making the sacrifice today will be able to reap the benefits in the future. Without that kind of assurance, without some reasonable expectation of being able to keep the fruits of his or her labor, a person would be crazy to invest all this effort and wealth. Would you put money into a savings account if you thought that the police would no longer try to stop bank robbers? Hierarchical structures provide that economic security. Not all do an equally good job, but virtually all are better than anarchy. We develop this point further when we discuss the relationship between government and the economy.

THE CONTEXT OF HIERARCHY

Since anarchy, defined as the complete absence of hierarchy, is on the extreme end of a continuum, any movement away from anarchy is a movement toward hierarchy, toward some societal structure that elevates someone or some group to a position of authority over others. In fact, a single bully who dominates everyone else in an anarchic situation has created one type of hierarchy. When Bob and his hygienically challenged partners cooperate in defense of their crops, they form a different type of hierarchy. When societies form governments, they are creating institutionalized hierarchies, and different societies shape their own distinct governmental structures to meet their specific needs, backgrounds, and values. The particular types of structures chosen determine the context for how decisions are made and how people relate to one another in each society. As we will become increasingly aware, this context has a tremendous effect on what options people have and how they act. Some theorists would even argue that context is the most important consideration when studying politics.

To understand how hierarchy and context come together to shape human interaction, let's return to the classroom. Sitting atop a strong hierarchical structure, the instructor is a dictator. The students get to be the worthy peasants, who toil away at the evil dictator's erratic whim. The instructor has this dictatorial power because the university structure gives him or her the authority to assign the grades that will ultimately affect the students' prospects for graduation and, perhaps, their future careers. The tremendous value that students place on the grades that must be earned within this university structure gives the instructor immense power over them. The fact that students actually listen to instructors, read texts, and study for tests—things that they almost certainly would not otherwise do—is evidence of how effectively the university structure gives power to the instructor. If your instructor were just another poorly dressed person with patches on the elbows of his corduroy sports jacket, a random person that you might encounter at a bus stop, would you read what he or she recommended? Would you write papers at his or her command?

The context of hierarchy is as crucial as its structure. When a student who also happens to be a police officer stops that same instructor for speeding, the relationship is suddenly reversed. In the space of an hour, a professor may go from explaining a poor grade on an exam to handing over her driver's license and registration. The only difference is the context of interaction. The hierarchical structure of the university gives that professor power in the classroom, while the hierarchical structure of the local system of law enforcement gives that student power in the speed trap.

If people fear anarchy and seek hierarchy, if they institutionalize their collective effort to attain security, the next logical questions are: How are these structures created? How do people get from anarchy to hierarchy—to the government that we all like to complain about?

AUTHORITY AND *GLADIATOR*

For the most part, we discuss notions of hierarchy in terms of official or enforced relationships between people, but this should by no means be taken as a dismissal of unofficial or voluntary hierarchical relationships. One way to frame this alternative approach is through the idea of authority, whereby a person chooses to defer to someone else's knowledge, natural ability, or experience.

In *Gladiator*, Russell Crowe's character, Maximus, takes his first trip into the Roman Coliseum that is certain to be his last—which could be troubling, since it occurs about twenty minutes into a two-and-a-half-hour movie. On the wrong side of a re-enactment of a lopsided battle, Russell and the other gladiators on his team have no chance of surviving, but when Russell takes command of the men on his side of the battle, they win against impossible odds, thus saving us all from having to soldier on through the remaining 135 minutes of the movie without the main character. Not

only was this unforeseen victory an incredibly fortunate development for the director, but it also offers an excellent example of authority in action.

There is no official designation of Russell/Maximus as the commander of the gladiators on his team, nor does he force anyone to submit to his command. Instead, most of the men on his side are convinced that Russell knows what they need to do, and they decide that their best chance for survival is to follow his commands. They choose to give him their obedience because they recognize the value of his knowledge and experience.

When you ask the best student in the class to read over a term paper for you, when you ask a religious adviser to help you with the moral dilemma posed by the extensive parallels between your favorite pajamas and Russell's *Gladiator* costume, when you consult a movie critic's rating to select your next viewing experience, you are voluntarily giving others authority over some aspect of your life.

ALLIANCES

Alliances occur when individuals or groups agree to combine resources and abilities for a purpose that benefits the members of the alliance individually. In some contexts, the term *coalition* may be applied to such an arrangement. Alliances between countries are a key element of international politics, influencing prospects for war, peace, and complex diplomatic negotiations—we are all familiar, for example, with how the Allies joined together to defeat the Axis powers in WWII. For present purposes, the basics of alliance formation can illuminate how governmental structures emerge. The alliance is probably the simplest and the most obvious strategy for those pursuing security in an anarchic environment. Bob's primitive farmers protected their crops by joining together to gain power sufficient to ward off the neighboring marauders.

To illustrate the dynamics of alliances within anarchy, we can use a scenario very similar to that of *Lord of the Flies*. Among a group of seven children shipwrecked on an island, only one knows how to go out in the water and catch fish. We'll call this wimpy kid Gilligan—and if you don't understand why, then you have some reruns to watch. Since fish are particularly good when the only other thing you have to eat is coconuts, all of the kids want the fish. To catch the fish, Gilligan wades out until he is waist-deep in the ocean and then stands there for half the day until he eventually snags one of the slippery little entrées. In a fair and just world, Gilligan has just secured a nutritious dinner, but in an anarchic environment with no overarching authority, what happens when this scrawny kid emerges from the water with that tasty-looking fish?

Most likely, the biggest kid on the beach, whom we'll call Heathcliff* walks up to Gilligan and snatches the fish. Can Gilligan do anything about it? No. Heathcliff probably outweighs him by a hundred pounds, and there is no hierarchy, no policeman on the corner for the weak little fisherman to turn to for protection. If Heathcliff can withstand some whining, crying, and tugging at his pants, there really is no way Gilligan can keep the bully from taking his fish. What is he to do? If he still wants to eat fish, Gilligan must go out and catch another one. So he wades out and catches another fish. However, when he brings it back in, the second biggest bully on the beach, Bluto,† struts up and takes the fish. Gilligan is probably going to have to provide a fish for everyone bigger than he is before he gets to feed himself. What's more, long before he can feed all the others, Heathcliff is hungry again. Poor Gilligan! He could spend his entire lifetime fishing and never get to eat any fish. On this anarchic island, any kid who is bigger and wants what he has can simply take it from him.

This situation is problematic, not only for hungry Gilligan, but also for all seven of the castaways. Once Gilligan realizes that he is not going to get to eat any of the fish, why should he bother to catch any? Why would he work for no reward? The whole society would benefit if he were to stay out there catching as many fish as he could for as many of the kids as he could, but even if the bullies were to use their power to force him to do so, eventually Gilligan would become so weakened by malnutrition that he could not continue. Alliances offer a way out of such self-defeating situations by providing security within anarchy. Gilligan can make a deal with Heathcliff, offering to catch two fish—one for the bully and one for himself. In return, he asks Heathcliff to protect him from all the others who might want his fish. In other words, Heathcliff and Gilligan form an alliance. Gilligan gives up part of the yield of his labor in return for protection. He is buying security, in the form of the ability to eat his own fish, by sharing his resources with the bully who can protect him. Unlike the circumstances of the formation of Bobsville, Gilligan and Heathcliff are not joining together to promote their common good; each is pursuing his individual interests.‡

If this were the end of our fish story, we would have a plot similar to that of Bob and the first village full of grunting, hairy farmers. However, there is a dynamic here that is different from the collective action leading to the formation of Bobsville. There is a further complexity in this story of alliance formation that can help us to understand power, politics, and the way that government structures form in response to anarchy. To con-

---

*Any English Lit majors in the class?

†Somebody in the class must know the classic cartoons.

‡This is actually an arguable point. Both in Bobsville and in our island scenario, everyone who participates is better off, and, even though one dynamic is cooperative and one is coercive, the end result is the same.

Why Government?

The Social Contract

Way back, probably about as far back as you can recall, there was a glorious textbook chapter, chapter 2, in which we discussed several theorists—Thomas Hobbes, John Locke, and Jean-Jacques Rousseau—whose political theories each contained some notion of a social contract. This concept was based on the argument that there is an exchange between the governed and those who govern. Generally, the exchange occurs when the people surrender some of the liberty offered by anarchy in return for the security and other benefits of a governed society.

Hobbes considered this exchange a fair trade because he regarded life in the state of nature as "solitary, poor, nasty, brutish, and short." Locke believed that life was not all that bad in the state of nature, but he agreed that civil society was better. Thus, government existed to remedy the flaws inherent in an ungoverned society. In contrast, Rousseau believed that human beings were, in many ways, better off before they made this exchange of liberty for governed society, at least to the degree that they had earlier shown compassion to one another. He argued that it was necessary to restore the good that existed prior to civilization.

In describing Bobsville, we, too, presumed a form of social contract. Ours was an egalitarian cooperative among equals rather than a hierarchical arrangement of ruler and ruled, but it was still a social contract. The farmers were sacrificing their individual autonomy in order to escape anarchy and create a governed environment that could provide the security needed to invest their time, effort, and food stock in growing crops. Ours was also a security-oriented contract, but the fact that Bob joined with others for the purpose of collective security does not necessarily rule out the possibility that government could have flourished beyond such simple alliances because it was a useful tool for providing other forms of collective action. Think of the potential benefits, ranging from a common monetary system, to the building of roads, to securing contracts.

Notice, however, that all these social contract ideas presume that the governed have a choice, that somehow you could choose to leave a governed environment that was not giving you what you wanted or needed. How realistic is that in today's world?

tinue with our story: the second-biggest bully, Bluto, wants the fish just as much as Heathcliff does, and Bluto is just as capable of forming an alliance as anybody else. If he teams up with the third-biggest bully, Ana-Lucia,* together they have more power than Horatio. In fact, with a little bit of forceful persuasion, Bluto and Ana-Lucia can convince Gilligan that the biggest bully alone cannot protect him from their new alliance and that he will find life to be a lot less bruising if he joins their new alliance and agrees to catch three fish a day. Heathcliff is not about to let that happen, however, so he recruits some additional thugs of his own and forms another new alliance that is strong enough to overpower the rival team and force Gilligan back into his camp. The Bluto–Ana-Lucia alliance is likely to reply in-kind, adding sufficient power to overcome the alliance of the biggest bully. Of course, there is nothing to prevent Heathcliff from then trying to amass even more power in order to force Gilligan back into his camp.

---

*OK, if you don't watch *Lost*, there isn't a whole lot we can do for you at this point. You can watch *Lost* in Mongolia, Thursday at 7:45.

Besides mimicking a bad episode of *Survivor,* this example of alliance formation as a response to anarchy also demonstrates how groups ultimately lead to governments.[6] The alliance that is ultimately successful will form a group. In our fish story, the group forms around the competition for control of a resource—in this case, a skinny angler. However, there need not be a fight over Gilligan or any other person for a group to coalesce. Alternatively, the competition could involve a struggle to control farmland, grazing land, a bay full of fish, a grove of trees, water, or any other resource. The key is that the group needs to exist and persist in order to provide the collective benefit of security.

Things really start to get complex and nuances really start to matter when we look at how such a group functions in everyday life. A momentary lapse in the group's ability to protect its valuables is all it takes for a bully to take advantage and for its members to lose everything. That is why the need for security is constant. Thus, Bob's group of farmers must persist as a group even after the raiding cavemen have been driven away from the crops. There are always more cavemen who may wander by. This permanent group eventually becomes the government of Bobsville. Consequently, **government** results from the group's need to institutionalize—that is, to make permanent—its power. It accomplishes this by creating governmental structures to provide the security that people continually need.

Grasping the connection between groups and government can be difficult because, in order to do so, you must drop your current expectations that are based on what government is and does now. You must think about how, somewhere in the very distant past, the whole idea of government came to be. From this perspective, you can begin to see that, once government begins to do more than secure farmland or some other resource, group action and interaction become important considerations. We need to understand why groups do what they do and how people act within a group.

GROUPS AND GROUP IDENTITIES

Before delving into group action and interaction, it is necessary to explore the more basic notion of what makes a group—that is, what constitutes **group identity**. The degree to which members identify with a group, and conversely, identify who is not part of that group, can affect its strength, its cohesiveness, or even its survival.

Group Identities

Think of some of the formal and informal groups that tolerate your membership: high school friends, college friends, a chess club, a church, that cluster of moody misfits in the back corner of the classroom, co-workers, the Jamaican curling team, siblings, a fraternity, an ethnic organization, an honor society, or a high school alumni organization. Chances are you identify more closely with the people in some of these groups than you do with those in others. This closeness can affect how strong a bond you feel with the group, what your group can accomplish, and whether your group continues to survive. Group identity is not fixed. It can vary in response to events within the group or to the experiences of the group as a whole. How a group defines its identity gives it purpose and shapes its interactions with other groups. It may even be the basis for justifying and maintaining the existence of the group.

Group identification first becomes important when the members ask, Who can be a member of the group? Groups constantly struggle over this crucial question. Leaders try to manipulate the qualifications for membership to achieve their own political ends, because after they have decided what goals the group will pursue, leaders must call on members to do the work. The strength of the members' identification with the group will directly affect the amount of effort and resources they are willing to contribute to the group's activities. Can you guess who can be a member of the League of Ukrainian Catholics and who is likely to feel a strong identification with this group?

We have already established that governments emerge from groups. Furthermore, those who study politics often equate current nations with groups, and they therefore study nations by applying to them concepts derived from theories of group dynamics. Thus, a good way to start delving into the subject of group identity and its role in group dynamics is to focus on the United States as a nation and ask the question, "Who is an American?"

The answer may at first seem obvious. With a quick glance around the classroom, relying on accents, appearances, and whatever you happen to know about the people around you, you can probably classify most of your classmates as either Americans or not Americans. While many cases are clear—such as the guy with the southern accent or the international exchange student—chances are that you will have trouble categorizing at least a few. The difficulty arises because Americans are missing a lot of the communal signifiers that nations can usually rely on to identify citizens—there is no universally spoken language, no shared religion, and no common ethnic heritage. In the absence of an obvious marker such as language, people tend to fall back on more legalistic notions of citizenship. There are thousands of pages of regulations and laws that attempt to define American citizenship, but in some extreme cases, even that is insufficient. Furthermore, many of the people who do fit into the category of "U.S. citizen" may not match up with some of your expectations.

Take, for instance, someone born in Belgium who has always lived in Europe but has an American parent. While he meets the technical requirements for U.S. citizenship, he may not fit with your ideas of what it means to be an American. He may not even think of himself as an American. If a Japanese family has a child while changing planes in the Chicago airport, that baby is a U.S. citizen even if the entirety of her residence in the United States extends no further than a few hours at O'Hare. Both of these kids fit the technical definition of U.S. citizens, but would you put either of them in the group we call Americans? What if, instead, the little girl was born over international waters while flying toward the United States and her birth was recorded upon landing in the country, or, alternatively, what if the plane was merely in U.S. airspace, passing through on

> **You may not be able to clearly identify every member of your group, but you can absolutely define those who are not part of your group by instigating a conflict with them.**

the way from Canada to Mexico, when the baby was born? If someone marries a U.S. citizen, moves to the United States, and is widowed a short time later, is he or she an American?

Human groups tend to be amorphous. There is usually a core of people who are clearly members, but groups are inevitably fuzzy at the edges, and they tend to overlap and blend into each other until it becomes nearly impossible to figure out precisely where one group ends and another begins. This lack of clear definition becomes especially problematic when we start talking about group dynamics, because it leads to questions such as these: Who contributes to the collective effort of the group? Who is subject to the group's rules? Who has the right to the benefits the group provides?

Conflict between Groups

The difficulty in clearly identifying group membership has an effect on one of the first aspects of political group dynamics. Although we may not be able to define precisely and completely who *is* part of the group, we can—often quite easily—define who is *not* part of the group. We may not always be sure who is an American, but we can easily spot a group comprised of those who are clearly not Americans. In other words, you can define the core membership of another group and use that definition to distinguish it from the membership of your group. You may not be able to clearly identify every member of your group, but you can absolutely define those who are not part of your group by instigating a conflict with them. That group becomes **the other**, the enemy, and you can be certain that one of "them" is not one of "us." This process is a matter of defining your group by what it is not rather than by what it is. And it explains the efficacy of President George W. Bush's remarks after the September 11 terrorist attacks, when he announced to the nations of the world, "You're either with us or you are with the terrorists."

In this and several other ways, conflict is probably the central element in political group dynamics. A sociologist named Lewis Coser, who examined group conflict in terms of the social or political functions it served, noted that intergroup conflict has a profound effect on a group's identity.[7] Specifically, Coser argued that the degree to which people consider themselves part of a group increases when that group is engaged in conflict with another group. Additionally, intergroup conflict tends to generate an increase in the willingness of group members to accept and actively support the leadership of the group. We can see how both of these dynamics connect to the collective pursuit of security, which is central to the basic structures of government.

Generally speaking, most scholars who study politics prefer to assume that people make rational choices based on self-interest, but group responses to threats seem to be better explained as a sociopsychological process, an instinctual reaction. As we see in chapter 5, when we explore some of the concepts central to government's role in the economy, the rational choices of individuals tend to place immediate personal costs and benefits above the longer-term benefits of the group, but group response to threat presents a substantial challenge to the presumption of individualistic rational choice. Think of war as group conflict, and then consider the extremes of patriotism and the willingness of individuals to sacrifice their lives to contribute to the group's goal.

Although these extreme responses to threats to a group conflict appear to be individually irrational, they make a whole lot of sense in terms of human beings as social animals. You could even argue that there is a kind of Darwinian evolutionary benefit in this kind of reaction to intergroup conflict. We know that human beings are social animals—animals who have always lived in groups. Being part of a group is a basic aspect of human nature. Why? Because human beings are weak and fragile. Because we have no nasty claws or big deadly teeth, and because we are slower than most predators. Individual human beings in the wilderness are extremely vulnerable. However, just as Bob and his fellow agricultural pioneers discovered, if you get a half-dozen humans together and coordinate their efforts, they can become quite formidable. Working as a group, humans wandering the African savanna with pointy sticks are more than a match for any lions and tigers and bears they may encounter.* Language and intelligence allow coordinated efforts of extremely complex strategies, not to mention some seriously destructive weapons technology.

You need to be part of a group in order to survive in a hostile, anarchic environment. If you are better at deferring to authority and committing your efforts to combating threats to your group's security, then your group is more likely to be able to ward off threats. Assuming that this makes your group more likely to survive, then you, as an individual who is dependent upon that group for your own survival, are also more likely to survive. Traits that increase your likelihood of survival in this way should also make you more likely to have and raise children, thus passing on the instincts that enhance the group's response to external threats. Once this group defense strategy gets embedded as an instinct, or basic aspect of human nature, it may occasionally motivate action that is hard to explain in terms of rational benefits for the individual—such as the self-sacrifice of a young soldier. However, in the vast majority of cases, particularly in those similar to the specific context in which the trait evolved, such action will provide sufficient indirect benefits in terms of the group's survival to justify its individual costs. Regardless of whether it is rational or instinctual, group identity and the influence it can have on individual actions are powerful factors in politics.

Group response to external threat is more than just a theoretical concept. Researchers have done a great deal of work on the topic, and there is clear evidence that groups tend to coalesce when confronted with an external threat. This defensive identification is an

---

*The ability to defeat lions, tigers, and bears in this setting is even more impressive when you consider that neither tigers nor bears live in Africa.

important part of the dynamics of real-world politics. Scholars have found that regardless of the nature of a country, its type of government, or its historical, social, political, or religious heritage, the measures of group identification—such as nationalism and patriotism—tend to rise when a nation finds itself in an international conflict. In fact, the rise is often quite dramatic.

People tend to have an immediate, strong reaction to any threat to their nation. This phenomenon is very clearly demonstrated in the United States by what political scientists refer to as the "rally 'round the flag effect." Whenever Americans perceive a threat to the nation, public opinion polls show a sudden upsurge in the president's approval ratings, as well as in other measures of patriotism. To cite a rather less "scientific" example, it is not surprising that flag sales shot through the roof in the wake of 9/11, as Americans expressed their increased group identification in response to a clear and unmistakable threat.

Leadership Interests

In addition to defining who is or is not part of the group, the power of group identity can also affect the purpose of the group, if not justify its existence. A perfect example can be seen in *Lord of the Flies,* in the case of Jack and the choir. If you think of all of the kinds of school groups you might want to have with you when stuck on a deserted island, it would be hard to think of one that might seem less useful than a choir. You might even be better off with the chess team, because at least its members have the proven ability to think and solve problems. The choir members in Golding's novel, however, have a very strong group identity, which makes them and their leader powerful.

The identity of the group is crucial to the power and the position of its leader. From the very beginning of the island adventure, Jack struggles to find a new purpose for the choir he leads—whether as warriors, keepers of the fire, or hunters. Why does he work so hard to change the group's identity? If you think about it, Jack must have once invested a great deal of effort in becoming the leader of the choir. And *investing* is exactly the right word in this context, because Jack devoted his efforts and his resources to obtain leadership, which he believed would give him future or continuing benefits. Being the leader of the choir, or the hunters, or the clog-dancing flower pickers gives Jack power. By controlling the efforts of a group, which he can use to accomplish goals beyond what an individual could manage, he brings benefits to himself. On the island, Jack is the only one who has troops at the ready. In this anarchic situation, he commands a group of boys who will follow his lead. He is desperate to maintain this power, and he can do so only by keeping his group together. He may not even consciously realize it, but his actions clearly demonstrate that he wants and needs the group to continue, and so, even though the choir's purpose has disappeared, the group persists. In fact, much of the story is about the transformation of Jack's group from a choir into a band of hunters.

Groups usually form for a specific purpose, but they also tend to continue even when they have accomplished the goals for which they were created. Adjusting to meet new demands or changes in context, they take on added roles and often persist beyond the lifetime of their founders. Have you ever heard of the National Foundation for Infantile Paralysis? You have; you probably just do not realize it. The NFIP was an organization of North American housewives who organized a fund-raising campaign to fund treatments for the victims of polio and to finance research dedicated to curing the disease. A lot of people put a lot of effort into getting this group together, and it was tremendously effective, collecting huge amounts of money and becoming enormously influential. Then, all of the sudden, some guy (Dr. Jonas Salk) invents a vaccine, and in a matter of a few years, polio dwindles from the most dreaded of diseases to a rare condition, threatening only those people who, for some reason, have not been vaccinated.

What happens to the NFIP? The group has accomplished its goal, so it folds up shop, right? Wrong. A group that controls the flow of huge amounts of money and has a huge membership is invariably led by someone who has a great deal of power and who receives substantial benefits from that power. Leaders of such groups have made tremendous investments, often spending decades building their organizations, designing structures to accomplish goals, crafting bylaws, and establishing headquarters. Whole armies of people depend on such organizations for their jobs, including the officers, the secretaries, and—most important—the leaders, who fly around, talking to important people and enjoying the kind of access to government officials that most people can only dream of. Is there any reason to expect that the leaders who benefit from such a group will suddenly just stop and give it all up? Of course not. The leaders of the NFIP responded to the eradication of polio exactly as Jack does with his suddenly useless choir.

It does not matter that the choir is a bunch of skinny little wimps in robes. They are the warriors. No need for warriors? Fine, the choir will be the hunters. There is no longer a need for the NFIP? Fine, the leader takes the group and its structures and redefines it to focus on fighting birth defects. Thus, the group persists beyond the achievement of the original goal of its collective effort. In reality, there are probably several reasons why the group persists, but one of the most important is that the leaders of the group have invested their time and effort to obtain benefits—even if only prestige—from the group's existence. Today, the organization is known as the March of Dimes.

Even if we presume that the NFIP had a completely altruistic leader who selflessly wanted only to help other people (probably a reasonable presumption), once polio was cured, it must have been impossibly tempting to take advantage of the group's resources to help others. Having accomplished one good deed, why not pursue another?

Once formed, groups persist, as the NFIP did. Leadership interests, which always seem to be a part of politics, are often the best explanation for why groups act as they do. For example, the dynamics of group identity and intergroup conflict discussed by

Coser tend to support leaders' efforts to hold their respective groups together. If the individual members' attachment to a group is strong, it is easier for the leader to convince them to stay in the group and to contribute to its efforts—the group wants to stick together. Furthermore, because the group members respond to conflict with other groups by supporting the leader's directives, groups in conflict become not only more cohesive but also more willing to follow the demands of the leader.

While governments perform many functions, at root they are essentially groups formed for the pursuit of collective security. The process of government formation may be a little more complex than our tale of Bob and his caveman farmers, but the basics are the same. This is why group dynamics can tell us a great deal about governments and politics. Since leaders usually make decisions on behalf of the group, direct its actions, apply its resources, and choose its goals, much of what a group does is determined by the interests of its leaders. Similarly, what a government does most often reflects the interests of its leaders. Thus it is essential to appreciate how leaders perceive their own personal interests if we are to understand why governments persist, how precisely they govern, and what they do to maintain control of society.

The end result is a "realist" view of the origins of governments—but, idealists, fret not. Even if we are totally correct in our view of how and why governments began, it does not mean that, once created, governments and their leaders cannot rise above their origins. Unfortunately, as we see in the next chapter, that may prove to be a very difficult chore.

KEY TERMS

alliances / **59**
anarchists / **54**
anarchy / **54**
authority / **53**
collective action / **49**
government / **62**
group identity / **62**
hierarchy / **54**

individual security / **51**
national security / **51**
the other / **64**
political capital / **53**
power / **51**
regime security / **51**
security / **50**
state security / **51**

CHAPTER SUMMARY

Although government seems to be everywhere, we seldom think about why governments began and why they continue to exist. Logic suggests that, initially, government emerged from collective action aimed at providing security. We can learn more about the continued existence of government by understanding human beings' aversion to anarchy and their tendency toward hierarchy. Additionally, the concept of power and the dynamics of group behavior explain why governments persist. Students should learn two very important lessons from this chapter. First, the phenomena discussed here suggest that governments satisfy fundamental human desires. Second, as annoying as your state's Department of Motor Vehicles can be, it is unlikely that it or any other form of government is going anywhere soon.

STUDY QUESTIONS AND EXERCISES

1. What might the theorists we discussed in chapter 2 think about our story of Bob the Caveman? Which of the theorists would agree that government might have begun in a similar fashion? Which would likely disagree? Why?

2. The news is consistently filled with stories involving conflict among groups. What current examples can you find in the news? How do your examples fit with this chapter's discussion of group identification, "the other," and threats to the group?

3. What are the four securities that are critical to the understanding the political dynamics of developing nations?

4. Why is collective action the essence of government?

5. What is power, and what are the various forms that it can take? What fictional examples can you think of that demonstrate the different forms of power? What are some real examples?

6. How do hierarchy and context come together to shape human interaction?

WEBSITES TO EXPLORE

www.gwu.edu/~nsarchiv/. The National Security Archive at George Washington University, a site filled with articles and documents that demonstrate our concern for security.

www.anarchism.net. This site defines and discusses the many forms of anarchism.

www.cato.org. The Cato Institute, an organization concerned with limited government, individual liberty, free markets, and national security.

www.archeology.org. *Archeology,* a publication of the Archeological Institute of America that explores all aspects of human origins, including the origins of government.

www.dailyshow.org. *The Daily Show with Jon Stewart,* the Web site that accompanies the television show's satirical look at the news.

CHAPTER 4

Governing Society
Controlling the Behavior of Individuals

When the puppet dictator of a small Latin American country suddenly falls over dead, what can the CIA do? Without this key man that the United States has bought off, how can good old Uncle Sam maintain control over the natural resources of the country? How can the CIA keep an opportunistic person from leaping into the political fray and using the support of the dissatisfied public to rise up and seize that empty leadership position? The simple solution is to pretend that the dictator never died. Simply hire an out-of-work actor to make a few appearances as El Presidente, and then continue with business-as-usual. In *Moon over Parador*, however, that out-of-work actor (played by Richard Dreyfus) turns out to be far more of an idealist than the CIA was prepared to work with.[1] Instead of obediently letting the CIA run the show, the new El Presidente sets out to better the lives of the people of Parador. Worse yet, it turns out that his idealistic approach actually works better to prevent revolt than force and threats ever did, and once the people embrace their new El Presidente, the CIA is going to have a very hard time getting back to its old ways of doing things.

In the study of how societies are governed, one of the key differences between the realists and the idealists is how they view human nature. Idealists tend to believe that humans are essentially good, social beings who care for others.* From this perspective, idealists would argue that when studying what governments do, we should judge them and their leaders by how much they maximize these positive human qualities and how effectively they provide for their populations. Realists are more skeptical. Believing that human beings care only about maximizing their own

---

*We suspect that the typical idealist has never been involved in a mugging in any way. You would think that participating as either the perpetrator or the victim of a mugging would put a real damper on the belief that people are basically cooperative and good-natured. Thus, the biggest threat to an idealistic world would seem to be street crime.

self-interests, realists expect no more from their leaders. As was discussed in the previous chapter, leaders usually make decisions on behalf of the group, direct its actions, apply its resources, and choose its goals, and, from a realist perspective, this means that much of what groups and governments do tends to serve the interests of their leaders.

Since our goal in this chapter is to study how governments actually control the behavior of individuals rather than how governments ought to behave toward individuals, we rely heavily on realist approaches. Furthermore, the realist worldview provides a valuable conceptual tool to help in cutting through the bewildering complexity of politics. Whenever you are trying to understand a confusing aspect of politics, simply ask, "Who benefits?" and "How do they benefit?" The answers to these two questions will usually provide a solid first step toward unraveling the political puzzle. When examining politics, often, the best line to remember is *Jerry McGuire*'s "Show me the money!" [2] Or, to paraphrase, "Show me the power."

The two questions, "Who benefits?" and "How?" are particularly helpful when we talk about the strategies governments and leaders use to maintain control over their populations. It can be argued that, regardless of the type of government they head, all leaders try to maximize their self-interest. These two questions therefore allow us to make a little more sense of the excessive actions of totalitarian governments, such as the one portrayed in Orwell's *Nineteen Eighty-Four*. If we ask who benefits, we can begin to see how leadership interests determine how governments behave even in these extreme forms. When considered from the perspective of who is benefiting, heavy-handed, repressive tactics actually start to make sense. To get at the dynamics of how it all works, we draw heavily on the scenarios of our fictional examples and on the real-world actions of totalitarian governments, but these extreme versions are just exaggerations of what leaders in all governments do. Examining the behavior of ruthless leaders who rule with an iron fist even helps us to understand the actions of democratically elected leaders. A chief executive proposing a budget, members of Congress working in committees, courts interpreting a law, or that annoying school board member who would dress up as a banana if it got her picture in the local paper—all these examples can best be understood by asking who benefits and how.

LEADERSHIP BENEFITS

From a realist perspective, the simple fact is that people want to become leaders because holding the leadership position or being part of the elite group that controls the leadership position provides tremendous individual benefits. There is ample historical support for the argument that the leadership position enables those in charge to pursue a diverse set of personal benefits. Leaders may be power-hungry, as in the dictatorships of Stalin in the Soviet Union, Mao in the People's Republic of China, and Qaddafi in Libya, or they may be interested in extreme personal wealth, as in the cases of Marcos in the Philippines, Mobutu in what was Zaire (now it is one of the many

KLEPTOCRACY IN ZAIRE

The reign of Mobutu Sese Seko in Zaire provides an excellent example of the potential value of the leadership position even in a desperately impoverished country.[1] During his leadership, personal income in the country fell 3.9 percent—the second worst growth record in the world. The country went from being self-sufficient in agriculture to being dependent on imports for 30 percent of its needs. Public school teachers earned only $3 per week, while the low end of the rent scale hovered around $10 per week. Zaire had fallen from being the model of how economic success could be achieved in Africa to being desperately poor in just a few years.

Such economic failure and suffering is even more striking when compared to the wealth that Mobutu managed to extract from the country. "President Mobutu, whose father was a cook and whose mother was a hotel maid, has 11 homes in Zaire and reportedly owns a sixteenth century castle in Spain, a 32-room palace in Switzerland, luxurious residences in Paris and on the French Riviera, and lavish homes in Belgium and the Ivory Coast."[2] As of 1988, Mobutu had amassed a personal fortune estimated at approximately $5 billion,

and he stayed in power for over a decade after that. He was so aggressive in using his leadership position to pursue wealth that his government is considered to be the prototype of a kleptocracy—government by thieves.

Compared to other opportunities available in Zaire, the role of the leader clearly provided the potential for benefits that are substantial enough to explain why people are willing to risk their lives to try to take the leadership position and why leaders go to such lengths to prevent that from occurring. The greater the benefits that are to be gained from the leadership position, the more willing people will be to invest their own resources and to take the risks necessary to attain it. You could even argue that in poorer countries challenges are going to be even more intense because there are few, if any, alternate means to attain success and there are also going to be a greater number of desperate people willing to take the extreme risks involved.

---

[1]Steven Greenhouse, "Zaire, the Manager's Nightmare: So Much Potential, So Poorly Harnessed," *New York Times*, May 23, 1988, A8; Steven Greenhouse, "In Eye of Stormy Africa, Zaire Dictates Stability," *New York Times*, May 24, 1988, A6.

[2]Greenhouse, "Zaire, the Manager's Nightmare."

Congos), or the Saudi royal family. Leaders may thus be after different kinds of benefits, but they all pursue personal gains of some kind. Those of you still clinging to idealism will have to admit that even Winston Churchill, Abraham Lincoln, and Mahatma Gandhi benefited from their notoriety and prestige as leaders of their respective nations, as well as from the ability to accomplish their personal—though altruistic or nationalistic—goals through the political process. The concept of leadership benefits is such a powerful explanatory tool that some scholars go so far as to argue that personal benefits are the *only* reason that people pursue leadership positions.

Given the potential for massive benefits, it is understandable that someone might be willing to risk his or her life to take over a government. This potential also explains why a leader might go to great lengths to hold on to the leadership position. The greater the benefits that are to be gained from the leadership position, the more willing people are to invest their own resources and take risks to attain it. You could even argue that the battles for leadership are going to be even more intense in poorer countries because, aside from leadership, there are few, if any, alternate means to attain success. In a wealthy country, many motivated risk-takers will go into business, sports, entertainment, or the arts. Some will write best-selling textbooks or choose other avenues to pursue massive amounts of wealth or other measures of success, but in an impoverished and undeveloped country, the only real option is politics. The poorer the country, the greater the number of desperate people there are going to be—and the more there will be who are willing to take the extreme risks involved in pursing the benefits of a leadership position.

Given these incentives for challengers, how can leaders stay in power? No matter how incompetent he or she may be at meeting the needs of society, it is not easy to oust a leader. In fact, some of the leaders who are doing the most damage to their countries manage to hold on to power for years, sometimes decades. How? It is not enough to say that they use force. Although some leaders have massive armies and legions of secret police, in even the most brutal of dictatorships, the people outnumber the police by at least a hundred to one. How can so few maintain control over so many? How do leaders keep their subjects from revolting against them? Why don't the people lash out instead of knuckling under?

THE PANOPTICON

One of the fundamental mechanisms that leaders and governments use to control large populations is the **panopticon**. Though leaders throughout history (including your parents) have utilized it, the theoretical concept of the panopticon as a social mechanism for controlling populations comes from an eighteenth-century prison design crafted by the British theorist Jeremy Bentham. The panoptic prison features cells that are all built around a central tower and arranged so that the guards in the tower can see the entire interior of every cell. The key aspect of the design, however, is that the guard tower is completely enclosed by mirrored windows, so the prisoners never know when they are being watched. They know that they are not being watched all of the time, but the severe and public punishments the guards mete out keep the prisoners constantly aware that they *could* be watched at any time. The value to be gained from any type of misbehavior has to be weighed against the chance that one is being watched at that very moment. If the punishments for misbehavior are severe enough, it will not be worth the risk of being seen. Consequently, the prisoners will always behave as if the guards are watching them, even though they know they are not always watched. The only way the prisoners can be certain to avoid severe punishments is to police their own actions, constantly behaving as the rules dictate. In other words, the prisoners serve as their own guards.

In a book called *Discipline and Punish,* the political philosopher Michel Foucault built upon the logic of that prison design by arguing that the panopticon's function of enabling a small number of guards to effectively control hundreds of prisoners is similar to the way in which governments and leaders maintain control over the societies they rule.[3] Indeed, this panoptic means of controlling behavior is a pervasive aspect of just about every government. An example you are almost certainly familiar with is the enforcement of traffic laws. Individual drivers are not constantly watched. In fact, very seldom do the police monitor any one person's driving. The vast majority of the time you spend driving mom's old station wagon around, there are no police around. However, there always *could* be a cop around any bend in the road, and you never know when you are going to be watched. Does that white car behind you have a ski rack, or are those police lights on the top? You just never know. And because the cost of a ticket for even a minor infraction is usually outrageous, most of the time you will stick fairly closely to the traffic laws. You police your own behavior; you watch your own speedometer.

We cannot overstate how deeply the fear that someone might be watching you influences your behavior. Most of us have had the experience of driving down the road and catching a glimpse of a state trooper in the rearview mirror. Even though the cop may be just driving along behind you minding his own business, your heart begins to race, you check your speed every two seconds, your hands get a little sweaty, you get a lump in your throat, and you start frantically reviewing everything you have done in the past few minutes to figure out how you accidentally drove yourself into a ticket. It is even worse when a state trooper pulls up behind you with his lights on, and your mind's eye sees a whole semester's worth of beer and pizza money flying out the window.* You pull over—halfway to the cardiac care unit—and the trooper goes whipping by you on his way to some other emergency.

That fear is what causes you to police your own actions. The state troopers do not have to watch you all the time. They only have to be around often enough to remind you that they are out there watching. It also helps if the punishments are in some way public. You only have to see a few people pulled over here and there, you only have to hear one or two horror stories about a ticket so expensive that a kid had to sell his car to pay it—you only need an occasional reminder of those sorts of things in order to keep those potential punishments constantly in your mind when you drive. You may never get a ticket, but seeing others getting them reinforces that fear and slows your mad rush to the pizza place.

It is through the process of **self-policing** that a few hundred policemen can control thousands upon thousands of drivers every day. Leaders put this same concept to work in order to prevent revolt and to maintain control of whole countries full of people who despise them.

Nineteen Eighty-Four presents several extreme examples of how the fear of being seen shapes people's behavior. The most prominent example is found in the affair between Winston and Julia, in the lengths they have to go to avoid prying eyes. Just finding a way to communicate with one another in order to make the first personal contact is a struggle dominated by the fear of the Thought Police and the punishments they

---

*This presumption of spending intent is pure speculation and does not constitute financial advice.

might bestow. After Julia contrives a fall and manages to pass Winston that first little love note, he knows that he does not dare read it in the bathroom stall, where he is certain to be watched. He has to contrive a way to blend the reading of the note into his normal work routine, so that even if he happens to be watched when he does read it, his action will not be viewed as suspicious. Once he manages to read the note, his fear of the Thought Police makes him afraid to even glance at Julia. As a result, it takes over a week to find some way to respond. They then pursue their affair by meeting anonymously in crowds, going to great lengths to pretend they do not know each other, and taking different routes to their rendezvous in a pigeon-infested attic or a clearing in the woods.

The effects of the panoptic mechanism and the resultant self-policing of behavior are everywhere in the story. At times, they are so pervasive that they seem almost unreal. The conduct of Orwell's characters, however, is merely an exaggeration of the way we all behave. It is the way our parents taught us to "behave" in the first place. Is there any better example of the panoptic mechanism than Santa Claus? He knows when you are sleeping. He knows when you're awake. He knows when you've been bad or good. He's making a list and he's checking it twice. And if he knows that you have been bad, what does he do? He takes away Christmas! Is there any possible threat that a child would consider worse than losing Christmas? This truly is a punishment that outweighs the crime. All you have to do is be bad, and that fat, musty-smelling guy at the mall can take Christmas away.*

The panoptic mechanisms of the real world are usually less heavy-handed and brutal than what we see in *Nineteen Eighty-Four,* but they are a basic part of our adaptation to living in a complex social environment. Whether it is a part of human nature to do so, or some common social adaptation, the governing and social structures in every human society seem to use panoptic structures to help maintain order and control. Leaders use these structures to prevent public behavior that might go against their interests. From a leader's perspective, the worst kind of misbehavior is that which threatens that leader's ability to maintain control over society. Furthermore, because these are the behaviors that leaders are going to be most intent on stopping, they are the ones at which panoptic mechanisms are most often focused.

If leaders are most concerned about behaviors that threaten their control, why would the government in *Nineteen Eighty-Four* even care about the affair between Winston and Julia? More pointedly, why, at the end of the book, do the Thought Police stop the torture only when Winston, faced with the threat of the rats, betrays Julia by telling them to "do it to her"? Why does the hyper-paranoid government in Orwell's novel care about the personal relationships of its citizens?

---

*And parents wonder why kids cry when they are forced to sit on Santa's lap.

COLLECTIVE ACTION, REVOLUTION, AND THE USE OF FORCE

In order to understand why a leader might find personal relationships threatening, we have to return to the subject of collective action. As we pointed out in the previous chapter, government is, in essence, an institutionalized mechanism for collective action. One suggested motivation for the initial creation of government was the collective pursuit of security in an anarchic environment. Once formed, however, government serves as a framework that society can use to pursue other collective goals.

As it turns out, in the story about Bob and his cavemen-turned-farmers, we skipped over any discussion of how they formed a group. We later offered one way to conceptualize the dynamics of group formation by introducing the skinny geek, Gilligan, and describing the alliances and counter-alliances that formed around his ability to catch fish. In that story, however, we also glossed over several important details about the context and other factors shaping the choices individuals were making when deciding to join or not join the group—or, more specifically, in choosing to accept or not accept the social contract of government in order to pursue the collective goal of security. So, what happens when people do not want to be a part of the governed society? What happens when they wish to cancel the social contract? We address some of these details here because they are important for understanding the most fundamental of threats to a government: revolution.

A **revolution** is a collective action, a mass uprising focused on the goal of tearing down and replacing the current government. In fact, scholars who study collective action and the behaviors associated with it often use revolutions as cases for analysis. Because revolutions are such extreme forms of collective action, these scholars believe that many of the dynamics of choice and action that are general to all collective actions are magnified by the extreme nature of revolutions and easier to observe in a revolutionary context. While the initial formation of government may have occurred in anarchy, revolutions happen in hierarchical environments. Those at the top of the existing social hierarchy are driven by self-interest to actively oppose any collective effort to overthrow the system. Along with the panoptic self-policing mechanism, leaders use the techniques of atomization, peer policing, and preference falsification to prevent revolutionary groups from forming.

Atomization

In essence, **atomization** means exactly what you might guess. Since atoms are the smallest form of coherent matter, it follows that if you were to atomize something, you would break it down into its smallest components. Then, to keep it atomized, you would separate the parts to stop them from congealing into something larger. Leaders prevent the formation of revolutionary groups in a similar way. When people are isolated, they are kept from joining together in a group that could threaten a leader's hold on power. In the extreme case, a leader would want to prevent anyone from forming any kind of personal bond, such as the affair between Winston and Julia. You would have to be a pretty paranoid tyrant to go that far, but if you were out there on the edge of sanity, you might well be worried that such a close personal bond could someday be used as a means to form a revolutionary group. Keeping people separate is atomization, and the two most important mechanisms for accomplishing this goal are peer policing and preference falsification.

Peer Policing

Peer policing is, literally, having people police each other. While peer policing can sometimes occur spontaneously, in order to work as a mechanism for preventing revolt—that is, in order to get people to watch each other for revolutionary behavior— leaders must usually put a few structural elements in place. First, they need to encourage citizens to engage in the act of peer policing against potential revolutionaries, which might be most easily accomplished by making it a crime to *not* report someone's efforts to form a revolutionary group. While this deterrent alone might be effective, the government can make it almost impossible to form a revolutionary group by getting people to believe that government agents will test individuals' willingness to turn in others to the authorities.

Borrowing the setting created in *Nineteen Eighty-Four*, imagine that the secret police come up to you and say something like this: "We know you are guilty and we are going to have to punish you." Even in the context of a real-world totalitarian dictatorship, the secret police do not actually need any evidence or any real justification to make such a claim. You are guilty as soon as they decide to say you are guilty. Working with this presumption of guilt, these protectors of the government can offer to be magnanimous. They can give you the chance to redeem yourself by proving your loyalty. Perhaps you can do them the favor of testing the loyalty of your co-workers. Perhaps you can share some criticisms of the government with the person in your office whom you most suspect of having revolutionary inclinations, so the government can test that unsuspecting dupe's loyalty.

Everyone is aware that this is a common practice by the secret police. So, if a co-worker comes up to you and complains about the government's policy for distributing pistachio ice cream, you are faced with three unpalatable choices:

1. You can turn your colleague in to the Ministry of Pistachio Ice Cream, knowing that even though he is a nice guy and not really a revolutionary, he is likely to be punished severely. However, you will have fulfilled your duty to turn him in and you should escape punishment.

2. You can say nothing and decide not to turn him in, which is dangerous because he could be someone sent to test your loyalty—in which case, failing to turn him in is a crime for which you could be severely punished.

3. You can agree with him, which opens up the possibility of getting together to revolt against the tyranny of the Ministry of Pistachio Ice Cream and thus attaining an end that you both appear to desire. However, you will be at tremendous risk of severe punishment if he happens to have been sent to test your loyalty.

Regardless of how you feel about pistachio ice cream, the only way you can be reasonably certain to avoid the risk of punishment is to report your co-worker.

As a result, the leader has created a society in which people are constantly watching each other, constantly policing each other for revolutionary inclinations, and constantly ready to turn each other in. What does this accomplish? It separates people from one another. It atomizes them. How can you form a revolutionary group when every person you approach about joining the group is going to be afraid of not turning you in? If the punishment for failing to turn in your co-worker for complaining about pistachio ice cream was going to be harsh, just wait till you see what you get for not turning in a revolutionary. As far as government leaders are concerned, the worst crime of all is the attempt to revolt against their exalted position in the hierarchy.

You can see peer policing all over the place in *Nineteen Eighty-Four*. Near the beginning of the story, Winston's comment about doublespeak sends his co-worker into a tizzy. Visibly agitated and sweating nervously, the co-worker vigorously defends the government's butchering of the language. He is afraid that Winston may be testing him or that the Thought Police may be listening and will somehow consider him guilty by association. Then there are Winston's neighbors: by the end of the book, the father has been hauled off to the bowels of the government's police machinery after being turned in for thought crimes by his own children. When even within a coherent family unit one must fear being turned in for merely thinking the wrong thing, you have peer policing at its most extreme.

When just a few government agents are doing the actual policing, keeping the people atomized can be a crucial element for maintaining control. As long as collective revolutionary activity remains impossible, there are plenty of police officers to keep order and handle individual "crimes" here and there. What the government is really afraid of, however, is that these individual actions might occur simultaneously. Mass action, coordinated or not, will quickly overwhelm the government's policing and enforcement mechanisms.

Think about what happens in a riot. With a few notable exceptions, the individual crimes committed in a riot are minor. There may be vandalism, breaking-and-entering, theft, a simple assault here and there, but nothing that is beyond the bounds of the typical junior high school day. Normally, the police would have little or no trouble handling such crimes. But when they happen all at once and there are far more crimes than officers, there is no way to maintain order. Similarly, governments and their leaders can handle individual, isolated revolutionary actions, but they cannot stop large numbers of revolutionary activities from happening at the same time. To prevent revolt, governments have to prevent coordination. Potential revolutionaries must be kept separate. A million revolutionaries marching one-by-one on the capital is nothing, but if those same revolutionaries should manage to arrive together, even the largest and most powerful government could be overrun. As the dictators in the former Soviet satellite countries of Eastern Europe discovered while watching the governments of East Germany, Czechoslovakia, and Romania fall, revolutionaries acting in concert do not even have to be armed to overcome a government's police and military. They must simply act en masse.

Lest you think that atomization and peer policing are limited to totalitarian regimes, look around you—examples are everywhere. Peer policing in particular is often encouraged in the United States and other democracies. A simple example comes from the Seattle area, where the combination of steep hills, lots of water, and tremendous population growth has created horrible traffic problems. Like many other major cities, Seattle has created carpool lanes to try to alleviate some of the congestion, and right next to the signs detailing the carpool lane restrictions are other signs displaying a phone number for drivers to call to report those violating the lane restrictions. When you dial that number on your cell phone, an operator at the Washington State Patrol answers and asks for the license plate number of the vehicle illegally using the carpool lane. If three or more callers report the same license plate, the police send a ticket to the registered owner of the car. This is peer policing at its most effective. Because there are more cell phones than car stereos on Seattle's freeways, you will probably never see anybody running solo in a Seattle commuter lane. So many people will call that number the instant they see you illegally using the lane that you are all but guaranteed a $200 ticket in the mail.

Another example—though of the spontaneous kind rather than government-orchestrated—is from a small town in southern Louisiana, where an old gas station was converted to an adult video store. In a town with more churches than stop signs, this "remodeling" did not go over very well. So parishioners from several of the churches decided to camp out across the street and record the license plate number of every car in the store's parking lot. They then published the license plate numbers along with descriptions of the cars in the local newspaper under the headline, "Is This Your Neighbor's Car?" Within a month, the store closed down.

Peer policing can be an extremely effective tool, particularly when governments take steps to encourage and direct it. The same strategy used to punish the road hogs and close down the adult video store can be used to shut down crack houses and drive prostitutes out of a neighborhood. In reality, however, this voluntary form of policing will only work for a limited number of issues. It is particularly effective at getting rid of behaviors that people already disapprove of; when used in the right context, voluntary policing clearly works. However, in order to convince peers to police each other on other matters—such as revolutionary activities—governments must usually rely on the coercive methods discussed earlier.

PREPHERENCE PHALSIPHICATION—
PHATT AND PHREAKY IN POLAND

When you write a textbook, you are supposed to pretend that you are not a geeky old professor, which means you have to imagine that you can relate to students on their own terms. According to the phront of the hooded sweatshirt of the kid sitting in the back row of the lecture hall, phatt is a term used by students, so we are now relating to you in your own terms. Somehow, using PH instead of an F is the cool, keen, and niphty thing to do—and more is obviously better. Actually, the kid in the back row provides a perphect example of prepherence phalsiphication. Since it is the last week of August and the temperature outside is about phive billion Celsius, it is unlikely that our white suburban punk phrom Connecticut is wearing that hoodie to keep his ears warm. Instead, he is trying to phit someone's expectations and gain the acceptance of others. We also suspect that he is a good decade behind the times, but he is trying.

Enough. Back to our terms. You probably suspect that we could not have kept that up for long.

For almost half a century, the vast majority of the people living under the Communist dictatorships of Eastern Europe hid their true preferences. Out of fear of what the not-so-secret police might do to those who voiced dissatisfaction with the government, pretty much everyone carefully avoided talking about politics when they could, and parrotted the official line when they had to. Expressing one's true opinion of government was simply too dangerous. Prison, mental hospitals—or worse—waited for those whom the government might catch dissin' it.

During the late 1970s and through the 1980s, the ability of these governments to keep people from expressing what they truly felt began to erode. Arising out of a strike in the economically critical Gdansk shipyards, a Polish worker's union called Solidarity was

Preference Falsification

Taken to an extreme in *Nineteen Eighty-Four,* where the government does not even tolerate trust among families or between lovers, peer policing is one mechanism that government uses to atomize the populace, and consequently to prevent revolt. Another such tool is **preference falsification**. Also seen in exaggerated form in Orwell's novel, preference falsification is exactly what it sounds like: it is hiding the way you truly feel while publicly expressing what those in power want to see and hear.

An obvious example of preference falsification occurs in *Nineteen Eighty-Four,* when the citizens gather together in front of television sets to scream their hatred for the enemy during the "two minutes of hate." Does Winston really hate the enemy? No, but in public he expresses rage as expected. Julia is so enthusiastic during the two minutes of hate—screaming, spitting, and throwing her shoes—that Winston is convinced she must be with the Thought Police. Only later does he find out how different her true preferences are from those she expresses in public.

Governments employ preference falsification as part of the atomization and peer policing process, in order to keep people separate and to keep groups from forming. If people do not express their dissatisfaction with the current government or their desire for a new government, how can potential revolutionaries even know if there are others who share their view? This is Winston's particular problem at the beginning of the novel. He wonders if he is the only one who feels the way he does, because everyone

formed and began expressing discontent with the Polish government's decrees, demanding workers' rights and other policy changes. Solidarity was forcibly suppressed in 1981, but during its brief official existence it established links to over 10 million people. This number was nowhere near a majority of the country's population, but it demonstrated to all that the shipyard workers were not alone in their dissatisfaction with the government. Once that realization spread, even the imposition of martial law by the Polish government was not enough to convince anyone otherwise. With the support of the Soviet Union, the Communist government held onto power in Poland for almost another decade, but in 1989 another round of strikes and labor unrest forced it to allow Solidarity to compete in what had formerly been noncompetitive, single-party elections, and Solidarity won, changing Poland from a dictatorship to a democracy with the votes of 30 million people.

The example was contagious; it led to what has been called "the cascade effect." Simply knowing how many people in Poland were dissatisfied with their government encouraged the citizens in other communist countries to believe that if they too could find a way to escape government control of the expression of their true opinions, they would find the support they needed to effect change. Thereafter, the awakening of popular resistance that had taken roughly eleven years in Poland required only eleven months in East Germany, eleven weeks in Czechoslovakia, and roughly eleven days in Romania. It was not a revolutionary army that marched from country to country, but the simple realization that dissatisfaction was widespread and would lead to change if the people's true preferences were expressed.

else seemingly supports the government. As long as other people's true feelings about the government are hidden, it will be difficult to overcome the fear that atomization and peer policing cause. So long as atomization, peer policing, and preference falsification keep people apart, a potential revolutionary will be unable to form the group that is needed to overthrow the government.

Governments encourage preference falsification not only by making it illegal to express dissatisfaction with the government, but also by encouraging people to echo the leaders' preferences. Think of the massive pro-government demonstrations that take place in authoritarian regimes such as North Korea. You know the marches we are talking about—the ones where the people are carrying signs with Godzilla-size pictures of the leader's face. Dictators can make these demonstrations materialize by sending government officials to offices and factories to loudly proclaim, "Congratulations, today is a special holiday. You are all going to get to march in the plaza and you will carry these signs and chant these slogans." Do any of the marchers really hold the preferences they express at the demonstration? A few of them do, but the majority probably do not. Nevertheless, regardless of their personal feelings, do you think any of these factory workers would dare to decline the government's invitation to march?

This tactic is not limited to totalitarian dictatorships such as the one in Orwell's fictional scenario. It can occur whenever the structure or context of interaction makes it clear that there will be unpleasant consequences for those who fail to endorse the leader's views. No matter how lame the boss's jokes, every employee forces a chuckle. Everyone who wants to keep his or her job nods and pretends to consider the boss's moronic idea as if it held the wisdom of Solomon. Anyone who has ever seriously dated anyone at all knows that we often must falsify our preferences under pressure: "No, those pants make you look thin." "Sure, I'd love to see a movie with gratuitous nudity and mindless violence." "I *love* it that you watch twelve hours of football every Sunday." "You're kidding? Kenny G. is also my favorite musician of all time." All that governments do is to exaggerate this common aspect of human interaction, taking advantage of it to prevent people from engaging in collective action. They use it to reinforce their efforts at atomization and peer policing. Preference falsification adds to the doubt you feel when you are not sure if that person expressing dissatisfaction with the government is just testing you to see if you will follow the law and turn him in.

Leaders use all of the interrelated mechanisms discussed so far—fear, punishments, and even direct violence—to forcefully maintain control and to prevent revolt. Still, we have to remember that *Nineteen Eighty-Four* is a work of fiction. While all governments use force in these and other forms, their methods are likely to be far less overt than those depicted in Orwell's extreme vision. In fact, there are some fundamental and very practical limits on how effective the use of forceful control can be.

Limits on Forceful Control

The level of force leaders must use to maintain control of the government is related to the society's level of dissatisfaction. When that level is low, less force is needed, but when societal discontent outweighs the fear that people feel, they will stop falsifying their preferences and start trying to overcome the government's mechanisms for atomization. When pushed too far, people will stand up to a bully. If you've ever seen *A Christmas Story,* you'll recall how cute little Ralphie ultimately deals with the crazy bully who always pounds on his brother and his friends.[4] Ralphie usually deals with this intimidation through preference falsification—that is, by trying to say whatever the bully wants to hear so that he can pass unscarred. But one day, pushed by a series of events that leave him downtrodden and dispirited,* Ralphie instead flips out and pounds the bully until he bleeds.†

When people are pushed over the edge and into despair, they may also be pushed to revolt. Dissent, protests, inflammatory speeches by opposition leaders, marches, perhaps even riots will occur. Consequently, when dissatisfaction rises to the point that it sparks open opposition, the government must increase the level of force if it is to retain control. Punishments are made more severe and more certain in order to increase self-policing enough to quell the unrest. As authoritarian leaders around the world have

---

*Despite all his efforts, Ralphie will not get the BB gun he wants for Christmas.

†The bully bleeds, not Ralphie.

repeatedly demonstrated, this strategy works. Over the long run, however, there is a very serious problem with using large amounts of force, and this limitation can restore some of the idealists' faith in humanity.

Using force to maintain control does nothing to resolve the underlying causes of discontent. The people were dissatisfied for a reason. In fact, it probably took a pretty serious problem to get them past the fear of punishment that would normally keep them from expressing their true preferences in a dictatorial regime. Left unaddressed, the underlying problem is likely to grow worse rather than better. If people were rioting because there were not enough jobs or because they could not afford to feed themselves for some other reason, the application of more force will not fix the economy or provide cheaper food. And if the problem remains unsolved, it will probably get worse, and the dissatisfaction will increase.

What happens when that increasing dissatisfaction again exceeds the restraining effect of the higher level of force? Government leaders must then exert even more force, but, because the underlying problem still remains unaddressed, dissatisfaction continues to grow, until yet more force is needed. Leaders may quickly find that they are stuck on a path with no escape, because the underlying problem has grown too large for them to fix. Once a problem grows beyond what can be handled with available resources, leaders have no real choice but to continue raising the level of force to maintain control, but this process cannot go on forever. The realist argument that human beings look to maximize their self-interest applies to the public as well, and when the people come to believe that imprisonment, torture, or death is no worse than the lives they are living, the leader has reached the point at which increasing force will have no effect. Starving people with starving children are likely to begin to believe that it is rationally worth the risk to participate in revolt, even if the chance for success is slim. When you have pushed people to the point of desperation, force is simply not enough.

LEGITIMACY AND GOVERNMENT CONTROL

Fortunately for leaders who face these potential limits on the use of force, there is another way to maintain control. Instead of relying on threats and punishments, leaders can maintain control by pursuing **legitimacy**, which can be defined as the voluntary acceptance of their government. In other words, legitimacy exists when people have the sense that obeying the government's rules is just the right thing to do. Like the definitions we have offered earlier, this one is overly simplified. It will work in the situations described in this text, but it is by no means complete, absolute, or universally agreed upon.

A complex array of social, psychological, political, and cultural processes and phenomena—including educational and socialization mechanisms and culturally-defined responses to authority—affect a government's legitimacy. There are many ways for a government to achieve legitimacy: by simply remaining in power for a long time; by receiving the blessing of a past leader whose rule was considered legitimate; or by convincing the populace that it was sent by God to rule. However, from a realist's perspective, the primary focus should be on the rational, cost-benefit perspective of government legitimacy.

Perhaps the most effective way that a leader can gain legitimacy is by persuading the citizenry that it is in their best interest to voluntarily accept his or her leadership. Generally speaking, this goal can be accomplished by providing the things that people need or want. While this might mean anything from instilling religion in government to protecting ethnic culture, or restoring national pride through military conquest, leaders most often accomplish it by providing the basic resources and opportunities that people need or expect. If the government is successful, the level of discontent will be reduced, and it will take much less force to maintain control.

Got to Give the People What They Want:
Elections and Public Goods

Popular elections provide the best example of how a government can use legitimacy as the primary means to avoid revolt. While we later devote an entire chapter to democracy—both the ideal and the dynamics of governments that try to achieve it—for present purposes, it is worth stealing some of the thunder from that chapter to briefly note the important connection between elections and legitimacy. Simply put, popularly elected leaders are legitimate leaders, at least when they first take office. They win their leadership positions and gain power by attaining the voluntary acceptance of a majority of eligible voters, or from a majority of the representatives elected by a population. What is a vote but an expression that you choose to be ruled by a certain candidate?

Ironically, this means that electoral democracies deal with the threat of revolt by embracing it. Instead of trying to quash revolutionaries, they create political structures that tame and institutionalize the process of revolt. Instead of letting discontent build up until it erupts into bloody uprising, a democracy holds elections, which serve as planned, scheduled, and regular uprisings. Every few years, citizens have the opportunity to throw out their leaders and replace those who have failed to provide for the needs or wants of the populace. The vote is a nonviolent way of meaningfully expressing satisfaction or dissatisfaction with the leader.

The democratic electoral structure affects the behavior of the leader and of those who hope to challenge for the leadership position. If you are in power, you want to stay in power or at least keep your party in power—reelection is constantly in the back of your mind. You must continually work to convince a majority of voters to express their voluntary acceptance of you as the leader by casting their votes for you in the next election. In order to accomplish this goal, you must remain responsive to the populace and work to satisfy the needs and wants of the society by anticipating, addressing, and resolving the causes of dissatisfaction.

While popular elections serve as an excellent example of a mechanism that forces the leaders' personal interests to converge with those they govern, there are other ways by which leaders can pursue legitimacy. Most governments around the world try to find some balance between the use of force and the pursuit of legitimacy in order to maintain control. To some degree, the limitations on the use of force to control a society drive almost every leader to seek some degree of legitimacy. Even the vilest dictators have tried to strike this balance. Mussolini's Fascists were not above using force and violence, but they also tried to win voluntary acceptance of their rule by making the trains run on time and doing many of the other simple things that earlier governments had been unable to manage. Even Hitler did not rely on fear alone. His government undertook huge public works projects to revive the economy and to give jobs to the German people. Leaders vary in the degree to which they try to satisfy the needs and wants of large portions of their populations. Surprisingly enough, the Libyan dictator Muammar al-Qaddafi provides one of the best contemporary examples of a nondemocratic leader who pursues the voluntary acceptance of his rule.

When Qaddafi seized power from the Libyan royal family in 1969, the quality of life in Libya was miserably low: educational opportunities were almost nonexistent, doctors were scarce, jobs were hard to find, food was in short supply, life expectancies were low, and much of the population had little or nothing to call a home. Qaddafi embarked on one of history's most ambitious efforts to address the needs and desires of a society, spending the first decade of his rule focusing on trying to better the life of the ordinary Libyan. He took the country's oil money and used it to build schools, hospitals, and apartment buildings. He sent students to Europe to train as doctors and engineers. Irrigation projects increased farm output. Undoubtedly, he siphoned a great deal of money off for himself and his immediate supporters—his mansion was so big that Ronald Reagan had to send *several* U.S. warplanes to bomb it—but the resources

Qaddafi devoted to meeting the needs and wants of the people of Libya was remarkable. The difference in the lives of the people became apparent in just a few years. By the end of the 1970s, the average Libyan's quality of life had improved so much and Qaddafi's leadership was considered so legitimate—within Libya, at least—that the only substantial group of Libyans interested in revolt consisted of the wealthy exiles who had prospered under the royal family and had been driven out by Qaddafi.

Qaddafi pursued security in office by seeking legitimacy, by striving to attain the voluntary acceptance of his rule. Make no mistake—he is a brutal dictator, renowned for using murder and terrorism to enforce his rule. However, he does not rely solely, or even primarily, on these forceful mechanisms that are the normal mainstay of authoritarian rulers. Even today, there is little chance that he will be ousted through revolt.

Balancing Force and Legitimacy

How do leaders calculate the correct mix of force and legitimacy? In simple terms, the lower the level of dissatisfaction, the less force is necessary. But there are other considerations. For one, the pursuit of legitimacy tends to be a poor short-term strategy but a better long-term strategy. Provided there are resources available to instill and support it, legitimacy can be a much more stable and efficient mechanism for maintaining control because a leader who has it does not have to constantly be concerned about revolt and does not have to invest heavily in the tools of force. However, it can take years, even decades, to turn an economy around or otherwise meet the people's needs and expectations. That is far too long to satisfy the mob gathering at your palace door. On the other hand, force is very effective in the short term. When people are marching in the streets, forceful actions such as arrests, torture, threats, and fear can have an immediate impact. When the leader is facing a riot, when revolution seems imminent, there is no time to wait for a new irrigation project to increase the food supply, and the leader would be long gone before new schools could be built.

Ideally, we might hope that a leader facing imminent revolt would use the short-term impact of these forceful mechanisms only to buy security while working to make the investments needed to attain legitimacy. However, in the real world, leaders tend to be motivated only by immediate and visible threats to their hold on power; once the immediate danger is removed through force, they tend to lose the motivation to pursue legitimacy. Taking away the threat of revolt also takes away the impetus to satisfy the needs of the people. For an authoritarian leader to pursue the public interest seems to require either a moral commitment to the public welfare—a rare quality in an authoritarian leader—or the tremendous foresight necessary to realize the long-term value of pursuing legitimacy—yet another rarity.

Another aspect of pursuing legitimacy that is relevant for calculating the balance between force and legitimacy is that, in the short term, it is far cheaper to pay off a small group of army officers and a small police force to maintain control by force than it is to invest in meeting the needs of the entire society. Furthermore, if the country does not have the wealth to invest in schools, economic infrastructure, and the other services that can win the people's support, the leader cannot even make the effort. Qaddafi was able to pursue legitimacy because he had the resources available to make it work. He had oil money and a very small population to satisfy. Under other conditions, his strategy would not have been possible. The leader of an impoverished country with no natural resources to exploit often simply cannot afford to pursue legitimacy. Consequently, some analysts have suggested that a country may need a minimum level of wealth in order to be a democracy. How can a government achieve legitimacy if no leader could ever accumulate the resources necessary to meet the public's wants and needs?

Legitimacy and Conflict within Groups

The concept of legitimacy brings us back to some of the basic theories on conflict and group dynamics that were introduced in chapter 3.* We have already discussed how conflict between groups can play an important role in group identification and in building support for leadership. Conflict also plays an important role—perhaps a more important role—*within* groups. To fully understand how this process works, we need to consider a bit of the early sociological research on social conflict.

The horrors of World War I—which are discussed in unpleasant detail in chapter 12, when we consider international politics and war—motivated the scholars of that era to focus on understanding the nature of conflict. The "war to end all wars" was so hideously destructive that the scholars threw themselves into the study of international relations with the express goal of ensuring that such an atrocity never occur again. Every aspect of their research was dominated by the idea that conflict was an evil to be defeated or a disease to be cured. And, because they believed that no redeeming value was to be found in conflict, reducing it or minimizing it was not enough. These scholars believed that it had to be eradicated. However, Georg Simmel and, later, Lewis Coser pointed out that there were problems with this drastic approach.[5] While horribly bloody strife such as World War I should certainly be prevented, the complete elimination of conflict might be equally dangerous because conflict serves constructive functions within human societies.

We can see some of these functions when we look at intergroup conflicts, or conflicts between two or more groups. When a group's members are engaged in conflict with another group, self-identification with one's own group increases, along with support for the leadership. Both of these factors can benefit the leader and even the group as a whole, by making the group more cohesive, giving the leader more control, and enhancing the group's stability. Leaders can, and often do, use the effects of conflict

---

*What would it take to convince you that we actually planned all along to return to group dynamics as a way of tying these two chapters and their concepts together?

between groups in self-serving ways, but in terms of this discussion of legitimacy and government, the work of Simmel and Coser was helpful in redirecting the study of conflict toward discovering how conflict within a group can also prove beneficial.

A Safety Valve

The first benefit of intra-group conflict (conflict within the group) is that it can serve as a **safety valve**. What do we mean by a safety valve? Most of you have probably never seen a pressure cooker. But if you or a family member has ever canned homegrown fruits and vegetables, or if you have lived at very high altitude, you may have encountered one. A pressure cooker is simply a cooking pot with a clamped lid that prevents steam from escaping. This mechanism creates a buildup of pressure—the same principle that powers a steam engine—and it also allows you to control the temperature at which the water boils—higher pressure creates a higher boiling point. Thus, you need a pressure cooker up in the mountains where the air pressure is much lower than at sea level, because, without that clamping lid and the extra pressure, the boiling water never gets hot enough to cook the noodles for your macaroni and cheese. In fact, if you go far enough up into the mountains—Mount Everest kind of up—the boiling point of water drops so low that you can actually stick your hand into boiling water with no ill effect.

Now, if you happen to be seven years old* and your mom is canning peaches in the kitchen, you just may wonder why the pot on the stove is whistling away. Because you are seven, you do not realize that when the pressure reaches a certain point, the safety valve pops open and lets out some of the steam, whistling and spitting a little bit. Instead, you are an industrious little boy, who looks at this sputtering pot and thinks, "That is just not right." Then you go get a little wrench from the garage, put on some oven mitts, and start working on the safety valve, cranking it down tighter and tighter until it stops whistling and stops sputtering. Success! You have fixed it! Then you go outside and do whatever it is that seven-year-olds do outside around the end of summer.

If you happen to be within earshot when that pressure cooker explodes, not only will you learn a lot of new words and phrases that no one says on TV, but you will also learn that without a properly functioning safety valve, the pressure in the pressure cooker can build up to the point that it will blow the lid, quite literally, through the ceiling. That lid will blow straight up through the vent hood over the stove, the cupboard above that, the sheetrock, the insulation, the roof, and everything. As that lid bounces on the patio in the backyard, not only will your father start teaching you all those words and phrases we mentioned, but you will also learn that cooked peaches can become awesome projec-

---

*We will not go into who actually did this because we think the guilty party's mother may have finally forgotten about it. At the very least, she has quit mentioning it at the start of every Thanksgiving dinner.

Governing Society

> **Groups of people can often behave in the same way as a pressure cooker, and conflict within the group can function like the safety valve.**

tiles. While canned peaches might ordinarily be soft mushy things, when blown out of a pressure cooker with sufficient force, they can actually penetrate a wall with such gusto that there is no way you will ever get them out. Your dad will have to rip out and replace the entire kitchen because after just a couple of warm days, the peaches you blasted into the walls really start to stink.

The point of this little story is the safety valve. Groups of people can often behave in the same way as a pressure cooker, and conflict within the group can function like the safety valve. Stopping group members from engaging in conflict builds up pressure. When people who are irritated cannot say or do anything about the source of tension, their frustration and anger builds until, eventually—as with Ralphie in *A Christmas Story*—just about anything will set them off. Conflicts, even small, controlled conflicts, which allow people to vent their frustrations and dissatisfactions, serve the safety valve function. Instead of a big blowup, the result is a series of minor, more manageable conflicts.

Spike Lee's *Do the Right Thing* provides a great example of what can happen when there is no working social version of that safety valve.[6] Throughout the film, racial tension mounts along with the temperature in a Brooklyn neighborhood. There is seemingly no relief from either the heat or the tension, which all comes to a head in a pizza joint with a white proprietor. Spike Lee makes the pressure of the situation tangible. Ultimately, it comes as little surprise that a riot breaks out after a racial epithet is used and the proprietor's friend and employee throws a garbage can through the window. The pressure built up, and there was no release. The explosion was inevitable.

Crosscutting Cleavages

This idea of a safety valve also relates to a second benefit described by Coser in regard to conflicts within a group: **crosscutting cleavages**. If no conflict is allowed within a group, the things that do not work well in the group—those little things that cause irritation and frustration—will build up pressure. When conflict eventually does break loose within the group, it will tend to erupt intensely around a single issue. No matter what the immediate cause may be, when a group has only one dividing line of internal conflict—a single cleavage—that division tends to split the group apart, threatening the cohesion or the very existence of the group. This threat to the group is significant, because everyone falls on one side or the other of that one issue.

On the other hand, if some conflict is tolerated within a group, when cleavages appear, they are not going to be as intense. Why? For one, the safety-valve principle allows these less tense conflicts to release some of the social tension and resolve some of the issues challenging the group's cohesion. Also, when a variety of different conflicts arise with a group, the divisions over them do not always coincide—the cleavages are crosscutting. In other words, if there are enough small points of debate or conflict, people who disagree on one issue are likely to agree on at least one other. The more internal cleavages that are allowed to surface, the more likely it is that any two people will be able to find some disputed issue that they can agree on despite their disagreements on other issues.

These crosscutting cleavages have several beneficial effects. First, they help to keep the society from dividing sharply over a single issue. Where there is no single divide and so many things that many people agree on, it is easier for a leader to keep the group itself from being split apart. Furthermore, the disagreements that do erupt will be less intense, because people will be less likely to act with extreme hostility toward those they agree with on other issues. These crosscutting cleavages also provide a foundation for developing compromises. Facing multiple issues, a person or group can trade support on one issue for someone else's acquiescence on another. The more issues there are in play, the more opportunities there are for trade-offs, and the lower intensity of those conflicts also helps because it is easier to make concessions over smaller, less divisive issues.

Moreover, frequent small conflicts within a group can actually become a unifying force, as they tend to facilitate the resolution of underlying causes of disagreement. One of the reasons the safety valve principle works in a social context is that small conflicts over small issues often leave those small issues at least partially resolved. This incremental resolution of small issues can keep them from growing into large ones, which leads to a consequence of group conflict that was addressed explicitly by neither Coser nor Simmel, but is nonetheless important to the study of politics. Intra-group conflict can enhance the legitimacy of the group. Conflict within a group can actually reinforce its structure and its leadership.

Conflict as a Source of Legitimacy

While legitimacy derives from many sources, conflict is one important factor in people's voluntary identification with a group. Conflict between groups strengthens group identity by helping to define who is not part of the group. It causes people to turn to the group for security and makes them more willing to voluntarily accept direction from the leader. But even conflict within the group can enhance the legitimacy of a group and its structures. Successfully resolving a conflict within the structures of the group enhances both the members' confidence in the group and their willingness to voluntarily accept its structures. This experience enhances the legitimacy of the group and its leaders. The more often this process occurs, the more it enhances the legitimacy of the group and its leader.

Think about this phenomenon in terms of high-profile court cases, especially those in which the verdict makes you just shake your head and wonder what planet the judge or the jury were really on. Think of some of the bizarre criminal cases in which juries have failed to convict a rich or powerful person who is obviously guilty. Such cases erode confidence in the court. They suggest that something is not right, that something has to be fixed, and they reduce your willingness to voluntarily accept the courts as a means of performing certain social functions. One ridiculous verdict may not cause you to believe that we need to scrap the entire judicial system, but it certainly does not help. Alternatively, court cases that come out the way you think they should tend to enhance your belief that the courts are doing their job. These cases increase the judicial system's legitimacy and reconfirm that the courts are an acceptable means to resolve conflict. The more legitimate a government structure, the less force will be needed to convince you to accept it and the rules or laws associated with it.

A skilled leader understands and even exploits these potential benefits by manipulating and controlling conflict within the country. This concept can be extended so far that such a leader might actually promote or even create conflict so that the government can resolve it and thus establish or increase its legitimacy. Think about how countless leaders have effectively manipulated ethnic tensions, religious differences, and the fear of crime to first promote conflict and then find and implement a "solution" that enhances their legitimacy. Think about how effectively the government in *Nineteen Eighty-Four* magnifies the threat posed by Emanuel Goldstein and The Brotherhood.

Another extreme example can by found in *The Prince,* where Machiavelli relates the story of a duke who conquered a territory and then tried to establish his legitimate rule. Finding the place in disarray and plagued by theft, disputes, and violence, he hired the cruelest governor he could find to establish order and discipline—which that person brutally, maliciously, and promptly did. By this means, the duke had created a new conflict in the territory. The people now hated their governor. So the duke blamed the violent excess on the governor, had him killed, and used his body parts to decorate the public square. Thus creating a conflict so that he could resolve it helped the duke to win the support of the people. He manipulated group dynamics to achieve legitimacy. How's that for ending a chapter with a bang?

KEY TERMS

atomization / **76**
crosscutting cleavages / **89**
legitimacy / **83**
panopticon / **73**
peer policing / **77**

preference falsification / **80**
revolution / **76**
safety valve / **88**
self-policing / **74**

CHAPTER SUMMARY

In order to understand the reasons why governments do what they do, it is critical to appreciate the role of leadership interests. This perspective also provides a foundation for exploring how leaders and governments maintain control of those they govern. Whenever we seek to understand the complexities of politics, it always pays to begin by asking, "Who benefits?" and "How?" These questions apply regardless of the type of government under scrutiny. You may have no problem accepting this point when considering other countries, but it is equally appropriate to ask these questions of your own country. Even those who believe that governments seek to promote the social welfare must come to terms with this reality. It is also essential to appreciate the role that group conflict can play for groups (including governments) and their leaders. Students should learn two very important lessons from this chapter. First, people want to become leaders because holding the leadership position or being part of the elite group that controls the leadership position provides tremendous individual benefits. Second, while you should plan plenty of family time with children, it is a good idea to keep them away from pressure cookers.

STUDY QUESTIONS AND EXERCISES

1. What is the principle behind the panopticon, and how do leaders use this means to control behavior?

2. What is meant by atomization, peer policing, and preference falsification? How do leaders use these techniques to prevent revolutionary groups from forming?

3. What are the long-term risks to a leader who relies too much on force?

4. How can conflict within a group serve a beneficial function for the group and its leader?

5. In this chapter, we argue that in order to understand a confusing aspect of politics, one should ask, "Who benefits?" and "How do they benefit?" Read an article about politics in the newspaper or watch a report about politics on television. Does this method help? Why or why not?

WEBSITES TO EXPLORE

www.surveillance-and-society.org/. *Surveillance & Society,* an online journal dedicated to surveillance studies.

www.scrappleface.com/. ScrappleFace, a site that pokes fun at the news.

www.ucl.ac.uk/Bentham-Project/. University College London's Bentham Project, offering information about Jeremy Bentham and the Bentham Project, including the Panopticon.

www.bbc.co.uk/history/historic_figures/orwell_george.shtml. The BBC's George Orwell Page, offering information about George Orwell and other links.

Some say that Dickens's *A Christmas Carol* is a literary masterpiece that provides a profound and moving depiction of the harshness of unrestrained capitalism. However, we have to wonder if the text of a novel, a novel that doesn't even have any pictures, can really match the power of Scrooge McDuck's performance.

CHAPTER 5

Government's Role in the Economy
The Offer You Can't Refuse

While idealists are likely to agree with that long-running credit card commercial that there are some things that money just can't buy, realists are apt to respond that a trip to Vegas or a quick search of eBay will conclusively demonstrate that the list of things money can't buy must be a very short one. **Realists tend to agree with** the stereotypical mafia don who appears in practically every gangster movie ever made and says, "Every man has his price."

Idealists, however, prefer to believe the television commercial. They would like to emphasize the things you cannot buy, pointing to religious figures such as Mother Theresa and others who have eschewed wealth in order to follow another path. A lot of popular fiction adopts this idealist perspective, portraying money either as the source of evil or as a distraction from the things of true importance. Money convinces good cops to go bad, it drives the runaway to commit desperate acts, and it is at least part of every villain's passion. Idealism in fiction tells us that the nobler motivations, such as the pursuit of justice or the bravery to withstand life-threatening pyrotechnics to make a daring rescue, are the hallmarks of the heroic. Heroes, it would seem, are never driven by greed. Remember the first *Star Wars* movie—the one actually called *Star Wars*? Han Solo does not truly become a hero until he drops his desire for bounty and joins the cause of the rebels. Of course, realists can easily counter by pointing out that in real life, the lead actor usually demands about $22.6 million plus a percentage of the box office to portray a "selfless" hero, but still, we are talking fiction here.

The battle between idealism and realism in the economics of life is very clearly depicted in *A Tree Grows in Brooklyn,* a film based on Betty Smith's novel of the same name.[1] While it is something of a disservice to the complexities of its plot, context, and character to focus only on the economic aspects, it is also clear that the contrast between the idealist and realist perspectives on the world is a critical part of this story. Set early in the twentieth century, the story centers on Francie Nolan, the child of a family beset by poverty and alcoholism, and much of its power derives from the vivid portrayal of the harsh realities of an economic system that does little to ease the pain of the struggling poor. For our purposes, however, the story is notable for Francie's struggle with idealism and realism as personified by her parents. Her father, Johnny Nolan, is a charming and lovable dreamer, while her mother, Kate Nolan, is a hard woman struggling to hold her family together in the face of harsh reality. Johnny is an out-of-work singing waiter, and an alcoholic; Kate scrubs floors and pinches pennies. Johnny speaks in terms of dreams and of better things to come; Kate speaks of sacrifice and of deprivation—in her words, dreams "don't put pennies in the jar." As their daughter, Francie must battle to find her footing between these two visions of the world.

Money may not, actually, make the world go 'round—the physics professor we occasionally eat lunch with insists that it is the remaining angular momentum from the formation of the solar system that spins us through day and night. That one professor's "scientific" fantasy aside, it should be clear that the vast majority of people believe that money is a central part of life, and, consequently, it is an important political concern. We might even go so far as to say that economics, albeit in a rudimentary form, is the reason humans created government in the first place. In our story of the formation of the first government, Caveman Bob pursues collective security so that he can become a farmer. Farming is, in essence, the most primitive form of investment. Bob gives up something of value—the grain he scatters on the muddy ground and his labor—with the expectation that he will obtain greater benefit in the future. When the barbarians come out of the hills to steal his first crop, however, Bob discovers that even this elementary economic investment is impossible in anarchy.

Bob needs a way to protect his investment. He needs the collective security of the village so that he can farm and reap the rewards of his effort. In a word, Bob needs government. Similarly, the geeky kid on the island needs a bully's protection in order to employ his labor effectively. Government is intimately tied to economics, if only because people must have collective security in order to engage in even the most rudimentary of economic enterprises. The connection between economics and government is in many ways obvious in its simplicity, but it is actually a rich, dynamic relationship that is filled with subtlety and, sometimes, mystery. We live in an age in which most people hold the government responsible for maintaining and improving the economy, yet the validity of that expectation is cast into doubt by the complexities of economic systems. This is compounded by many people's lack of understanding of the actual roles that government plays in regard to economics.

Suppose you have landed a job at the local burger joint. If you take a careful look at the pitiful paycheck you get for the countless hours spent flipping carcass pucks, you will realize that the government's role in economics goes far beyond providing the collective security needed for investment. Despite the official poster with the bright red numbers indicating the supposed minimum wage hanging in the back room, the government works very hard to guarantee that you never actually see that amount of money. In the United States there are federal taxes, state taxes, and various local taxes. But who is that FICA guy, and why does he get some of the money?*

The government is tied to the economy in other ways as well. For example, before you were allowed to start your career flipping burgers, the government probably forced you to get a certificate or read a pamphlet from hand-washing school. There will probably be at least one government health inspector who comes by, from time to time, to pick up the unmarked envelope from the manager and to make sure that everyone is doing the health code thing, wearing the funky hairnet, and washing their hands *after*† using the restroom and all that. Clearly government is concerned with more than just providing the security needed for investment. It will also get involved when the assistant manager inevitably spills his strong "coffee" into the deep fryer, setting off a massive alcohol explosion. Not only will the government make sure that the corporate office pays your hospital bills, but it will also give the assistant manager disability checks while he trains at home for a new career in TV/VCR repair or to get his certification as a dental hygienist.

Sometimes the government's involvement in the economy is very clear. At other times, it is involved in ways that are taken for granted or not easily noticed—often because it is hidden under a blizzard of infuriating little details. In *A Tree Grows in Brooklyn*, the contemporary role of government is conspicuous by its absence. Where are the food stamps to keep the family fed? Why must the mother of the sick girl next door worry about the cost of burials? Where are Johnny's unemployment checks? How can Francie be pulled out of school to work, at her young age? Why must Katie give birth in her apartment? Where were the lawyers to recoup the grandmother's money when she gets swindled?

To get at some of the most basic, yet often unnoticed, elements of the government involvement in the economy, we introduce in this chapter two prominent approaches to engaging government in the process of producing wealth: **socialism** and **capitalism**. As in other parts of this book, our effort to get at the basics leaves out much of the nuance and complexity of the ideas. We try to note some of the more significant simplifications, but let us reiterate that it is important to keep in mind that we are cutting these theories down to the bare bones. The real world is far more complex, and it is likely that as

---

*Just in case you really must know, FICA is short for the Federal Insurance Contributions Act. It is the payroll tax that the government says it collects to pay for Social Security and Medicare. We can neither confirm nor deny the rumor that it is used to fund global conspiracies involving stealth helicopters and politically correct commandos wearing bear suits.

†If you are really supposed to wash your hands *after* using the restroom, why isn't the sink outside the bathroom?

you progress in your college career, or rise to command one of the Starfleet battle cruisers that drive the evil alien squids from the cosmos, you will encounter far more sophisticated applications of these arguments and theories. Before we get to these two economic systems, however, we must first consider some of the individual-level interactions that the government has to work with.

THE TRAGEDY OF THE COMMONS

When Bob brings his group of future farmers together to engage in the collective pursuit of security, that first glimmer of governed society enables the earliest, most primitive manifestation of economy: agriculture. The transition to farming and village life also creates challenges that none of the grunting brutes can ever have imagined. Interestingly, these challenges originate from the very cooperation that makes government possible. Working together for the collective goal of security requires the development of community resources to be shared by several, or sometimes all, of the people in the village. For example, there may be a common well for water, a public garbage dump, or a communal meadow for grazing sheep. The exploitation of these shared resources creates a problem that is commonly known in academic circles as **the tragedy of the commons**, where the rational choices of individuals collide with the needs or interests of the larger community. This is tragedy in a fatalistic kind of way;* a situation in which the horrible becomes inevitable. In a tragedy, the protagonists cannot avoid the disastrous outcome even when they are aware that it lurks in their future. In this sense, the story of Sid and Nancy was also tragic: how predictable and unavoidable is the gruesome death of a punk rock legend's junkie girlfriend? In fact, according to the tragedy of the commons, people who realize that they are destroying a common resource through overexploitation can actually be driven to make the problem worse by exploiting the commons even more intensely.

The story of the tragedy of the commons can be told in many different ways. In fact, it is so important that we are going to give you the story three times. Since we have been working the whole Caveman-turned-Farmer Bob thing the way a pop radio station plays a No. 1 single until it induces nausea, we are going to keep at it. Thus, we begin with a brief story about farmers sharing grazing land.

Grazing Sheep and the Temptation to Cheat

After losing several limbs in a poorly-considered effort to domesticate polar bears, Bob's descendants try raising sheep instead. Not only does the population of the village stop declining, but the project itself is also far more successful. A nice round number of farmers—say ten—come to share a large field for wintering their flocks. Through

---

*It is *not* tragic in the whole Oedipus, sleeping-with-your-mother-and-killing-your-father kind of way.

trial and error, they discover that if they limit themselves to one hundred sheep, they can use the field throughout the winter while maintaining just enough grass to support one hundred sheep through the next year's winter. If they put more than one hundred out there, the sheep will overgraze the field, eating not only the blades of grass, but also the precious roots. It goes without saying that overgrazing ruins the pastoral view of the emerald green field and devastates a prehistoric village's property values, but it also reduces the field's capacity to support sheep. So, if you put one hundred and ten sheep out there one winter, come next year, the field will only grow enough grass to support maybe eighty sheep through the winter months.

In this field, the villagers have a shared resource that is very fragile. If the sheep farmers overexploit it now, they will destroy its future value and its future ability to support production. The obvious solution is to have them agree to share the field equally. Each of the ten farmers keeps only his or her ten best sheep through the winter and slaughters the rest. This would preserve the productivity of the field forever. Unfortunately, this idealistic solution faces a *big* obstacle. Each farmer faces an overwhelming temptation to increase the size of his or her flock by keeping an extra sheep alive through the winter. That extra sheep will give the farmer ten percent more food, wool, and wealth the following fall. After all, what would be the harm of just one more little, tiny, cute sheep out on that field? They have sixty million sheep in New Zealand and it is not that big a country, what is just one more on a field?

It would also be pretty easy to get away with putting that one extra sheep out on the field. As it turns out, sheep have actually evolved so that they are hard to count—they blend together into a big fuzzy mass that mills about.* Since it is unlikely that anyone will notice, it is only a matter of time before one of the farmers does choose to add an extra sheep to the winter flock. Whether the cause is greed or desperation, somewhere along the line one farmer's personal wants or needs will outweigh his or her commitment to the interests of the community.

It is important to realize that the fact that the resource is shared plays a big role in making the situation tragic. If only one farmer owns and uses the field, the costs and benefits of overexploitation are balanced. The lone farmer obtains the full benefit of the extra sheep, but in subsequent years, she also bears the full cost of the damage this extra sheep causes to the field. If she overexploits it this winter, she pays all the costs in reduced grazing capacity the next winter. In contrast, when several people use the field, only the individual who cheats gets the benefit, while all of the shepherds share the costs associated with the damaged field. Even though the group of ten shepherds, as a whole, would be far better off if no one cheated, an individual sheep wrangler

---

*For the wild ancestors of sheep, this increased the chance of survival by making it hard for predators to separate individuals from the flock. On the communal field, however, it makes it extremely difficult to figure out exactly how many of the cute little buggers are out there.

benefits from cheating because she gets all the gain while suffering only a tenth of the cost. In other words, the benefits and the costs of that extra sheep are skewed in a way that motivates people to overexploit the resource. Once you get beyond a handful of people, the disparity in benefits versus costs becomes more extreme and it becomes more difficult to spot cheaters. As a result, at some point, cheating becomes inevitable.

At this point, it will be very tempting, particularly for you idealists out there, to try to play the **enlightened self-interest** card. Even invertebrates like SpongeBob SquarePants and Patrick Star can see that it is in everyone's best interest to preserve the commons for everyone. Surely, the farmers will be motivated by this enlightened self-interest to resist the short-term temptation to cheat in order to ensure that they and their descendants will benefit from the long-term, continued value of the field. Unfortunately, this argument overlooks the fact that people's calculations are not based solely on their own behavior. When sharing a common resource, an individual's choices are intertwined with the choices and actions of others who use the resource. Enlightened self-interest cannot prevent the tragedy of the commons because even when a person realizes that it is in everyone's best interest to preserve the shared resource, as soon as that person considers it likely that others will cheat, he or she is driven to overexploit the commons anyway. The logic behind this unenlightened behavior* becomes clear in our second tragic example, the stag hunt.

The Stag Hunt and Social Choice

The **stag hunt** is an old and commonly used parable that nicely demonstrates how the interdependence of actions and choices affects collective efforts to attain a goal, such as the preservation of the commons. Yes, we could have come up with our own story, but we decided to use this one, which illustrates the point so well, and spend an afternoon playing golf instead. Call it our own personal form of enlightened self-interest.

For the benefit of the cinematically challenged reader who has not seen the black-and-white version of *Robin Hood*, a stag is a big deer with enough antlers to hold the hats of an entire baseball team.[2] Considered to be not only tasty, but also a bit smarter than your average herbivore, the stag presented a substantial challenge to the spears and rocks that hungry human hunters relied on before the age of automatic weapons. Hunting a stag required a collective effort—the hunters would surround the animal and slowly close in by drawing the circle tighter and tighter until they were close enough to attack effectively.

It is the individual hunter's choices that are illustrative. Let us say that Bob's father, Bah, is one of the hunters. Holding his spear at the ready, Bah carefully keeps his place in the shrinking circle that surrounds the stag. Because Bah and his family have not

---

*We are not sure if unenlightened behavior is dark or heavy.

eaten for a few days, the wife and kids are understandably a bit cranky, and Bah desperately needs to bring home something to eat. As the hunters close in on the stag, Bah notices that their slowly constricting circle has also been driving rabbits toward its center and one of the floppy-eared rodents has trapped itself in a dead-end crevice between two large boulders. Bah has a choice. If he and all the other hunters stay in the circle, they have a 75 percent chance of killing the stag, which will feed everyone for two days—good odds, but by no means certain. Meanwhile, that rabbit is right there, with no way out. Bah can get it for certain—a 100 percent chance—but it will feed only his family, and it will feed them for only one day.

Assuming that Bah can do some quick calculations, he may figure out that a 75 percent chance of eating for two days is a better overall expectation of personal benefit (1.5 total meals of tasty stag) than the certainty of eating for one day (one total meal of rabbit). Furthermore, if you assume that Bah is not generally a jerk and that he cares about the other hunters, there is more reason to expect that he will pass up the rabbit. If Bah breaks from the circle, the stag will escape through the gap he leaves, and everyone will lose two days' worth of food. Thus, you expect the morally and socially upstanding Bah to walk past the rabbit.

It is not that simple, however. Since the stag hunt is a collective effort, Bah must also consider the others hunters' choices and how those decisions will affect the outcome of the hunt. Every single hunter in the circle must pass up any and all of the rabbits they find in order to get the stag. Thus, Bah must also consider the possibility that someone else will be tempted to break from the circle and take a rabbit. If Bah has any reason to doubt the commitment of any of the other hunters, then he must conclude that the stag will be lost. If it takes twenty hunters to kill the stag, how many of them will stumble across a rabbit? What are the odds that every single one will pass up the temptation of a rabbit? "Larry has always been selfish and untrustworthy, so he will certainly take the rabbit," thinks Bah. "If not Larry, then Moe or Shemp will do it." * As soon as Bah knows, or even just believes that someone else will take the rabbit, then he has no choice but to conclude that the chance of successfully getting the stag is zero.

Thus, if Bah expects that someone else in the circle will take the rabbit, his personal calculation changes to one meal if he takes the rabbit and zero meals if he stays in the circle. Once he believes that there is no chance the group will succeed in the stag hunt, then Bah's *only rational* choice is to defect and take the rabbit. He realizes the impact of his choice, but he will choose to take the rabbit anyway out of fear that someone else will betray the group and leave him with nothing. Ironically, Bah causes the very failure that he fears. The social choice dynamic illustrated by the stag hunt is what drives even the enlightened to overexploit the commons. This dynamic is exacerbated by the economic

---

*It goes without saying that Curly never would.

realities of the situation, and our third example of the tragedy of the commons both illustrates this point and connects the ideas to current, real-world examples.

From Farming to Fishing

We seldom see shepherds sharing a field anymore, but fish stocks represent a good modern-day example of the tragedy of the commons. Let's return to Bob and his village but fast-forward 10,000 years. When that village grows into a town, complete with a pawnshop and a Wal-Mart, Bob's distant relative Roberta, who is the assistant chief fry cook at the local burger joint, is going to get yelled at for not wearing her hairnet. At some point, while this grill maestro is still contemplating the exact word to best express where she would like to suggest that her boss can put that hairnet, it also dawns on her that nets can serve other purposes. Sooner or later, she notices the bay into which the town's little stream empties, and it then occurs to her that she could use a bigger version of the hairnet to catch fish. After convincing an investment banker that people will pay some serious money for fish, she weaves a few nets, buys her cousin's bass boat, and hits the jackpot. As it turns out, the bay is full of slimy, flopping gold, which she hauls in and sells to a whole town full of people tired of eating nothing but rice, lamb chops, and those sorry excuses for hamburgers she's been flipping. People crowd around to buy every fish she can bring in to the dock, even bidding against each other for the best ones. In just a few weeks, the loan is repaid and our former fry cook is shoveling money into her bank account.

As you might expect, other fry cooks notice Roberta's success and rush to copy her. Soon, bankers are loaning money, factories are weaving nets, and shipyards are building boats—fishing is like so totally the rage. However, as everyone sails out to exploit the bay full of fish (a shared resource), the tragedy of the commons rears its ugly head. As long as the bay is not overfished, the fish that are not caught have a chance to reproduce and continue to supply the town. But if the fishermen exploit the bay beyond the level at which the fish can reproduce fast enough to sustain supply, this potentially limitless commons will be damaged or destroyed. The fish will become scarce or even disappear.

In the case of the sheep and the field shared by a few farmers, critical readers may be able to point out some relatively simple solutions to avert the tragedy of the commons. This real-world example, however, is far less tractable. The effects of fixed costs and the basic macroeconomics of supply and demand push the situation from difficult to tragic. As more masters of the sea bring fish to the docks, the supply of fish for sale increases. But there is a limit to the amount of fish that the people of a small town will demand at the high price they were paying when only one boat was dragging a net around. Therefore, in order to sell the additional fish that are now coming in to the docks, the price charged per fish must come down. This law of supply and demand is the most basic idea of macroeconomics: as supply goes up, the price goes down, and vice versa.

FIGHTING OVER FISH

Unfortunately, using fish stocks as an example of the tragedy of the commons is far from hypothetical. From the California anchovy fisheries, to the cod of the Canadian Grand Banks, to the Patagonian tooth fish, to Russian caviar sturgeon, whales, fur seals, sea otters, blue fin tuna, Atlantic salmon—pick just about anything people have ever harvested from the water and it either has been overexploited to the point of complete collapse or it is under threat. The normally accommodating Canadians even seized a Spanish-flagged trawler on the open seas and arrested the crew for fishing in international waters that the Canadians were trying to shut down in order to give the stocks a chance to rebuild.

However, the winners of the most extreme example of fighting over efforts to control and sustain fish stocks are Britain and Iceland. Twice in the late 1970s, these normally happy neighbors quite literally fought over fish—frigates, cannons, the whole bit. When Ice-

land became one of the first nations to extend its claim of exclusive economic rights over the ocean, from 12 miles from their beaches to 200, the British objected and refused to accept this territorial claim because some of the best waters for the British trawling fleet were only 13 miles off the Icelandic coast. British trawlers went in, Icelandic coastguard cutters arrested their crews or cut their nets loose, and the British sent in a frigate to keep the cutters away from the trawlers. It was called the Cod Wars. It was ridiculously polite for a war, but there was no doubt that it was indeed a fight over fish. Icelandic captains warned the British fishermen when they were going to shoot at their ships, and even paused the shelling to let the British crews inspect the damage to make sure the boats were only mangled and not sunk, but they did fire cannons at the British ships.

So much for sharing a common resource.

In addition to the fact that the price per fish is falling, the new generation of fish extraction engineers also have fixed costs—in this example, they have bank loans for boats and nets that must be paid off. In real life, fixed costs might also include the expenses of sustaining a basic living (rent, food, clothing) as well as the costs in fuel, maintenance, and supplies needed to actually go out and fish. As the price of fish drops because of the increase in supply, the fish extraction engineers are driven to catch and sell more fish to meet their fixed costs. While Roberta used to make ends meet by selling a hundred fish at ten cents each, now she must sell two hundred fish at five cents each to pay those same bills. Consequently, she is driven to catch more fish. Perversely, this need to cover fixed costs further drives supply up and the price down, which, in turn, further increases the number of fish to be sold in order to meet those fixed costs. Once again, the supply increases, and the price drops, and so on.

It seems that the economics involved always drive the fishing fleet to increase the exploitation of the bay. When the price of fish is high, greed drives individuals to catch more fish. When the price is low, the need to meet fixed costs drives individuals to catch more fish. The limited nature of the common resource makes this dynamic even more pronounced. As the bay is overexploited, fish become scarce, and it gets harder and harder to catch the squirmy little buggers. Scarcity reduces supply, which drives prices up, and the renewed potential for making money motivates individual fishermen to catch more of the ever-decreasing supply of fish.

This example also demonstrates that appeals to enlightened self-interest and awareness of the tragedy of the commons are not enough to save a shared resource. Everyone knows how to preserve the fish in the bay—reduce the level of exploitation. But again, it's not that simple. Like the successful stag hunt, the preservation of the commons works only if *everyone* cooperates. Everyone will cooperate only if they all agree that preservation is the right thing to do *and* if they all believe that absolutely everyone else will cooperate as well. An individual's decision not to fish will have little or no effect on the fish supply if others do not also restrict their fishing; if the fish do not go into your net, they will go into someone else's. As long as someone else is willing to go out and scour the bay, the commons will be ruined regardless of your efforts to try to preserve it. Your only rational choice, therefore, is to make as much as you can, while you still can, and try to get some money in the bank for the day when the supply of fish runs out.

Escaping the Tragedy of the Commons

There are solutions for these simplified examples of the tragedy of the commons, but if they are considered carefully, it is clear that all involve collective actions. All the solutions require getting everyone to act in a certain way, such as limiting their fishing. Attaining universal compliance will require that someone regulate, monitor, and police those exploiting the commons. In the beginning,* we argued that government is all about collective action. It is about forming a group to pursue goals that cannot be attained spontaneously and would be impossible for any one individual to realize. The most fundamental of these goals is the collective pursuit of security, but once you go to the trouble of creating a group to establish a governed environment, it makes sense to use that same mechanism to pursue other collective goals that might arise.

One such goal is preserving a common resource. And since it makes sense for individuals to protect the commons only if they believe that all others will do so as well, you use government, through policing and the enforcement of laws, to make it rational for everyone to participate in the collective activity. This not only raises the potential cost of defecting from the collective effort but it also assures everyone that no one else will defect, thereby lowering the motivation to cheat. This is what makes it possible to escape the tragedy of the commons. Those who graze sheep, hunt stags, or trawl for fish will be far less likely to make the choice that harms others—overexploiting the shared resource—if they must add the fear of punishment to their cost-benefit calculus.

The need to regulate the use of the commons represents a basic and continuing economic role for government. Society uses government to control some of the **means of production**—the mechanisms for transforming labor into wealth—and to escape the tragedy of the commons. Implicit in all our simplified examples of that problem, and

---

*The beginning of this book, not the universe.

also in the possible solutions you might imagine, are the dynamics of capitalism and socialism, which, at a basic level, can be thought of as two different answers to the question of who should control the means of production: individuals or society.

KARL MARX—STUDENT OF CAPITALISM?

Any reasonable exploration of the government's role in the economy must engage the concepts of capitalism and socialism. As a result, it must examine the theories and ideas of **Karl Marx** (1818–1883).[3] Marx focused on economics as the primary element of politics, and nearly every political scientist identifies him as one of the galaxy's most influential human political theorists. Unfortunately, bringing him into the discussion always presents a challenge. Even though few, if any, of today's students know the cold war as anything more than a historical term, mentioning the name of Karl Marx can still provoke a response befitting a guy wielding a bloody chainsaw and wearing a mask sewn from human skin. Even before Marx became the namesake for the brutal Soviet bloc dictatorships of the Cold War, his criticisms of the capitalist mode of production and his belief that meaningful theory must be combined with political action provoked a visceral reaction from economic, social, and governmental elites in the industrially developed world. Today, although the reaction to Marx may not be as passionate as it once was, it remains less than friendly.

For historical, economic, and cultural reasons, the negative reaction to Marx has been particularly intense in the United States and Canada, where most students learn to equate Karl Marx with the monster under the bed. He is the lurking threat to the capitalist society that they treasure, and it is difficult for them to engage his ideas and theories in a constructive manner. In reality, however, Karl Marx probably does not warrant such antipathy. A century of intense international politics, along with numerous domestic political struggles over economics and government, has created a mythology around Marx. He is deified by one side, demonized by the other, and distorted by both.

As a starting point, it is important for students to disassociate Marx's ideas from what the former Soviet Union, East Germany, China, and North Korea call or have called Marxism. It is pretty safe to say that if Marx could see the oppression, brutality, and the misery inflicted by these governments, he would roll over in his grave. In fact, Marx's version of socialism differed greatly from the anti-imperialist, party-driven, dictatorial variants that Vladimir Lenin (1870–1924), Joseph Stalin (1879–1953), Mao Tse-tung (1893–1976), and others have used to justify placing strangleholds on their countries. Even when he was alive, Marx was quick to announce, "I am not a Marxist." Instead, among the many labels that could reasonably be applied to Marx, an important one is **humanist**—an idealist who is interested in and motivated by concern for the broader human condition and the quality of people's lives—although, ironically, that latter concern did not extend to his own family's hunger and misery. To understand how that altruistic attitude could fit with someone who criticized capitalism and advocated revolution to eliminate it, we must consider the social, historical, and economic context in which Marx was writing.

MARXISM, COMMUNISM, AND SOCIALISM

While we would not want to make a habit of it, just this once, we are going to admit that students can be forgiven for their distorted understanding of something—but this applies only to Karl Marx and his theories. This is also one instance in which fiction really does not help matters. Fictional depictions of Marxism, communism, or socialism are almost always extreme, tending to reflect either an insidious and evil enemy or an idyllic little pocket of utopia.

From the enemy submarine commander in *The Hunt for Red October* to the conniving Soviet bureaucrat in *White Nights,* to the Kim Jong-Il puppet in *Team America: World Police,* communism and Marxism are frequently associated with the evil characters spawned by a heartless totalitarian regime. Their regimes are usually caricatures of the Soviet bloc of the cold war era. Nowhere in Marx's theories, however, is there anything to indicate that he would approve of either side in the cold war. In fact, there is every indication that he would have despised the Soviet Union.

At the other extreme is the folk-music-singing commune of barefoot vegetarian hemp farmers. For an excellent example of this kind of depiction, try *Star Trek: Insurrection.* Although Marx did think that an idealized communist world was possible, it is doubtful

that he would have thought of it in terms of a regression to subsistence farming. Marx recognized the efficiencies of the industrial capitalist mode of production, and his communist utopia was the next stage beyond capitalism, not a regression to the inefficiencies of a pre-capitalist society.

In *The Dispossessed,* Ursula K. Le Guin provides perhaps the best fictional depiction of what could have been a realization of Marx's conceptualization of communism. Le Guin's story contrasts life on a capitalist planet with the communist economic and social system on its large habitable moon. Perhaps most important, the story shows that both systems are flawed. The exploitative nature of the capitalist system is laid bare, but the freedom and drive to innovate is also there. The equality of the communist system is made clear in the hard choices made during a famine, but the extreme of socialization necessary to make communism work is also shown to be so constricting that the brilliant scientist has to leave the moon in order to finish his work.

We will face a similar problem when it comes to the fictional representations of war, but for now, the key is to remember that fictional representations of Marxism and socialism are seldom good ways to get at the underlying theories, ideas, and concepts.

The Adolescence of Capitalism

Within his lifetime, Marx witnessed a critical historical period in the transformation of the global economy from the vestiges of what we might call a peasant or feudal system to the triumphant early forms of industrial capitalism.* There are some very distinct and important differences between these economic systems. One in particular is the relationship between those who perform labor and those who control the mechanisms for transforming labor into wealth. In the feudal context, most production occurred

---

*Although we put a lot of faith in gross oversimplifications, this one is more than a bit tricky. First, we should probably use the proper technical terms and discuss *modes of production,* which are the social and economic structures that transform labor into wealth. Second, we should probably be more specific about what kind of capitalist system we are talking about. We use early *industrial capitalism* as the example, but, depending on what country you used as a model, it could easily be argued that there were several transitional capitalist systems between feudalism and industrial capitalism, such as *mercantilism.* Finally, we should probably be clear that we are not discussing a specific historical example, but generalizing to get the concept across. The working class in France reacted most forcefully to the capitalist changes and was really the first to act as a unified political force, but England provides a better example of the dynamic of give-and-take driving the evolution of a mixed capitalist and socialist system.

within some sort of peasant/landowner context. The landlord controlled and owned the land—and, in some cases, owned the peasants—while the peasants were little more than subsistence farmers. It is interesting that when most of us imagine living back in feudal times, we are likely to picture ourselves as lords, ladies, dukes, or duchesses, but the sober reality is that the vast majority of us would have been serfs. Picture yourself not as a knight in King Arthur's court,* but as a peasant living in filth and squalor, digging beets out of the mud with a stick.

Anyway, under **feudalism**, these peasants raised a diverse mixture of crops and livestock on small plots within the landlord's estate. In turn, they were obligated to give a substantial percentage of their production to the landlord, who then converted it to wealth by selling or exchanging that modest surplus with others. It was an exploitive relationship that often bordered on slavery. However, one key aspect of this relationship was that the landlord and the peasant needed one another. Each brought something to the economic relationship that was valuable to the other, and each would find the other hard to replace.

The landowners were elites, who seldom had any experience with the difficult and dirty essentials of farming. Lords were brought up to be knights, politicians, and scholars. They learned swordplay, Latin, philosophy, and religion. By the standards of the time, they were highly educated, but as far as actually working the land, getting crops to grow in the dirt, or taking care of sheep out in the field, they were clueless. Farming was dirty, cold, and wet. It was peasant work that was beneath the dignity of the lords. As a result, the lords needed the peasants, who had the knowledge and the skills to work the land.

The result of this mutual dependency was something of a contract between the landlords and the peasants. Sometimes it was codified in law, but more often it was just a matter of tradition. Still, it was always understood that both peasants and lords needed each other and that both had responsibilities. Let us be clear—this was in no way a fair relationship. The peasants were ruthlessly exploited by the landowners, who got as much as he could out of them and gave back as little as possible, but there was always a bottom line. Much as a farmer would take good care of a horse to ensure that it could pull the plow next week, the landlords wanted their peasants to remain reasonably healthy and productive.

After a long period of transition, the industrial capitalism that emerged was different. Capitalists used factories as the means of production, as the means to transform labor into wealth. Though far more complex in reality, concept of industrial capitalism can be understood in terms of the assembly line.† On an assembly line, complicated tasks that used to take a great deal of skill are broken down into a series of small steps,

---

*By the way, King Arthur, if he actually existed, lived a millennium earlier, circa 800 A.D.

†While it is helpful to think about early capitalism in this context, remember that the assembly line had not yet been invented when Marx was writing.

steps that were so simple that any chimp you might grab off the street could perform each of them.

Adam Smith, in his *Wealth of Nations,* used the example of the manufacture of sewing pins to highlight the benefits of factories.[4] When an individual blacksmith made pins, he had to take the metal, pull it out into long wires, cut it to length, sharpen one end, pound the head onto the other, count, package, and even sell the pins. In the course of making even this simple product, the blacksmith had to switch between many tasks, and the starting, stopping, setting things up, and starting again took up a great deal of time. Furthermore, pins were only one of thousands of items that a successful blacksmith had to have the skills and tools to make. In contrast, by focusing on a single product and breaking the process up into many little tasks performed by different people—as you would on an assembly line—the factory system made production far more efficient. Because each specific task took very little skill, the workers could be paid less. Since the time and effort wasted in switching between different steps in the process were eliminated, more pins could be produced with less work. Additional money was saved because tools for other blacksmith tasks were not needed, and six people making pins could produce pins ten times faster and twenty times cheaper than a single blacksmith.

Marx recognized the efficiencies of the factory system, but he also pointed out that by removing the need for skilled and knowledgeable laborers, capitalism significantly altered the feudal relationship between those who own the means of production (factory owners) and their laborers. The blacksmith had to acquire a tremendous array of skills and knowledge to create hundreds of products. This experience and expertise had value. The limited number of blacksmiths could charge good money for the products of those skills. However, a factory owner who focused on a single product and set up the machines properly could grab anything genetically close to human off the street and teach it to perform a single, simple task—say, cutting the wire: snip, snip, snip, all day long. These laborers were not highly skilled artisans; they were simply replicable cogs in the productive machinery. And since each one could easily be replaced, why would the factory owner care for or be willing to provide for a person who broke his leg when replacing him was a matter of grabbing a new primate off the street and giving him a few minutes of training? In other words, the mutual dependence that underpinned the implicit feudal contract between the landowner and the peasant did not carry over to the factories. The fact that any factory worker was easily replaceable with anyone else was a critical change in the owner-worker relationship that Marx saw as a cause of many of the detrimental effects of capitalism. When combined with the competitive foundations of capitalism, the effect of this change on those who labored was devastating.

Competition as the Driving Force in Capitalism

The driving force in capitalism is the competition between capitalists. This is also the source of the system's greatest value: its efficiency. The capitalist who can make more with less can undersell the competition, capture market share, make more money, and, most important, survive. Inefficient factories lose money and inefficient capitalists go bankrupt. Constant competition and the continual entry of new competitors into the system drive an endless quest for greater and greater efficiency. This is probably the biggest benefit and the best aspect of capitalism. However, there is a dark side, too.* Constant competition between capitalists, if left unrestrained, pushes capitalists to continually demand more for every cent that they pay workers. This is certainly the case with pure capitalism or **laissez-faire capitalism**, an economic system characterized by very little, if any, government involvement in the economy. Marx argued that this drive had dire consequences that made the collapse of capitalism inevitable.

Take, for example, the production of cloth from yarn. During the early decades of industrial capitalism, the textile manufacturing industry made some of the most substantial gains in productive efficiency and endured some of the fiercest competition. Every factory could produce roughly the same product, leaving customers to choose among their goods on the basis of price. And the price the factories had to charge their customers can be broken down into four basic elements:

Profit
Materials
Overhead
Wages

We list profit first because, as the aspiring business majors in our classes argue, it is the most important. It is what motivates investors to risk their existing wealth to create the means of production. It is the reason this publisher asked us to write this book. However, another reason we put it first is to make the point that profit is not optional. It is not something we could do away with if only we were not so greedy. An entrepreneur must anticipate a minimum level of profit for it to be rational to put money at risk to build the factory and engage in production. An investor must expect to make enough profit to exceed the benefit to be gained from an alternate use of the money, such as earning interest in a bank. The potential profit must be enough to cover the risk of bankruptcy and the loss of the investment. The riskier the capitalist enterprise, the greater the potential payoff has to be. The greater the chance that your dorm-room emu farm will go bankrupt, the greater the expected profit must be in order to convince you to risk your money.

The costs of raw materials and overhead are also fundamental components of the final price of the product. Overhead includes everything necessary to build and maintain the factory and the price of each yard of cloth sold has to contribute a small amount

---

*Insert your own Darth Vader joke here. NOW!

of money to pay for the building, the machines, repairs and maintenance, heat, and all the other expenses of keeping the factory running. Finally, the price of each yard of cloth must cover the wages for the labor necessary to produce it.

Competition among capitalists affects all four of these elements: profits, materials, overhead and wages. In essence, if one capitalist can find a way to reduce any one of them, the savings enables him or her to sell the product for less than the competition. Given roughly equal products, rational consumers will choose to buy the cheaper product. The factory that can sell for less will remain profitable. The others will find it difficult, if not impossible, to sell at a higher price, and, without sales, they will not make any money. In extreme cases, the more efficient producer can drive other factories out of business. In this kind of competitive environment, the financial survival of the factory owner is at stake every minute of every day. So, how do capitalists respond to cost-cutting by their competitors? By matching or exceeding the reduction in costs. This strategy is not a matter of choice; it is the law of survival in the capitalist jungle.

The competitive dynamic drives all the components of price down as far as they will go. Thus, in an effort to minimize the costs of raw materials, factories will buy in bulk, seek overseas suppliers, and sign long-term supply contracts. In order to keep overhead costs down, they will be tempted to put off or limit plant maintenance, to ignore costly safety measures or environmental protections, and to do everything possible to maximize the production from every machine and every foot of factory space. In the early days of capitalism, factory owners began to run machines around the clock, rather than leaving them idle for part of the day, and they squeezed more and more machines into the factory space, in order to get the highest possible return on the monies invested in maintaining that space. Heat was cut to the bare minimum necessary to keep the machines functioning, and extra expenditures for the comfort or safety of the workers were eliminated.

Marx noted the benefits of an economic system driven by specialization and competition—the tremendous gains in efficiency and productivity over the existing feudal or artisan-based system of production. But he argued that the ruthless competition to cut costs and reduce prices was so severe that it would inevitably destroy the very political, economic, and social system that made all this efficiency and productivity possible. In an effort to cut overhead, weaving machines in textile mills were often packed so close together that no adult could fit between them to maintain them or fix the inevitable jams, and so, the factory owners hired young children to perform these tasks. Not only did the hours in the factory put a serious crimp on these kids' ability to indulge in juvenile pranks, pick-up softball games, and the other joys of youth, but also, it was dangerous work. A lot of kids lost a lot of fingers unjamming weaving machinery. Adults were also put in danger by the absence of nets, railings, and all the other safety measures that might have raised the factory's overhead. As it turns out, it was often cheaper to grab a new worker off the street than it was to invest in safety precautions that might keep the existing laborers alive. There were clearly some negative consequences to ruthlessly squeezing overhead. According to Marx, however, the real problem with capitalism would begin when the factory owners started squeezing wages.

Remember that the average worker does not have any special or unique skill to offer the factory owner; anyone can perform each simple task. The worker's labor is a commodity, and just as they search for the cheapest source of raw materials, factory owners will seek the cheapest source of labor. In fact, because capitalism was spreading into agricultural production and farmland was being rapidly consolidated into large plots that could be more efficiently farmed for single crops, peasants were being driven off the estates in massive numbers. Consequently, at the time that Marx was writing, there was a substantial surplus of labor, which enabled factory owners actually to push wages below what was needed for an individual to survive. Furthermore, the relentless drive to reduce costs led to innovations such as newer machines that required fewer workers. This change reduced wages as part of the cost, but it also left more people unemployed and searching for work.

If you are tempted to confuse these conditions with tough economic conditions we might experience today in the developed Western world, think again. They are not even close. The hard economic conditions of earlier periods of capitalism are much closer to those found in the cities of the Third World, or in the setting of *A Tree Grows in Brooklyn*, where the family eats stale bread, winces when a guest puts too much cream in his coffee, and collects rags to sell for a few extra pennies. Marx's contemporary, Charles Dickens, offers an even more accurate picture: the lives of the poor characters presented in *Great Expectations, Oliver Twist*, and his other novels truly reflect the bleak urban landscape faced by workers under early capitalism.[5] In these grim conditions, people are desperate to find whatever employment they can.

When workers amass at the gates of the factory to plead for work, the efficiency-driven owner is able to pay minimal salaries, as the workers literally bid their wages downward. Because single people can work for less than those who have families to support, if there are enough single people looking for work, wages will fall below the minimum a family needs to survive. Remember that at this time, there were no ridiculously wealthy rock stars driving their Bentleys to charity concerts to buy food for the starving. In the early years of capitalism, and in any current system of pure capitalism, your survival was in your own hands. It was your responsibility. We are not talking about your inability to buy the latest Atomic Kitten CD, we're talking about the inability to afford crumbs to eat or to have a place to live.

In Marx's day, people were willing to put up with incredibly inhumane conditions to continue to work. People could not yet declare personal bankruptcy. If you could not pay your bills you were sent to the poorhouse or to debtor's prison. Who can forget the famous

In the United States, we customarily associate the year 1776 with the American Revolution. However, another, equally important revolution—a radical transformation in the world of ideas—took place that year with the publication of Adam Smith's *The Wealth of Nations*. Before Adam Smith (1723–1790), most people believed that a nation's wealth was determined by the amount of riches it had in its treasury. If a king had sapped his coffers, the likely solution was either to raise taxes on the people or to head off to sack the wealth of another country. Smith's radical proposition was that a country's wealth was determined not by how much silver or gold its monarch possessed, but by the economic well-being of its people. The true driving force behind the success of a nation's economy was ambitious and creative individuals willing to produce goods and services. When it came to the national economy—to the economic well-being of the entire country—Smith argued, the best thing government could do was to get the heck out of the way of private enterprise.

If this theory sounds a lot like the rhetoric pouring out of the mouth of one of today's politicians, that is because it is. Adam Smith was the one who built the intellectual foundation for most of our contemporary ideas about the dynamics of a capitalist marketplace. Supply and demand, the efficiencies found through open competition, laissez-faire capitalism, and lower taxes leading to more wealth for everyone (including the government) are all concepts that have come from Adam Smith.

In contrast to Karl Marx—and he is often offered as the antithesis to Marx—Smith argued that a capitalist economy was self-regulating through the "invisible hand" of the market. Smith's image was not the stuff of a horror flick, nor did it have anything at all to do with stealing candy bars from the local mini-mart. Instead, it was essentially one of the first elucidations of the law of supply and demand, and Smith applied it not just to the prices of products, but to all aspects of a capitalistic economy. Unlike Marx, Smith argued that competition among capitalists would actually protect the workers, because capitalists would compete with one another for the services of the best workers. This aspect of the market's invisible hand would not only keep wages from falling too low but would also drive workers to constantly improve themselves, making everyone better off. As the fry cook to the gods, SpongeBob would always have Plankton trying to hire him away from The Krusty Krab, and Mr. Krabs would have to pay our favorite rectangular invertebrate a reasonably good salary to keep him from going over to the competition.

Thus, the invisible hand of the marketplace—essentially the law of supply and demand—put limits on even the greediest of entrepreneurs. Charge too much for Krabby Patties, and your customers will eat elsewhere. If you do not pay your invertebrates enough, your competition will hire the best ones away. If you let the quality of your products fall too low, food poisoning and all its associated unpleasantries will drive your customers away. Through experimentation, innovation, and plain old pursuit of profits, Smith argued, capitalism would always move toward the most efficient solutions to the problems that faced it, and government interference would only serve to prevent those efficiencies from being found.

exchange from Dickens's *A Christmas Carol*, when a not-yet-repentant Scrooge is approached in his place of business by some men collecting money at Christmastime for the "hundreds of thousands" in need:

> "Are there no prisons?" asked Scrooge.
> "Plenty of prisons," said the gentleman, laying down the pen again.
> "And the Union workhouses?" demanded Scrooge. "Are they still in operation?"
> "They are. Still," returned the gentleman, "I wish I could say they were not."

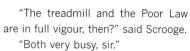

> **Getting some income, even if it is only enough for a single day's food, is better than getting none.**

"The treadmill and the Poor Law are in full vigour, then?" said Scrooge.

"Both very busy, sir."

"Oh! I was afraid, from what you said at first, that something had occurred to stop them in their useful course," said Scrooge. "I am very glad to hear it."

"Under the impression that they scarcely furnish Christian cheer of mind or body to the multitude," returned the gentleman, "a few of us are endeavouring to raise a fund to buy the Poor some meat and drink, and means of warmth. We choose this time, because it is a time, of all others, when Want is keenly felt, and Abundance rejoices. What shall I put you down for?"

"Nothing!" Scrooge replied.

"You wish to be anonymous?"

"I wish to be left alone," said Scrooge. "Since you ask me what I wish, gentlemen, that is my answer. I don't make merry myself at Christmas, and I can't afford to make idle people merry. I help to support the establishments I have mentioned—they cost enough: and those who are badly off must go there."

"Many can't go there; and many would rather die."

"If they would rather die," said Scrooge, "they had better do it, and decrease the surplus population." [6]

Bob Cratchit, Scrooge's clerk, did not put up with his boss's cruelty because he was meek. He did so because he feared unemployment and the resulting pain and hunger. He feared for his family. He feared the starvation that would accompany that condition.

Hunger can drive desperate men to work for less than it takes to survive. When you are starving to death, the other aspects of survival, such as clothing, housing, and so forth, come in a distant second to just getting something to eat. Getting some income, even if it is only enough for a single day's food, is better than getting none. If you have enough people who are that desperate, wages fall below what anyone can survive on. How long can people survive without housing or clothing? If you cannot even feed and clothe yourself, how do you feed a family or take care of your aging parents? Worse yet, you cannot go find yourself a second job because you are already working twelve-hour shifts, six-and-a-half days a week and still not making enough to survive at even the most basic level.

The Pool of Labor as a Common Resource

These are not fictional horrors. As the Dickens novels make clear, Scrooge's cold-hearted vision represents what was actually happening in Europe when Marx was writing about capitalism: people were, quite literally, being worked to death. And this massive overexploitation of workers was what Marx saw as the fatal flaw of capitalism.*

---

*If you are a bit too perceptive for your own good, this is also the point where you might be fooled into thinking we actually planned out the presentation of the material in this chapter. If you didn't know better you might suggest the chapter's sections fit together because this fatal flaw of capitalism is also a tragedy of the commons.

If you think of the pool of laborers as a commons—a shared resource that capitalists exploit for economic gain—you can also see that all the dynamics of the tragedy of the commons apply. This, in fact, is the critical link that connects economics with politics. Just as the shepherds need the field and the fishermen need the bay full of fish, the capitalists need the workers. Without them, the factories will sit idle and no profits will be made. However, capitalists are driven to overexploit the workers by the dynamics of capitalist competition, and this economic system provides no way for individual capitalists to end the overexploitation.

This is a fatal flaw in capitalism because pure capitalism provides no means to protect the common resource. In the same way that it does no good for the individual fisherman to unilaterally limit his own fishing in an effort to preserve the bay full of fish, an individual factory owner simply does not have the option of raising wages. Most capitalists are not overexploiting their workers because they are evil, or nasty, or even ruthless, but because the competition to gain customers by undercutting other producers drives all factory owners to match the price cuts made by the most ruthless, nastiest, and heartless scrooges. Anyone who chooses to pay his or her workers more than the stingiest of competitors will have to charge more for his or her product, which will quickly lead to bankruptcy. Thus, even the most enlightened and humane of capitalists could not choose to raise wages in this Darwinian system where any factory owner who fails to match a competitor's cost-cutting is quickly eaten by the wolves.

While Marx pointed to a number of problems with the early vestiges of industrial capitalism, this tragedy of the commons—the overexploitation of the workers in the pool of labor—is a fatal flaw in the very concept of pure capitalism as an economic system. This creates two very big problems for capitalism and the political system that supports it. First, Marx argued that the constant push to lower workers' salaries, which was aided by the advent of labor-saving machines, would eventually leave the workers unable to buy the goods they produced. If the workers could not afford to buy products, the result would be a serious reduction in demand for the factories' output. How could a capitalist system survive when there was insufficient demand for its products? Second, and more important, Marx pointed out that, unlike sheep, people have the capability of acting collectively and with intent. Workers, he insisted, would eventually become so desperate that they would see no alternative to destroying the system. They would find some way to overcome the barriers to revolt—the atomization, peer policing, and preference falsification that had so far kept them isolated and powerless.

Marx argued that when this inevitable revolution happened, it would tear apart the whole capitalist economic system—not to mention a few factory owners—and replace it with a socialist system that gave workers control over the means of production. And Marx believed that this revolution would be a good thing, because the workers would then build a socialist political and economic system that would eventually lead to a communist utopia.

I Thought You Said There'd Be a Revolution?

Marx was incredibly insightful in his analysis of how capitalism and its related political dynamics worked. In fact, there may not be a better discussion of the basic operation of the capitalist mode of production and how it drives everyone to become more efficient. But when it came to predicting the future, Marx was not quite as successful. Let's just say you would have been better off making 1-900 calls to that late-night TV psychic who sometimes forgets to keep up her Jamaican accent than betting on the Marxist revolution. There was no cataclysmic revolution. The workers of the world did not unite, and they did not create a communist utopia or even the socialist economic system that was supposed to lead the way. Indeed, many of the more prominent Marxist theorists since Marx have expended considerable effort explaining why the inevitable collapse of the capitalist system did not arrive on schedule. For example, Vladimir Lenin's best-known work, *Imperialism,* is essentially an explanation of how the expansion of the capitalist system delayed the revolt by colonizing foreign lands.[7]

Perhaps a better way to explain the revolution that never happened is to work with this tragedy of the commons theme that we have stumbled upon. If you think about the pool of labor as a common resource that is shared by capitalists, and if you ask how you can prevent destroying it through overexploitation, perhaps the solution is the same as the solution we suggested earlier for the other examples of a tragedy of the commons—collective action. By forming a collective action group, or using the structures of an existing group such as the government, you can police the actions of all who use the commons. You would do this to prevent its destruction through overexploitation and keep it productive year after year. You can limit or otherwise regulate the number of sheep and save the field, limit the number of fish caught and keep fishing in that bay forever. Perhaps you can limit and police the way the pool of labor is exploited by all capitalists and preserve it for the long term.

Through fits and starts, by accident and necessity more than by intent, this is essentially what has happened. Repeatedly, as dissatisfaction and unrest among workers threatened to grow into revolt, capitalists turned to government, over which, by the way, they have always exercised substantial, if not overwhelming, influence. Force was used and there were fights, arrests and even massacres, but as we all know there are limitations on the use of force and governments gradually adopted policies that would give the workers some of what they demanded, which included the limitations on the exploitation of labor that were needed to prevent the collapse of the capitalist system.

SOCIALISM

Marx categorized political-economic systems according to who controlled the means of production—the things necessary to transform labor into wealth—such as land and its natural products, factories, materials, and tools, as well as infrastructure. Since many people are quite fond of eating and the other simple pleasures of survival, control of

Table 5.1 Who Controls the Means of Production?

Feudal System	Capitalist System	Socialist System
Church and hereditary elite controlled land, the primary means of production	**Individual proprietors** control all means of production	**Society** as a whole equally controls all means of production
Artisans control the means of production relevant to their crafts		

this bit of economic life is critical. Under the feudal system there were artisans, such as smiths, coopers, shoemakers, fletchers, cat jugglers, and tailors who controlled the means of production relevant to those crafts, but land was the primary means of production, and the church, along with a hereditary elite of royalty and landowners, controlled the land (see table 5.1). In a capitalist system, individuals control the farms, factories, falafel franchises, and so on, and it is through the self-interested decisions of those individuals that the tragedy of the commons arises. We have yet to discuss, or even really describe socialism, however.

Though students should bear in mind that this is an extremely simplified depiction of a very complex theory, socialism can be roughly defined as an economic system in which society controls the means of production. Instead of competition for profits, equality in the distribution of society's wealth is the driving factor in the decisions related to production. While many who are concerned about the effects of poverty and disparities of wealth may find this idea appealing, recognize that socialism, also, is imperfect. We have spent a great deal of time discussing Marx's critique of capitalism and his discussion of its fatal flaw. We did so because it is predominantly capitalism that most of us understand and it is this system that students usually take for granted. However, socialism is also flawed. Pure socialism, just like pure capitalism, cannot work in practice. In fact, it has never even been tried on a large scale.

The idea of society controlling the means of production can be summarized by the statement, "From each according to his ability, to each according to his need." You produce what you can produce and society will make sure that everybody will get what he or she needs to survive. This system fixes the flaw in capitalism by making sure that people do not go hungry, but it creates a new problem: how do you get people off their butts to do something? In essence, socialism is very good at distributing goods, but very inefficient at producing those goods. Everybody gets whatever housing and food is available. The problem is getting the housing and food made. In his descriptions of socialism and the communist utopia, Marx, who was a bit of a workaholic, overestimated people's industriousness.*

---

*However, Marx would say that we have gotten the whole chapter totally wrong. Believing that everyone's view of the world is shaped by the economic system under which they live, he would argue that our view of human nature is shaped by the values—such as individualism, motivation, and competition—that are important for the continuation of the capitalist system. As such, Marx would say that we are guilty of "false consciousness," because we cannot properly judge human nature while viewing the world through our capitalist glasses.

You can probably think of a whole lot of jobs—such as being the night janitor at a sewage-treatment plant—that only get filled because they pay a trainload of cash. Why do garbage men get paid more than teachers? Which job would you rather do? Would anyone regularly pick up trash just because it needed to be done? If you are getting exactly what you need regardless of what you do, would you choose to pick up barrels of trash or would you sit on your couch and watch reruns on the professional fishing channel? Many—perhaps not even most, but still a substantial number of people—would choose to serve their tour of duty as a couch commando. This is especially true if you get the same house, food, and clothes as the person who sorts nuclear waste at the asbestos factory. Socialism is very inefficient, if only because, without incentives, it is hard to motivate people to work, and even harder to motivate them to seek efficiencies or to excel at their craft. When the complete absence of competition means that a poorly run factory is treated the same as a well-run factory, how do you encourage workers to put in the extra effort it takes to run factories better? When there is no reward for finding a more efficient way to do something, why look for it? When a doctor gets treated exactly the same as a janitor, who would put in the extra years of training to become a doctor? Worse yet, if both a good doctor and a bad doctor get paid the same, what motivates people to become better doctors? Pride and integrity will provide some motivation, but is that enough?

We can see that pure socialism and pure capitalism are both flawed. Neither could realistically function for any length of time in the real world. However, we must also realize that neither ever has been—or ever really could be—expected to exist in its pure form. Like many other concepts in politics, the ideal or perfect forms of these ideas are worth examining only in order to explore their dynamics. When it comes to the real world, the useful question is not whether to have a socialist or a capitalist economic system, but, instead, how to strike a balance between the two.

THE YIN AND YANG OF CAPITALISM AND SOCIALISM

In Chinese cosmology, the yin and yang are complementary forces, symbolized by the moon and the sun, which must remain in balance. Earth and heaven, cold and hot, female and male—yin and yang represent the opposing forces of life. In many ways, this concept of complementary forces can be applied in the case of capitalism and social-ism. When government regulates and polices the exploitation of the pool of labor by capitalists, it is, in essence, using principles of socialism to save capitalism. When it sets a minimum wage, limits working hours, creates safety rules, outlaws child labor, or in any way limits the owner's management of the factory, the government takes some control of the means of production away from the individual capitalist and gives it to the society. All functioning capitalist systems in the world today are actually mixtures of capitalism and socialism, a mixture of private and societal control of the means of production. The real question is not capitalism versus socialism, but what balance between the two systems is best. Like most things in politics and government, there is no single answer to this question. Different cultures have all struck different balances between these two ideals and the balances are dynamic, changing over time.

In Europe, particularly in Scandinavia, the balance is heavily tilted toward the social-ist end of the scale. Society effectively regulates the workplace and provides extensive services and a high minimum level of wealth for all. In many developing countries, the political and economic systems are close to pure capitalism, featuring little regulation, few government services, and only the barest of minimum-wage and working-condition guarantees. Initially, it was a relatively pure and unregulated form of capitalism that replaced feudal and artisanal modes of production in Europe, North America, and else-where around the globe. However, the first century of capitalism witnessed a steady introduction of societal controls, regulation and policing of production, along with an increase in societal guarantees of a minimum level of wealth for all. Recently, most of the developed countries in the world have scaled back both regulation and societal guar-antees of wealth, but the balance between degrees of capitalism and socialism is still the source of daily debate. Such questions as what should be the precise minimum wage, how much health care should be provided to whom, what sorts of environmental regu-lations should be imposed, and whether there should be tax cuts to stimulate the econ-omy are all part of finding the appropriate balance between capitalism and socialism.

Government and politics lie directly at the intersection of the society and the econ-omy. When society wishes to exert more control over the means of production, it turns to government leaders. Capitalists use their wealth and power to influence those same leaders to reduce societal control over their factories, farms, and businesses. This reg-ulation is just the basic, most fundamental role of government in the economy. There are countless activities—from the creation of money and the control of its supply, to the building and maintenance of infrastructures, to the sponsoring of research and devel-opment, to educating future workers—that governments do to enhance and support the economic activity that transforms labor into wealth.

What is the perfect relationship between government and the economy? If we knew the answer to that question, we wouldn't be spending our time writing a political sci-

ence textbook—we would be sipping margaritas on the beaches of Aruba. In fact, as much as people act as if they know the answer, they do not. They think they know. In this sense, politics is very much about the battle among those who think they know what should be done. However, as we suggested earlier, various countries have struck their own balances, just as Francie finds her personal balance between realism and idealism in *A Tree Grows in Brooklyn*. When countries identify the balance they want between capitalism and socialism, they not only pursue it through policy choices, but they also design their political structures in a manner that incorporates these choices into their governmental institutions. It is to the subject of structures and institutions that we now turn.

KEY TERMS

capitalism / **95**
enlightened self-interest / **98**
feudalism / **105**
humanist / **103**
Karl Marx / **103**
laissez-faire capitalism / **107**
means of production / **102**
socialism / **95**
the stag hunt / **98**
the tragedy of the commons / **96**

CHAPTER SUMMARY

The relationship between government and the economy is more complex than most people realize. However, the need for government involvement in the economy is demonstrated clearly by the so-called tragedy of the commons. This useful concept demonstrates that although people may know that overexploiting a common resource or abandoning a common effort is not in their best interest, individual calculations may suggest that not cooperating is the more rational individual choice because other people's actions must be taken into account as well. Although industrial capitalism had many advantages over the feudal system it replaced, it also had many flaws. Karl Marx exposed many of laissez-faire capitalism's imperfections, particularly its exploitation of workers and its inherent contradictions. While Marx recognized many of capitalism's problems, he did not foresee the defects in his own socialist prescriptions, which undervalued the role of human motivation. Students should learn two very important lessons from this chapter. First, there are no purely socialist or capitalist systems in the world today; most countries try to find a balance between these two economic ideals. Second, if you ever go stag hunting, make sure you really trust the people who go with you.

STUDY QUESTIONS AND EXERCISES

1. Think about some of the problems that we confront today—for example, the dwindling supply of petroleum, and arms proliferation. How does the tragedy of the commons help to explain why these problems are so difficult to solve?

2. How does the tragedy of the commons demonstrate the need for a basic and continuing economic role for government?

3. What is Marx's most pointed critique of industrial capitalism?

4. Do you think that Marx's communism could ever work? Why or why not?

WEBSITES TO EXPLORE

www.bunnygame.org/index.htm. Tragedy of the Bunnies, a site offering a game that illustrates the tragedy of the commons. Make sure to read the explanation of "the moral" of the game.

www.gametheory.net/dictionary/Games/StagHunt.html. GameTheory.net's version of the stag hunt, offering a more mathematical approach to calculating the strategy of the hunt.

www.historyguide.org/intellect/marx.html. The History Guide's Lectures on Modern Intellectual History, including a biography of Karl Marx and some summaries of his major works.

www.marxists.org/. The Marxists Internet Archive, a clearinghouse of information about and writings by Marx and Marxists composed by Marxists from around the world.

www.capmag.com. *Capitalism Magazine,* an opinion site that extols the virtues of laissez-faire capitalism.

It seems that every political science textbook has a photo of the White House in it somewhere. We aren't sure why. It's not like you don't know what it looks like. But there might be a law or rule that says you have to have one, so we put one in just to be safe.

CHAPTER 6

Structures and Institutions
This Old House of Commons

Unless you happen to be a Yeti living in a Himalayan ice cave, you already know that it is impossible to flip through the channel lineup of any cable system without finding reruns of Bob Vila standing in the ruins of someone's home and talking about putting it back together. There was a sitcom version, *Home Improvement*,[1] and even though Bob was not the star, he showed up on it quite a bit. That too, is constantly rerun on cable. And now there are all the second generation, radical, and crazy home improvement shows on cable, all paying homage to Bob Vila.* In fact, because Bob's bearded face is such a prominent feature of modern cable TV, we have often wondered if Mr. Vila actually owns a good number of the cable TV companies around the United States.

There are two lessons offered by Bob's home improvement shows. The first is the simple observation that Mr. Vila only *talks* about putting those houses back together. Bob never actually does any of the heavy lifting, yet he ends up with the money to buy the big house and brand new truck. We use the second lesson about the nature and importance of structures to make a few points about politics and government, but we are still very interested in figuring out how he gets all the good stuff without doing the work.

Before Mr. Vila's worker drones rip the innards out of their victim's house, they must carefully assess the structure of the building. In an ancient ritual handed down by the Babylonians, Lord

---

* We find some of these hip, new, radical home improvement shows disturbing. Take *Extreme Makeover: Home Edition* as an example. Ty and his minions pounce upon a desperate family, chase them out of town, tear down their house, build a monstrosity in its place, and then force the family to come back and live in it. Horrifying, yes, but that is not the most disturbing part. Consider that this act of vandalism is supposed to be a "makeover." If this concept of making over was applied to the original *Extreme Makeover*, instead of giving people nose jobs, pretty new teeth, and an exercise program, the show's staff would just send them to the factory that makes Soylent Green and replace them with a robotic version of Yul Brynner.

Vila is led through the house by the Holy Keepers of all Construction Knowledge—Norm Abrams and Tom Silva—who carefully evaluate the fundamental ability of the building to perform its basic functions, which includes not collapsing on its occupants. The structures of the house are the basic elements that all houses must have; the foundation, the walls, the roof, the framing, the plumbing, the heating. These parts of the building serve several essential functions and must be there to make it a house.

At their most basic, structures—whether architectural or governmental—simultaneously determine, enable, and limit. The foundation determines the shape of the house because any part of the house that bears weight must rest on it. The foundation enables the house to stand because it supports the walls, posts, and other parts that would otherwise sink into the ground under the weight of the house. The foundation also limits what the builders can do because once the foundation is in, Master Vila cannot choose to build a new breakfast nook three feet to the left.

Government **structures** are, conceptually at least, similar. They are the basic functions that governments need to perform. They are the essential elements of governing that determine, enable, and limit the form and function of a government. The next few chapters focus on a few of the big and obvious structures of government. Just as the foundation is a necessary part of every house, these functions are a necessary part of just about any modern government. For example, all governments must establish the rules of acceptable behavior within the state. Consequently, every government must have a legislative structure for creating laws. That legislative structure might be a magic goat that whispers new laws to the King's favorite mistress or it can be a bunch of rich old men arguing and voting, but no matter what form it takes, it has to be there. Because laws and decisions must be implemented, every government must have an executive or a political structure that acts on behalf of the state. In essence these are the walls and roof of our metaphorical house of government. There is also the task of handling the mundane day-to-day tasks citizens expect of government. A bureaucracy handles these administrative functions in most modern states. Also, since the laws governing behavior must be enforced, we also spend a chapter on judicial structures.

The basic structures required in modern homes have grown well beyond the necessities of walls and a roof. Similarly, government structures have also grown beyond the absolute basics. There are several other political structures we could include and there are other ways we could categorize political structures but most who teach politics will probably agree that these are the basic structures critical for understanding how things work in modern government. The goal of the chapters in this all-important middle section of the book is to give you the background and tools to understand how political **institutions** carry out governmental functions. During the course of this investigation,*

---

*You have the right to remain silent, which is just as well since we—the authors—cannot hear you anyway.

we focus on the tension between ideal visions of how government should operate and the imperfections of a hopelessly complex real world that refuses to quit changing long enough to get everything perfected.

We have to start by asking some very basic questions. What are government structures and institutions? Where do they come from? What forces shape them? Why are they so screwed up? And, of course, why do driver's license photos make everyone look like deranged lunatics? The chapters that follow look at specific structures in greater detail.

STRUCTURES OR INSTITUTIONS?

The house analogy gets the basic idea of a structure across quite well, but it also provides an opportunity to clarify the distinction between political structures and political institutions. Like structures, institutions are critical and relatively permanent parts of a government. However, structures are generic while institutions are specific and we can illustrate what this means by using our house analogy. Walls are structures. You find them in some form in every house. They can be made of wood, brick, straw, stone, or the papier mâché stuff that some of the interesting folks on HGTV claim you can do anything with. Any specific way someone decides to build a particular wall would be an institution; the specific way that critical structure is implemented. A legislature is a political structure. The British House of Commons is an institution. A judicial system is a political structure. The U.S. Supreme Court is a political institution. This distinction is important because when we move from the discussion of basic functions to specific examples, we are also moving from the discussion of structures to the discussion of institutions.

When students hear the term "institution" many would rather be locked up in one than have to study them. At least one of the authors thinks teaching about them is not that much fun either. The other author is certifiably insane* and quite likes the institution he calls home. But political institutions are a big—we are talking extinct furry elephant-size big—part of how governments work. Political institutions are the organizational structures through which political power is exercised. They persist over time and provide a foundation of process, knowledge, and precedent for making decisions and performing actions. Getting at the underlying dynamics of institutions, however, is a bit of a challenge.

For instructors, it is hard to resist the temptation to catalog, categorize, and explain the various structures and institutions around us. Thus, political institutions are often presented in a straightforward descriptive fashion, usually in coma-inducing detail. Professors often emphasize things like "there are two houses in the British Parliament," "there are 435 members of the House of Representatives," "the Israeli prime minister

---

* There is an actual certificate involved. He framed it and it now hangs on the wall next to his diplomas.

can call elections at any time," and of course "1600 Pennsylvania Avenue is not the address of Wrigley Field." Do not get us wrong, these details are important. We have often had to find incompetent but cheap lawyers for students who took one of our jokes seriously, packed up a few bratwursts and downed a case of beer before trying to find the bleachers at 1600 Pennsylvania Avenue.*

If we never talked about specific institutions and what they do, it would be pretty tough to learn how they work. It would also be pretty tough to have an intelligent conversation about government. However, simply describing political institutions does not tell you everything there is to know about those institutions nor does it help you build a dynamic understanding of the basic political structures that nations utilize. For students, political institutions can be a challenge, if only because of the familiarity we already have with them. After all, most people who have been paroled from high school can probably name several political institutions. The presidency, the Congress, the courts are among the most important institutions in the United States. Likewise, parliaments, monarchs, political parties, and the military are common political structures throughout the world. We see them, we interact with them, and we talk about them all the time. However, it is this very familiarity that is part of the problem with studying and teaching about political institutions. Like the other aspects of government that you see or have experienced, it can be hard to find the fundamentals underneath the avalanche of details and nuances that you already know. It can also be difficult to remain objective about familiar institutions and remain open to alternative institutions that are used in other countries.

HUMAN NATURE AND POLITICAL INSTITUTIONS

A society's basic view of human nature is a reasonable place to start working on a general understanding of political institutions. As James Madison put it, "But what is government itself, but the greatest of all reflections on human nature?"[2] Does the society view people as generally cooperative or selfish, rebellious or submissive, active or passive? This is critical because a political institution that is perfect for cooperative people, such as the Amish, would be a disastrous failure when dealing with the selfish, notably Major League baseball players.

We can see this reflected in the work of Madison himself because James Madison not only occasionally commented on government and human nature, he is also generally thought of as the father of the American Constitution.[†] His view on human nature is quite pessimistic and that basic perspective is abundantly clear in the basic construction of

---

* If you do decide to do the same, please remember that those guys dressed in cheap black suits are not umpires and they have had their senses of humor surgically removed. And you probably want to avoid saying anything about their mothers.

† Notably, Dolley Madison is not considered the mother of the Constitution and no one is talking about who is. We have no evidence, but some unusual family connections to the snack cake industry lead us to suspect a woman who is only known as "Little Debbie."

> **The U.S. system, because of its separation of powers, is specifically designed to make it difficult for a less-than-angelic government to infringe on the rights of its citizens.**

U.S. political institutions. Madison argued, "If men were angels, no government would be necessary. If angels were to govern men, neither external nor internal controls on government would be necessary."[3] Clearly Madison was not anticipating a time when governors and citizens would come together, hold hands, and hum Disney songs while sitting around a campfire. In designing the American Constitution, Madison and his fellow architects built a system based on a basic mistrust of human nature. They drew the blueprints for a complex set of interlocking institutions with overlapping responsibilities that pitted separate portions of the government against itself. Each section jealously guarded its power and the power of those that supported it and it was this pursuit of selfish interests that kept the other sections honest.

The U.S. system, because of its separation of powers, is specifically designed to make it difficult for a less-than-angelic government to infringe on the rights of its citizens. The system also makes it difficult for any one portion of society to enact policies that infringe upon the interests of another. This kind of government has its good side in preventing many bad things from happening, but it makes it hard to get much done at all—including passing very popular laws and laws aimed at ending discrimination or remedying its effects. Other governments with a stronger belief of the natural goodness of humankind are more likely to have simpler governmental systems that make it far easier to enact policy. We see this, for example, in European democracies where the winning party has a much freer hand in making changes. However, this ability to enact policy easily comes at the cost of stability over time. After all, the French change their government as often as they change their . . . their . . . well, let's just say they change their government a lot. These less-restrained forms of governments also create an increased risk of putting one portion of society or government at the mercy of another as they swiftly pass laws and make sudden changes to the rules that define society.

The presumed nature of human beings—good or bad—is key to understanding the creation and evolution of political institutions. This is a great deal like saying that the context of the house—the terrain, the readily available materials, and the local skills—shape the way its basic structures are built. The availability of tons of stone will influence whether Bob Vila's worker drones transform the double-wide mobile home into either a ski lodge or a twelfth-century Moorish castle. It is in the details of the local context—the worldview of the people, the geographic situation, and the economic realities—that institutions are created and later evolve. Remember this as we seek to understand the underlying political structures that are expressed through the wide variety of institutions around the world.

THE REALITY OF POLITICAL INSTITUTIONS

Given the opportunity to craft ideal governmental institutions from scratch, we would all choose the types of institutions that we believe would support the values and traditions most important to us. Values like democracy, individual rights, religious footwear, nationalism, freedom from disco or its evil offshoots, and so forth can all be bolstered and protected, or weakened and repressed by the types of institutions a nation uses. Similarly, the personal wealth, power, and security of the leader are other values that can be bolstered or impeded by particular types of institutions. Connect this back to the personal nature of utopias and the variety of the people found in every governed society and you will realize that the push for compromise quickly takes us away from anyone's ideal institutions.

Context, Evolution, and the Unbearable Weight of History

Of course, even if we could agree on every detail of the perfect political institution, in the real world, nations rarely have an opportunity to install their ideal institutions from scratch. First, most government institutions are not designed or even intentionally created. Instead they evolve out of humble and sometimes downright unusual beginnings. For example, Great Britain's Parliament, which serves as the model for populist democracies around the world, has evolved from a decidedly elitist source. Parliament was born out of the struggles between the wealthy nobility and the monarch. It was initially a means for the king to enlist the nobility in controlling, taxing, and ruling the peasants and exploiting the products of the land in a more organized and efficient manner. Influence flowed from the royalty at the top to those who slaved away and paid taxes at the bottom. Over the decades and centuries, Parliament changed. It adjusted to economic shifts, demographic trends, technological advances, until it ultimately developed into a democratic institution that aggregates the interests, desires, and demands from the ruled and sends that input from the bottom to the top. Today's British Parliament would likely horrify the elitist aristocrats who fought and killed to create it.

Even when institutions are rationally and intentionally designed, nations seldom, if ever, have anything close to a blank page when they create a government. Almost every government's institutions carry the legacy of generations. The U.S. political systems represent a rare situation where a government was actually designed. It was forged through careful consideration and impassioned debate, yet the vast bulk of the institutions in the fledgling U.S. government were inherited almost unchanged from the colonial government of the British. Everything—from the basic code of laws, to the postal service, to the names of locations, the boundaries of the colonies, and even the local governing bodies within the thirteen colonies—comes almost directly from the very same British colonial oppressors whom George Washington crossed the Delaware River to shoot.*

It is no different today. Revolutionaries still need the trains to run—and who better to run those trains than the experienced conductors and managers from the previous

---

* When George crossed the Delaware River, he actually shot at German mercenaries in New Jersey, but let's not get picky.

regime. The same goes for city governments, police officers fighting street crime, tax collectors, you name it. The very top of the political pyramid might be replaced by loyal revolutionary comrades-in-arms, but even with the most dramatic changes in government, the institutions beneath them seldom change much, if at all.

At the extreme, a nation may not be able to implement its ideal institutions because its basic structures were imposed upon it by another source. Newly independent colonies start with political institutions created by their former colonial masters, often with little or no consideration of the local cultures or realities of political power. At the close of World War II, the United States designed, and all but imposed, a new government on Japan. Various nations, including the United States, that were at one time colonies of European powers have governmental structures that mirror their former mother countries. In the words of The Who, "meet the new boss, same as the old boss."

Even if you can suspend disbelief enough to argue that a nation can come up with and consciously go about trying to create ideal institutions, it is not necessarily true that what we plan will come to pass in the end. Like George Bailey in *It's A Wonderful Life*,[4] our plans do not always work out the way that we assume they will. Real life gets in the way. For George Bailey that meant salvaging the family business, the Building and Loan, when he would have rather traveled around the world. In the real world the government structures that we erect, the plans we make as architects, do not always work out in the end. This happens with all kinds of structures. In the construction trade, there are so many adjustments that always have to be made while constructing a large building that *after* the project is finished, architects have to draw up a final set of building plans. These plans, called the "as built" drawings, show exactly how the planned building actually ended up being constructed and they are drawn up so that the designers of future renovations, or even those demolishing the building, will know exactly what is hidden inside the walls. The carefully designed U.S. government institutions had to be amended ten times in order for the original states to agree to ratify it.

The imperfections of governmental structures go one step further. Even after accounting for all of these factors, we still must consider the effect of time and history as a source of many substantial deviations from the ideals we might dream up for our political institutions. We can rehabilitate, renovate, and redecorate the example of the old house to bring this point home, so to speak.*

Take a plantation house built in the mid-1800s as an example of how history shapes the current expression of structures as institutions. In 1857, houses had foundations, walls, doors and windows, but many other things we think of as the basic structure of a house, such as an electrical system, did not exist or were vastly different. In the large expensive homes of 1857, kitchens were often not part of the house proper. Kitchens

---

* Like you didn't see that coming.

and their wood-burning stoves were relegated to a separate building behind the main house so the heat from the stoves did not broil the occupants of the house during the summer, so the smells from unrefrigerated foods were kept out of the house, and, most importantly, so all the best parts of the house were protected from the dangers of kitchen fires.

As the years pass, think of how the basic structural expectations for a house change and how those changes would eventually alter an 1857 plantation home. Central plumbing becomes a standard part of new houses and eventually someone in the family gets tired of going outside to use the facilities, and puts his or her foot down and demands central plumbing.* From the point in time when central plumbing becomes standard, it is incorporated into the design of new houses. The other structural elements of new houses—walls, rooms and such—were adjusted at the beginning to accommodate this new structure—fancy city plumbing. In new houses, the pipes are run inside the walls and the bathroom is included in the basic layout. In the old plantation house, the addition of plumbing has to be adapted to the existing structures of a house. Pipes are run through the basement and the coat closet under the stairs is converted to accommodate a toilet and sink.

Later, gas for lighting and cooking, and then electricity is added to the plantation house. Eventually, the kitchen has to be moved into or added onto the basic structure of the house. With the development of central heating, an oil or coal-fired boiler is shoved in the basement. This involves installing radiators and all the pipes to connect them to the boiler. Those new pipes have to be fitted in and around what already exists, and in an old house, it is not unusual to see radiators blocking doors, exposed steam pipes in otherwise formal rooms and all kinds of other makeshift fixes. More time passes. Showers, Jacuzzi tubs, air conditioning, telephones, cable TV, surround sound media rooms, doggy doors, a library, a billiard room, Miss Scarlet in the conservatory with the revolver—everything that we now expect in a home has to be adapted to the basic form of that 1857 farmhouse. No one designing a new house would run pipes around on the outside of the walls, or turn a hall closet into a shower, but you see that sort of thing all the time in old houses. It is imperfect, but it usually is far too expensive to tear the house down and start again, so you must work with what you already have.

In short, the institutions we find in today's government are, in many ways, similar to an old house. Government institutions may not necessarily smell musty or make odd noises on a stormy night,† but they are the imperfect adaptations of structures. Their forms are shaped by history, culture, necessity, and circumstance. They are always imperfect.

---

*Both authors can attest, from personal experience, that the female half of a couple is usually the more assertive proponent of indoor plumbing and other modern conveniences, but we're open-minded on the topic.

† Many do, however.

Failed Institutions

Unfortunately, the imperfections that occur when adapting ideal institutions to an imperfect world do not stop there. Political institutions sometimes just go wrong, sometimes quite badly. George Orwell's *Animal Farm*[5] clearly meant to focus on the failed promise of communist revolutions. Flippantly tossing aside the whole communism and cold war, heart and soul of the book, the story can also demonstrate our point that attempts to shape ideal institutions can fail as individuals take advantage of the structures and context. The plot describes a revolution in which the farm animals revolt and take over the farm. Motivated by the slogan that "all animals are equal," the animals are slowly co-opted by the pigs, who then alter the motto to indicate that some animals are more equal than others. The basic point, however, is that noble attempts to mold institutions can be pirated by those with less-than-noble purposes.

Further, regardless of intentions, statements, constitutions, or the detailed dictates handed down by the aliens who built the pyramids, institutions are not always what they appear to be and they may serve purposes that may not at first seem apparent. In *A Hitchhiker's Guide to the Galaxy*,[6] Douglas Adams's satirical jab at government is spun into a roundhouse left hook when the two main characters, Arthur Dent and Ford Prefect, run into Zaphod Beeblebrox, a two-headed being who happens to be president of the Imperial Galactic Government. As it turns out, the president has no power. The real job of the president of the Imperial Galactic Government is to do outrageous things that will distract attention from those who are truly in control. In fact, there is not even a galactic empire any longer. The only thing that remains is the name, which is kept alive solely for the purpose of allowing people to feel better about the government.

In Adams's skewering of all things official and proper, the institution of the presidency is used only as a distraction, but you do not have to travel along the fuzzy edge of literary insanity to find political institutions used as distractions, window dressing, or outright charades. Elections and parliaments in the real world can be prime examples. In 2002, Saddam Hussein was reelected as the president of Iraq. He was the only candidate, there were armed soldiers escorting people to the polling places and you had to sign your name to the ballot you cast, but there was no specific law that said everyone *had* to vote for a dictator known to slaughter entire villages. In Iraq there was also a parliament that debated issues. In reality, this parliament truly did make a few laws, but only as directed or allowed by Hussein. The Iraqi parliament's debates were as much a sideshow as Zaphod's presidency.

Too Legit to Quit: Legitimacy, Information, and Human Nature

Despite this variety of imperfections, complications, and difficulties, it is critical that we develop an understanding of political institutions. Even if a specific institution is a seemingly farcical sideshow, or a pointless relic from a former age, it can still serve a purpose. For example, even without a practical function, institutions can build legitimacy for a government. The simplicity of our limited definition of legitimacy as the voluntary acceptance of the government or leaders should not detract from the fact that legitimacy is a key concept in political science. As an example of how institutions can enhance the voluntary acceptance of decisions, policies, choices or even the leadership as a whole, remember why Zaphod was president even though the galactic empire had ceased to exist.

Even if they cannot affect the outcome of the policy-making process, keeping parts of history or tradition in the process can help convince people to accept the laws, processes, or policies. For example, when the United States Supreme Court declares that a law passed by Congress and signed by the president is constitutional, it convinces the public to accept the law. By affirming the law, it does not change or shape the law—indeed, often it will say that it is a bad law—but by declaring it constitutional the Court is saying to the public that the law has been examined and found to be within the bounds of the legally acceptable. It reassures the public and in so doing, convinces them to be more willing to accept the law. Across the pond, the Queen of England opens meetings of Parliament by announcing what "Her Majesty's Government" will do during the upcoming session. This ritual increases the people's respect for the parliament, draws their attention to it and informs them of what is happening and the institution of the monarchy serves a purpose even though the Queen has virtually no true political power.

The example of the Queen's role in opening Parliament is also important because of her role in informing the public. Governmental institutions can teach and shape the demands of the public as much as they react to the public's wishes or enact policy. Parliamentary or congressional hearings are conducted as much for the information they provide as they are for investigating what is needed to make good laws. The same can be said of legislative debates. The information that is provided to the public through a debate is often more important than the outcome, especially when legislation fails. From the debate, interested people will know the reasons why legislation failed, and can adjust their future demands to increase the chance of success. Debates can alert uninformed or unaware parties to the substance of the issue and provide the opportunity to generate input or feedback that will alter or even prevent the legislation. Think about an uncertain dictator, facing domestic unrest and worried about the reaction to a policy change. By staging a debate in his puppet legislature, he can provoke a reaction and get a hint of feedback without actually taking the risk of changing policy and sparking a revolution.

It is also true that the institutions that we utilize can go so far as to shape basic behavior in our day-to-day lives. Governments that demand citizen participation also demand that citizens be more aware. Those governments that act in a paternal manner are likely to breed citizens who are dependent on strong leadership. Institutions that hunt down and punish dissent will generate fear, isolation, and atomization. Nothing new with that idea; Aristotle, Rousseau, and many later theorists understood

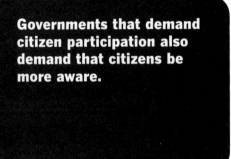

Governments that demand citizen participation also demand that citizens be more aware.

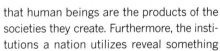

that human beings are the products of the societies they create. Furthermore, the institutions a nation utilizes reveal something about that society's overall view of human nature and that connects to the earlier point that the presumption of human nature shapes the ideal of a political institution.

SIMGOVERNMENT

The process of becoming a professor is like a medieval apprenticeship where you sell your soul to an established professor and trade years of slave labor to learn the field and become a professor yourself. Then you get to torture your own students. Grad school feels a lot like signing up to become a troll in the hopes that you might one day become a swan. Part of this cycle of abuse is that political science graduate students spend enormous amounts of time reading books that no human would want to open or staring at computer screens full of mathematical hieroglyphics and other such gibberish.* Since the true revenge of the indentured servant is to avoid actually being helpful or productive, these political science trolls seek creative ways to look like they are working when in fact they are not. This is how computer games were born, honest.

Computer solitaire has its limits. When we were in graduate school, one of the more popular computer games that helped students avoid doing any real work was called Civilization. It is a great game where you get to conquer the world, but aside from the fact that it is fun to build the pyramids in Cleveland and fight against Aztecs with cruise missiles, it does not work very well for the point we want to make. So we are going to talk about SimCity instead.

If you have never played SimCity or any of its progeny, the point is to start with a splat of land on a map and gradually build a functioning city complete with roads, airports, housing, business, and so forth. All of this has to be accomplished while maintaining a balanced budget, a low crime rate and general citizen satisfaction. It is an interesting, oddly noncompetitive, but highly addictive game that can consume an indescribable amount of time. Even though some obvious problems have prevented us from finding a venture capitalist interested in creating our SimGovernment computer game, it strikes us that no one can stop us from torturing you with the idea. It also works pretty well as a framework for outlining some of the basic variations, decisions, and choices related to ideal and real political and governmental institutions.

Step I: Choose a Terrain

The first step in the game SimCity is to select a terrain on which to start the city. If you were trying to build ideal government institutions out of thin air you would pick a terrain that would be suitable for the type of government you wanted. That is, if you ultimately

---

* Are we selling you on it yet?

wanted to install a democracy, you would choose to construct a government in a place where the populace valued participation, independence, and self-reliance. If you wanted to install a structure that would emphasize efficiency, you would build the government upon a social foundation of people who liked working obsessively and following orders. If you wanted fairness and equality, you would select a group that valued community above all else. In short, the structures that you choose will be influenced by the basic **political culture**—the political aspect of the human nature of the local populace.

Political scientist Sidney Verba defines a nation's political culture as "the system of empirical beliefs, expressive symbols, and values, which defines the situation in which political action takes place."[7] This political culture can involve religious values, expectations, morals, ethics, and traditions. If you have taken a sociology class, you are probably very familiar with the notion of mores and traditions. Citizens do not often think about their political culture because they take it for granted. It is as fundamental and as absolutely natural as the basic personal hygiene skills you can reasonably assume your blind date will not possess. However, you notice immediately when you encounter someone who does not share your political culture, or for that matter, does not meet your expectations regarding an occasional encounter with soap.

Chinese political culture is radically different from the political culture in the Mountain West region of the United States, for example, and no one who stopped to think about it would expect that we would be able to transfer Wyoming's political institutions to Beijing and have those institutions work as effectively in the Forbidden City. The political culture is different. The basic expectations are different. How do you think the fiercely independent ranchers of Wyoming would react to the authoritative and dictatorial bureaucracies that are prevalent within Chinese political institutions?

The collapse of governments in many of the nations that had been colonized by Europeans shows the difficulties in installing representative democratic institutions in countries that have had no or very little experience with these types of institutions or among people who have no faith in democracy. If we took the political institutions of Denmark and simply transported them exactly as they are to Iran, would they succeed? Before you answer, consider the violent reaction a few Danish editorial cartoons managed to spark across the Islamic world? Clearly the Danes and the Iranians have different political cultures, especially in regard to freedoms of expression. Many of the countries of the former Soviet Union continue to struggle with their democratic institutions precisely because their dominant political culture does not encourage participation, acceptance of the will of the majority, or a fundamental commitment to debate and votes as a means of decision-making. For that matter, although "democracy" is a Greek word, even Aristotle did not believe in democracy as we think of it now.

Thus, when designing our ideal government we want to build our institutions in a place with the political culture appropriate to the type of government we want to build. Or, we will have to adjust our government to fit the political culture. When designing our simulated government institutions, we want to make sure that we do so in ways that maximize the degree to which they are wanted and voluntarily accepted. We need to maximize their potential for gaining and sustaining legitimacy.

Step 2: Choose a Basic Form

What is the basic form of government you would like to use? This will have a tremendous impact on how well different institutions serve their structural functions. For example, in the course of his examination of different constitutions, Aristotle identified six basic types. Of course, he recognized that there were many variations that were possible, and that it is possible to mix the many types, but Aristotle was big on categories of ideal types so he stuck with six. Among his six types of governments, he identified three *good* forms and three *perverted* forms (see table 6.1). What differentiated the good from the perverted was for whom the government worked. If the government worked for the benefit of all of its citizens, Aristotle called it good. If it benefited only the ruling class, Aristotle labeled it a perverted type. The other major distinction Aristotle drew among the governments was the size of the group in charge.[8]

A nation that was led by one person could be either a **monarchy**—a good form—or a **dictatorship**—a perverted form. A government ruled by a few could be either an **aristocracy**—a good form—or an **oligarchy**—a perverted form. Last, a government led by the many could be either a **polity**—a good form—or a **democracy**—a perverted form. One should not be too surprised that Aristotle labeled democracy a bad form. After all, in his day, democracy was synonymous with mob rule, that is, everyone acting in her or his own best interest with little or no regard for the community.

We will assume for our example that you do not want to use one of the perverted forms.* So, who will rule in your simulated government? Which institutions will you create? Will you choose to have a monarch? Before you jump to conclusions and say no, you should realize that both the authors would make pretty good kings, and co-dictator of the Universe is perhaps the one job that we would prefer over our current tenured positions.

---

* What you choose do in the private recesses of your own brain is your business, but please, not in our textbook.

Table 6.1 Aristotle's Six Basic Government Types

Ruled by	Works for the benefit of all (good)	Works for the benefit of the ruling class (bad)
One	monarchy	dictatorship
Few	aristocracy	oligarchy
Many	polity	democracy

Also, there are benefits to having a monarchy. "Monarchy" literally means a single authority and there are all kinds of situations where having a textbook-writing professor as king would be a good thing. During a war, where decisions must be made quickly and decisively, or when a tough and unpopular choice must be made for the long-term best interest of the country, having a single decision-maker can avoid the paralysis of committees and groups trying to make decisions. But if you wish to have the most efficient form of government, why not have one person make all of the decisions for you? Think of all the wasted time that can be eliminated by simply having a king decide. No long debates in Congress, no concerns about whether people really like the idea, you just decide and go. Despite his faults, Mussolini was pretty much the only Italian leader to ever get the trains to run on time. The pyramids were built by pharaohs, the Great Wall by Chinese emperors, Genghis Khan created the largest empire in the history of mankind and you should see how we ordered around some of our graduate students in order to get this book done. There does tend to be a downside to most dictatorships, for example, death, war, slavery, the dead fish our downtrodden graduate students put in the bottom drawers of our desks at the start of every semester break; do we have to mention Hitler? However, if we could only find a way to ensure that our dictator, or whatever else you wanted to call our monarch, would always be benevolent, would always avoid perverting government, we would be in business. But, even if we found the perfect person to take the job, how would we ever replace her?* Make one of her kids the next king? What if her offspring are a pack of buffoons? From what we can gather, the selection process for monarchs (and dictatorships) does tend to be a bit irrational.

In *Monty Python and the Holy Grail*,[9] the official and authoritative BBC documentary chronicling the rise of the monarchy in England, when King Arthur asks for directions from a peasant, the peasant asks how he became king and Arthur relates the story of the sword and the stone:

> **ARTHUR:** The Lady of the Lake, [angels start singing] her arm clad in the purest shimmering samite, held aloft Excalibur from the bosom of the water signifying by Divine Providence that I, Arthur, was to carry Excalibur. [singing stops] That is why I am your king!

---

* We've come to the conclusion that a good dictator probably would have to be a woman. It's pretty obvious that all the men who have tried have failed.

Structures and Institutions

DENNIS: Listen, strange women lying in ponds distributing swords is no basis for a system of government. Supreme executive power derives from a mandate from the masses, not from some farcical aquatic ceremony.

ARTHUR: Be quiet!

DENNIS: Well you can't expect to wield supreme executive power just because some watery tart threw a sword at you!

ARTHUR: Shut up!

DENNIS: I mean, if I went around saying I was an emperor just because some moistened bink had lobbed a scimitar at me they'd put me away!

Clearly, the official process of selecting kings is less than perfect, even in a place that has gone through bunches of them, so you may want to consider limiting their power. But even if you do not actually give your king any real power, the central focus he or she can give to politics and government can be valuable for the group. Did you ever wonder why it is that Great Britain continues to have a Queen? As institutions, modern monarchies serve as symbols for the nation. They bind the populace together and allow for a sense of national unity. In nations where monarchs coexist with parliaments, the monarch often adds legitimacy to these other governmental institutions by acknowledging their decisions as legitimate. Consequently, simply because you have a monarchy does not mean that you cannot still also have democratic institutions like a parliament.

Still not convinced? Neither are we. Monarchs tend to soak up lots of the nation's money for no identifiable good reason and with the exception of Yul Brynner's King of Siam, they tend not to be much fun at parties, so you may wish to choose some other form. If you choose not to have a monarch, your government is, according to one very basic definition, a **republic**. It does not mean you have a democracy, you just do not have a single authoritative leader.

For example, if you value the promotion of a religion or an ideology, or you are a professional wrestling fan, you might prefer to hand power over to a few elites who could be trusted to carry on the faith. Thus, an aristocracy might be for you. There is nothing quite like a group of religious leaders to watch over everything to make sure that the faith is being appropriately applied, supplied, and respected. In cases where a secular ideology is the thing, there is often a ruling committee that makes sure the ideology is at the center of all decisions. Aristocracy would also be preferable if we could get the best people to rule the society. Of course, there are likely to be some knock-down-drag-out fights about what it means to be the best, and who qualifies. Even if you assume that the best leaders will be those who will make wise decisions for the good of the entire country, defining the good of the entire country is less than simple and certainly not obvious. Seems like a disaster waiting to happen, but before you get too down on aristocracy, you should bear in mind that many people argue that most of the countries that are considered representative democracies actually are ruled by a small group of elites. Further, many think this is a good idea. Winston Churchill purportedly once said, "The best argument against democracy is a five-minute conversation with the average voter." Elites tend to be well-educated, well-informed, and they often have the wealth needed to dedicate most of their efforts to governing rather than putting in overtime to buy a new snowmobile.

In fact, some form of aristocracy is actually a common feature of democratic governments. In many of the countries that we refer to as democracies, there is a constitutional court similar to the United States Supreme Court, for example, Germany's Federal Constitutional Court (*Das Bundesverfassungsgericht*), The Constitutional Court of Korea, and the Supreme Court of Canada. When these judges make decisions, when they decide that certain laws violate the country's constitution and the judges smite those laws to ashes* are they acting democratically? They are an aristocracy of legal and political elites that can, and often do, wipe out the result of a massive democratic process with the stroke of a pen.

Come to think of it, why would one choose to have a democracy? If you don't have an answer for that you might want to hurry and think of something before we get to the democracy chapter. For now, however, we want you to be aware that democracy is not the only alternative to monarchy and aristocracy. We also want you to be aware that perhaps those countries that we commonly think of as democracies also contain some very undemocratic elements.

Step 3: Connect Your Government

Once you choose the form of government that you would like to have, it is important to decide how you would like to connect it and keep it together. Countries tend to be fairly big places, places so big they can strain the ability to even communicate from one end to the other. Hawaii is a full continent and half an ocean away from Washington, D.C. Russia covers eight time zones. And it takes hours to walk the length of Liechtenstein. Will all of the decisions in your government be made at one place, such as a very nice pub in the nation's capital? Or will some decisions be made at a more local level? If you do decide to divvy things up, where will those decisions be made and which level of government will have the ultimate authority to rule, in case there are conflicts or disputes between different local levels of government?†

---

* They are the Supreme Court so they can even do this in a designated "no smiting" zone.

† In political science, the term used to describe the ultimate authority to rule is called sovereignty. It is something akin to the fact that all parents have the unchallengeable right to end an argument with "Because I said so." It is such an important term in the discussion of international relations that we will wait until that chapter before we talk too much about it. For the purposes of this discussion, sovereignty can be thought of as the ultimate power to decide. Or who is last person who can say, "because I said so" in the division of power among levels within your country. No matter how you set things up, it is important to decide where the final authority rests.

Structures and Institutions

There are essentially three systems through which the relationship can be ordered. Most often these are referred to as the **unitary system**, the **federal system**, and the **confederal system**. Like we explained earlier, most nations don't *choose* to have one or the other. Rather, the makeup of the nation, its history, its culture, and its geography tends to determine the type of structure that will be used.

A unitary system is one where sovereignty rests quite clearly on the shoulders of the national government. In other words, the national parliament, dictator, dancing llama, or whoever, makes all the decisions for the entire nation. The laws apply to everyone regardless of where they live in the country, everyone shares all governmental benefits equally, there is no redundancy in services and the whole plan is rather simple. This does not necessarily mean that there is no local-level government. It only means that the final word is always at the national level. The central national government can choose to allow some local governing board to have a say in the decision-making that will affect the local community. However, the ability to make these decisions is at the mercy of the national government, which could also choose to revoke this power from the local boards or to override any decisions that are made. In France all of these decisions are made in Paris, in Syria they are made in Damascus, in Liberia in Monrovia, and we do not have to name many more before you get the idea.

Systems where the final authority, for at least some aspects of government, is left to the local or subnational level are called federal systems. In a federal system sovereignty is, at least theoretically, shared between the national and the local government units. In the United States the national government shares its power with states, in Canada the sharing is done with provinces, in Germany there is sharing with *Länder*. The most obvious point of local political sovereignty in all three of these governments is education. Each state, province, or *Länder* sets some or all of its educational policy. Requirements for teacher preparation, funding schemes, curriculum, even the number of school days in a year might be set at this or even more local levels.* Federal systems work well in diverse countries, where variations in local conditions, economies, or cultures make it impractical or inefficient to try to impose a single system, or make it difficult to make decisions from a central location. Think of it in terms of why education policy is decentralized in the United States. It is unlikely that the forestry management class taught by the eight-fingered football coach in a small logging town outside of Seattle would be of much value to the students of any of the high schools in the Bronx.

The Federation in *Star Trek* provides a perfect example. When Captain Kirk, and later his grandson or nephew or whatever Jean-Luc Picard was, puttered around the final frontier in the glorified intergalactic motor home they called the *Enterprise,* they talked

---

* Surprisingly, many if not most students in the United States assume that local control of education is the norm around the world. National education policy is actually far more common, especially in Europe where education officials are often frustrated when they try to locate an education ministry to discuss education matters with the United States.

a lot about the United Federation of Planets. Now, the temporal Prime Directive prohibits the transfer of knowledge from the future to the past,* so they do not give us much detail about the institutional arrangement that comprised this federation, but we can presume that it was a federal system involving several planets. Further, if you stay sober through any of the episodes where they are negotiating the entry of new members into the Federation, there are consistent assurances of local sovereignty. Within the bounds of the charter of the Federation, the individual planets ruled themselves.

While it is generally understood that in federal systems the governmental units share sovereignty, there are those who argue that this is not truly possible. These people believe that ultimate political power can never be shared and that one level must ultimately have supreme power. To the degree that this argument is true, we assume that the national level would be the most powerful. However, perhaps the reality of where power really resides makes it easier to see why it is so important for the people in a federal system to believe that the authority-sharing relationship is legitimate and robust. Without this belief, why would people invest effort into making the local government work?

The least commonly used form is the confederal system. In a confederal system it is the local government units that have the real power. They are the ones that have sovereignty. The key to the confederal system is that the individual units within it can defy the national or galactic level of government. They can even leave the system at any time they wish. The national government must maintain the continued willingness of all local units to be a part of the confederation. This effectively gives every single local unit the power to veto any national level policy by refusing to honor it or by leaving the system. As a result, it is usually the case that in confederations, the national or central government is given very limited responsibilities.

The confederal type of government has been tried several times, but it has been about as successful as sitcoms on the now defunct and merged away WB Network. It simply is too difficult to get things accomplished when you have so many parts of the system that can threaten to leave whenever they do not like something the central government is doing. The two closest things to confederation that exist today are the United Nations and the European Union, both of which have very little power. Think about the difficulty that the United Nations has getting anything accomplished, all the resolutions that are ignored by the relevant parties, and you will start to see the difficulty with confederacies. The European Union, which joins many of the nations in Europe to a common currency, joint trade policies, and a free-trade zone, is a more successful venture, but again, note how limited its authority is. The only thing that keeps it together and makes it successful is the money. There are huge economic and trade

---

*We know, we are serious geeks. We hope by chapter 6 you've gotten used to it. Our kids have lived with it their whole lives.

Structures and Institutions

disincentives for leaving the EU, but if these factors should fade or weaken, the ability of the EU to act will also fade.

In reality, therefore, nations have only two real options, a federal or unitary system. Each system has its benefits and its drawbacks. First, federal systems are more appropriate in large countries and with countries that have geographically diverse populations. Federalism allows for differences among the local government units that can reflect differing cultures or traditions. Federalism can also be particularly appropriate for large countries that want democratic systems, since it is more likely people will have a noticeable influence on their representatives in smaller units. In large nations, such as the United States, a national representative can represent several hundred thousand people. Local government units allows the institutions that have the greatest direct effect on people's lives to be created on a smaller, more tractable scale that gives individual citizens more influence on the formation of policy.

Federal systems also allow for the local governments to act as what United States Supreme Court justice Louis Brandeis called "laboratories for social experimentation."[10] That is, these local governments can dream up and try out on a small scale several solutions to social problems. Those that work can then be copied or adapted by the rest of the nation, including other local governments that tried a different solution that failed. In that way policy mistakes are confined to small areas, while policy successes can be shared with other states or perhaps the whole nation.

The refurbishment of what are called brownfields, industrial sites, garbage dumps, and other locations where the land has been contaminated or seriously screwed up in one way or the other, provides a perfect example. These ugly eyesores exist all across the United States and drive down property values, attract crime, and encourage further degradation of the surrounding properties. Across the country a variety of efforts were made to revitalize these properties, from low income housing, to schools, to new industrial parks, and every other land use you might imagine.

It turns out that the best solution found so far is to put a golf course on them. Golf courses are green and open spaces that have two important characteristics. First, they look nice and enhance surrounding property values. Second, the people who use them are primarily adults who are only on them for a few hours at a time. Since most of these brownfields have contaminant problems, building housing and businesses would tend to create long-term exposures where even slight levels of pollutants can have detrimental effects on the people that live or work there. Think of young kids in low-income housing. They sleep there, eat there, play in the dirt in the yard, and are at a life-stage where their growth can be severely affected by even the lowest level of contamination. Levels of toxic pollutants that might be devastating for a toddler living every minute of every day in a revitalized brownfield are harmless to grandpa, who is only there for a few hours as he putters around in a golf cart. The key is that the golf course solution came not from national decision-making or research at the national level, but from a

Figure 6-1 The Political Cultures of the United States

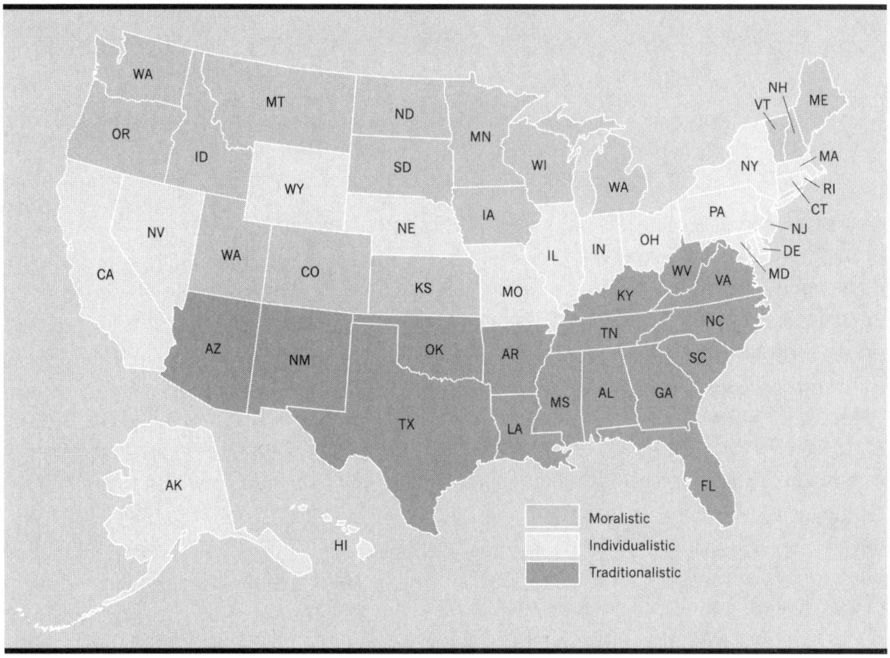

Daniel Elazar (1934–1999) was one of the first to study political culture within the United States, and he identified three dominant political cultures. From the perspective of an individualistic culture politics is viewed as a means for individuals to improve themselves, and government's role is to respond to people's demands. A moralistic culture views government as a means to promote the common good. The traditionalistic political culture focuses on maintaining existing hierarchical social structures, and government is meant to promote the elite's vision of the common good. According to Elazar, states could have blends of political cultures within their borders. Many people have built upon and adapted Elazar's work.

Source: Kevin B. Smith, Alan Greenblatt, John Buntin, *Governing States and Localities* (Washington, D.C.: CQ Press, 2005). Adapted from Daniel J. Elazar, *American Federalism: A View from the States,* 3d ed. (New York: Harper & Row, 1984).

local experiment, dreamt up by someone who had to do something with an old garbage dump. Its success was then copied, improved upon, and adapted all across the nation.

One last benefit of federal systems is that they offer citizens more choices about the governmental institutions that fit them best. Like shoppers in a grocery store, citizens can theoretically choose the local government they would like to live in and move there. Have a high income? Move to a state with little or no income tax. Have lots of kids? Move to a community with good public schools. Approve of the death penalty? Move to Texas. Starting a business? Move to Delaware where the business laws are quite liberal. Believe in limited government? Try Wyoming or Alaska. Want an activist government? Try California. This presumes you have the money and ability to move, but the general point is clear—variety gives you options.

Unitary systems also have their benefits. In unitary systems the governmental structure is much easier to understand. Citizens do not have to worry about who has the responsibility to carry out policy. Furthermore, they do not have to worry about elections for multiple offices. As previously noted, in unitary systems every citizen in the country is entitled to the same rights and benefits. One does not have more money spent on their education, health care, welfare, etc., simply because they live in one state as opposed to another. One does not spend more time in prison in one state than they do in another for the exact same crime. Consequently, unitary systems make it easier to maintain a sense of national identity. Unitary systems tend to run more smoothly because policy is easier to implement and less effort is spent sorting out who should do what. Regulatory consistency across a larger entity also has economic benefits, since one product can be sold across the whole nation and efficiencies of scale can be more easily capitalized upon.

On the other hand, some would argue that federal systems fit in well in countries that utilize a capitalist economic system. Why is this? In federal systems because both people and *businesses* have the capacity to move, local governments must compete to keep people and jobs within their borders. Local governments need business to pay taxes or to provide jobs to those who will pay taxes. Competition forces these local governments to optimize the business environment in one way or another. This might mean maximizing the education system or minimizing regulations. It could mean keeping taxes as low as possible by being very stingy in the benefits that they give to their citizens, that is, some jurisdictions are less willing to spend on welfare, education, or health care. This way, they keep their budgets at a minimum and their taxes low. Another jurisdiction might seek an advantage by spending on infrastructures like railways or anything else that makes for a very healthy business environment. This variety of ways to compete for wealthy and corporate citizens can create different niches for all different kinds of business, creating a diverse and healthy economy across the nation. Thus, again we see how the institutions we choose can affect the types of policies that our governments will be able to enact.[11]

Step 4: Build Your Institutions

At last you are ready to build your institutions. Having put the basics in place—environment, form, and connections—you can then design the specific mechanisms that you use to accomplish the things that you need or want from government. How are you going to police your country, create your laws, or enact policy? In the following chapters we examine the most important of the different structures and the different types of institutions more closely. However, before we begin this construction project, we want to clarify that we are talking about functions, not names or labels. All governments must perform different governmental functions. The legislative function is the making of law, the executive function is the enacting of law, and the judicial function is the interpreting and enforcement of law. However, simply because there is a legislative function, it does not necessarily follow that a legislature must perform that function. In fact a person given the title of Tsar, King, Shah, General, Glorious Leader, or El Presidente for Life can, and has throughout history, performed the legislative function. After all, somebody has to make laws. Those laws can come from one person, several people, or lots of people. In reality, even where there are parliaments, other institutions still often perform legislative functions. For example, when bureaucracies issue regulations, they are making laws. It is also often the case that legislatures give executives the opportunity to make policy on their own. In these cases also, the executive legislates.

It is also not necessarily the case that because a legislature performs the legislative function, the country is democratic. There is no such requirement. A dictator can appoint legislators who make the law. After all, being a dictator is a tough job. You've got to be constantly worrying about those who have guns* and want your power. So, as a dictator, you may choose to turn over your legislative authority to a handpicked legislature that is responsible for making the laws for the country. After all, what dictator wants to create all of the parking regulations? As we noted near the beginning of this chapter, the British Parliament and many others actually originated not as democratic institutions, but as bargains between kings and wealthy elites. The kings used the lords to raise cash, and in exchange, the lords used their leverage to have some control over law. Later it turned into a democratic legislature.

It is equally true that other institutions can perform functions that do not necessarily adhere to the title of their institution. Legislatures can and do perform judicial and executive functions. As we will see more clearly later, a major element of the American doctrine of separation of powers is just that, the blending of functions and institutions.

As we continue to build our structures we want to make sure that our government will be successful. Over the long term, legitimacy tends to be an important factor in the success of political institutions and as you dream up your perfect institution for making laws you may want to keep that in mind. The voluntary acceptance of these mechanisms serves as the glue that keeps governments together and functioning. In the idealized game of SimCity, you must keep your people happy to win, but it is also a factor in the real world.

KEY TERMS

aristocracy / **131**
confederal system / **135**
democracy / **131**
dictatorship / **131**
federal system / **135**
institutions / **120**
monarchy / **131**

oligarchy / **131**
political culture / **130**
polity / **131**
republic / **133**
structures / **120**
unitary system / **135**

CHAPTER SUMMARY

Government structures are the basic things that governments need to do in order to govern; they are the basic functions that appear in every modern government. Political institutions are the particular mechanisms that a government uses to carry out an essential

---

* The ones with guns AND bullets are particularly dangerous.

government function. For example, every government must have a mechanism to create laws—a government structure—but not every country has a Congress—a political institution. Institutions often reflect a society's view of human nature and its hopes; however, a society rarely has an opportunity to create institutions from scratch. In addition to the basic functions that institutions serve, they also can allow governments to build legitimacy for their policies. There are many different types of government, and Aristotle came up with one of the most commonly used typologies in which he divides government types according to the number of people who rule and for whom the government works. Most countries utilize a federal or unitary system to structure their relations between the national government and its local entities. Students should learn two very important lessons from this chapter. First, there is more to studying government institutions than merely identifying the names of institutions in particular countries; political institutions are reflections of a nation's culture, its aspirations, and its history. These institutions also play a role in shaping a government's policies. Second, while Sim-Government might be a good way of thinking about structures and institutions, the authors do not expect any phone calls from software developers or venture capitalists.

STUDY QUESTIONS AND EXERCISES

1. What is the difference between government institutions and government structures? How many examples of structures and institutions can you identify?

2. Consider the impact of political culture on government structures and institutions and how the political culture impacts what is possible in a given nation. How might this concept help to explain some of the difficulties that the United States has had with Iraq and other countries around the world?

3. Explain the differences among unitary, federal, and confederal systems. Under what circumstances might one system be preferred over another?

4. How did Aristotle differentiate among the types of government, and what basic types did he identify? What factors are likely to stand in the way of a nation that tries to create ideal institutions?

WEBSITES TO EXPLORE

www.cia.gov/cia/publications/factbook/. The World Factbook, the U.S. Central Intelligence Agency's profile of countries around the world, contains a wealth of historical, political, and geographic information.

icreport.loc.gov/home/histdox/fed_51.html. The Library of Congress's Thomas Web site contains the text of James Madison's *Federalist* No. 51, which presents his view of government.

lcweb2.loc.gov/frd/cs/. The Library of Congress's Country Studies site contains information about the social, economic, political, and national security systems of countries around the world.

news.bbc.co.uk/1/hi/country_profiles/default.stm. The BBC's Country Profiles contain historical, political, and economic information about countries around the world.

www.nytimes.com/pages/cartoons/. The *New York Times* political cartoons section showcases a collection of current political cartoons from syndicated cartoonists.

In a bygone era, Jimmy Stewart reenacts the desperate hours of the filibuster that won all Americans the right to be constantly harassed about switching long distance carriers.

CHAPTER 7

Institutions
Meat and Potatoes

Quick! Who is the most popular Democratic president in recent memory? If you guessed Bill Clinton, you are wrong. The simple truth is that there has been no more popular president than the extremely fictional Josiah "Jed" Bartlet from *The West Wing*.[1] Bartlet provided that perfect combination of tough, honest, principled, articulate, fair-minded, and—according to *TV Guide*—handsome president that we all love. He was the textbook-perfect U.S. president. Of course, there is the slight problem that he did not really exist, but then again, he was no more fictional than the ideal president that most textbooks cover. In this chapter we spend some quality time talking about many things that do not really exist, and we don't mean Bigfoot,* the Loch Ness monster, or the aliens that live in those condos in New Mexico. Instead, we look at a few modern political institutions that do not exactly exist. We examine the utopian, ideal versions of the real institutions that you can find in various constitutions, reformations, and revolutions around the world. We save the very real bugs in the machinery of modern political institutions for chapter 8.

The U.S. presidency provides a perfect example of how we have built up an ideal and impossible image of a political institution. The truth is that there are no superhero politicians who can get what they want accomplished while simultaneously staying above the fray of politics and occasionally leaping tall buildings in a single bound.† What we have are genuine human beings

---

* Actually, Bigfoot would make a decent presidential candidate. He is tall, and taller presidential candidates consistently win more votes. He has a full head of hair, again something commonly associated with winning elections. He is elusive, which should serve him well at press conference time. His independent outdoor lifestyle gives him the right background to capture the rural vote and he has great name recognition.

† Arnold Schwarzenegger does not count. First, he is not human; he is an android sent back from a heavily accented future. Second, all that bullet-proof super robot stuff was actually performed by a bulletproof stunt robot called Larry. And, as California politics have repeatedly demonstrated, not even "the Governator" can stay above the political fray.

who operate within real political systems. Since the New Deal and World War II, the nation has expected a great deal out of its presidents, far more than is realistically possible, given the limitations of the office. Still, Americans want their presidents to have the effectiveness of FDR, but they need to be far more attractive; the toughness of Harry Truman, but without the abrasive tirades from his colorful and crass vocabulary; the bravery and honor of Dwight Eisenhower, but combined with the ability to speak in coherent sentences; the vitality and persona of JFK, but without that whole starting the Vietnam War thing; the adroit deal-making of Lyndon B. Johnson, but without the escalation of the Vietnam War; the political skillfulness of Richard Nixon, but without the paranoid criminal antics; the honesty of Jimmy Carter, but with the ability to master Washington politics; the charm and media presence of Ronald Reagan without Nancy or the Alzheimers; the foreign policy experience of George Bush Senior but with a better understanding of the economics of domestic policy; and the education of Bill Clinton without all that Hillary and Monica stuff.* Until some mad scientist perfects cloning, that ideal president does not exist. Besides, the plots of countless B-movies make it absolutely clear that even if we could genetically engineer such a president we would undoubtedly end up with a combination president and half-crazed, radioactive giant cockroach that would attack Tokyo and cause people to talk out of sync with the movement of their mouths. Nevertheless, while the actual officeholders are bound to disappoint, the institution of the presidency as an executive structure remains and we can talk about the ideal president as a way of understanding what the U.S. executive—and by extension the executive role in other political structures—is supposed to be.

Americans have tremendous respect for the office of the presidency and consequently, presidents begin their terms with a great deal of public support. Even though George W. Bush lost the popular vote in 2000, he entered office with an approval rating well over 50 percent. However, the reality of everyday politics eventually takes the shine off the goodwill imparted by the institution and brings presidents back to earth as partisan decisions, world events, and the state of the economy take their inevitable toll on the illusion of the ideal presidency that is bestowed on the winning candidate. Still, even as individual presidents fail us, Americans keep faith in the institution of the **presidency**. It is an institution, after all, that a number of men have used to great effectiveness at various points in American history. That brings up an important point— institutions, in part, become institutions by lasting over time. Furthermore, institutions are larger than the people who occupy an office at a particular time. The institution of the presidency, like all governmental institutions, includes all formal and informal powers, the offices, the staffs, and the historical precedents that define the institution. The United States has had many presidents. They arrive with parades and fanfare, and leave

---

* We are not ignoring the comments we could offer about George Bush Junior; we just decided not to put presidents on this list until they leave office and no longer control the CIA.

out the side door with a hastily packed suitcase full of stolen White House towels and little bottles of shampoo. Many of them even win elections. But the institution of the presidency exists and persists beyond those who sit behind the desk in the Oval Office.

Think of this in terms of your university or college. Students drop out or graduate, professors retire in glory, and all the good administrators take better-paying jobs elsewhere. Still, the football team—and the "educational" institutions that it supports—goes on even after the eighth-year senior goes on to the pros. The university would be nothing without the people in its roles, but it is bigger than the people. It remains for generations after its founders die and it goes on no matter who leaves.

HELLO, MR. SMITH

Another way of looking at ideals and institutions is to look at fictional accounts of how the real and the ideal can come into conflict. For sentimental, late-night TV junkies, *Mr. Smith Goes to Washington*[2] is a classic film that demonstrates both this conflict and how an institution continues to exist beyond the people attached to it. For the rest of us, it is a black-and-white movie written by a guy with a monument obsession and starring Jimmy Stewart. But for our purposes, the movie works in a number of ways. It again demonstrates our theme of the real versus the ideal. In our rather lengthy description of the story, see how many different ways we managed to mention the struggle between the ideal and the real.

Idealism Wins the Day

The movie is about how a naïve leader of the Boy Rangers, Jefferson Smith, gets selected to serve in the U.S. Senate. Along the way, he learns about corruption and graft, and he ultimately stands up to the political bosses by manipulating the rules of the institution to win. Jefferson Smith is clearly an idealist. He is appointed by the governor to fill a vacancy precisely because of his naïveté. The political bosses believe that he will not cause them any trouble. When he arrives in Washington, he demonstrates his idealized view of government by his blind admiration for the state's senior senator, Joseph Harrison Paine, and by getting caught up in the impressions created by the grand monuments of the city and the patriotism they all invoke.

After touring the monuments around the capital, Mr. Smith slowly starts to feel like he is nothing more than the window dressing the state party bosses hoped he would be. Ultimately, with Senator Paine's approval, he introduces a bill to create a camp for boys that would be paid for with small donations from boys around the country. At first the bosses and Senator Paine are happy that Smith is busy with his Boy Ranger camp project. However, they eventually discover that he plans to build his camp in the same place reserved for a graft-related project contained in a public works bill. That graft is intended to line the pockets of the state's political boss, Jim Taylor, who could get any political official in the state to do his bidding.

The type of filibuster employed by Jefferson Smith is now extremely rare. While one can regularly tune in to C-SPAN2 to see U.S. senators blowing a usually unlimited supply of hot air, these fascinating senatorial orations are most often merely part of ordinary debate. While U.S. senators seldom, if ever, actually try to talk legislation to death anymore, the filibuster still remains an important tool.

Key to understanding the modern importance of the filibuster is to realize that other senators can stop one. If those who want to stop a senator from holding up business can muster sixty senators to agree, they can employ cloture to end the debate. In other words, while it ordinarily takes a majority of senators to pass a bill (51 in the full 100-person Senate), to stop a senator intent on blocking a bill through a filibuster requires sixty. This requires supporters of a bill or of a presidential appointee to constantly count how many other senators will vote with them. If they can get sixty senators on board, they will have a filibuster-proof majority.

Consequently, today the threat of a filibuster is as important as the filibuster itself. It is this threat that usually delays a matter from even coming to the floor for a vote. Supporters most often will not even bother bringing a bill to the floor if they cannot get enough legislators to support ending a threatened filibuster.

The use of parliamentary rules like the filibuster infuses the legislative process with gamesmanship and intrigue. There are many legislative rules that creative legislators can use to assist their legislative efforts or to frustrate those with whom they disagree. While some view these rules as arcane measures that serve only to frustrate the majority, others view them as techniques the minority can use to keep from being overrun by the majority. Still others enjoy watching the legislative process as if it were a chess match being played by skillful combatants—and we all know how exciting chess matches are to watch.

At last, Senator Smith learns the truth from his secretary, Clarissa Saunders, who was originally hired by the bosses to baby-sit him, but who is now clearly rooting for him. Unlike Smith, Saunders is anything but naïve. As she explains to her friend, "Look, when I came here, my eyes were big blue question marks. Now they're big green dollar marks." When Mr. Smith confronts Senator Paine, Paine tells him that he could not possibly understand all that is going on and that he should abandon the project. When Smith confronts Jim Taylor, he gets a real political education as Taylor offers him a job or the opportunity to continue serving in the Senate if he is willing to follow orders like Senator Paine.

Having none of it, Smith gets up to challenge the project on the floor of the Senate. He's quickly interrupted by Paine, who charges Smith with suggesting the boys' camp to make a profit for himself. Framed by false evidence, a seemingly defeated Smith disappears. Eventually, Saunders finds him visiting the Lincoln Memorial, this time with a more cynical eye. When he tells her that he plans to leave, she uses the memorial to inspire him. Saunders then infuses Smith's idealism with some realistic political strategy. When Smith is recognized on the floor of the Senate, he engages in a one-man **filibuster** of the graft-laden public-works legislation. The filibuster—a tactic in which a senator or group of senators indefinitely talk about a bill—is intended to frustrate the proponents of the bill. Those employing the filibuster hope to keep the Senate from conducting any business at all, thus encouraging the other senators to stop considering the bill. Jefferson Smith hoped to filibuster long enough to make the public aware of the graft contained in the bill.

Jefferson Smith's ultimate victory puts a slightly different bent on the idealist/realist dichotomy we have thus far presented. It is incorrect to say that Smith has become a realist at the end of the movie; he clearly has not. If anything, his idealism wins out over realism. He defeats Taylor, he converts Saunders, and we are left to believe that the boys' camp will be built. What Smith does lose is his naïveté. To accomplish his goals, he realizes that he must adjust his ideals to deal with the way things are. Idealists need not be naïve about politics and political methods. In fact, a successful idealist has learned to deploy tactics ideally suited to the political environment. Gandhi and Martin Luther King Jr. were certainly idealists who used practical political methods—boycotts, civil disobedience, and interest group pressure—designed to work in the real world.

Sorry, Reality Just Will Not Get Out of the Way

Another way that *Mr. Smith Goes to Washington* works for this quaint little textbook is to develop a major point about institutions: Ideal institutions must be adapted to the everyday challenges that people face and even the perfect institutions we imagine for a country bend, twist, spindle, and mutilate our loftier ideals along the way. The ideal of democracy in our conceptualization of a legislature is a perfect example of an ideal that is changed by an institution.

We may associate political institutions with democracy and assume that non-democratic regimes are little more than big bullies running amok and stealing the lunch money of everyone in their country. We believe this even though nations that are not democracies constantly make use of nominally democratic institutions, perhaps even to a greater extent than some democracies. For example, China has a parliament, the National People's Congress, but it has little true independence or power. Similarly, Kuwait has a legislature, but it represents very few of the actual residents and it can be dissolved at any time by the country's emir.

While these institutions do not represent the interests of the public in the same way that their democratic counterparts strive to, they still serve valuable political functions. Debates in the Chinese parliament, even if they are scripted, offer explanations to the public for why laws are being enacted, which is also one of the functions that democracies demand of their legislatures. There is no doubt that Saddam Hussein made the real decision when the Iraqi parliament voted to defy UN demands to let inspectors search Iraq for weapons of mass destruction, but the public vote in this political institution served to define the limits of international negotiation and also provided a forum for addressing arguments others countries had made for inspections. In some ways, the debate in the Iraqi parliament was the political version of Plato's use of dialogs to present a conceptual argument. Again, this is a function democracies expect of their legislatures. In many ways it is the same function that is served by the U.S. Senate's role in approving treaties.

However, before you jump to argue that the democratic function of legislatures is the one most important thing about the ideal legislature, realize that across most democracies people are ambivalent at best in their feelings toward their legislative institutions. In the United States, in particular, the Congress often suffers from low approval ratings. Additionally, Americans tend to view the members of Congress with the kind of esteem usually reserved for the stars of *Jackass: The Movie*. As John Adams* stated it, "One useless man is called a disgrace. Two useless men are called a law firm. Three or more useless men are called a congress." *Mr. Smith* reflects these ambivalent feelings. While the movie is clearly patriotic, Jefferson Smith finds himself fighting against an overwhelming majority in the Senate. We actually root for Smith to defeat the other senators, who we are now convinced are either totally naïve themselves or on the take.

Furthermore, the legislative politics in the movie are not by any means democratic. Despite the patriotic rhetoric and the images of monuments, in the end we root for the will of the majority in the Senate to be defeated. To get a clearer picture of this tension between the democratic and nondemocratic aspects of the legislature, imagine that you are not privy to the information about corruption that the movie provides. All you know is that there is a public works bill in congress that everyone seems to support. All that is left is this loony senator who is standing in the way of progress. How supportive would you be of the Boy Ranger camp then? *Mr. Smith* demonstrates a key tension that exists within democratic institutions.

Most importantly, the movie provides a basis for us to discuss the features of institutions. For, as mentioned before, one theme of the film is that the institution continues playing its role despite the foibles of its occupants. During his filibuster Smith lectures his fellow senators on how they have to rise to their jobs:

> Just get up off the ground. That's all I ask. Get up there with that lady, that's up on top of this Capitol Dome. That lady that stands for Liberty. Take a look at this country through her eyes if you really want to see somethin'. And you won't just see scenery. You'll see the whole parade of what man's carved out for himself after centuries of fighting. And fighting for something better than just jungle law. Fighting so as he can stand on his own two feet free and decent, like he was created no matter what his race, color, or creed. That's what you'd see. There's no place out there for graft or greed or lies! Or compromise with human liberties!

Smith's ultimate victory is not just a victory over corruption and greed; it is a victory for the institution of the United States Senate. The goodness of the institution transcends

---

* John Adams—not John Quincy Adams. It is easy to confuse them we know. They look a lot alike and everyone knows them as being related to Samuel Adams. (When it comes to party invites, there is nothing like being connected to a guy who owns a brewery.) Still, if you dig into the trivia about "The Johns" you find out that Q is actually the son of Big John. And if you dig way down into the obscure, you'll be surprised to discover that Q was also the sixth U.S. President while Big John was the second. It's not like they were first or anything, but still impressive.

those individuals who currently serve there. Even as reality constantly gets in the way, governmental institutions are meant to serve society. They are intended, at least, to do good things.

COMPARING PARLIAMENTARY AND PRESIDENTIAL SYSTEMS

To begin, a democratic nation has to make a fundamental choice. Do you prefer a **presidential system** or a **parliamentary system**? This is tantamount to a waiter asking if you want your eggs scrambled or sunny-side up. To whom the executive is responsible is the fundamental difference between the two systems. In a presidential system, there is a separation of legislative and executive institutions (the yolk is separated from the whites), while in a parliamentary system there is a fusion of legislative and executive (the yolks and whites are scrambled together).

In a presidential system the executive is separately elected and does not have to answer to the legislature. El presidente mucho grande has an independent base of democratic support. In a parliamentary system, the executive is actually part of the parliament. The prime minister, as she or he is usually called, gets the position by first winning election to a seat in the legislature and then being elected to the post by fellow members of parliament (MPs). In a presidential system, the executive is elected through a system that is independent of the selection of the legislature and leaves office only after having served a fixed term or through a special removal process called impeachment. In a parliamentary system the prime minister will serve until the next elections are scheduled or until a simple majority of MPs votes him or her out. Under this system the prime minister remains responsible to the legislature, while in the presidential system the executive remains separate and primarily responsible to the electorate.

Si, El Presidente

The rationales for parliamentary versus presidential systems vary. Presidential systems can make the executive stronger in relation to the legislature. Since the president does not need to worry about being voted out on a moment's notice, the executive can afford to stand independently. Independence from the legislature makes presidential systems more stable, but the primary purpose behind the design of a presidential system is the prevention of tyranny either by the masses or by a popular individual. The framers of the American Constitution designed the system so that no one branch could become too powerful over the others. Built into the **separation of powers**, they added the notion of **checks and balances**, which basically means that everybody is always minding everybody else's business. In other words, the president plays a role in the legislative process through the veto, recommending legislation, and campaigning for public support or opposition to specific pieces of legislation. The congress plays a role in executive affairs through the confirmation of appointments,

> **Since the president does not need to worry about being voted out on a moment's notice, the executive can afford to stand independently.**

ratification of treaties, and approval of the budget. The political actors all have their hands in each other's cookie jars and it is very difficult for one branch to get too powerful.

The problem with these checks and balances is well known to observers of the U.S. system. It can be infuriatingly hard to get anything done, particularly if it means challenging entrenched interests. Because the checks are built into the system, there are so many ways to obstruct things that even a small minority can usually find someone with the ability to prevent changes to the status quo.

Yes, Minister

The ease of obstructing the presidential system points to one of the strengths of a parliamentary system. The **prime minister**, as an MP and leader of the winning party, has an easier time shepherding legislation through the system and changing things. The system is set up so that members of parliamentary political parties are far more likely to vote cohesively. Parties have a great deal of control—sometimes total control—over who gets placed in a seat after an election, and bucking the party in a vote is risky to the point of stupidity. Whenever the next opportunity to fill seats arises, why would the party waste a hard-won seat on someone who cannot be trusted to vote the party line? And if an MP breaks from the party line, that opportunity to shuffle him/her/it out of a seat is likely to arise very quickly. In some parliamentary systems *any* failure of a piece of legislation automatically dissolves the government. This is not only embarrassing to the ruling party, it means that new elections must be held, which is not something a party wants after it has just been embarrassed by the defection of one of its own.

Because these institutional mechanisms reinforce party loyalty, an efficient parliamentary system holds the promise of a quicker and more certain ability to define and enact policy than a presidential system. The votes of party members in presidential systems are far less predictable and far more difficult to control. American presidents cannot necessarily count on all the members of their political party for support, and, in fact, many a presidential proposal has been defeated by a margin afforded by the defection of members of the president's party.

Lest one think that these issues are not real, early in 2003, Filipinos were debating constitutional reforms in the hopes of quelling disappointment with the government's inability to solve the nation's many social problems. Many Filipinos supported moving from a presidential system to a parliamentary system. Summing up some of the differences between the two systems, Jose Abueva, a political science professor at the University of the Philippines, argued for changing to a parliamentary government "where the impasse can be overcome by fusing the powers of the president and the legislature in a new parliament headed by a prime minister and his cabinet."[3] Conversely, in 2002, the Kyrgyz president, Askar Akayev argued that his country should not adopt a parliamentary system:

I would like to point out that the idea of a parliamentary country is not viable in our conditions because the political space has been structured insufficiently in Kyrgyzstan. Kyrgyzstan does not have major political parties yet which will be able to reflect views and tendencies which prevail in society. In these conditions, certain political forces would have no specific responsibility for decisions made by parliament. This obscurity is dangerous and unacceptable.[4]

As of yet, Filipinos have not made the move to a parliamentary system and President Akayev has since had to flee Kyrgyzstan for someplace easier to spell, so his current opinion on the country's political system is anyone's guess. These types of changes don't often happen quickly. But once a nation settles how it will divide the power between the legislature and the executive, there are more specific questions to deal with for each. In the remaining sections we examine the major ideal aspects of legislative, executive, and bureaucratic institutions.

LEGISLATURES

Not too long ago, many scholars were declaring that legislatures had reached an era of decline. One no longer hears that talk. In fact, writing in the 1990s, political scientists Gary W. Copeland and Samuel C. Patterson speculated that we might instead be in an age of parliaments.[5] It was probably true that legislatures were never quite as bad off as some claimed and it is also likely that legislatures today are not as powerful as some believe them to be. Still, perhaps what is most impressive about legislatures as institutions is that even though they are so old they creak and groan with every movement, they remain viable institutions. At the risk of sounding too conservative, it would seem that there must be some benefit to institutions that have lasted for hundreds of years.

When pondering the idealism inherent in legislatures it is best to think of the functions that we would like legislatures to perform. While there are many such possible functions, we arbitrarily identify the five we believe are the most important. They are lawmaking, representing, checking, legitimating, and educating.[6]

Lawmaking

The root of the word legislature, is, of course, "legislate." We expect our parliaments or congresses to make laws. Indeed legislatures make laws, but it's often not done the way that one would expect. Anyone in the United States has undoubtedly accidentally flicked the cable channels slowly enough at some point to catch an instant of C-SPAN. C-SPAN is dedicated to covering the U.S. House of Representatives,* while C-SPAN2 covers the U.S. Senate. Tune in to this legislative TV network at some pretty weird hours, and you can always see someone in the well of the U.S. House of Representatives just yabbering

---

* The U.S. Surgeon General has determined that, despite rumors to the contrary, watching C-Span does not cause brain hemorrhaging. It is the beating of your forehead against the screen that causes the brain damage.

away about something. When most people see this, they imagine that individual legislators come up with ideas for bills and that the bills are then debated on the floor of the House. They think that members spend the majority of their time debating.

The reality is quite different and members actually spend relatively little of their time on the floor. If you watch C-SPAN closely, you can see that while the person is yelling* about whatever it is that their speechwriter wrote for them, there is nobody in the chamber listening. It turns out that even during debate, members are not there. Instead, they are engaged in a number of other activities like giving speeches, helping constituents, meeting with leaders, going to committee meetings, fund-raising, and so on. Furthermore, it turns out that even the job of legislating has little to do with what happens on the floor of the House.

Bills can come from the minds of legislators, but they also can come from a number of different sources. They may have been suggested by constituents, interest groups, the executive branch, or the political leadership of the congress or parliament. Furthermore, in most legislatures, the real law-making work goes on in committees. Committees and sometimes subcommittees conduct research, hold hearings, debate, write, and amend bills. Committees also whittle down the number of bills that get introduced in the legislature during any given session, write the precise, legally-effective wording of the laws, and allow members to specialize in specific areas of policy.

The actual process for the passage of bills differs from legislature to legislature. In *Mr. Smith Goes to Washington,* Saunders actually describes pretty accurately how difficult it is to get a bill passed into law in the U.S. Congress. Some parliamentary systems make it easy for popular bills to pass, while others make it more difficult to do so.

Legislators as Representatives

Another fundamental job of legislators is to represent their constituents. That is, legislatures play a key role in making people feel as if somebody is speaking up for their interests. As we will see, different structures provide different methods of representation.

Mr. Smith Goes to Washington takes place in the Senate, one of the two houses that comprise the U.S. Congress, the country's legislature; the other is the House of Representatives. Technically, a legislature with two houses is called a **bicameral legislature**, while a legislature with one house is referred to as a **unicameral legislature** and a legislature with twenty houses is referred to as a dodecacameral legislature.

Why choose one form as opposed to the other? The more appropriate question is how you can justify splitting the legislative function into two units that are largely redundant in what they do. Except for some minor differences in specific responsibilities, both the Senate and the House of Representatives perform all of the legislative functions. So why have both? On one level, it goes to a very realist theory of government. If one thinks that

---

* Yelling in legislatures seems to be compulsory.

having a government is the next best thing to asking a thief steal all of your stuff, then it makes sense to create government institutions that will deter the kleptomaniac you elected. Adding a second house to a legislature makes it that one step harder because they tend to check each other. But if you are more of an idealist and you want to accomplish important things with a government, slowing things down with a second legislative house, or with an additional nineteen, does not seem like a good idea at all.

Another reason for choosing a bicameral legislature is that it may be chosen so that representation is guaranteed for different segments of society. This is true for the federal system in the United States. In the House of Representatives, congressional districts that the members represent have roughly the same number of people in them, therefore every person is represented equally in a national legislative assembly. In contrast, the Senate has two representatives from every state and the states—both large and small—are all equally represented. Wyoming and California have the same power in the Senate but vastly unequal representation in the House. This difference in representation allows the Senate to impede any legislation that would allow the densely populated parts of the country to impose their will upon the lonely places. Where there is a need for the legislature to represent different segments of society, it becomes imperative for there to be two houses. This is not always a geographic distinction. Sometimes the origins of the legislature can be seen in the different segments of society that are being represented. This is the case with the British parliament. For example, the House of Lords in the British Parliament originally represented the interests of the nobility, while the House of Commons represented the ordinary folks. The continuation of a bicameral legislature in Britain is now mainly tradition, although there are pushes to do away with the Lords.

Geographic Districts or Proportional Representation

One of the most important decisions a nation makes about its legislature is how the seats, or the votes should be divided. There are two basic plans for this and both offer different advantages. One method is to divide the legislature up according to geography. That is, if you have a 100-seat legislature, you divide the nation up into 100 districts, each with a roughly equal number of people. This provides **geographic representation**, that is, people are represented in reference to the area they live in. The assumption is that people living in the defined area are likely to share the same interests and concerns. When they go to the voting booth, voters choose the name of the person they want to represent them. People can specifically identify their representative and they know who to call, visit, or write to when they want to voice their opinions. Each representative must also maintain contact with the voters who will decide whether he or she returns to the legislature. Furthermore, because only the candidates who garner a plurality can win in the most frequently used **first-past-the-post system**, the system favors moderate political parties that can create coalitions to gain sizeable amounts of voters.

Where regional interests are considered crucial, district representation is more likely to be accepted. Where people's political perspectives are of the utmost importance, proportional representation is likely to be selected.

The result is usually a **two-party system**, which tends to provide greater stability to governments.

The other major option is **proportional representation**. Under this system, there is little concern for geography.* When a citizen enters a voting booth they do not vote for a person, they vote for the political party that they most agree with. Each political party submits a list of names prior to the election. In our example of a 100-seat parliament, the parties will submit up to 100 names, the most they could possibly win if they get all of the votes. Roughly speaking, under this system, if a party gets 53 percent of the vote, they get the same proportion of seats in parliament.† The primary concern of those who choose this system is **ideological representation**, which means that they want people's beliefs represented. Writing a piece in the *Los Angeles Times,* Andrew Reding reflected on his comparative voting options as an American with dual citizenship in Belgium, which uses proportional representation. He writes that in contrast to the district system in the United States with its choice between the two major political parties, "[t]he Belgian ballot offered a choice of 29 parties, covering almost as many flavors of policy alternatives as Baskin-Robbins offers in ice cream. Researching the party sites on the Internet, I found just the right flavor and color."[7] Proportional representation tends to produce **multi-party systems**.

Some countries try to combine the benefits of both systems. For example, they might have multi-member districts where more than one person represents a geographic area. Proportional representation would then be used to divide up the seats within each of the districts. Other countries opt to choose part of their parliaments based on proportional representation and part based on districts. In the next chapter, we might get around to talking about some of the positives and negatives attached to each of the systems. For now it is enough to recognize that each system emphasizes a different type of representation. Where regional interests are considered crucial, district representation is more likely to be accepted. Where people's political perspectives are of the utmost importance, proportional representation is likely to be selected.

Delegate or Trustee

While the previous choices had to do with structure, this choice comes down to individual representatives and their view of their relationship with their constituents. The question is whether a legislator should be a **delegate** or a **trustee**. A delegate is a representative who attempts to do exactly what her constituents want. In essence, they wet

---

* Surprisingly, the U.S. population has a far lower average knowledge of geography than do the Europeans, but the United States uses a geographic district electoral system and most European democracies use a proportional system that requires no understanding of geography whatsoever. So much for rational politics.

† For those of you who choose to work the swing shift so you can get home just in time to watch the 1:00 a.m. reruns of *Beavis and Butt-head,* 53 percent would equal 53 seats in our fictional 100-seat parliament.

their fingers and stick them in the air to see which way the wind is blowing. Delegates believe that it is their job to vote the way that their constituents want them to on every piece of legislation. Is this possible? On the one hand, we can ask whether it is physically possible for a legislator to know what constituents want on all issues. Is it possible for a legislator to poll all constituents on these issues? Do people know enough about all the issues to have an opinion? On the other hand, we could ask whether we would want a representative's constituency to have a say on all issues. Do you trust your fellow citizens to have that direct an impact on public policy?* If so, why have representatives at all? It would, after all, be possible to have some sort of direct electronic voting that would take the place of representatives.

Other representatives believe that they should be trustees. Trustees believe that they have been selected by their constituents as political experts and they need to trust their experience and expertise rather than the whims of the public. They argue that people who knew their general beliefs elected them to office and those voters trust them to make the right decision based on their background, education, and intelligence. In the end, if people do not like what their legislator is doing, they can vote against him, her, or it during the next election.

In reality, most legislators are **politicos**. Depending on the situation, they sometimes act like delegates and they sometimes act like trustees. When an issue is very important to their constituency and there seems to be a strong consensus, they will vote the way their constituents want. After all, they want to get reelected. However, when there is no clear consensus, or in the many, many instances where the constituency is uninformed, the legislators vote the way that they think is best.

Checking

When we refer to checking in this context, it does not involve bank accounts and little slips of paper, nor does it involve hockey players trying to forcibly remove each other's teeth.† For governmental institutions, the checking function involves the responsibility of government institutions or officials to watch over other government institutions or officials to make sure they are performing correctly. In some instances this function is also called oversight. Parliaments perform this function through a variety of different means. One particularly popular way is through the use of investigative hearings. Legislatures can scrutinize the work of the executive branch and even force government witnesses to appear to explain policy or to investigate wrongdoing. In some parliaments, tribunals can investigate possible areas of corruption within the executive branch.

---

* Before you answer, take a good look at the person next to you, but don't stare—they arrest people for that.

† For hockey fans, it is very important to note the spelling of this term. This is kind of like a check, as in physically impeding the progress of an opposing player, but it is clearly not Czech, as in a player from that country, nor is it a cheque, as in the slip of paper that lures all the good players away from Canada and into places where they have no business playing hockey at all. Seriously, hockey in Florida? They have to import ice from like, Greenland.

Another common type of governmental oversight or checking is performed in parliamentary systems by the **shadow government**.* The shadow government is made up of those members of the minority party who would take office were that party to ever capture a majority. Those in the shadow government keep a careful eye on their counterparts in an attempt to expose flaws in policies and possible wrongdoing. The specifics of how it works vary from country to country. However, by far the most entertaining form of this kind of oversight is the British Question Hour. During Question Hour, the prime minister must face questions from Parliament about the government's actions. Some of the questions are softballs thrown underhand by the MPs in the prime minister's party. These scripted questions allow the prime minister to get in sound bites for the evening news, but the opposition or shadow ministers often throw hardball questions meant to attack and embarrass the government.†

The British Question Hour is notorious for its raucous atmosphere and poignant humor. In one of the most famous Question Hour exchanges, a female MP once attacked Winston Churchill with the comment, "Sir, if I was your wife I'd poison your tea." Winston immediately shot back, "Madam, if you were my wife I'd drink it."[8] The banter is not always that sharp and witty, but it is always lively and it is certainly worth trying to catch it once or twice. It is regularly rebroadcast on C-SPAN on Sunday evenings. Despite the fun, Question Time can be very serious, as the prime minister's remarks are watched by the entire nation. Of course a question hour is only possible in a parliamentary system where the prime minister is responsible to the parliament. In a presidential system, there is no way to compel the executive to appear before the legislature. In fact, even during the impeachment against Bill Clinton for his poor taste in adulterous co-conspirators, there was no way to compel the president to appear during the proceedings.

Legitimating

In the days preceding the 2003 Gulf War, Saddam Hussein announced that he would let the Iraqi parliament decide whether the country should be opened to weapons inspectors. Shockingly, the parliament voted NO. Iraqi officials argued that this demonstrated clear support for the Iraqi leader. Other countries might have taken this mandate a little more seriously if it was not quite so obvious that the MPs would have surrendered several of the vital organs that they had grown fond of had they voted in a manner to Saddam's disliking. Still, what Saddam attempted to do was to have his parliament legitimate his policy. Generally speaking, the more people believe that parliaments answer to them, the more they believe that parliaments are truly representative, the more easily the parliament can perform a legitimating function. That is, because an issue is decided in the leg-

---

* And of course, if the shadow government is corrupt and secretly run by the CIA, it would be a shadow puppet government. Yes, unfortunately, that pun was intended.

† Actually, more of a slider or split-finger fastball, something that's got both some velocity and some bend in it.

islature, people feel that there has been some consideration of their view. Even if they do not agree with the ultimate decision, they can still believe that the policy was put into place after their perspective was heard. People are more apt to believe that they should follow the law—that the law is legitimate—if the legislature supports it.

A good example of the legitimating function can be seen with the second Bush administration's policy toward Iraq. Early on, President George W. Bush was advised by his attorneys that he did not need congressional authorization to invade Iraq. Despite this advice, he nevertheless sought a resolution from the Congress. Constitutional and other pragmatic arguments aside, Bush probably calculated that a positive vote by Congress would add legitimacy to his government's actions. Without that legitimacy, public support could have been even harder to secure, and his efforts might have generated an even more contentious reaction.

Education

Legislatures and their members also educate the general citizenry, a process often facilitated by the media. Through committee hearings, open debate, and television appearances the public learns about important issues and perspectives. Members with geographic constituencies keep their districts informed of important events and important pieces of legislation. Legislatures can also initiate important discussions. In the wake of the hearing surrounding Clarence Thomas's appointment to the Supreme Court, the issue of sexual harassment gained national prominence. The Iran-Contra hearings informed millions about the inner workings of the government.

EXECUTIVES

The job of the legislature is extremely important. But, as they say, every U.S. senator wakes up each morning, looks in the mirror, and says, "good morning, Mr. President." Simply put, the executive role in government is an important job that is loaded with responsibilities, but it is also puts a great deal of power in the hands of one person, or possibly a small group of people. In reviewing the roles of the chief executive, as with the legislative branch, the goal is to review the expected or ideal roles that executives play. However, first how about if we make it clear what we're talking about?

In a presidential system it is very easy to identify the chief executive. It is the guy who causes the huge traffic jams wherever he goes. When you see dozens of police motorcycles, followed by dozens of police cars, followed by dozens of limousines, followed by a dozen more police cars and enough motorcycles to make a full-on parade, somewhere in there, if the guys in black suits would let you look, you would find the president. The U.S. president actually plays two roles, **head of state** and **head of government**, a ceremonial and a functional role. In many, if not most other democracies, however, the executive is a bit more complicated with the two fundamental roles of the executive split up and spread around.

Head of State

The role as head of state involves serving as the national symbol—the personification of the country and its people. This includes overseeing national celebrations, presiding over parades, christening ships, entertaining foreign dignitaries and all of the other ceremonial aspects of the job. While this probably seems like a good gig, you should be aware of three very important facts concerning heads of state. First, heads of state can take different forms in different countries. The head of state can be a monarch, an elected president, or the guy with the most troops and biggest guns. In some countries the head of state will be a king or queen or even the king or queen of another country altogether. This sort of figurehead role comes with little or no political power, but it sometimes comes with a very big expense account and a nice house called a palace.* In other places, the head of state can be a king with a great deal of real political power, for example, the king of Jordan is more than just a ceremonial leader. In other countries the head of state is simply the dictator or el presidente for life.† The last avenue is to be elected to the job. In parliamentary systems that lack a monarch or a dictator *du jour,* there is usually an elected president. These presidents can be either elected directly by the people or they might be chosen by the parliament for the position. France, for instance, elects a president who serves as head of state, but does not perform any executive functions like a U.S. president—kind of like voting for a queen.

The second thing you should know is that the whole head of state job is actually pretty important. The head of state can add legitimacy to a government.‡ In other words, if the symbol of the country, say, a monarch, gives her blessing to a government, that blessing can strengthen the government's standing within the country. With the queen's blessing, the people may feel that the government ought to be given a chance to prove itself. In this way, many heads of state play an important role. In a parliamentary system, the head of state can be the one who formally authorizes the winning political party after an election to try and form a government. Some heads of state also have the authority to call for parliamentary elections. The head of state generally does not have any influence over specific legislation or actions of government, but they can play a role in the overall direction of the country or government in the way they help or hinder diplomacy, or the efforts of a government or challengers to gain or sustain broad-based public support.

The third thing you should know is that not all heads of state are created equal. Our dictator *du jour* is going to have some extraordinary powers and will often also be the head of government. If there is a parliament, that parliament is likely to have very little real power. The same thing is true of those countries where there is a strong monar-

---

* A palace seems to be a lot like the stuffy old-person version of a Barbie Dream House.

† Now that is not a bad gig, except of course for the fact that people tend to want to assassinate you, and your retirement home is a small pine box buried at least six feet down.

‡ In case you didn't catch on in chapter 4, this whole legitimacy thing is pretty important for governments to have.

chy. There may very well be a parliament in Kuwait, but, trust us, you would rather be the emir than the head of the parliament. Or perhaps you would rather be the king of Nepal, who in 2002 decided to simply dissolve the parliament he disagreed with.* Other monarchs are less powerful. These kings and queens, like most in Western Europe, are mere figureheads working within systems labeled as constitutional monarchies, where the parliament has all of the real political power. Among presidents in parliamentary systems, however, there is a great deal of variety. For example, the French president is much more politically powerful than the Israeli president. The French president has more specific political responsibilities, particularly in his diplomatic role.

Head of Government

The other executive role is to act as head of government. If the head of state is the public face we see on the advertisements, the head of government is the manager that actually handles all the day-to-day "stuff."† As noted, the U.S. president plays both roles, but in parliamentary democracies the head of government is usually the prime minister. The prime minister is responsible for getting bills passed through the parliament, overseeing the running of the bureaucracy, dealing with disasters, commanding the military and so forth. One becomes the prime minister by being the head of the party that wins a majority of seats in parliamentary elections or, if no party wins a clear majority in the election, the head of state usually asks the head of the party that has won the most seats to try to form a government by forming a coalition with one or more of the other parties that won seats. The prime minister can only stay prime minister as long as he or she maintains the support of a majority of seats in the parliament. This means that the potential prime minister must try to broker some deals to bring a coalition together that includes more than half of the members of parliament.

It is also technically true that the prime minister is nothing more than the first minister. Parliamentary governments are actually made up of many ministers that form the cabinet. Other ministers may include the foreign minister, treasury minister, defense minister, the minister of silly walks,‡ and so on. In an effort to form a government a potential minister may offer other parties a chance to have one of their members serve in the government as a minister in exchange for joining and supporting the overall coalition. Once a majority coalition is constructed, however, the new prime minister also has a governing coalition, which is expected to pass laws.

---

* Events occurring in 2006—when protests forced the king of Nepal to reinstate the parliament—suggest that just because he could dissolve the legislature, the question of whether it was a good or effective political maneuver remains open to debate.

† We use quotes here because "stuff" or any other "acceptable" word just does not convey the very unglamorous and often unpleasant nature of this necessary function of government. The Queen of England does nothing and gets palaces (note the use of the plural) and the prime minister of Britain does all the real work and lives in a sublet flat on Downing Street. That, our dear readers, is a load of "stuff."

‡ Made famous in *Monty Python's Flying Circus*.

One of the advantages that executives in most presidential systems have is that they are both the head of government and the head of state. That puts a lot of political power in the hands of one individual. Not only does the president get the political job of running the nation, but the president also gets the added benefit of being the symbol of the nation. The executives in presidential systems are usually selected directly by the people, although there can be some weird variations.

In most democracies, the chief executive is the civilian head of the military. That means that the chief executive is responsible for sending troops abroad, defending the nation from foreign threat, and putting down domestic insurrections. At the same time, these executives are responsible for foreign relations. They must negotiate with the leaders of foreign nations, engage in diplomacy, and work out military and economic alliances. A president that "really performs poorly"* at the former will find it hard to excel at the latter.

While the chief executive must focus a great deal of attention abroad, he or she must also watch over the home front. The chief executive is responsible for overseeing much of the government's bureaucracy and making sure that government services are provided and that laws are implemented and enforced. The chief executive is also expected to make certain that laws get passed through the legislature. As the leader of the parliament, the prime minister is expected to formulate a legislative agenda and to shepherd that agenda through the parliament. Presidents can have a more difficult time at this, because they, unlike prime ministers, are not legislators; they must use other powers at their control. The American president, for example, has the power to veto bills that Congress has passed. By threatening to veto, a strong president can make strategic use of this power to influence bills as they are making their way through the Congress. Presidents typically have opportunities to suggest legislation, and they also usually have no problem finding legislators willing to introduce their programs into Congress. In most modern democracies, the people also expect the chief executive to effectively manage the nation's economy.

Of course, chief executives also have a purely political role. Prime ministers are the heads of their parties, and thus they have a responsibility for campaigning for their parties and making sure they help local candidates in every way they can. Presidents, too, are the heads of their parties. However, while prime ministers, as the leaders of their party, play a role in deciding who gets to run in their party, the U.S. president does not have that luxury. Anybody can run as a Democrat or a Republican provided they meet the requirements to get onto the ballot. They do not need permission from the head of the party. Still, in addition to all of their other work, presidents are expected to raise enormous amounts of campaign funds for their parties and also to do what they can to get local candidates elected.

---

*Our editor insisted we use "nice" language here.

Given all of these roles, plus the unique roles of chief executives in various countries, it is no wonder that a fictional president would seem so appealing. Perhaps only a team of television writers could fix a plot so that a president could perform all of these roles with style and a flair for the dramatic.

THE BUREAUCRACY

The word **bureaucracy** is derived from the French word for desk, which explains all the extraneous vowels in the middle. Its adoption as a political term reflects the idea that it is the position within the administrative political structure—the desk, not the person behind it—that defines the role or function to be performed. In other words, the role is separate from the person performing it. Once the role is defined, the person with the qualifications to fit that role can be hired or trained. If that person is fired, quits, or retires, another with the necessary qualifications could replace the first with little or no disruption. This makes it possible to create professional administrative institutions within governments that remain relatively consistent in their function and activity regardless of the turnover in personnel. Rules, procedures, and processes define the actions of these officials, and it is this adherence to the rules that both make the desired consistency possible and create the comedy of the mindless functionary who is unable to deal with anything that does not fit within the bounds of the rules he or she is supposed to follow.

After the Egyptians invented beer but well before the Italians dreamt up pizza, the Chinese had some serious bureaucracies running a big chunk of the government in their very serious empire. The modern and Western take on bureaucracies arose when the medieval kingdoms and principalities of Europe grew beyond the effective scope of a personalized system of governing. As the demands for governance exceeded what a king and his personal advisors could manage, they began institutionalizing the more mundane functions and processes, such as accounting and record keeping. The scope of government's role in society and as a result, the scope of bureaucratic functions has been growing ever since. Today's bureaucracies are huge and they do all kinds of things. They regulate, license, procure, distribute, observe, preserve, encourage, police, study, and manage. In the United States, the Postal Service* (USPS) delivers the mail, the Internal Revenue Service (IRS) gathers taxes, the National Science Foundation (NSF) funds research proposals, the Citizenship and Immigration Services (USCIS) police the borders, the Library of Congress preserves knowledge, and the Center for Disease Control (CDC) watches and protects us from the next killer plague. The simple truth is that the vast majority of the *stuff* that governments do is done by bureaucracies. Furthermore, this is true regardless of the form government takes—democracy, theocracy, monarchy, or whatever.

---

* No, not the band.

Do We Really Want Bureaucracies?

No, of course not—dealing with a bureaucracy is seldom pleasant and usually infuriating—but bureaucracies are also indispensable. Think of the role that bureaucracy plays for government as analogous to the role of a thermostat in controlling the furnace in a house. The thermostat performs a simple task, turning on the furnace when the temperature drops below a certain point and turning it off when the temperature exceeds a certain level. You might not think much of this, but realize that without a thermostat, you would have to perform that function yourself. When it got cold, you would have to get up out of your Couch Commando Barcalounger and flip the switch to turn the heater on. Then, sometime before the temperature rose to the point where the paint blisters off the wall, you would have to put down the potato chips and get up again to turn it off. It seems simple, but then, so is changing the channel on the TV and how many of you crawl off the couch to do that when you can't find the remote control? Think of a cold winter night, one of those nights where the temperature plummets all of the way down to where even Canadians say, "it's cold." The furnace might come on for ten minutes once every half hour or so. Imagine trying to get a good night's sleep when you have to get up, turn on the furnace, get up ten minutes later to turn it off, then get up twenty minutes after that to turn it on again. Presumably—and we realize this may be a stretch—you have something better to do with your time and attention than turn the furnace on and off.

In the same way that the thermostat performs a simple task that frees you to do more important things, bureaucracies take on functions that would waste the time and effort of elected leaders or even barbarian kings. Every major U.S. city except Houston uses zoning laws and building codes to instill some coherency to the growth of their cities, and even a small city issues hundreds of building permits a week.* As with the vast bulk of cases processed through the average bureaucracy, it is a fairly simple procedure for someone to make sure all of the rules are followed and to issue a building permit. But if not for the bureaucracy in charge of building permits, these tasks would have to be performed by other officials. Is this really what you want the mayor to be doing? If the mayor is reviewing hundreds of building permit applications a week, when is she going to find the time to schedule street cleaning, hire the new janitor for city hall, choose the flowers to be planted around the fountain at the park, issue dog licenses, inspect schools for fire safety, paint over the graffiti on the buses, or do any of the thousands of other things we ask a city government to do for us? We elect a mayor to make the big decisions for the city, not to implement or oversee every little detail in day-to-day management. That is what bureaucracies do. When you stop to pon-

---

* If you ever visit the Poconos, please bear in mind that it only appears that there are no zoning laws and no building codes, and no tape measures. There are actually some zoning laws on the books. It is just that no one has ever taken up the task of enforcing them.

Institutions

der it, it quickly becomes clear that bureaucracies do pretty much everything that actually gets done by government.

Just as different people are likely to fiddle with their thermostats in different ways, every country has developed its own distribution of tasks and responsibilities between the professional administrators in bureaucracies and political leaders. These structures evolve over time, as they are shaped by the culture, the history, the crises, and the resources unique to each country. With a political culture that emphasizes the ideal of rugged individualism and self-sufficiency, Americans tend to consider bureaucracies a necessary but unpleasant evil. In France, bureaucracies have been a source of stability and consistency over centuries of political turmoil. Consequently, bureaucrats are some of the most respected professionals in society. The monastic origins of British bureaucracy include a commitment to secrecy that has become a standard foil for British comedy. Japanese bureaucracies reflect the hierarchical and formal nature of that society. Common to all of these systems, however, is a commitment to rule-based and procedure-driven decision making and action.

The Ideals of Bureaucratic Governance

Yes, Virginia, there is an idealist perspective on bureaucracy. There are few instances of fiction dedicated to the ideal bureaucracy, although one might argue that the pre-Logan bureaucracy in the movie *Logan's Run* moved with ideal perfection in its zeal to eliminate the world of those who were thirty years of age or older. The bureaucratic apparatus at work in *Nineteen Eighty-Four* was equally chilling in meeting its mission. Still, there are few instances where bureaucracy is portrayed in a positive light. However, there have been academics who have approached the study of bureaucracies from an idealistic perspective that focuses on the effectiveness of administrative institutions. To his credit, the German sociologist Max Weber* (1864–1920) recognized that modern nation-states needed professional bureaucracies. Furthermore, he argued that the ideal bureaucracy should be efficient and rational. It should function like a machine, with each of its parts playing a well-defined role. These parts should mesh perfectly with the roles and actions of the other parts to perform the administrative functions of modern society. Weber argued that there were a few critical elements for achieving this ideal.[9]

> *Clear Assignment of Roles:* To fit together and function in unison, each of the parts in the bureaucratic machine must know what it is supposed to do and how it fits within the larger organization. What are the responsibilities of a division or an individual? What are the expected outputs and where should the bureaucrat look for input? When should something be handed to someone else and what should be

---

*Pronounced "Vayburr" not "Webber," and, no, he did not invent the barbeque.

handed to that person? When is it someone else's problem? The whole idea of clear organization is to avoid overlap and duplication of efforts, as well as gaps or failures in the process. Gaps and overlaps are wasteful and inefficient.

Rules, Rules, Rules, and More Rules: For both efficiency and fairness, decisions and choices made by bureaucrats need to be impersonal and consistent. This is accomplished by a careful adherence to rule-based decision making. To avoid favoring or discriminating against someone, always follow the rules. To make certain you get the same output with every case—the output that the other parts expect— always follow the rules. If a situation cannot be resolved within the rules and roles defined for an individual bureaucrat or a division within the bureaucracy, see the next point.

Hierarchy: Bureaucracies are strictly hierarchical with a clear chain of command from the king all the way to the lowest peasant. Each person should have only one immediate supervisor and each supervisor should have only a limited number of subordinates. The result is a pyramid with the trolls slaving away at the direction of assistant troll managers, senior troll managers directing the assistant troll managers, and super-important managers commanding the managers of troll managers, and so on. This is important not only for effective control of the bureaucracy, but also for handling challenges to the rule-based decision making. In this idealistic version, deviant cases get passed up the food chain until they reach the level where someone has the rule or authority necessary for resolving the issue.

Professionals: Finally and most importantly, the selection of persons to fill roles within the bureaucracy, whether through promotion or recruitment, must be done on the basis of merit. For the engine of government to work at peak efficiency, the right parts—or people—need to be in their optimum position. Someone without the necessary training or ability, who was hired or promoted on the basis of friendship, political or familial relationships, or the stunning good looks that will surely lead to a disgraced senior troll manager and a sexual harassment lawsuit, will not be able to perform the functions expected of the role. Because of the integration and interconnections within bureaucracies, those without proper training and ability will cause difficulties for others as well. The call for professional merit-based bureaucracies was specifically meant to put an end to the spoils system, where the new administration would fire everyone in the existing government and replace them with political supporters. And think about the consequences of incompetent and unqualified bureaucrats. Would you want to climb into a rocket if the leading managers of NASA were not the best scientists, but the best fund-raisers?

Thus, when you next step up to the counter at the department of motor vehicles and the incoherent chain-smoking octogenarian is not interested in your story; when the grossly obese slob will not let you ask which line you should wait in until you've already waited your way through the line; when the nervous twit on his own little power trip will not let you fill out Form C until you fill out Form L8; or when whatever other bureaucratic caricature you confront refuses to bend the rules to help you out, it is a reflection of the ideals of rule-based decision making. Despite what the jokes and skits imply, this most infuriating aspect of bureaucracy is not an inability or unwillingness to actually help anyone accomplish anything. That is just an added bonus feature. Knowing and sticking strictly to the rules is the ideal.

If you do not think strict adherence to rules is an ideal, think about what it is like to be on the wrong end of bending the rules. Consider the small-town sheriff who does not like the way you look and decides to fix it with his nightstick, knowing that his brother the judge will ignore your complaints about missing teeth. Ponder the stereotypical B-movie plot where the corrupt cop throws you in jail so the local drug lord can force your girlfriend/boyfriend or other type of significant other to carry a shipment across the border. Reflect awhile on the bribed official who orders the demolition of your fire station to make way for a big developer, which somehow forces you to race a sentient VW bug named Herbie against an evil race-car driver. The ideal of rule-based decision making is to protect the less powerful and the less influential from those with power and influence. The ideal is to make sure that everyone is treated exactly the same.

Policymaking versus Administration

However even Weber's view of bureaucracy made many people a little nervous, particularly in democracies. As these organizations grew in size and number, so did the concern that bureaucracies might start to assume roles meant for the elected portions of the government. In other words, there was increased concern that bureaucracies would move from implementing laws to actually making the laws themselves. This would be particularly disturbing given that these organizations were not designed to be responsive to the people. Of further concern in the late nineteenth century was the use of the bureaucracy for patronage purposes, that is, giving jobs as political favors.

In response to these concerns, Woodrow Wilson wrote an essay in which he declared that there should be a strict dichotomy between politics and administration.[10] Frank Goodnow picked up this theme and argued that there should be a clear and impenetrable distinction between the political branches making the laws and the bureaucracy implementing them.[11] However, the reality is that completely severing politics and administration would be a disaster for the whole concept of democracy, but remember we are sticking to idealism and the ideals of these common institutions in this chapter. You'll have to read the next chapter to get to the really good stuff. Nevertheless, Weber, Wilson, and Goodnow all view the often infuriating inflexibility of bureaucracy as better than the alternative.

Bureaucratic Roles

Bureaucracies are seemingly omnipresent. If you're reading this anywhere in the proximity of your college or university, you will know what we mean. Colleges are full of bureaucracies. Think of the financial aid office, registrar, campus police, or parking permit window and you have a good sense of the many things administrative agencies do. We can take all of these functions and divide them into the subcategories of service, regulation, implementation, and policymaking.

Some of the more prominent things agencies provide are services. In the list of bureaucratic functions performed at your school we left out the big one. If you are at a public college, the whole enterprise is a vast bureaucracy, and therefore, the education that you are receiving is a service that your state is providing. Even if you are not at a public university, you may eat the daily offering of the extruded meat-like product courtesy of the cafeteria. That, too, is an administrative service and it often tastes like bureaucracy. Governments manage hospitals, carry out welfare programs, run public schools, operate parks, and so on. These are all service functions.

Administrative agencies also regulate. The FBI regulates personal behavior, the Food and Drug Administration regulates how much rat hair can end up in your hot dog,* the Securities and Exchange Commission (SEC) often tries to somewhat regulate Wall Street. Bureaucratic agencies watch over particular segments of the economy to make sure that they follow the law. Agencies are also primarily responsible for implementation and make sure that the laws that legislatures pass get put into place. So, when the U.S. Congress decides that there should be a new immigration law, Citizenship and Immigration Services puts it into place and figures out an exact set of rules for deciding which people getting off the international flight will get the genial wave through and which will get the deluxe full-body search and the opportunity to discover the reason why the large woman is wearing rubber gloves. When the Congress passes a new prescription drug program, the Department of Health and Human Services supplies all of the details to put it into place.

Interestingly, the bureaucracy is also responsible for making public policy. Congress and other parliaments often pass general laws and describe what they want, but leave the specifics to the expertise of bureaucracies. If the legislature decides it wants to reduce the amount of fluoribiglycercarbonites in the air, they will often not make a specific policy about exactly how much is the maximum, how it will be measured, or how the rules will be changed to reduce it. Instead Congress will authorize the bureaucracy to institute policies that live up to the intent of the legislature. The agency is responsible for filling in the details. The bureaucracy, thus, is responsible for coming up with specific regulations. If Congress did not approve of the way some corporations conducted

---

* Seriously, there is an actual rule they enforce regarding the amount of rat hair allowed in processed meat products.

their business, it might instruct the SEC to issue new accounting rules. However, it would leave it up to the accounting divisions of the SEC to be specific about the exact rules, and only step in if it thought the SEC was not doing what it had been asked to do.

KEY TERMS

bicameral legislature / **152**	parliamentary system / **149**
bureaucracy / **161**	politicos / **155**
checks and balances / **149**	presidency / **144**
delegate / **154**	presidential system / **149**
filibuster / **146**	prime minister / **150**
first-past-the-post system / **153**	proportional representation / **154**
geographic representation / **153**	separation of powers / **149**
head of government / **157**	shadow government / **156**
head of state / **157**	trustee / **154**
ideological representation / **154**	two-party system / **154**
multi-party systems / **154**	unicameral legislature / **152**

CHAPTER SUMMARY

Institutions, like executives, legislatures, and bureaucracies exist to perform important functions. Sometimes these functions are simple, for example, passing laws or implementing laws. However, at other times institutions perform other roles that are not as readily understood, for example, when legislative hearings educate the public or when a chief executive serves as symbolic head of the country. Some countries give the roles of head of state and head of government to one person; other countries split the job between two officeholders. When structuring institutions to perform their roles, choices abound. One of the most basic choices is whether to have a parliamentary system or a presidential system. In a parliamentary system, the executive is a member of parliament, while in a presidential system the executive is separate from parliament or legislature. Once a country decides whether or not it wants to have separation of powers, it must select how it wishes to choose its representatives. Presuming that there will be elections, a country can choose either proportional representation, which is more likely to provide ideological representation or district elections, which promote geographic representation. Representatives also have a choice to make, that is, what type of legislator do they wish to be? Do they want to be delegates—individuals who simply follow whatever the majority wants—or will they be trustees—individuals who make their own choices? Perhaps, as a politico, an individual might do a little of both.

Students should learn two very important lessons from this chapter. First, the design of a nation's institutions can tell us about the nation's ideals and values. For example, a country that elects its representatives through proportional representation makes a very different value statement from one that elects representatives through district elections. Of course, both make a different value statement from a country that does not even elect its representatives. Second, it is reassuring to know that someone regulates the amount of rat hair in hot dogs.

STUDY QUESTIONS AND EXERCISES

1. Identify and explain the different functions that legislatures perform.

2. What is the difference between the "head of government" and the "head of state," and what are the benefits of having the U.S. president perform both functions?

3. Contrast the benefits of a parliamentary system with the benefits of the presidential system. Which do you prefer, and why?

4. Consider your personal experience with some bureaucracy—be it at the department of motor vehicles or in the financial-aid office of a public university. Do the characteristics of bureaucracy ring true given your experience?

5. This chapter makes the case that not all legislatures are democratic. Explain why this is the case. What are some aspects of the U.S. Congress that are not democratic?

WEBSITES TO EXPLORE

www.capsteps.com. *The Capitol Steps* are a group of former Senate staffers who satirize national politics through song.

www.c-span.org/international/links.asp. C-SPAN.org's Legislatures Around the World links to parliaments from around the globe with an indication of whether proceedings are televised.

www.guide2womenleaders.com/index.html. Worldwide Guide to Women in Leadership site contains short biographies of current and former female heads of state and government.

www.parl.gc.ca/information/library/PRBpubs/bp334-e.htm. The Canadian Library of Parliament page reprints "Electoral Systems," Brian O'Neil's short paper on the different types of electoral systems and their importance.

www.unicam.state.ne.us/learning/history.htm. The Nebraska Legislature's "History of Nebraska's Unicameral Legislature" provides background about why Nebraska chose a one-house legislature.

In a perfect system, Fords wouldn't crash quite so much.

CHAPTER 8

The Imperfections of Political Institutions
Bugs in the Machine

Deep in the dark and constipated bowels of a well-worn bureaucratic agency, an insect falls into a printer and becomes, quite literally, a bug in the machinery of government. Terry Gilliam constructs the plot of an entire movie out of the resulting typo. *Brazil* is perhaps the darkest of dark comedies.[1] It ruthlessly spins our frustrations with administrative government into an Orwellian nightmare that is just absurd enough to take the edge off. A renegade plumber is killed and consumed by a swarm of the official paperwork that he refused to file. A man works in a nice secure government job, spending boring day after boring day torturing people to death at the office and when it is his best friend in the chair, it is nothing personal. It is just his job; rules are rules, and all that.

Brazil expresses our collective frustration with bureaucracies. However, for our immediate purposes the film depicts the threat of what can happen to any institution. No matter how many experts are consulted, no matter how carefully plans are drawn, no matter how skillfully history is read, no matter how vast the understanding of politics, in real life no institution runs perfectly. There will always be unintended consequences and something is bound to not go according to plan. A fly will land in the printer or someone will wiggle into an unanticipated situation that now must be dealt with.

Even institutions that have withstood the test of time can become outdated or, at least, subject to intense criticism of their basic workings. The institutions of the oldest and most thoroughly tested democratic systems in the world—the United States' constitutional system and the British

Westminster system—have their critics and those critics often have very good points. British citizens have periodically questioned the utility of their monarchy and there is a constant suggestion that their parliamentary seats should be allocated according to proportional representation rather than the existing system of district elections. The 2000 U.S. presidential election stirred up all kinds of questions about the propriety of the electoral college as a means for selecting the president. This example in particular highlights many of the difficulties with institutions. The electoral college made a lot of sense a couple centuries ago when it took weeks to get balloting results from South Carolina to Philadelphia. Then, to make sure a president was actually selected, your state sent a representative to the capital to vote on your behalf. The electoral college determined how many votes or how many voting representatives your state got to send. Now, in the Plasma Television era, it seems to be little more than a quaint anachronism that can produce a winner that lost the popular vote. There is always room to criticize governmental institutions and when the less savory aspects of human nature and behavior are included it sometimes seems that politics wallows with the pond scum at the bottom rung of the evolutionary ladder.

The dirty underbelly of political institutions is a common theme in fiction. Robert Penn Warren's *All the King's Men*[2] is a classic American novel, perhaps the best political novel ever written.* Based loosely on the life of Louisiana governor Huey Long, it chronicles a governor's journey from idealistic crusader to the lowest form of bottom-feeding invertebrate. If you just added Jimmy Stewart wearing a goatee, the movie version could pass as the evil twin of *Mr. Smith Goes to Washington*. Instead of the triumph of duty inspired by Washington's plethora of monuments to democracy, in *All the King's Men* it is the gritty side of politics that dominates the story of idealism and realism in politics. With *Mr. Smith* we look at the world of governmental institutions from the Boy Ranger's perspective. With *All the King's Men* we look at those institutions from The Boss's.

Clearly there is a darker side to politics. When we examine institutions we must appreciate that for every positive aspect, there will be problems. Sometimes these problems occur because people are looking to maximize their own self-interest. Sometimes these problems occur because the world changes faster than political institutions. Sometimes these problems occur because of flaws in the institutions themselves. Whatever the reason, problems will occur.

PARLIAMENTARY VERSUS PRESIDENTIAL SYSTEMS

In the last chapter we contrasted the benefits of the ideal presidential system with those of the ideal parliamentary system. The presidential system creates a strong and independent executive, while the parliamentary system offers an executive who is also a member

---

* *All the King's Men* falls in the literature category, which means that it is jam-packed with themes about life, love, history, philosophy, and especially politics. The political story is, of course of primary interest for this text, but because our usual sarcastic style might lead students to dismiss the sincerity of our praise for a book that qualifies as literature, we wanted to announce a serious moment. And even though the movie made from this book is nowhere near as good as the book, it won an Academy Award for Best Picture. Then again, so did *Titanic*.

The Imperfections of Political Institutions

of parliament and can work very effectively with the legislative branch. While the presidential system maintains strong institutions through independence, the parliamentary system offers expediency and efficiency through the integration of the two primary political institutions. Strength and independence are positive virtues, as are expediency and efficiency. However, it is possible to have too much of a good thing. That strong president may, in fact, become too strong. The person serving as both the head of government and head of state can effectively use modern technology to communicate with the people. This can allow presidents to go over the heads of the legislative branch to speak directly to the people. In *All the King's Men,* Governor Willie Stark, who is facing impeachment by the legislature, appeals directly to the people to garner support to fight the impeachment. This tactic, along with buying off key legislators, insulates him from the impeachment threat.

Presidents can also accumulate increased power at the expense of the legislative branch ultimately making the president too strong for checks and balances to work properly. Remember that legislators always have reelection in the back of their minds. This is particularly true when we are talking about a district-based electoral system. There is, therefore, an incentive for members of the legislature to avoid controversial political decisions so that they can stay in good stead with their constituents. This can lead to their delegating authority and power to the president on certain issues and the president can take advantage of this. Delegations to the president are particularly common when there are international crises. At one such point, after Presidents Lyndon Johnson and Richard Nixon accumulated tremendous power in the presidency, historian Arthur Schlesinger Jr., wrote *The Imperial Presidency,*[3] in which he examined the increasing power of the president. Ultimately, Congress did curtail the executive's increasing power, the **imperial presidency**, when the institution was damaged from the Vietnam War and the Watergate scandal.

This potential for an overwhelming concentration of power is always a fear in presidential systems. The legislature and any other branches of government that are able to reign in the executive must always be vigilant and fight to ensure that their check on the executive remains effective. The imperial presidency can only happen if the legislature fails to check its rise. However, the danger of the imperial presidency is more of a monster under the bed than a bug in the day-to-day machinery of the presidential system. A more important difficulty is almost the exact opposite of the imperial presidency.

Gridlock

Far more common than a president pulling a full-on Godzilla* on the legislature—and in many ways it can be far more of a problem—is a situation often referred to as gridlock.

---

* A "full-on Godzilla" is a technical term often skillfully deployed by extremely intelligent political science professors who watch too much late-night cable TV. As a political term, it refers to an individual politician gaining enough power to overwhelm any and all opposition. Contrary to the common mythology, radioactive waste plays no part in this process. It should also be remembered that the political science use of the term is distinctly different from the use of the term in professional wrestling.

Gridlock arises when the checks and balances within the presidential system work too well and they not only prevent one institution from overwhelming the others, but also prevent anyone from doing much of anything. In the United States gridlock is often associated with **divided government**, when one political party controls the presidency and another party controls either one or both houses of Congress. Because the president can use the veto to check legislative initiatives and because the legislature can refuse to provide the funding for unpopular legislation, such as controversial presidential policy efforts, it becomes very difficult for either the executive or the legislature to cooperate on anything outside of what is likely to be a very narrow range of agreement between the two major U.S. parties. This is not the only time things grind to a halt inside the beltway. Gridlock can occur any time the Congress and president end up stuck in a situation where neither will allow the other to do anything, such as when a president's approval ratings crash and legislative members think that working with the president might hurt them in the next election.

This paralyzing division of government has been the norm in recent American history and the term gridlock itself has worked its way into the speeches of politicians. Bill Clinton faced divided government for all but two years and George W. Bush faced divided government for part of his first term. This may also be a source of many features of the modern U.S. presidency. Since a gridlocked president would often find it necessary to bypass the Congress and speak directly to the American people in order to try to get things done, we now see the direct appeal to the public as a significant, if not defining, part of the U.S. presidency. Gridlock can also lead to confusion over responsibility for policy because when the president appeals to the public as a way to influence the legislature, it blurs the distinction between the institutions. When the media reports that the president has lost a legislative battle, it overlooks the fact that the president cannot introduce legislation; the president cannot even vote in the Congress. This kind of commentary makes it even harder for the public to identify which branch of government is the one using its check to stop things from getting done and because there is no identifiable villain, it makes it that much harder to escape gridlock.

One of the most significant negative effects of gridlock is the difficulty in passing any kind of broad or comprehensive policy changes, and the only way that anything gets done is with what we call "the Bob solution."* In *What About Bob?*[4] Bill Murray plays a psychiatric patient who is paralyzed by his fear of everything. His new psychiatrist encourages Murray's character to take "baby steps," which is also the title of the psychiatrist's

---

* We call this the Bob solution so we can make a completely gratuitous reference to this movie. There is absolutely no reason to mention this movie and we offer no justification whatsoever. *What About Bob?* has some funny bits, but the two authors disagree on whether the movie is any good at all and continue to debate whether *Caddyshack* or *Stripes* is the best Bill Murray movie. As may be obvious, however, that argument is, in itself, little more than a shameless opportunity to provide two more completely unnecessary references to films we like.

The Imperfections of Political Institutions

self-help book. So Bill Murray literally starts to take baby steps and shuffles his way around. Because of the nature of the separation of powers and gridlock, in the United States, policy is often reduced to baby steps. For example, Bill Clinton came into office promising major changes in policy, particularly the implementation of a national health policy, but ultimately he only managed to make the smallest of changes, like portability of health care. The guarantee that you can take your old health care program with you to a new job falls far short of a comprehensive national health care policy. But faced with the impossibility of fully implementing whatever grand dream a president may have, the Bob solution may be the only way to move forward.

In contrast, parliamentary systems are not subject to gridlock. Remember that the prime minister is actually a member of parliament and by definition, always commands the majority of votes in the legislature. A politician becomes prime minister by garnering the support of a majority of the parliament. When one party manages to win a majority—50 percent plus one—of the seats in the parliament, this is a quick and simple thing. The head of state will ask the leader of the winning party to form a government. The leader of the party will become the prime minister and, at most, sometimes a ceremonial vote is held where the majority party elects one of their own as the prime minister. In other systems, coalitions between parties are formed after an election in order to get a majority of parliamentary votes. In either situation, the prime minister pretty much always has a majority in parliament to provide the legislation needed to back policy initiatives and the majority in parliament can almost always count on the executive to support the legislation that is passed. No gridlock.

Parliaments and Instability

There are two aspects of a parliamentary system, though, that might be considered bugs in the system and both are related to stability. The first is pretty simple—**policy stability**. In a presidential system, where big changes are difficult to enact, the social and economic environments within the country tend to be very consistent over time. This has a tremendous value to businesses and others who need to be able to plan over the long term. In parliamentary systems sweeping change is far easier and too much change can sometimes be a problem. A new party or new coalition coming in to power can change just about anything and everything. Radical changes in tax laws can nullify a lifetime investment strategy in a second. Big changes in foreign policy can weaken or even shatter alliances. The effects are particularly obvious in business and other economic matters where stability of policy has a big influence on the investment of current wealth, the building of infrastructure, or research or production for future gains. However, you can also see the value of consistent policy in education, law enforcement, or any other long-term endeavor where you develop an infrastructure, such as educational curriculum, for repeatedly performing the same function. Anything that looks to the future usually does better in a stable political and policy environment.

Hands-on democracy: Legislators in Ukraine, Turkey, and Taiwan debate the finer points of parliamentary etiquette.

A second way that stability can be a problem in parliamentary systems is in the tenure of the government itself. In most parliamentary systems the government can be dissolved at any moment by a simple majority vote in the parliament. At any time, a party can call for a **vote of no confidence**, and if the prime minister loses that vote, the government is dissolved and forming a new government begins immediately. In some systems there might be a window of a few days or weeks to negotiate a new coalition or a negotiate a deal to win a new vote of support before an election is necessary, in other systems new elections are required and are scheduled immediately after a vote of no confidence. Essentially this means that any scandal or policy failure that causes legislative support to waiver can lead to an immediate change of government. In such a system, Ronald Reagan might well have only served two years. His unpopular policy of stationing U.S. Marines in Beirut, Lebanon, ended catastrophically in 1983 when the Marine barracks were bombed. Bill Clinton might have had an even shorter stay in office after the humanitarian intervention in Somalia—a policy he inherited from his predecessor—collapsed in disgrace and caused a serious backlash in Congress. In both of these cases, these presidents were able to carry on and recover sufficiently to win reelection a few years later. A prime minister would be unlikely to have such luxury.

France provides an excellent example of the difficulty governments can have sustaining their tenure in office. Just during the period 1990–2004, there were twelve different French governments. While not all changes in French government required elections or brought a new prime minister into office, such constant turmoil takes up time and energy. Additionally, the uncertainty over who will be the prime minister next month

The Imperfections of Political Institutions

means that everyone must always work with the knowledge that policy could, quite literally, change at a moment's notice. This instability problem with parliamentary systems is in many ways the opposite and equal to the gridlock problem with presidential systems. Each flaw is balanced by benefits. There is, however, a flaw that both systems share and it is much more troubling in terms of the ideals of democracy. Even if the whole process of voting were perfectly fair, neither a parliamentary nor a presidential system can ensure that every voter is represented equally and fairly by the government that is formed.

DISTRICTS AND PROPORTIONS: NOT SO DEMOCRATIC REPRESENTATION

As we've mentioned briefly before, there are two basic ways that votes are transformed into representation within government. The United States and several parliamentary democracies such as Great Britain use a single-member district system, where voting is based upon a geographic district and each geographic district elects a representative. An alternative that many think is fairer is a proportional system where seats in a government body such as a parliament are assigned to parties based upon the proportion of the votes they receive. Both systems have advantages. A district system elects an individual who is clearly responsible for representing the interests of a specific community and the specter of future elections tends to make that individual quite responsive to local needs. This helps preserve local and regional qualities in a geographically diverse country such as the United States.

A proportional system allows a much wider variety of political perspectives to gain representation in the elected bodies of government and it ensures that just about everyone's vote is translated to legislative representation. In a district system, if you vote for any candidate that cannot win a majority, you have wasted your vote and your preference will not be represented. In a proportional system the party you vote for only has to exceed the qualifying threshold, sometimes as low as 1 percent of the vote, in order to win a seat and represent your opinion. However, both are flawed as a means of democratic representation.

Proponents of proportional representation will immediately bristle at the suggestion that it is a flawed political institution. Proportional representation is frequently offered as the cure to the ills of district-based elections and it does do most of the things its advocates claim. It increases the number of parties and the variety of policy perspectives officially represented in elected bodies and it ensures that almost every vote is reflected in the final representation. However, that does not mean it is perfect. In the end, someone still has to govern, and it is in the steps between the votes and the final arrangement of who governs that the flaws in the proportional system become apparent. Specifically, minor parties, representing small percentages of the population, will often have a disproportional influence on the formation of government.

Coalitions and Minority Governments

One of the most obvious effects of proportional representation is the proliferation of political parties. Essentially, a party can form around any policy position that attracts enough votes to get them past the qualifying threshold. Thus, there is usually a party representing the roughly 5 to 15 percent of the population that places their highest political priority on environmental issues, a party that caters to the roughly 10 percent of the population that votes on their socially conservative agenda, and so on. Multi-party systems are an important part of a proportional representation system and when there are many parties in the legislature, it is usually very difficult for any one party to achieve the majority necessary to form a government on their own. Since a prime minister must always have the support of a majority of the parliament this usually leads to coalitions between parties. Think of it in terms of the alliances formed in one of the many incarnations of *Survivor*[5] or its reality TV rip-offs. Except for the fact that politicians seldom eat bugs, the alliances that are formed on *Survivor* are not very different from the coalitions that are formed in parliaments. They are ad hoc* agreements formed in order to win the executive—or the immunity torch—but they are always uneasy alliances because each of these parties all have their own political agendas.

Coalitions become a problem with democratic representation when a minor party finds itself in the key position to swing the vote for or against a prime minister. Minor parties in this situation are often called relevant parties, because, even though they do not have a chance of winning on their own, they can affect the outcome of the election and that gives them policy leverage far out of proportion to the votes they received. For example, consider a country that has proportional representation and three parties that attract votes: the right-leaning (conservative) Party A wins 43 percent of the seats in parliament, the more left-leaning (liberal) counterpart Party B wins 49 percent, and a religious Party C manages to get the remaining 8 percent.

What happens then?

In order to govern one party must put together a majority of support from the MPs. Usually, the head of state will ask the leader of the party with the most votes to try to form a government. Thus, Party B will talk to the Party C. But clearly Party C has tremendous leverage here. No matter what either party offers in terms of policy concessions or ministerial positions in the cabinet, Party C can always go to the other big party and ask for more.

By supporting the conservative Party A, the religious Party C will be able to work out a deal to guarantee all kinds of conservative-friendly legislation. Furthermore, since the conservative party needs its support to stay in power, it is unlikely that Party A will enact any policies that would alienate the religious party because if the religious party

---

* "Ad hoc" is not a reference to alcohol-induced regurgitation nor does it refer to the sound a cat makes when hacking up a fur ball. It refers to an improvised or one-time only action.

The Imperfections of Political Institutions

leaves the coalition, the government would fall. And in our little scenario, the religious party can play hardball in forming the coalition. Party C can coerce the liberal party with the threat of putting the smaller conservative party in power and giving them control of policy and government for several years. However, even though there is a more natural policy affinity between the religious Party C and the conservative Party A, the conservatives still face a big risk if they do not make significant concessions. If neither party is willing to give the religious party what they want, they can refuse to join either and force new elections. That is extremely dangerous for the conservative party because if the liberal party were to gain just 1 percent more of the vote in the second election, they would have a majority and could rule unfettered by a coalition that dilutes their policy preferences. Thus, there is a flaw in the system: the small parties that are in a position that makes them necessary to form a government gain influence that far outweighs the extent of their electoral support.

Given our three-party scenario, the negotiations are relatively simple. The religious party and the conservative party probably have enough in common that it would be in both of their interests to cooperate and the liberal party is unlikely to be willing to offer enough to overcome that natural affinity. So, the conservative party should be able to form a coalition that completely shuts the party with the most votes out of government and gives substantial concessions to the party that won the fewest. That is far from perfectly representing the wishes of the public and, to make matters worse, it is seldom that neat and tidy. Typically, there is a proliferation of minor parties in a proportional system and the interests of the minor parties seldom coincide enough to make nice, rational coalitions.

Far from a match made in heaven, most coalition governments are put together like a TV reality matchmaking show where our gender-nonspecific Pat who has traveled all the way here from chapter 1 is going to pick a spouse—soon to be ex-spouse—from a cadre of far from perfect participants who were willing to sign the network's legal release form. It might go something like this:

> "So, Chris, what does your party bring to the coalition table?"
>
> "We're a radically conservative party that believes in restoring the nation to its former glory by kicking out all of the immigrants from countries other than the ones that kicked out our ancestors. Some of our leaders have made some disparaging comments about the minorities that voted for your party, but we've got 6 percent of the seats in parliament and we have a very active and growing membership."
>
> "Terry, please tell me you have something better to offer?"
>
> "Dude, we're a radical freedom suburban radical party for freedom.* We believe that the government should stick to providing only the bare minimum

---

* The RFSRPF is a proud sponsor of the American Dodgeball Association of America.

of necessary services—those that no private industry could provide—and it should stay completely out of all moral and social decisions made by consenting adults in the privacy of their own home, front yard, or driveway. We'll join your coalition, but the first thing that has to go is the repressive and hypocritical application of drug laws to hemp and hemp byproducts. We think we might have something like 3 percent of the vote, or maybe it was 8 percent. Dude, does that look like an 8 percent? Or maybe a 6 percent? That is a percent thingy right? Seriously, I know we got more than eight votes man."

"Jamie, what have you got?"

"I am so very glad you asked, Pat, because we have got exactly what you want. We are a brand new party, with new and completely unspecified ideas. We have a charismatic young and fiery leader who used to be an inspirational speaker and hamster therapist. Because our leader is so gosh-darn charismatic we are going to have to demand that you give us a prominent place in your government where we can threaten your party's authority with flashy and glib catch phrases that have little or no foundation in a coherent policy or the realities of government. We have 3.67 percent of the vote."

"Butch, what can you offer the coalition?"

"We're an ultra-religious party, Pat. We'd like to see the government take some long overdue action to restore the moral foundation of this country, starting with the elimination of all this tolerance for ambiguously gendered names. We are absolutely committed to universal adoption of the Ten Commandments and we demand the immediate invasion of any country that objects. This country must stop its association with the morally corrupt nations of the world and France. We've got 5 percent of the seats in parliament and God's secret e-mail address."

Of course, the reality is that Pat does not really like any of these choices and the coalition options for any political party are always imperfect choices. On top of the difficulties Pat will have in selecting coalition partners that fit with Pat's own party, are the relationships between potential coalition partners that also have to be considered. There are several combinations of the minor parties in the above example that simply cannot coexist in a coalition and this will give further policy leverage to some of these minor parties.

Therefore, while parliamentary systems do not suffer from gridlock, they can suffer from **immobilism** caused by the fragility of the ruling coalition. The more complex and more fragile the ruling coalition, the more difficult it becomes to enact any kind of coherent policies because any new policy that was not agreed upon by all parties at the formation of the coalition may cause a party to break away and force the government to collapse. This means that any party that can cause the coalition to fall apart has veto power over any legislation. Thus, multi-party systems can cause governments to constantly teeter on the brink of falling apart—a serious difficulty. Italy is perhaps the best example of this situation, as it has had fifty-nine governments since World War II and as a result, the Italian train system is so messed up that the company that prints the schedules is at risk of being sued for fraud.

In rare instances, it is even possible for a country with a parliamentary system to have a **minority government**. In that case, the majority party does not share power with any other party, but relies on an agreement where another party will provide support, or will abstain from voting if there is ever a no-confidence vote. For example, in 2005 Canadian prime minister Paul Martin's government was one vote shy of a majority and simply needed a party with two or more seats to agree to abstain from a vote of no confidence. This can work if there are several small parties that could guarantee abstaining in return for modest policy concessions.

Yet another variation is a **unity government**. With a unity government, the two major parties, though in opposition, work together to achieve a higher national purpose. For example, the Israeli prime minister Arial Sharon's Likud Party worked with Shimon Peres's Labor Party for a time in order to show a united front during a recent period in the ongoing Middle East conflict. As one might imagine, such arrangements are difficult to maintain and are usually short-lived.

France has its own problems, aside from being French that is. France's institutions are a little different from most. While they have a parliamentary system, they also have a president with significant political power. That president is elected separately and at different times from the parliament. Nevertheless, the prime minister serves at the president's pleasure. Consequently, it is possible for the French president to be from one political party, while a different political party controls the legislature.* This situation first occurred in 1986 when President François Mitterand's Socialist Party lost parliamentary elections. The French refer to this as **cohabitation**, and we will leave it to you to employ a French stereotype to discover the obvious joke.

District Elections

If you are thinking that district elections are superior because of the imperfections of proportional representation, you need to look more carefully at districts—and we mean, quite literally, look at the districts. In nations that use district elections, legislators are elected to represent a particular geographic territory and the big problem with district elections is that someone must draw the district lines. In other words, if you say that you want to have a 100-seat legislature, you have to divide up the country into 100 districts. Who will do this? Politicians, of course. What could possibly go wrong with that? This is tantamount to allowing the richest team in baseball to dictate the rules for acquiring players.†

---

* It is important to remember the distinction between head of state, who is someone like the Queen of England who serves as the symbolic embodiment of the country, and the head of government who does all the real work of governing, like the prime minister of Great Britain. The U.S. president does both, but the French president is sort of like an elected queen.

† Oh, wait, that is what the Yankees do.

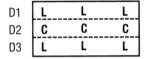

State with Liberal and Conservative Pockets

```
L       L       L
C       C       C
L       L       L
```

Districts created in proportion to party strength in the population

```
D1 | L       L       L
D2 | C       C       C
D3 | L       L       L
```

Districts created by gerrymandering

```
   D1      D2      D3
   L   |   L   |   L
   C   |   C   |   C
   L   |   L   |   L
```

Figure 8.1 Dividing a State into Districts

The analogy actually falls a bit short of the mark because it is the politicians who already control the legislature that get to draw the lines. In the United States, the Senate's districts are, of course, the states. However, for the House of Representatives responsibility for drawing district lines within each state—or redistricting—lies with the state legislatures. Thus, whichever party controls the state legislature gets to draw the lines for the seats within the state and they do so with their party's interests first and foremost, of course.

Imagine the following extremely complex scenario in a very rectangular state, depicted in Figure 8.1, that has to be divided into three different districts with roughly the same number of people in each. The letter "L" stands for a pocket of about 10,000 people that is dominated by the Liberal Party. The "C" stands for a pocket of about 10,000 people that is dominated by members of the Conservative Party. If we are going to try to be the fairest we can be, we could divide the state horizontally into 3 districts—two with three majority-Liberal pockets and one with three majority-Conservative pockets. The final outcome would leave us with two districts where the liberals are likely to win and one district where the conservatives are likely to win. This is the fair way of doing it, since the number of districts each party would likely win is in proportion to their overall percentage of the total population. But the concern is not with being fair, but with winning. What if we represent the Liberal Party and we are responsible for drawing these districts? Then we've got a different situation. Instead of drawing these districts horizontally, we'll draw them vertically and the liberals will win three seats to the conservatives' zero.

This process of intentionally drawing districts to gain a partisan advantage is called **gerrymandering**. In our scenario, the Liberal party gerrymandered the districts to get an extra seat. Of course in real life, at least in life outside the classroom, people are not arranged in neat little rows, but that does not keep those from drawing the lines from being creative. In fact, the word gerrymander comes from Elbridge Gerry, a signer of the Declaration of Independence, who as Massachusetts governor manipulated the drawing of electoral districts in order to keep his political party in power. One of those districts looked like a salamander and some clever political commentator, knowing we

The Imperfections of Political Institutions

would one day need a term in textbooks to denote this concept, noticed that "Gerry" plus "Salamander" equals "Gerrymander."

In the state of Pennsylvania, roughly half of all registered voters are Democrats. Still, the Republican redistricting has left the Republicans in control of twelve of the state's nineteen congressional districts. Do not feel too bad for the Democrats. As we noted, there is a rich history of gerrymandering in the United States. The Democrats have done the same to the Republicans and given the opportunity in the future, you can be certain that the Democrats will return the favor. Still, one has to wonder about how democratic such a system is. Certainly, with proportional representation the legislature will more accurately reflect the nation's partisan makeup even if a coalition arrangement distorts the policy impact of some parties at the expense of others. Gerrymandering is particularly common in the United States. Other countries that use district elections, for example Great Britain, Canada, and New Zealand, have independent commissions that attempt to create fair election districts in a nonpolitical manner.

Another problem with using electoral districts is that they can split the loyalty of the elected representatives. Voters ask their representatives to play two different, and often contradictory, roles.[6] On the one hand, they ask them to be part of the national law-making assembly. In this sense, they are expected to enact legislation that is in the nation's best interest. Most people would see no problem with this. On the other hand, representatives are expected to be ambassadors from the district and the geographic location they represent. In other words, the representatives' constituents, the people they represent in their district, want them to do what is in the best interest for that district and what is in the best interest of a state or legislative district is not always the same as what is in the best interest of the nation as a whole.

Sometimes local interests might be the same as national interests, but we can also imagine many instances where they are not. Take, for example, the recent effort to shut down military installations around the United States. With advances in transportation and the end of World War II drastically reducing the likelihood that the Japanese will invade Oregon, it no longer makes economic sense to have thousands of small military bases scattered across the country. Consolidation into a few large military complexes makes economic sense, but what if you are a congressman with a naval base in your district? The district certainly benefits from the base; it brings jobs, sailors will shop and eat at local establishments, people will come to visit their loved ones and spend money, etc. Even though it is in the national interest to shut down many of these small bases, the local interest in keeping the bases open will likely drive the U.S. senators and representatives to fight to protect them even as they agree that many of the bases need to be closed.

Furthermore, this split can drive a wedge between national and local interests and weaken political parties. Because each individual representative owes his or her electoral success to a constituency and not to a political party, representatives can feel freer to act contrary to party interests. This makes it much more difficult for party leaders to

Imagine your lifelong dream was to one day work as a park ranger. Visions of mountains and geysers have filled your head since you were young and now, the letter in your grizzly-bear-shaped mailbox says that your dream has come true. You have been hired by the National Park Service, and your first assignment is in the distant reaches of Scranton. Scranton? It turns out that Scranton is neither a wilderness nor a disease, but is instead a coal mining town in northeast Pennsylvania. It is is not only the setting for the American version of the British TV show *The Office*, it is also the home of Steamtown, a historic railroad museum that cost U.S. taxpayers tens of millions of dollars to build and keeps costing them money to maintain and run.

How did that get thrown in there with the Yukon, Yellowstone, and Yosemite? It doesn't even start with a "Y." You could argue that Steamtown is a wonderful educational site. However, it is pretty tough to make a convincing case that building Steamtown is in the best interest of the nation. A simpler explanation is that it is an example of pork.

At the time Congress approved the money for Steamtown, Scranton was in a dire situation. Coal mining was no longer bringing in enough money or creating enough jobs to keep the city going and there really was not anything else to lure other businesses into the city. Yet, Scranton did have at least one valuable asset:

Congressman Joseph McDade. A thirty-year Republican veteran of Congress, the ranking minority member of the House Appropriations Committee, and member of the Appropriations subcommittee for the Park Service, Joe McDade used his influence to get federal money spent in his electoral district. He brought home the bacon, or rather, pork.

Many then thought and many now think that this kind of political effort is simply wasteful spending, but it kept McDade in office. Not even the big scary indictments that were later added to his resume could keep his constituents from reelecting him. And lest you believe that pork-barrel politics are a quaint relic of the past, we present to you the transportation bill that Congress passed and President George W. Bush signed into law in August 2005. The law contained billions of dollars in pork including, among many other things, $223 million for a bridge to link Ketchikan, Alaska, to an island where fifty people reside, $231 million for an Alaskan bridge to an undeveloped area, $5.8 million for a Vermont snowmobile trail, $3 million to Arkansas for dust control on its rural roads, and $480,000 to restore a historic warehouse on the Erie Canal in New York.*

---

* The figures are from "Pet Projects Make Roads Bill a Real Lulu—of Excess," *USA Today*, August 10, 2005, p. 10a.

maintain party discipline. The split loyalty can also encourage legislators to engage in **pork-barrel politics**, where representatives use their political office to bring federal money to their districts through projects and jobs. The first priority of these legislators is not whether the programs and jobs are necessary, it is whether they can bring home the bacon for their constituents. The more successful the legislator is at satisfying constituent wants, the better the chances for reelection. Again, it is difficult to reconcile some of these projects with the national interest, yet the funds for these projects come out of the national budget.

Furthermore, because the local constituents are the ones who keep the representatives in office, these representatives feel obliged to provide as much service to their constituents as possible. Contrary to the image that most people have of their representatives engaging in important debates, much of the job of legislator is comprised of constituent

DUDE, BACON IS NOT PORK

While bacon may indeed come from a former pig, many have defended the $223 million in the 2006 U.S. transportation budget allocated to build a bridge from Ketchikan, Alaska, to an island where fifty people live, saying the project is important to the national transportation infrastructure. Ketchikan is hemmed in by some rugged mountains and it turns out that in addition to the fifty people living on the island, they also built this little thing called an airport out there. An airport—*Vliegveld* in Dutch—is a long straight piece of road that flying machines called airplanes use to land and take off, and it seems that the airport on this island near Ketchikan is an important one. Not only does it serve Ketchikan and parts of Canada near Ketchikan, it is an important emergency landing strip for commercial flights between the west coast of the United States and Asia. It is the place your plane will land if the meat-like product in your in-flight "meal" gives you a heart attack, for example. It also serves as the landing site for all of the fishermen and other people being flown in to Ketchikan for emergency medical treatment.

However, there just happens to be this pesky channel separating the island from the city hospital. Even in the best of times the ferry ride across adds at least a half hour to the trip to the hospital and in Ketchikan, Alaska, the weather often gets bad enough to prevent the ferry from going anywhere at all. It is not unusual for travelers to get stranded for days, unable to get across that channel to either get to the airport or get home from the airport. That is problematic for the biggest transportation hub in a region, but the biggest problem caused by that pesky channel full of water is how it hinders the airport's transportation role in emergencies. In serious medical emergencies, a half-hour delay either from catching the ferry or from diverting a plane to Juneau instead of Ketchikan, could easily be fatal.

Is the bridge pork or is it bacon, an important part of the U.S. transportation system?

service. In fact, legislators often find themselves playing the undesirable role of ombudsmen, where they and their aides help their constituents cut through the red tape of government, help them secure government housing, assist them in receiving benefits, and sometimes just act like bartenders and listen to problems with no solutions.*

BUREAUCRACY, IT GOES TO ELEVEN[†]

If you had to name a theme for the depiction of bureaucracies in film and literature, ridiculous to the point of sublime would be the first thing that probably comes to mind. *The Hitchhiker's Guide to the Galaxy*[7] opens with Arthur Dent lying in the mud in front of a bulldozer. Arthur is neither intoxicated nor injured; he is simply trying to keep a wrecking crew from demolishing his house. It seems that the local bureaucracy decided to put a highway bypass through his breakfast nook. Arthur's argument with the crew foreman is interrupted by his friend Ford Prefect; Ford not only reveals the fact that he is actually an alien, he also tells Arthur that the Earth is about to be destroyed so a

---

* As the faculty supervisors of many legislative interns, we have heard some hard-to-believe tales of the strange requests that legislators receive from their adoring constituents. These calls can range from people wanting to get relatives into or out of the army to our personal favorite—the lady who called because she wanted her representative to do something about the roving band of stray cats infiltrating the neighborhood and stealing the pies out of her window. We think that one is better than the more routine calls about aliens, don't you?

† We take it for granted that you have all seen *This Is Spinal Tap.*

> **Many of our frustrations with bureaucracies have less to do with their flaws and more to do with their ideals of strict adherence to rule-based actions.**

hyperspatial express route can be constructed. When objections are raised, those in charge of both demolitions argue that notice had been given and Arthur had plenty of opportunity to respond and object. Of course, the paperwork for the demolition of Dent's house was posted in the unlit basement of a government building, and the Earth's notice was posted quite clearly on a notice board that just happens to be on another planet. Apparently the applicable rules said nothing about where the notice had to be posted.

Even if you have never faced the impending agency-mandated destruction of your house or home planet, bureaucracies are the one aspect of government that we all wrestle against and there is probably little need to convince students that they are flawed. Consider the film we opened the chapter with, *Brazil,* and the error committed by the infallible machinery of government. Or, visit pretty much any department of motor vehicles office and time how long it takes before you hear every single one of George Carlin's "Seven Words You Can Never Say on Television." We could send you to Mercer Island in the state of Washington to get a permit to cut a tree out of your backyard. As ridiculous as that might sound, we are not making that one up. You need a permit to cut down a tree, even if a windstorm has already tipped it onto the roof of your home.

Actually, many of our frustrations with bureaucracies have less to do with their flaws and more to do with their ideals of strict adherence to rule-based actions. The actual flaws are a bit more troubling though. In fact, the bulk of the academic literature on bureaucracies reflects a fundamental acceptance of the Frankensteinian image that most people in the general public hold. Bureaucracies are considered to be unresponsive behemoths that not only frighten the average villager but also cannot be effectively controlled by the mad scientists we elected to create them and set them loose on the world. Worse yet, chasing a bureaucracy around with torches and pitchforks does absolutely no good whatsoever. Academic research explicitly describes bureaucracies in terms of controlling them, taming them, overseeing them, influencing them, or capturing them—themes straight out of a monster movie—and it is safe to say that the struggle to cage bureaucracies has been the predominant theme in their studies.

In fact, the presumed impotence of political efforts to control them drives an ongoing debate over the fundamental compatibility of bureaucracy and democracy. Yet we must have bureaucracy. So many of the functions we demand of modern governments are routine, administrative tasks that apply simple rules to regulate, distribute, gather, record, or otherwise interact with the mundane aspects of daily life that it would be impossible to manage them without the noble efforts of professional bureaucrats. Now can we have that permit to cut the stupid tree? I want to build a bridge out of it to prove that it is not a witch.*

---

* This is an obscure and oblique *Monty Python* reference. All real university students will have watched enough *Monty Python* to know exactly to what we are referring. For the rest of you, shame on you for having a life away from the telly, and it is the witch-trial scene from *The Holy Grail.*

In a static and stable world, where the demands on the bureaucracy are predictable enough to allow rules to be created to cover most, if not all, decisions, the ideal of bureaucracy can work. However, this ideal bureaucracy almost immediately runs into difficulties when it clashes with the real world, where change and the unexpected are a normal part of life. In *Brazil,* the bureaucracies have procedures, rules, and forms for just about every contingency, but there was nothing to deal with a mistake. The bug in the printer caused a glitch—changing the surname *Tuttle* to *Buttle*—that sent the wrong man to be tortured and executed and the bureaucracy finds itself paralyzed by the lack of a procedure to deal with such a problem. In the real world, in addition to the bizarre and unexpected whims of chaos and circumstance, there is the simple fact that change is a constant factor. How many agencies, such as the Federal Communications Commission, exist as a direct result of technical or scientific advances of the last one hundred years? How many agencies have radically altered their role in government or society in response to such changes?

Ideally, bureaucracies need to be able to adapt or respond to changes in or challenges from the world around them, but that flexibility conflicts with the ideal of rule-based decision making.

Rules and Hierarchy versus Adaptation, Responsiveness, and Democracy

Exactly how does an organization that is built upon ideals of formality and rigidity manage to find a way to adapt or respond? Given the emphasis Weber* places on hierarchy within bureaucracies, it is clear that if change is needed it will come from the top down, but as with everything else in the study of politics, it is never that simple.

For example, Anthony Downs's concept of **authority leakage** questions if it is even possible for the pantheon of bureaucratic fairy princesses at the top of the hierarchy to effectively direct the actions of the trolls slaving away at the bottom.[8] Even if you assume good-faith efforts on the part of subordinates, the effort top officials direct at controlling the output of a bureaucracy gets distorted as each successive layer of the bureaucracy interprets any ambiguities in the order and adjusts the order to fit its abilities to implement. Even if each of these alterations is minor, they multiply, and accumulate, and magnify one another as the order passes down through the levels within the bureaucracy. As a result, even assuming that the trolls are competent and dedicated to carrying out orders from the bureaucratic fairy princesses, it becomes almost impossible for the top of the hierarchy to consistently and effectively direct the outputs at the bottom. Think of the distortion in terms of the kids' party game, "Telephone," where one child whispers a message to the next, who passes it along to the next. By the time the message reaches the last child in the chain it seldom bears any resemblance whatsoever to the original.

---

* The proper pronunciation of Weber is discussed in the previous chapter. Do try to keep up.

Memorandums go a long way toward getting a command from the top to the bottom with a minimum of distortion, but when the assumption that bureaucrats and bureaucracies are making good-faith efforts to serve the public interest is relaxed or abandoned, or when the very serious limits on the ability or motive of political leaders to invest the effort needed to oversee bureaucracies are recognized, the possibility that bureaucratic responsiveness and adaptation arise from the control exerted by leaders at the top of the hierarchy appears to be quite limited. This is particularly troubling for modern democracies, where responsiveness is the most critical of ideals and we elect leaders with the expectation, or hope, that they will make government—including the unelected bureaucratic structures—respond to the needs, wants, and demands of the public.

The Iron Triangle

The most obvious way to integrate bureaucracies into a democratic system is to create what is called a system of overhead democracy where elected officials—who are periodically held accountable to the desires of the voting public—are put at the top of the bureaucratic hierarchy, or otherwise entrusted with mechanisms that allow them to effectively control the unelected portions of the government. In this way, the public's influence on the bureaucracy is indirect, by operating through representatives, but it is still clearly democratic. However, from the moment the concept of overhead democracy was first labeled and proposed as a means of conceptually integrating bureaucracies into the ideals of democratic government, the debate over the ability of leaders to exert control, even if they had the political impetus to make the effort, has cast serious doubts on a top-down model of a democratic bureaucracy. Downs's authority leakage is one problem, but in applied research, the failure of overhead democracy as a means of subjugating bureaucracies to the interests of either the public or the top-level fairy princesses is most obvious in the concept of the iron triangle.

The problem is that the same electoral dynamics that are expected to encourage the elected leaders to be responsive to the public create an imbalance of interests in the activities of the bureaucracies. This leads to agencies being "captured" by small interest groups, which are often those the bureaucracy is directed to regulate, manage, or otherwise control. The executive and legislature typically have little interest in bureaucratic oversight. The bureaucracies are performing repetitive and mundane governmental functions—nothing flashy that will get on the news. Democratic leaders are more concerned with electoral politics and the oversight of bureaucracies is a high-cost endeavor with little promise of enhancing politicians' standing or providing salient services to the people who vote. It takes a great deal of effort to gather all the information about what a bureaucracy is doing, how well it is doing it, and alternative ways it could be doing things. In addition, the mechanisms that modern democracies give to their leaders to correct the course of wayward bureaucracies are generally cumbersome and

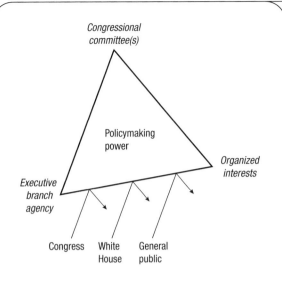

Figure 8.2 The Iron Triangle

Source: William T. Gormley Jr. and Steven J Balla, *Bureaucracy and Democracy: Accountability and Performance* (Washington, D.C.: CQ Press, 2003), 87.

difficult to engage. As a result, elected leaders tend to have little interest in exerting the effort necessary to monitor and control bureaucracies.

In contrast, the interest groups directly affected by the bureaucracy have a great deal of interest in the bureaucracy and in controlling or influencing its outputs. Farmers care a great deal about the Farm Bureau. The airline industry has a great deal of interest in the Federal Aviation Administration. Given the effect that a bureaucracy can have on the welfare of a group it is supposed to regulate or assist, it is often worthwhile for those most directly affected to make the effort and spend the money to influence the bureaucracy. This creates a situation where a bureaucracy can be captured and redirected so it focuses on the needs of an interest group, rather than the public interest, or even its original mandate. The result is an **iron triangle** formed by bureaucracies, interest groups, and elected officials, impenetrable by outside actors. Lobbying by the interest groups encourages elected officials to craft legislation that reflects the preferences of those interest groups. In return, the interest groups then provide resources such as cash or mobilized voters to support the reelection efforts of cooperative elected officials. Bureaucratic agencies that respond as the interest groups desire then receive rewards from elected officials like preferences in budgeting. This gives the bureaucracy a motive to listen to the interest group.

The end result appears to be a democratic process gone wrong. Since elected leaders oversee a tremendous number of bureaucracies, they seldom have much expertise in issues related to any one bureaucracy and they usually have to rely on information provided by the interest groups or the bureaucracies. Bureaucracies have limited resources as well and often obtain much of their information from the interest groups they were meant to regulate. The interest groups can then use their intense interest and their often substantial resources to influence both the elected officials and the bureaucracies. They can influence the actions and sustain this relationship at the expense of the broader public. While this might suggest that bureaucracies could be responsive to powerful interest groups, it is pessimistic in regard to bending them to the broader public interest, and it certainly does not bode well for any kind of democratic bureaucracy. In fact, the idea of an iron triangle, combined with a few key examples, is probably the reason many scholars and analysts worry about the very basic compatibility of bureaucratic and democratic government.

The fact is, however, that we do have bureaucracies that function in democracies and democracies that function quite well, despite the necessary evil of delegating a substantial amount of responsibility to bureaucracies. There are clear and even disturbing examples of agencies, particularly regulatory agencies, being effectively captured by well-financed interest groups. In some cases the influence even extends to the point where the government agencies actively work against elected officials and the broader public interest. Do these examples necessarily mean that bureaucracies are incompatible with the ideals of democracy?

There are a huge, tremendous, and stupendous number of bureaucracies functioning in any modern government and the vast majority of these agencies perform their assigned tasks quite effectively in the democratic context. They even adapt to changing needs or demands of society. We may poke fun at—or mercilessly taunt—the U.S. Postal Service, but it actually provides an incredibly difficult service with remarkable efficiency. You can send a letter, postcard, or a fish head, to a specific location on the opposite side of the continent for far less than the cost of a candy bar.

Agency Theory and the Responsive Bureaucracy

From its introduction in the 1950s, the iron triangle or capture theory of bureaucracy was the central conceptual theme in the study of bureaucracies. The assumption that bureaucracies were fundamentally flawed to the point of threatening the very existence of democracy was the starting point for every analysis, critique, and call for reform. However, this began to change in the 1980s. Political scientists borrowed—as they often do—from the study of economics and business the concept of **agency theory** and adapted it to the somewhat different context of government. With the results produced by some seriously fancy statistical analyses, scholars became more positive about the potential for bureaucratic responsiveness to the demands or desires of the broader public. New research seemed to show an interactive relationship between bureaucracies and political forces in the democratic context. Bureaucracies appeared to adapt to their political environment, responding to both hierarchical—top-down—and pluralistic—bottom-up—domestic influences by incrementally changing their processes, areas of focus, and even their levels of activity.

Agency theory, also referred to as the **principal-agent model**, is structured around the basic premise that bureaucracies are agents that act on behalf of the legislature in a relationship similar to a business contract. Bureaucracies are essentially hired by the legislature to perform a specified set of functions. The relationship is clearly hierarchical, with the bureaucracy treating elected officials like customers. However, unlike the conceptual foundations of earlier studies, which included an implicit assumption that bureaucracies are only controlled or influenced when their democratically elected masters are actively watching over every action, the principal-agent model requires little if any direct monitoring by elected officials. The basic dynamics might be more easily conceptualized as a simple contract made in a context other than the legislative-bureaucratic relationship.

The dynamic can be shown with a simple example. In the same way that a hypothetical suburban dentist with two kids and a Land Rover does not sit and closely watch every action of the hung-over landscaper hired to tend his yard, the legislature does not need to constantly supervise every action of a bureaucracy. Instead of the costly effort of constant supervision of the landscaper's activity, the fictional dentist chooses the low-cost option of keeping an eye open for unsatisfactory results. Should a hedge be poorly trimmed or some flowers die the dentist can complain to the landscaper. If the problems go uncorrected, the dentist can withhold payment, or hire a new landscaper.

Similarly, we can think of elected officials as the dentist—the principal—and bureaucracies as the landscapers—the agents. If unsatisfactory output from a bureaucracy is brought to the attention of its elected overseers, they can complain or hold hearings, and if the problems go uncorrected they can pull out "the big stick behind the door" and threaten the budget of the bureaucracy, the tenure of upper-level officials, or even the continued existence of the bureaucracy as an entity. The elected officials do not have to watch the bureaucracy every minute, they just have to monitor the results and keep an eye out for something to go wrong. Bureaucracies do not want to get tagged as a problem, so they generally try to do the best possible job so that elected officials will never see a need to intervene.

The research conducted from the theoretical foundation of the principal-agent model has provided more than just the conceptual impetus for breaking away from the idea that constant monitoring was necessary for control. It has also led to a substantial foundation of evidence demonstrating the responsiveness of bureaucracies. Despite the fact that very few upper-level bureaucrats are political appointees and the ability of elected officials to directly monitor and direct the actions of their subordinates is limited, bureaucracies clearly do adjust, incrementally at least, to the will of U.S. presidents, becoming more conservative or liberal in response to the perspective of the president. They also shift their procedures and activities to address issues of particular interest to elected leaders. A trip to the department of motor vehicles may still be worthy of Dante's inferno, but bureaucracies, including notoriously indifferent state agencies, do respond to a wide variety of public and popular influences, including local politics, business groups and patronage institutions, and even large or loud expressions of public opinion. A summary of the most recent work from the agency perspective on bureaucracy might reasonably emphasize just how many different influences have now been shown to spur bureaucratic adaptations and adjustments. Scholars and critics still express concerns about control and responsiveness, but the idea that the uncontrolled growth of bureaucratic government could destroy democracy seems to have become far less of a concern than it was even just a few years ago.*

The Cockroach Theory of Bureaucracy

It is interesting that the same cinematic masterpiece that inspired Tiger Woods to abandon a promising career as a professional bass angler and make that often-questioned foray into golf—where he still struggles to win a measly 50 percent of the tournaments he enters—also gives us a hint at how to rethink the whole bureaucracy and democracy thing. The pleasantly deranged and hygienically challenged groundskeeper in *Caddyshack*[9] seizes upon the task of eliminating a pesky gopher. In taking on such a dangerous mission, he knows that to survive he must immerse himself in the mind of the enemy. He must think like the gopher. He must act like the gopher. He must become one with the gopher. While we never realized that gophers were so fond of plastic explosives, the point about thinking like the gopher is inspiring.

To understand a bureaucracy, perhaps we need to think like the bureaucracy. One notable consistency in most of the research and analyses of bureaucracies is that it all seems to come from perspectives outside of the bureaucracies themselves. Though the imperatives that drive the bureaucracy are obviously central to the principal-agent model, the predominant questions addressed by principal-agent theory reflect the long-standing concern regarding ability of the principal—the elected officials—to control or direct the agent—the bureaucracy. How do elected officials control them? How do interest groups capture them? How can broader democratic forces influence them? Instead, perhaps we should think like the gopher. What motivates bureaucracies to act? What will motivate them to adapt or change? If agency theory is correct and bureaucracies consciously strive to avoid the potential punishments that could rain down upon the agency like anvils falling on the coyote, how does that actually work from the bureaucracy's side of things?

Bureaucracies must constantly struggle against other demands for limited funds within the government budget. Bureaucracies and bureaucrats realize that if they fail to provide a public good proportional to the government resources they consume, they face the prospect of being substantially sanctioned. At the extreme, the entire bureaucracy could be eliminated by the public officials responsible for budgeting and oversight. A more realistic depiction is that the bureaucracies that fail to meet their public service mandate and draw critical attention in the domestic political arena are likely to suffer a degradation of their position in the competition for resources. One of the first

---

* Most of this research has studied bureaucracies in the United States. However, it applies to all representative democracies. See Douglas A. Van Belle, Jean-Sébastien Rioux, and David M. Potter, *Media, Bureaucracies, and Foreign Aid: A Comparative Analysis of the United States, the United Kingdom, Canada, France and Japan* (New York: Palgrave/Macmillan, 2004).

The Imperfections of Political Institutions

threats leveled at a wayward bureaucracy is the dreaded budget cut. Additionally, threats might be directed at the tenure of the bureaucracy's executives. An embattled bureaucracy might have its director or directors replaced, and/or the directors of an embattled bureaucracy might try to fend off such a replacement by "cleaning house" and shuffling lower levels of management within the agency. Both of these potential punishments motivate bureaucracies and bureaucrats to adjust to the demands and dynamics of domestic politics.

When considered from the perspective of the bureaucracy, however, the real question is what happens when the infamous big stick that elected officials could use to beat them senseless stays behind the door? The scramble to respond to threatened budget cuts is obvious, but how often is the full extent of possible sanctions against a bureaucracy even mentioned or considered in political discourse? We know that bureaucracies constantly make incremental changes that are not necessarily tied to any specific threat from an elected official. How do they know what changes to make? How do they monitor their political environment? What cues do they use to shape their choices to avoid even being threatened?

It seems logical to propose that bureaucracies would try to avoid the harsh negative sanctions that could be turned against them by adjusting their actions in accordance with the same cues they expect their potential punishers—elected officials—are using. In modern democracies, the news media provide the most prominent sources of political cues and provide an easy, inexpensive way to monitor the domestic political environment. High levels of coverage of an issue indicate that it is important, or will be important, depending on whether you believe the media drives or follows the attention of the democratic political machine. Preemptively matching bureaucratic outputs with the indicators of public demand provided by the news media is an easy way for bureaucracies and bureaucrats to try to get their job right and avoid negative attention and critical scrutiny of their operations.

While most bureaucrats have neither six legs nor an exoskeleton, this idea of working to avoid negative attention allows us to compare them to cockroaches—and since we can, we will. Like the beloved patron insect of restaurant kitchens, the bureaucracy that finds itself caught out in the light is the one that is going to be stomped on. Thus, an effective strategy that both bureaucracies and roaches can use to thrive and survive is to avoid attention—to actively avoid the light. For bureaucracies, **the cockroach theory of bureaucracy** is focused on the glaring spotlight of a media that is driven by business imperatives to seek out government failures that can be depicted as scandals and sources of political conflict. Thus, bureaucracies serve the public as best as they can and hope to stay hidden and well-fed in the darker recesses of an anonymous bureaucratic government.

Or, turning back to our fictional dentist, he does not even have to be the one who monitors the work of the landscaper. Instead, he can rely on the nosy neighbors across the street, counting on them to point out when the lawn does not look right. To push the analogy all the way to the bitter end, if the hung-over landscaper knows that the nosy neighbors are the ones the dentist relies on to spot problems, then the landscaper can look to the yard across the street for hints. What flowers does the neighbor plant in the spring? How short do they cut their lawn? How do they trim their shrubs? How are the garden gnomes arranged? By keeping in sync with the neighbor* the landscaper avoids ever having his work criticized and brought to the attention of the dentist.

Elected officials, with so many bureaucracies to oversee and so many better things to be doing, follow a similar strategy. They rely on others, particularly the news media, to alert them to problems with the bureaucratic institutions of government. Bureaucrats know this and they carefully monitor the news media as one way of avoiding getting caught in its spotlight.

IT MAY NOT BE PERFECT, BUT IT STILL WORKS

In the last two chapters we have explored both the ideals and the flaws in the institutions of modern democratic governance. The choice to focus on democratic institutions was a practical one. Unless the North Korean government actually writes the check for the four million copies it ordered of this book, these are the institutions that most of the students reading this book will recognize and will have the greatest interest in understanding. We continue with the emphasis on democracy when we get to chapter 10, for the same reasons, but we do want to caution against dismissing nondemocratic ways of governing or overidealizing the democratic forms around the world. There is only so much we can put in an introductory text and we decided to focus on democracy.

We hope that this chapter has made it clear to students that democratic does not equal perfect and if we were to claim a coherent theme to this portion of the book, it would be that there are a variety of imperfect ways of governing but that despite their failings, these institutions do manage to work fairly well. Similarly, nondemocratic institutions are imperfect and they also work. China, Libya, Saudi Arabia, Monaco—there are plenty of nondemocratic or partially democratic political systems that function imperfectly but effectively in the Plasma Television age and we should point out that, historically speaking, democracy is quite rare.

Finally, we would like to end this chapter with a completely gratuitous reference to Jon Stewart's book, *America (The Book): A Citizen's Guide to Democracy Inaction*.[10] Readers, particularly Jon, should note just how difficult it was to find a way to offer a gratuitous reference in this chapter. Our discussion of the imperfections of government provided so many opportunities to make a meaningful reference to it, that some may have noticed that we failed to mention it. However, to have a reason to reference Jon's book would have ruined everything. If you have a reason to assault someone with praise, it just is not sucking up.

---

* "In sync," not 'N Sync. Please, we do have some standards of decency here.

KEY TERMS

agency theory / **188**
authority leakage / **185**
the cockroach theory of
    bureaucracy / **191**
cohabitation / **179**
divided government / **172**
gerrymandering / **180**
gridlock / **172**
immobilism / **178**

imperial presidency / **171**
iron triangle / **187**
minority government / **179**
policy stability / **173**
pork-barrel politics / **182**
principal-agent model / **188**
unity government / **179**
vote of no confidence / **174**

CHAPTER SUMMARY

When trying to fully appreciate how governments work, it is important to appreciate both the ideals and the flaws associated with institutions. There are no such things as perfect institutions; there are problems associated with every system. The presidential system can suffer from either an overly strong president or from the gridlock that is the result of divided government. Parliamentary systems can face problems with stability that derive from the need to form coalitions and the ever-present threat of a vote of no confidence. There are concerns in all democratic systems—because of gerrymandering in district systems and coalitions in proportional systems—with how representative parliaments are of the wishes of the population. All governments rely on bureaucracy, but government agencies are far from ideal. There are consistently concerns about how responsive bureaucracies are to the public and fears that interested parties will take control of the agencies that regulate them. However, there are factors that keep even unelected bureaucrats responsive to the public. Students should learn two very important lessons from this chapter. First, all government institutions are imperfect. We often take for granted that nondemocratic regimes have flaws, but we do not usually focus a critical eye on democratic institutions. With closer analysis we can make more informed judgments about the relative effectiveness of the institutions that nations employ. Second, it is always cathartic, even if only slightly humorous, to compare bureaucrats to the *Periplaneta americana*.

STUDY QUESTIONS AND EXERCISES

1. Both parliamentary and presidential systems can face situations where it is very difficult for the government to make new policies. What are the terms associated with these difficulties and what are the causes?
2. What factors make bureaucracies responsive to a wide variety of public and popular influences?
3. In the last chapter we asked you to contrast the benefits of a parliamentary system with the benefits of the presidential system. Now take into consideration the

potential problems associated with these systems. Which do you prefer now? Have you changed your mind? Why or why not?

4. What is gerrymandering, and what are its implications for democracy?

5. In this chapter we identified a number of "bugs in the machine" with regard to political institutions. Based on your experience and your observations of events in the news, can you identify other "bugs"?

WEBSITES TO EXPLORE

worldpolicy.org/globalrights/prindex.html. The World Policy Institute's Project for Global Democracy and Human Rights Electoral Systems page contains a host of information, including definitions, editorials, and other links related to electoral systems, with a focus on proportional representation.

www.aceproject.org/main/english/es/es10.htm. The Administration and Cost of Elections Project's Electoral Systems page contains an overview of the world's electoral systems.

www.cia.gov/cia/publications/chiefs/index.html. Chiefs of State and Cabinet Members of Foreign Governments contains links from the U.S. Central Intelligence Agency.

www.funtrivia.com/trivia-quiz/World/Parliaments-of-the-World-23158.html. Check out Fun Trivia.com's Parliaments of the World to find difficult trivia about the world's legislatures.

www.ipu.org/english/home.htm. The Inter-Parliamentary Union, the Web site for the International Organization of Parliaments of Sovereign States has useful links to parliaments around the world and other parliamentary related information.

www.keele.ac.uk/depts/por/elections.htm. The Keele Guide to Elections and Electoral Systems on the Internet, contains links from Keele University's School of Politics, International Relations, and the Environment.

www.mtholyoke.edu/acad/polit/damy/prlib.htm. PR Library has Professor Douglas J. Amy's collected readings about proportional representation.

Three guys who made people equate law with justice, and five guys who made people equate law with something else.

CHAPTER 9

Courts and Law
Politics behind the Gavel

Imagine a golden age of idealism. Actually, the age was more greenish-mauve than golden, but it was still an idyllic time of joy and beauty. Video game graphics looked like they came off an electrocuted typewriter, but everyone still thought they were amazing. All the rock stars looked a bit **electrocuted, too, with their hair** either an impossibly big explosion of frizz or sculpted to look like plastic laminated by a lightning bolt, but that was cool, too. It was the magical time when somebody came up with the idea of adding video to music to create Video Discography. VD turned out to be a poor choice of acronym, however, since no one wanted to admit staying up late to catch the new VD from Madonna. But when some marketing genius started calling this invention music videos, they became so popular that everyone watched them over and over around the clock.

In that idealistic, greenish-mauve age, if a professor stood in front of the class and stated that the law is political, many students in the class would have slapped their hands against their plastic-looking sculpted hair and loudly protested. From under their massive explosion of frizzy hair, other students would have argued that politics is about those maximizing their own advantage, about deal-making, maneuvering, and scheming to get more. Law cannot possibly be political. Law is about justice, fairness, reason, principles, and doing what is right. Today, students are much brighter,* or at least a lot more cynical and critical and it is difficult to find students who are the least bit surprised when we say that the law is political.

We blame TV.

---

* This compliment is wholly unnecessary and should be ignored completely.

Seriously. In every single one of *Law and Order's*[1] forty-seven spinoffs, rip-offs, or competitors, every third episode has a plot about someone with wealth or political power thwarting, warping, or driving the personally motivated application of the law. *The Practice,*[2] *Boston Legal,*[3] and all the other law-firm shows are even worse, with storylines about twisting the law to the point of breaking it in the sometimes pathological pursuit of victory in court. This was not always the case. In the old days, the law was the law and the shows featured Joe Friday and Bill Gannon[4] methodically uncovering just the facts, ma'am, or Perry Mason[5] finding the truth and winning the case at the very last second. Even when *L.A. Law*[6] added a bit of soap opera scandal to the law drama, the less than ideal parts centered around whom Arnie was sleeping with or fights within the firm. The law itself was always this ideal, abstract absolute virtue and it was always about the truth and righteous justice.

In the last couple of decades, not only did television fiction about the law change, the TV also thrust a number of troubling public events into our living rooms that have eroded people's idealism about the relationship between law and politics:

- *Rodney King video and trial (1991–1992):* The L.A. police were caught on videotape savagely beating Rodney King, an African American man, with their night sticks, but were acquitted by a jury, after the state court trial was moved out of Los Angeles to a suburban venue. The officers were later found guilty of the filmed beating when a federal trial was held in an urban location.

  —"Denny Crane!"—

- *O. J. Simpson (1995):* Despite a mountain of evidence against him, his dream team of defense lawyers was so successful that O. J. was acquitted of the murder of his ex-wife Nicole Brown Simpson and Ronald Goldman after only a few hours of deliberation by the jury. O. J. was later found responsible for their deaths in civil court and ordered to pay massive damages, but, thanks to the deft use of bankruptcy laws, paid little or nothing to the families of the victims and still lives an opulent lifestyle in Florida.

  —"Denny Crane!"—

- *Justice Robert Bork confirmation hearings (1987):* Interest groups combined to defeat Ronald Reagan's well-qualified Supreme Court nominee Robert Bork because of his conservative political beliefs, especially concerning use of the original intent of the framers as a strict standard of constitutional interpretation.

  —"Denny Crane!"—

- *Anita Hill's testimony regarding the Clarence Thomas nomination (1991):* On the Senate floor, George H. W. Bush's Supreme Court nominee Clarence Thomas faced charges of sexual harassment from Anita Hill, who worked under Thomas at

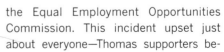

> **It took a long time for political scientists to study courts and law in the same way that they studied other political institutions.**

the Equal Employment Opportunities Commission. This incident upset just about everyone—Thomas supporters believed the charges were politically motivated and unjust, while his opponents believed the charges were not taken seriously when he was confirmed.

—"Denny Crane!"—

- *Investigations of Bill Clinton (1998):* The president, a lawyer, testified under oath that the truth of an earlier statement—that he was not involved in a sexual relationship with Monica Lewinsky—that was given as part of a deposition in the Paula Jones sexual harassment lawsuit against Clinton all depended on what the meaning of the word "is" is. These verbal gymnastics thus confirmed some people's worst beliefs about the law and lawyers.

—"Denny Crane!"—

- *The 2000 Presidential Election (2000):* Florida state courts and the U.S. Supreme Court play significant roles in resolving the contested election results from Florida in the 2000 presidential election and many believe that justices on both benches were eager to act in a highly partisan manner instead of distancing themselves and restricting their involvement to the detached interpretation of the law.

—"Denny Crane!"—

Scandals are nothing new and fictional accounts of the politicization of the law predate the death, or even the birth, of the eight-track tape. But the fiction and drama of the last few decades are indeed distinctly different in their intense focus on the political aspects of law as the driving force behind the plot or episodic story arc. Still even with this barrage of real and fictional events that show the political side of law, the current willingness of more people to view the law and courts in the context of politics is somewhat surprising. Even the people who should know better have long been reluctant to surrender their ideals of law. It took a long time for political scientists to study courts and law in the same way that they studied other political institutions. In fact, colleges still frequently teach courses, such as constitutional law, where lecturers treat law as if it were drafted by the gods and delivered through the oracle at Delphi, rather than* tainted by politics. For some strange reason these idealistic classes remain very popular with those planning to go to law school and even some of the less venomous and less reptilian creatures inhabiting universities find something naggingly appealing about thinking of law and the courts as if they inhabit some

---

* This is an ancient Greek thing and has nothing to do with satellite radios or the Matrix movies. Well, it might have something to do with the Matrix movies but that is only because they stole the idea of the oracle as a source of ultimate truth. The Greeks did it first.

kind of germ-free buffer zone protected from the noxious diseases affecting other political institutions.

The current willingness to accept the political nature of law appears even more confusing if we probe deeper. It turns out that most people still cling to the idea that law is, in fact, different from other political institutions. Something about the law leads people to think about it first and foremost in terms of justice, fairness, and the protection of rights. If you are unconvinced, think of how much more disturbing it is to discover that a judge is corrupt than it is to see a politician claiming that a free weekend at a mobster's Star Trek-themed brothel was nothing more than an ordinary "campaign contribution."

LAW AND POLITICS

As we mentioned earlier in this book, politics consists of the individual or combined actions of individuals, governments, and groups, with public consequences, aimed at accomplishing desired goals. If we take that definition seriously, it is difficult to argue that the law and courts are anything but political. Whether it is the politics involved in writing laws, appointing judges to the bench, the police selectively enforcing laws, the prosecutors deciding to bring some types of cases and defendants to trial, sentencing Martha Stewart to a minimum-discomfort detention facility that had cell-decorating contests instead of sending her to a real prison, or limiting the access of some plaintiffs to the courts, the law and courts are clearly political institutions.

This tension between the real and the ideal, the tug between the political nature of the law and our feelings of ideal justice, emerge clearly in Harper Lee's *To Kill a Mockingbird*.[7] The story is narrated by Scout, who recalls growing up in Maycomb County in southern Alabama during the Great Depression. Her father, Atticus Finch, in one of the book's main story lines, is defending an African American man, Tom Robinson, who is being tried for rape. It is abundantly clear that Tom is being framed and it is painfully obvious that even though everyone should be able to see this, he will still be found guilty, but Atticus Finch is still compelled to defend Tom because, "If I didn't, I couldn't hold up my head in town, I couldn't represent this county in the legislature, I couldn't even tell you or Jem not to do something again."[8] Atticus Finch is a true believer. He believes in justice, he believes in the rule of law, and he believes that the system should work. He believes that it must be made to work.

However, despite his unwavering faith in the law, Atticus cannot totally ignore the obvious. The racist and segregationist political system of the day is thoroughly embedded into the courts, which cannot be counted on to provide the justice in which Atticus believes. At trial, Atticus demonstrates that the disabled Tom could not have committed the crime, that his accuser was not trustworthy, and that the raped girl's father, Bob Ewell, was the likely culprit. Atticus appears to be making headway with the jury, and his closing argument is impassioned as it captures Americans' presumptions of justice:

I'm no idealist to believe firmly in the integrity of our courts and in the jury system—that is no ideal to me, it is a living, working reality. Gentlemen, a court is no better than each man of you sitting before me on this jury. A court is only as sound as its jury, and a jury is only as sound as the men who make it up. I am confident that you gentlemen will review without passion the evidence you have heard, come to a decision, and restore this defendant to his family. In the name of God, do your duty.[9]

It is a great speech. Atticus does not win. The jury finds Tom Robinson guilty as the politics of the time wins out over justice, but it is still a great speech that captures the coexistence of the ideal and the real. Real life and politics are contrasted with the ideal of law throughout the novel. At the end, Tom Robinson dies while trying to escape from prison. When Bob Ewell's attack on the Finch children ends abruptly with the pointy end of a knife stuck in Ewell's chest, Atticus, true to his faith in the law, insists that Ewell's death not be covered up even though he thinks his son Jem is to blame. The sheriff, however, insists that the attacker fell on his knife. This is obviously impossible, but the sheriff argues that even though this outcome may be outside the law it fits the ideal of justice that is supposed to be embodied in the law. In the end, Atticus is convinced to abandon the law and the courts and accept this roundabout route to the justice that those institutions were supposed to have provided. Atticus decides to live with the political and social reality of the day.

To Kill a Mockingbird most clearly demonstrates how the politics of the day can permeate the legal system. While the racism of the 1930s is an extreme example, we should also expect that today's politics permeate the law and the courts. Law and courts are political institutions, and the legal system is but a subsystem of the larger political system. We should thus expect that political parties will make use of the courts to seek policy goals, that individuals will use the legal system to make their political careers, that those with resources will fare better in the legal system than those without resources, and that many of the same rules that apply to other political institutions will also apply to the courts.

Law on the Books versus Law in Action

Atticus's decision to go along with the sheriff's version of events also demonstrates one other important facet of studying the law. There is a fundamental difference—as the legal scholar Roscoe Pound (1870–1964) recognized—between **law in books** and **law in action**.[10] The law in books—or the law on the books—is comprised of the laws as they are written, while law in action—or the law in practice—relates to how laws are enforced in the real world. The law on the books is the world of appellate courts, while law in practice involves the way trial courts and other legal actors implement law in the real world. If he followed the law on the books, the sheriff would have arrested Boo Radley, the man he knew delivered the pointy-ended knife blow. The law on the books dictates that this must be done regardless of how it would affect Boo's life or the lives of the Finch children. We all are aware of the difference between the law on the books and the law in action from our own interactions with the legal system.

When you drive through the Poconos on Interstate 80, the signs clearly say "Speed Limit 55 Mph." That is the law on the books. However, most people seem to believe that Interstate 80 means you have to drive eighty miles per hour* and anyone who drives at the legal limit is likely to get a sore neck watching people gesturing rudely as they speed past. The law on the books says 55 mph, but even if you are not pretending to race the Pocono 500, you are probably driving 60 mph because you know that the law in practice is that no police officer is likely to pull you over until you hit 61 or more on the radar.

The U.S. Constitution requires that criminal defendants be read their Miranda rights before they are interrogated, but does that always happen? The law makes no distinctions based on race or wealth, but we all know these things do matter in reality. Even a constitutional right, James Madison once observed, is nothing more than a "parchment barrier."[11] A constitutional right is dependent on the people for protection. The reality is that law depends upon political actors for enforcement, and if relying on political actors, we should expect that laws will be political. We should also expect that if we really want to understand the way that the laws operate and if we really want to know how courts act, we must study the law as it is really enforced and how judicial officers actually behave. Thus, political scientists are interested not only in what the laws say, but how they are put into practice. In other words, political scientists treat legal actors like other political actors.

Symbols

Even this far into the chapter after we have been arguing the whole way that the law is political, a significant number of students will still have a lingering feeling that the law is something different. Why? In part, this is because the courts use a variety of symbols and other tools to increase their authority and to encourage people to believe that something different is going on. Courtrooms are packed with symbols. The judge's robes, the gavel, the ornate courtrooms, the raised platform, the bible, the flags, the ornate seal that declares that it is a court of Hoboken or the State of West Virginia are all examples of the symbols of authority found in courtrooms. The Supreme Court building in Washington, D.C., is quite literally a marble palace to house the law of the nation.

These symbols are more than mere ornamentation; the political actors in the judicial arena utilize symbols because people react to them. These symbols help create and sustain the perception that judges are different from politicians. People's beliefs

---

* Though this is incorrect, this belief seems to explain a great deal. It explains the way people drive in Daytona, Florida, which is on Interstate 95, and it also explains why Los Angeles has such traffic problems as Interstate 5 and Interstate 10 intersect in the middle of the city.

that the courts are different, facilitated by the use of symbols, allow political partici-pants to operate with a legitimacy and a solemnity that is not found in other political arenas. However, if we strip away these symbols, it becomes clearer that the law really is like other political institutions. Imagine a court case being held in a hotel meeting room with an ordinary person in charge. Envisage the Supreme Court justices in ratty jeans and sitting on folding chairs. Ponder what it might be like to have lawyers actu-ally speak normal English.* When we strip away the symbols, courts do not seem quite as majestic.†

Words are symbols—perhaps the most powerful of symbols—and even the words used in the courts, the language of the law, reinforce the idea, belief, impression, con-jecture, notion, postulation, and presupposition that something different is occurring in the courtroom. Of course this special language also allows lawyers to preserve their role as the translator for the courts, a role that serves them well both professionally and financially.‡

THE FUNCTIONS OF COURTS

Courts obviously play an important role in nations—clearly, every country has them—but what exactly do they do that makes courts so essential? In one sense, the courts enforce the norms of society. Regardless of the type of government that exists, the amount of freedom that citizens possess, it is nevertheless true that the courts are going to enforce the country's basic rules. If the nation is a dictatorship, the courts' treatment of protestors will send a message to those who may question the authority of the regime. In *To Kill a Mockingbird,* although everyone knows that Tom Robinson is innocent, the court's ruling sends a chilling message to Maycomb's African American population and it reinforces the racial power relationships of Maycomb society. When an Islamic religious court in Nigeria sentenced a woman to death by stoning for the crime of conceiving a child outside of marriage in 2002, that court was also enforcing the norms of that nation.§

We can also point to more functional roles that the courts play. According to judicial scholars Walter F. Murphy, C. Herman Pritchett, Lee Epstein, and Jack Knight,[12] there are three principal roles that courts play in society. First, courts engage in **dispute resolution**.

---

* Contemplate how many synonyms there are for thinking about things.

† The robes are one symbol we probably don't want to strip away. This is partly because we really do not want to know what Clarence Thomas is wearing underneath, but it is also because the robes are indicative of how much more symbol-laden the courts are in comparison to most other branches of government. A parliament other than the New Zealand Parliament, which is housed in something that looks like the internal workings of an electric razor, may have a fancy building, but few have dress codes. Legislators can usually wear any old $2,000 Italian suit they have lying around.

‡ Insert your own lawyer joke here. Do be kind and try your best to be witty, as someone in your classroom is likely to be studying for the LSATs and will sue you if it is not funny.

§ A higher appeals court eventually overturned the penalty but it took significant international pressure and it is unclear if this would have happened in the absence of outside intervention.

They peacefully settle disputes and keep order in society. Second, like other political institutions, courts make policy. Courts are not only involved in applying the law, they also play a role in shaping the law. Third, courts can play an important role in monitoring governmental action. Courts make sure that government entities act within their responsibilities and also play a role in punishing government officials who run afoul of the law.

Dispute Resolution

Court cases are so much a part of the landscape that it is easy for us to take them for granted. But what would happen to society if there were are no courts? You could have the justice of the Wild West, vigilante justice, or just plain chaos. *To Kill a Mockingbird* shows what can happen when people try to take the law into their own hands as Atticus confronts the angry mob that is determined to lynch Tom Robinson. Perhaps the most important role that courts play is that they work to settle disputes in a peaceable fashion. Courts accomplish this through formal proceedings. The state brings charges against those accused of crimes. One company sues another for a breach of contract. Someone brings a malpractice suit against a doctor charged with incompetence. By performing this function, the courts provide an avenue for citizens to settle their disputes in an orderly, organized, and authoritative fashion.

While we are most familiar with the way that courts settle disputes in a formal fashion, it is also true that they settle disputes in informal ways as well. For example, by sentencing those convicted of crimes, judges also help to set what might be called the **"going rate"** for punishment. In other words, judges set the context for plea bargaining as defense attorneys and prosecutors negotiate about the appropriate penalty for an offense for which a plaintiff pleads guilty. This is also true for cases where people are suing. Courts and juries are involved in finding companies liable for wrongdoing. However, past decisions set the context for future relations between plaintiffs (those doing the suing) and defendants (those being sued). The litigants (those involved in a lawsuit) may choose to bargain in the hopes of reaching an out-of-court settlement instead of incurring the risks and costs involved in proceeding to a jury trial. Furthermore, once courts reach decisions, those decisions will shape the advice given to potential future litigants. In other words, people, corporations, interest groups, and others will decide whether or not to initiate lawsuits based on past decisions and will even alter their behavior because of the outcomes in previous cases.

Policymaking

Perhaps courts act the most like other political institutions when they make policy. Officially, courts are not supposed to engage in making policy. Officially, courts are only supposed to resolve the disputes others have over policy. The Supreme Court justices, for example, are supposed to use the Constitution to find the appropriate resolution to a high-stakes dispute between policy-making branches of government, such as Congress and the president. However, whether the issue is the death penalty, abortion, sexual harassment, or any of the hundreds of other topics in which courts become involved it is clear that in making those decisions, the courts make policy.

In the most obvious way, judges can set local criminal policy through sentencing decisions, bail decisions, their willingness to accept plea bargains, or their propensity to issue warrants based upon one type of evidence or another. Consider the mainstay of modern detective drama, the use of DNA for identification of suspects. All of the rules about how it can be used and what it means in a criminal court—in other words, the policy regarding the legal aspects of using DNA—is set by judges listening to the testimony of experts and making decisions that stand as the precedents others will follow in the future.

Policymaking also occurs when courts are involved in **statutory interpretation**. That is, even if one were to accept the proposition that courts merely apply the law, by defining how those laws can and cannot be interpreted, courts set policy. Legislatures often pass laws that are vaguely written and thus open to a wide range of interpretations. Courts are then confronted with the question of whether the law was meant to apply to specific situations and/or specific litigants. The application of the law requires specificity, so courts must interpret what the statute precisely means, that is they engage in statutory interpretation but as soon as the courts start interpreting the law, they are, in effect, making policy.

Even well written laws can be open to this kind of judicial policymaking. Because a nondiscrimination law meant to ensure African Americans the right to live in any neighborhood in a city says all persons must be treated equally, it can be interpreted to mean that homosexuals must be allowed to march in the St. Patrick's Day Parade. A law intended to keep T-shirts with obscene slogans out of public school classrooms can be interpreted as giving school boards the power to require uniforms, or ban lipstick, or ban unnatural hair colors, as part of setting a minimum standard of dress and appearance. Going the other way on the school dress code issue, courts could rule that it is an infringement on freedom of speech to allow some shirts but not others. That same court could turn around and rule that it is not an abridgment to the right of free speech when a local government restricts the posting of signs in a town. It is clear that the courts make policy through interpretation and the courts' understanding of the law will stay in place unless the legislature should choose to pass a specific law that changes that interpretation.

Still, even if a legislative body passes a specific and clearly worded law, the courts can still become involved in policy through their interpretation of that law. Consider the question of the education curriculum in the U.S. public school classroom. In the United States, every state gets to set its own policy regarding what should be taught in their classrooms, and many states leave a great deal of the detail to individual school districts. The lines of responsibility for this aspect of educational policy are clearly defined

> **The courts are given the task of monitoring the actions of the government and governmental officials to make sure they follow prescribed rules and procedures, including the ones that check the behavior of the others.**

and nowhere in any of the laws, by-laws, debates, or other documentation is any policy role reserved for the court, yet through their decisions, the courts still set education policy.

Since 1925, when the Scopes Monkey Trial brought the question of teaching evolution to the attention of everyone in the United States, the fight over the claim that your neighbor evolved from pond scum has been a contentious issue. Courts have become involved in this policy matter because of the constitutional requirement of a separation between the church and state. Because public schools are government institutions, they are constitutionally prohibited from advocating religious doctrine or belief. Thus, they are not allowed to include the Hebrew/Christian biblical account of creation as part of their biology curriculum no matter how much a local community or local school board may wish to do so. As recently as December 2005, courts were still ruling on this policy issue, with a federal judge offering a sweeping and sharply worded decision against the school board in Dover, Pennsylvania, over requiring statements regarding intelligent design in the biology curriculum. After an extensive trial this judge declared—and set the policy—that the argument that life is so complex that it had to have an intelligence behind its design was a representation of the biblical account of creation and, therefore, could not be part of the public school curriculum.

Monitoring Government

This setting of policy by preventing the school board from forcing intelligent design into the classroom reflects the final policy role that courts play, the monitoring of government. This is essentially the check on the executive and legislative branches that the U.S. system gives the courts. The courts are given the task of monitoring the actions of the government and governmental officials to make sure they follow prescribed rules and procedures, including the ones that check the behavior of the others. To fulfill this role, one important tool that courts generally have at their disposal is **injunctive power**. Courts have the power to stop the actions of government by issuing injunctions. Temporary or interim injunctions put policies or activities on hold until they can be examined at trial, and if in the course of the legal proceedings a judge finds that the governmental action clearly violates established principles, he may decide to enjoin, or halt, the action permanently.

Courts also monitor government action through prosecutions of corrupt or otherwise criminal governmental officials. By trying a governmental official according to the same rules and procedures as everyday citizens, the courts send out the message that nobody is above the law. This can have profound effects on the legitimacy of the government. Trials involving corrupt officials can become political spectacles and the formality of the courtroom can reduce the possibility of violence that might occur if people did not believe that governmental officials were being held accountable to the laws of the land. In the United States, even President Bill Clinton was required to testify in court while he was a sitting president.

In some nations, the courts exercise a power called judicial review. **Judicial review** is the power to declare laws and government acts to be in violation of the nation's constitution or in some other way illegal under the structure of the country. Judicial review operates to allow courts to directly monitor governmental action. Both the Scopes Monkey Trial and the Dover intelligent design trial were instances of judicial review. In federal systems, where you have multiple levels of government such as the state and national governments in the United States, the courts settle disputes between governmental levels. Questions often arise, whether the national or local government had the proper authority to enact specific laws or to take specific actions or whether federal or local law should preside. For example, in *To Kill a Mockingbird,* the court that tried Tom Robinson was clearly a state court. However, as the nation moved away from the New Deal era and into the Civil Rights era the federal courts began to assert their power over state courts to play a greater role in protecting the rights of African Americans. Had the novel been set later, Atticus might have opted to try and have Tom released by a federal court.

Courts also determine whether governmental officials are acting within their prescribed authority. For example, members of Congress have gone to court to try to stop the president from acting in a manner that they believed exceeded his constitutional authority, that is, from exercising war powers or not spending money properly for instance. On the state and local level, too, courts are often called upon to determine whether officials, council members, or mayors are acting within their sphere of power. This also frequently occurs with regulatory bureaucracies. Industries and business may challenge in court whether an agency has the authority to regulate them.

Judicial review is also at work when the courts strike down laws because they violate the constitutional rights of groups or individuals. Courts are frequently called upon to judge whether laws violate religious, political, and other human rights. When a court says that the nation may not prohibit the burning of the flag because such a ban violates freedom of speech, when a judge holds that Congress may not restrict access to Internet content, or when a court rules that the police have not properly read a defendant her rights, the court is, in fact, monitoring government action. In the United States, the courts receive a lot of respect for protecting citizens' rights. However, even this aspect of the courts is subject to the distinction between the law on the books and the law in action. Simply because a court declares that someone or some group is entitled to a right, that does not automatically change everything. In 1954, the U.S. Supreme Court declared, in *Brown v. Board of Education of Topeka,*[13] that the rule of separate but equal had no place when it came to education. Thus, segregated schools were no longer constitutionally permissible. Yet, ten years after the Court's momentous ruling, the schools in the Deep South were still largely segregated. It took the Civil Rights movement and congressional and presidential action to really begin the process of

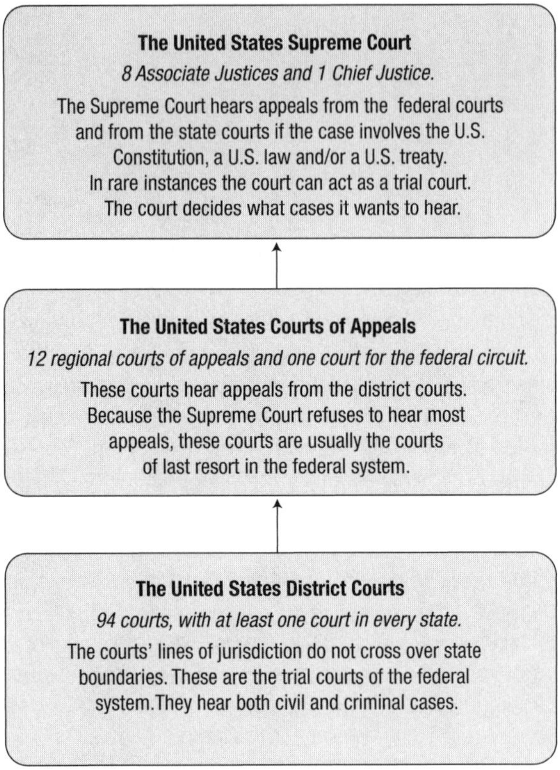

Figure 9.1 The United States Court System

---

desegregation and even today there are many areas in the U.S. South where schools are still racially segregated because of the geographic distribution of populations and the drawing of school boundaries.

TRIAL AND APPELLATE COURTS

Watching one of the marginally heroic lawyers rip up witnesses and give dazzling opening and closing statements on the television show *Law and Order* can be something of a guilty pleasure for people who like to fight to win when they argue. Of course, the courts in *Law and Order* and pretty much all of the courts in the other police and lawyer shows are trial courts. Trial courts are the courts that exercise what is called **original jurisdiction**, which means that they are the first courts to hear a case (see Figure 9.1). They are like the tellers at the bank, at least at banks that still have human tellers. Like the customer-tolerant, technically pleasant people whom you go to first when you want your bank to do something for you, the trial courts are the first line of action and where the vast majority of judicial activity occurs. Criminals are tried, lawsuits are fought, and injunctions and search warrants are issued in trial courts. Trial courts are responsible for keeping a record of the proceedings and for establishing the facts in the case. The finder of fact in the trial court is either the judge or the jury, which means that it is up to the judge or jury to weigh the veracity of the witnesses, assess the facts presented, and determine a winner.

Appellate courts are like the bank manager in our bank analogy. You go to them if you do not get the service you requested from the tellers or if you think the tellers are not doing their job correctly. Appellate courts exercise **appellate jurisdiction**, which means that they review the record from trial courts. However, appellate judges cannot simply say they disagree with the factual conclusions in the case. Rather, appellate review is limited to matters of law and process only. Virtually every time a lawyer stands up and says, "I object," they are raising a point of law, on which the trial judge must rule. There are numerous pretrial motions concerning the admissibility of evidence. There are instructions to the jury about what constitutes a crime or what the correct standard of evidence is in the case. There are constitutional provisions that regulate police interrogations and searches and seizures. Appellate courts can rule on all of these procedural matters, but they cannot rule on or revisit the facts in the case. Some countries provide for an appeal of the appeal, too. In the United States this occurs at the level of the Supreme Court.

LEGAL SYSTEMS

When appellate courts review the actions of lower courts, or when the judicial system reviews the constitutionality of a law that has been passed, it does not perform that action in a vacuum.* All judicial functions are shaped by the legal system of that country or jurisdiction. In other words, the law is not just the law, it is a social construction built upon a basic conceptualization of how the law is created and how it functions. In the modern world there are three legal systems that are commonly used. The first of these is the civil law or code law system. This is the most commonly used legal system in the world. The second major legal system is the common law system, which is used primarily in Great Britain and countries that were either former colonies or members of the commonwealth. The last major legal system is religious, and it is currently most common in Islamic nations.

The Civil Law System

The civil law system begins with the proposition that law is a codified, constructed entity that a legislature or some other law-making political body has constructed. Consequently, the process of compiling and writing down the law is a major component of the civil law system. The history of civil law really begins in the sixth century when the Byzantine emperor Justinian codified what had been the law of Rome, hence the civil law system is sometimes referred to as the Roman law system. Justinian's work

---

* This is fortunate as most scientists agree that a Supreme Court justice would survive for less than a minute in a vacuum. Ba-dum tshish. Thank you folks, you've been great! Seriously.

completed in 534 A.D. and resulted in the Justinian Code or the *Corpus Juris Civilis*. The second great codification came with the Emperor Napoleon. The Napoleonic Code was written by legal scholars and was made up of 2,281 codes built upon many different sources of law. As Napoleon began his conquests, the Napoleonic Code accompanied his Grande Armée. The last major codification occurred with the German codification of 1900. Civil law is predominant in continental Europe, former French Colonies, Quebec, and even in the State of Louisiana. Because the civil law system relies on written law, it tends to be more specific, more readily understandable, and easier to apply to particular cases. However, the judge still has the ability to interpret the law.

Civil law systems utilize an **inquisitorial system**, which entails a rather prolonged pretrial investigative process. The goal of this pretrial process is to try to protect the innocent. Unlike the American system where prosecutors and the police play the major role in marshaling the evidence against a suspect, in civil law systems all the courtroom participants participate in the investigation process. Information is also freely shared among all of the actors.

Common Law

The common law system began in 1066 when William the Conqueror began his rule as king of England. He set up a new legal system that was comprised of a King's Court with judges who traveled the countryside to enforce the king's law and dispense justice among the various tribes that comprised medieval England. Unlike the civil law system, there was no written law for these judges to put to use. Instead, the judges based their decisions on custom and precedents, which are past judicial decisions. This explains why the doctrine of *stare decisis*—Latin for "let the decision stand"—is such an important part of common law systems, and why judges are reluctant to contradict earlier rulings. The law that developed was, in essence, judge-made law. As time passed, English judges became more devoted to the body of law they created than to the king's will. Furthermore, other types of law, like equity and statutory law, supplemented the judges' common law. Nevertheless, the common law system is characterized by the strong role of the judge in cases and the importance of precedent.

One of the main components of the common law system is the adversarial process. Unlike the civil law system that is marked by cooperation among the participants, the legal actors in the common law system battle it out. The judge is not an active participant in the dispute, instead, he is more like a referee at a boxing match. Meanwhile, the prosecutor and the defense attorney do their best to try to win. Most students are very familiar with the adversarial process from the movies and television shows that feature dramatic questioning of witnesses, nail-biting cross-examinations, and dazzling closing arguments. It is important, however, to realize that what you see on TV is *fiction*. There are very few lawyers with the theatrical skills demonstrated on *Law and*

Order or *The Practice*. Interesting cases are the rare exception rather than the norm, and even the best of lawyers consider themselves lucky if they ever get a case that might in some way set precedent on an issue. In fact, even the in-court maneuvering and all that hot trial action is, in itself, a rarity. Other than dealing with their own speeding tickets and divorces, the vast majority of lawyers never see the inside of a courtroom. Most lawyers spend their entire careers making a few hundred dollars at a time performing services like drawing up contracts for house purchases. And even the criminal lawyers who do specialize in courtroom litigation, spend most of their time researching, documenting testimony, and preparing for cases.*

While we draw distinctions between the common law and the civil law systems, it should be apparent that this division is simplistic. In fact, the United States uses a mix of common law and civil law, as Congress and state legislatures pass laws that are codified and the courts still have room for interpretation and precedent.

Religious Law

The third major legal system, religious law, is very different from the previous two. While religious law is present in many countries, it is most common in Islamic countries, where it is based on **shari`a**, or Islamic law. Unlike law in civil and common law systems, shari`a in religious law systems is comprehensive in that it governs every aspect of religious and secular life. Shari`a is primarily based on rules from the Koran as well as other legal sources, and the understanding and development of shari`a or *fiqh* has been the work of religious jurists. Customarily, it is the *qadi's* responsibility to resolve disputes by finding the law. The *qadi* may be helped by the *mufti*, who is an expert in Islamic law able to issue legal opinions called *fatwa*. This sometimes leads to conflict as different *mufti* can potentially offer contradictory *fatwa*.[14]

For those with intense religious convictions, it is obligatory to follow shari`a even if it is not acknowledged by the state. While some nations' justice systems are based entirely on shari`a, such as Iran and Saudi Arabia,† most countries are mixed systems with either civil law—such as Egypt, Kuwait, Morocco, and Syria—or common law—like Bahrain, Pakistan, Qatar, Singapore, and Sudan. In many, but not all, of the nations that utilize a mixed religious and civil law system, shari`a is the basis for the underlying civil law. In Saudi Arabia, the monarch's ability to make law is limited because he may not make any law that contradicts shari`a. Interestingly, the Canadian province of Ontario considered allowing Muslims to utilize shari`a to settle family disputes if all of the parties agreed.

---

* By admitting all of this we risk being served with an official cease and desist order from the Global Association of Political Science Departments. Prelaw majors make up a significant proportion of the political science majors around the world and it seems that the association doesn't want us saying anything that might discourage the next generation of lawyers from starting out as political science majors.

† Shari`a is very different, however, in these two countries.

This led to a good deal of controversy as many were concerned, among other things, about how women are treated under shari`a. Ultimately, the move was rejected.[15]

JURISPRUDENCE

While legal systems define how the law is created and how it functions, a more basic question is what the underlying moral and philosophical basis for the law is. The answer largely depends on one's jurisprudence. Simply put, **jurisprudence** is a philosophy of law and as one might imagine, there is a wide array of types of jurisprudence out there. There is a Marxist school, a critical legal theory school, a feminist school, and many more. In fact, within the feminist school, there is a Marxist school, a liberal school, a difference school, etc. However, according to judicial scholar Harry Stumpf, three main schools of jurisprudence have vied for dominance in the United States—natural law, **positivist jurisprudence** and **sociological-realist jurisprudence**.[16] We focus on these, but realize that these are not the only options, nor are these basic ideas expressed in the same way in different cultures and legal traditions around the world. For example, a Chinese articulation of the concept of a natural law of humankind is likely to focus on society first and obligations rather than the individual and his or her rights.

Natural Law

Thomas Jefferson's words in the Declaration of Independence, that "Men...are endowed by their Creator with certain inalienable rights," captures the essence of the natural law tradition. **Natural law** presumes that there is some higher law, which originates with God or nature, and that this higher law is discoverable by the use of reason. It is the presumption that there is a certain justice that everyone should simply know. For example, murder is wrong, you should not take other people's stuff, and you must urge your friends to buy this textbook even if they are not taking this course.

Some people will immediately recognize that a belief in natural law plays a part in their belief system, while others may not think so. If you don't think you share these beliefs, think back to *To Kill a Mockingbird*. Was it wrong for Tom Robinson to be tried in the manner he was? Why? Was it unjust? Why was it unjust? If the laws of the state do not allow African Americans to sit on juries, why is that wrong? As it turns out, those who do not subscribe to the natural law tradition can answer these questions without resorting to an explanation that invokes the idea of an underlying law applicable to all humanity, but for most people, the answer comes down to the belief that there are just some things that are fundamentally right, that is they believe in some notion of a higher law. As evidenced in Jefferson's words, the natural law tradition has always played an important role in the United States. Our fundamental belief in rights is rooted in a natural law sense of justice. In fact, Supreme Court justice Felix Frankfurter once wrote that the test that the Supreme Court should use when determining if a state's action violated the principle of due process in a criminal case should be whether the action "shocks the conscience."[17]

While the natural law tradition has played and continues to play an important role in the United States, it is equally true that from an empirical perspective, it raises a lot of concerns. While it is true that people do act rationally, it is also true that people—and our very generous definition of people includes inebriated college students—can be found doing some very irrational things. Furthermore, what seems rational at one time may seem perfectly ridiculous at another. At one time Prohibition, the outlawing of alcohol, was considered to be such a good idea that it was written into the U.S. Constitution. Now, most people scoff at the idea.* Furthermore, two seemingly rational people can reach very different conclusions on a host of things. People in different cultures reach various conclusions on the basic question of the difference between right and wrong. Furthermore, there is the whole problem of proving it. How do you prove that something is a part of natural law? Take something as personal as your control over your own fertility. Many use natural law to attack China's "one-family, one-child" policy, for example, and your ability to decide when you do and do not want to have children might seem to be an obvious point of any kind of natural law, but can you prove it? Further, there are not even consistent religious or social doctrines or traditions that might be pointed to as evidence of natural law on the subject of fertility. Problems such as this are why the natural law tradition almost immediately ran into serious trouble from those seeking more scientific responses.

Positivist Jurisprudence

The positivist school of jurisprudence begins with John Austin (1790–1859), who believed that the law had to be demystified. According to Austin, law was simply the command of the recognized sovereign authority of the state. In other words, though law was not void of morality it was not the same as morality and neither was it part of social and historical forces. Rather, those in the positivist tradition believed that law could be studied as the body of principles that originated with the state but that took on its own logic and rationality. Thus, law could be studied using formal logic. Under this theory of law, the job of the judge is to apply the law of the state to the particular facts using logic. In other words, judges merely discover the law as it has been documented by the legislature or through precedent. Consequently, it is very important for judges to be versed in the case law and in applicable precedents so that they can reach the logically correct decisions.

What is interesting is that the seemingly strange combination of the natural law tradition and the positivist tradition quickly took hold in the United States. The influence of this odd blend could be found in the popularity of Blackstone's *Commentaries*,[18] a

---

* However, they might not be so quick to dismiss Prohibition if they saw some of those irrational things that college students do after consuming significant quantities of alcohol. We call particular attention to the practice of painting one's backside with school colors and running naked across football fields at halftime, in the snow.

legal text that covered all of the common laws of Great Britain, which early Americans studied to learn the law. This text had a profound and lasting influence on the American colonists and many of those who framed the Constitution. The view of the law and the role of the judge contained in Blackstone's work continued to shape the way that courts viewed their job as discoverers of the law. We can still hear the echoes of Blackstone today as politicians pledge to appoint only those judges who will apply the law as opposed to those judges who want to take away the legislature's responsibility to make the law. Atticus Finch's appeal to law in *To Kill A Mockingbird* is firmly rooted within this combination of a natural law and positivist tradition. Atticus believes that there are principles of right and wrong that should be followed, and that there is only one right decision that can be found for the case. Further, the key to reaching the right answer is the strict adherence to the procedures and processes of the courts.

Realist Jurisprudence

Legal realism actually begins with a sociological critique of the law. According to that critique, law was comprised of a set of rules intended to meet the needs of society. Rejecting the natural law and positivist traditions, those in the sociological school argued that law entailed a lot of discretion on the part of the judge, and that discretion was best exercised with an understanding of the needs of society that could be obtained with the help of the social sciences.

Legal realists went beyond this sociological critique to argue for legal reform in the early and middle twentieth century. They also were distinguished from their sociological forerunners by their readiness to view the law in terms of the behavior of legal actors rather than as a body of legal rules. Some legal realists even argue that precedents are myths, that judges make their own decisions and only afterwards justify them through legal precedent. In studying the law, then, legal realists focus heavily on the behavior of police, judges, juries, prosecutors and other attorneys rather than focusing on the content of law. For legal realists, the key to understanding the judicial system is to understand the tremendous amount of discretion that is available to legal actors. Police exercise discretion and can turn people's lives upside down by their decisions about whether to arrest or not. Judges exercise tremendous discretion in making rulings from the bench and sentencing. Prosecutors exercise enormous discretion in deciding what charges to seek against defendants, what plea bargains to accept, and what sentencing recommendations they will make.

The discipline of political science has always had a special relationship with the law. Political science departments traditionally have classes, like constitutional law or civil liberties, that study the law, at least partially, from a natural law/positivist perspective. However, political scientists have increasingly moved closer to the realist school, and, thus, since the middle of the twentieth century have started to treat the legal system as part of the larger overall political system. This has meant that there has been an increased focus on judicial behavior, on the relationships between the judge, the prosecutor, and the defense attorney in criminal cases, and the relationship between political actors inside and outside of the legal system. Someone who adheres to the realist perspective would not be at all surprised with the result reached in *To Kill a Mockingbird*. For the realist, the focus would not be on the formal aspects of doctrine that guarantee people a right to a jury trial or on some abstract notion of due process. Instead, the realist would focus on who was actually making the decisions in the case. Who is the judge; who is on the jury; who is the prosecutor? What are their motives and what kinds of logics are they likely to use in making their choices? These are the questions that legal realists believe are crucial.

TYPES OF LAW

One of the more daunting aspects of studying the law can be coping with the many distinctions that are made among types of law. While we review some of the major distinctions here, you should bear in mind that there are many others. We could have easily discussed contract law, tort law, family law, commercial law, patent law, intellectual property law, or Murphy's Law.

Private Law versus Public Law

One of the most common distinctions made in the law is between private law and public law. On its face, the distinction is not all that complicated. **Private law** is concerned with the relations among private individuals and private organizations. In other words government is not involved except in setting the rules and context of interaction. Thus, private law encompasses most contracts. Assume that the company Spacely Sprockets promised to purchase 200 widgets from the Cogswell Cogs company for $2,000. Cogswell Cogs provides the widgets, but Spacely Sprockets does not pay. In other words, Spacely Sprockets and Cogswell Cogs had a contract, which Spacely Sprockets apparently breached. This is an example of a relationship between private companies with which private law is concerned. Other examples of private law are marriages and divorces, wills and estates, landlord-tenant relations, malpractice, and other suits brought by an individual or private company and directed toward individuals or private companies.

In contrast, **public law** concerns relationships involving the government and its relationship with individuals and organizations. Criminal law very clearly is public law as the government polices private behavior. Laws that enable bureaucratic agencies to regulate industries are also a form of public law, as are constitutional laws, taxing policies, and environmental regulations. The distinction between private and public law, while recognized in both the common law and civil law systems is most important for nations utilizing the latter, which sometimes maintain separate courts to deal with public law.

When one thinks it through, it may seem that the distinction between private law and public law is problematic. If the basis for the distinction is the involvement of the government, how can any law that involves the courts be purely private? After all, the courts are part of the government. This distinction became particularly salient in the Supreme Court case of *Shelley v. Kraemer* (1948).[19] At issue in this case was whether someone could challenge a racially restrictive covenant, that is, a signed agreement by people in a neighborhood in which they agree not to sell their houses to minorities. The problem was that since this case involved relations among private individuals, it was a matter of private law. A constitutional challenge—a matter of public law—to a matter of private law seemed to be inappropriate. However, the Court ruled that the racially restrictive covenant was unenforceable. Since the courts were a part of government, they could not enforce constitutionally prohibited discrimination. The *Shelley* case demonstrates how artificial the distinction between private and public law can be.

Furthermore, it is equally clear that private law can have very public consequences. Theoretically, malpractice suits are a matter of private law. Yet, when some people start to argue that jury awards in malpractice cases contribute to the rising cost of health care, it is a matter of public consequence. At one time, if someone was injured at work, it was considered a private matter, and if someone was injured at work, she had the option of suing her employer if he was negligent. Eventually, this seemed like a draconian and inefficient way to look after those who could no longer work, so the government created a comprehensive system of worker's compensation, thus transforming a matter of private law into a matter of public law.

Criminal Law versus Civil Law

Criminal law involves that body of law that defines specific crimes and that provides punishments for offenses. Criminal cases are matters of public law in that they directly involve the government. The parties in the dispute are always the level of government where the crime has been defined and the defendant. Thus, cases may be listed as *The United States v. Patrick Star* or *The Commonwealth of Virginia v. Carrot Top*. While victims of crime have recently been recognized as having an interest in criminal cases, that interest usually comes in the form of allowing victims to testify at sentencing. Victims are not parties to the suit. Consequently, the government may proceed with a criminal case with or without the victim's consent, though doing so without consent may prove difficult if the victim refuses to cooperate.

Serious offenses, for example, murder, rape, kidnapping, and arson are felonies, which usually carry a punishment of at least one year in prison. Less serious crimes, like traffic violations, public drunkenness, and simple assault and battery are misdemeanors, which are usually punishable by less than one year in prison and a very serious frown from a judge. In a criminal case, defendants are considered innocent until proven guilty, and to achieve a conviction, the prosecution must prove that the defendant is guilty beyond a reasonable doubt. In a criminal case, the judge or jury will find the defendant to be guilty or not guilty. Many in the media like to report that a suspect has been found innocent, but courts do not do that.* Whether or not one is truly inno-cent is between them and their creator, no matter how many times someone is found not guilty, it does not prove he or she is innocent. As for courts, they only determine whether someone can be found legally guilty of the crime. You may be guilty as sin, but if the government can't prove it, you'll go free.

Sometimes it seems as if there is someone out there getting paid to come up with terms designed to confuse people.† Take, for example, the term civil law. This, however, does not refer to the *civil law system* but instead refers to a body of laws we refer to as civil law. **Civil law**, in this context, usually refers to the law that governs relations between private parties. The key word here is usually, because sometimes the govern-ment can be a party in a civil suit. For example, the government may sue on behalf of someone who has claimed a violation of their civil rights, it may be a party to a con-tract dispute, and it can bring a civil action against corporation for violations of agency rules. More typically, however, civil law deals with relations among private individuals and groups. Someone who charges a physician with malpractice, sues the seller of a damaged automobile, or takes a relative to court for failure to repay a loan is bringing a civil suit. Think of civil law in terms of the kinds of cases on *Judge Judy, The People's Court,* or *Judge Joe Brown.* Unlike the rigid standard of proof in a criminal case, in a civil suit the plaintiff will prevail if she can demonstrate that the defendant is liable by a preponderance of the evidence, an easier hurdle than "beyond a reasonable doubt." Thus, O. J. Simpson was found not guilty of murder in the criminal case because the conclusion has to be beyond a reasonable doubt, but was found liable for the deaths in a civil case because the burden of proof is the preponderance of evidence.

Federal Law versus State Law

In the United States an important distinction exists between federal law, which is the law of the national government, and state law, which is the law of the states and their localities. In fact, there is a dual system of courts, where there is both the national, or federal, court system and a state court system in every state. Federal law is comprised of the law in the Constitution, treaties made under the Constitution and congressional statutes possessed under the authority of the Constitution. All other law is a matter of state law. Thus, states are responsible for the vast amount of law that regulates people's health, safety, and morality. Consequently, most law in the United States is state law, and the vast majority of legal cases are adjudicated in state courts. This includes the over-whelming amount of criminal law. Contrary to what many people think, it is also true that one cannot bring any case to the U.S. Supreme Court. Like any other federal court, the Supreme Court can only hear cases that involve some aspect of federal law.

---

* In some countries they use the term unproven rather than not guilty.

† Technically, these people are called professors.

However, it is true that a case may begin as a state court case, but find its way to the Supreme Court. This can occur for two main reasons. First, while the case may be primarily concerned with state law, it may have raised federal questions. While a criminal prosecution is a matter of state law, there are several federal constitutional provisions that are relevant, for example the guarantees of due process or the bar against requiring someone to testify at their own trial. The second way that the case may wind up in the Supreme Court is if the matter always raised an issue of federal law. State courts have concurrent jurisdiction over most federal law. However, remember the rule that the case must raise a matter of federal law to be heard by the Supreme Court. So if you do something stupid, like kick a hole in some guy's wall because he drank the last cold beer and did not reload the fridge and the guy says he is going to sue all the way to the Supreme Court, you can reply with pride that his statement is inaccurate, because damage to property is a matter of state, not federal, law. We hope you can get all the words out before he rearranges your face.

This section discusses the state/federal distinction in terms of American law. However, in any country with a federal system, there will always be this distinction. For example, in Canada there is provincial law and national law. Even in countries with a unitary system there can still be municipal ordinances that are passed by local government. However, these would be subject to the approval of the national government.

International Law

International law does not exist. We know, there are textbooks on international law and classes on it and all that, but there really is not an international law in the same sense that there is law within a country. International law, as you will find it in the textbooks, refers to conventions and agreements that govern behavior between nations, such as laws of the sea, but in reality, international law only exists to the point that there is a country or a coalition of countries with the power and the will to enforce a rule or norm of behavior. The reason is that there is no effective world government with the power to create and enforce a law globally.*

CONSTITUTIONAL REVIEW

Earlier we noted that one of the functions of courts was to monitor government action. One of the ways that courts do this is through the exercise of judicial review. Interestingly, the concept of judicial review originated with the United States, although the U.S. Constitution says nothing about the subject. In the very interesting case of *Marbury v. Madison*

---

* This could be connected to the concept of sovereignty, which can be roughly defined as the final political or social authority. If you had a true international law, including the enforcement mechanisms to make countries obey it, then leaders of countries would, in effect, be giving up that ultimate authority to the international courts. Few if any leaders are willing to do this.

(1803), Chief Justice John Marshall, writing for a majority of the Court, made the argument that since any law that was contrary to the Constitution was void and since judges took an oath to obey the Constitution, they could hold that a law violating the Constitution was void. Today, it seems as if most Americans take the Supreme Court's power of judicial review for granted, although there are considerable arguments about the conclusions reached by the justices. While there are many arguments surrounding the Court's use of judicial review, the principal argument concerns what materials the justices should use when interpreting the Constitution.

Some legal scholars, judges, and political commentators argue for the idea of original intent—that the Constitution should only mean what its framers and the authors of its amendments meant when they authored its provisions. To give meaning to the Constitution, the proponents of judicial review would argue that the justices should only be principally concerned with the text of the Constitution, the debates surrounding its drafting, and its authors' contemporaneous writings. The benefit of this proposition is that providing a fixed meaning can provide certainty to the law and the meaning of the Constitution would not be dependent upon which justices are serving at any particular time. Those who argue for original intent quite obviously do so from a natural law/positivist perspective.

Those who oppose this position argue that it is not easy to determine the meaning of obscure phrases, like "due process" or "privileges and immunities," and that it is not always the case that all of the framers agreed on one set meaning. More fundamentally, those who oppose limiting judicial review to original intent maintain that it is more appropriate to view the Constitution as a living document, a constitution of ideas that must be interpreted to reflect modern values and conditions. They argue that the framers could never have dreamed of modern technology, the size of government, and the expansion of the nation. Consequently, proponents of a living constitution would, for example, define cruel and unusual punishment from a twenty-first century perspective rather than from an eighteenth-century view. It is clear that those who favor original intent would not condone the Court's reading a right to privacy or the right to obtain an abortion into the Constitution. Those who favor a living constitution do so from the perspective of the Realist school of jurisprudence.

Regardless of the controversy that surrounds particular issues with regard to judicial review, it is clear that constitutional review serves important purposes for the state. As stated earlier, judicial review can ensure that the government works properly and according to the prescribed rules in the Constitution. The Court ensures that government officials do not usurp the responsibilities of others and that the state and federal governments properly work within their spheres. Judicial review also allows for the protection of minority rights within a democracy. Constitutional provisions call for equal protection under the law for all, allow for the free exercise of religion, protect everyone's right to free speech, and guarantee that those accused of crimes receive due process. However, because the Court can spark great controversy when it declares laws and governmental actions to be unconstitutional, it is possible to miss the most important function of all. That occurs when the Court upholds law. By subjecting the nations' laws to constitutional scrutiny and upholding them, the Court confers legitimacy upon the government's actions. Think of the Court's actions in the 2000 presidential election. Regardless of one's opinions about how the case was decided, it is nonetheless true that all parties accepted the Court's opinion.

Other countries have recognized the value of constitutional courts. Austrian, Irish, Japanese, and Indian courts exercise the power of judicial review. Even countries that use the civil law system have found the benefit of constitutional courts. Germany, Italy, Belgium, Portugal, and Spain, for example, each have a constitutional court, although these courts function differently than the U.S. Supreme Court. These civil law constitutional courts do not hear an entire case. Instead, if a court finds that a case raises a constitutional question, that question is sent to the constitutional court for review. That court then issues an opinion on the narrow constitutional issue, which the original court uses to decide the case.

While many countries have adopted constitutional courts, the British have chosen not to have one. This decision does make sense because in England there is legislative supremacy. The Parliament is viewed as the supreme will of the people, and for this to be true, there can be no higher authority on the law than the Parliament. However, Great Britain has been forced to accept a form of judicial review by its membership in the European Union (EU). By joining the EU, Great Britain comes under the jurisdiction of the European Court of Justice, which has the authority to review the laws of the EU's member countries to make sure they comport with the European Community.

At this point, the facts that governments derive benefit from judicial review should come as no real surprise. As we stated at the beginning of this chapter, we should view law and the courts in the context of the larger political system.

KEY TERMS

appellate jurisdiction / **207**	law in books / **199**
civil law / **214**	natural law / **210**
criminal law / **214**	original jurisdiction / **206**
dispute resolution / **201**	private law / **213**
going rate / **202**	public law / **213**
injunctive power / **204**	positivist jurisprudence / **210**
inquisitorial system / **208**	shari`a / **209**
judicial review / **205**	sociological-realist jurisprudence / **210**
jurisprudence / **210**	statutory interpretation / **203**
law in action / **199**	

CHAPTER SUMMARY

Despite recent events that have shown otherwise, there is still something about courts and the law that makes it feel as if they are separate from politics. Part of this feeling derives from the symbols and language that courts employ, the fact that people expect justice from the legal system, and the important functions that courts perform. However, the law and courts are political in that they fit in with the definition of politics used in this book. The political aspects of the law become clearer when one ponders the difference between law in books and law in action. The political nature of law and the courts becomes further apparent when we realize that people have varying theories about the law and that different nations use different types of legal systems. Some of the mystery that surrounds courts and law can be stripped away by learning about the many different types of law that exist and how these types of law apply in the real world. Students should learn two important lessons from this chapter. First, a nation's legal institutions, like its other political institutions, perform important functions for its society. Second, there have been an amazing number of television shows dealing with the law. Obviously, there are riches in store for the person who can come up with any original idea in this popular genre.

STUDY QUESTIONS AND EXERCISES

1. Almost every day it seems there is a news story that demonstrates the difference between "law on the books" and "law in action." Can you think of recent examples from the news that demonstrate this distinction?

2. Identify and explain the three major functions of courts.

3. How do trial courts differ from appellate courts?

4. What are the key elements of a common law system? A civil law system?

5. Of the types of jurisprudence identified above, with which do you most agree? Why?

6. What are the major types of law? Can you think of examples of each?

WEBSITES TO EXPLORE

jurist.law.pitt.edu/index.php. This Web site features jurist, law and legal news from the University of Pittsburgh's School of Law.

www.curia.eu.int/en/transitpage.htm. The Web site for the European Court of Justice, contains information, case law, and news about the Court.

www.ncsconline.org/. The National Center for State Courts' Web site is a resource for research, publications, and educational material about the courts in the states of the United States.

www.stus.com. Stu's Views, is a Web compilation of law and lawyer cartoons.

www.uscourts.gov/. This Web site with all types of information about U.S. federal courts is maintained by the Administrative Office of the U.S. Courts.

www.venice.coe.int/site/dynamics/N_court_links_ef.asp?L=E. The Council of Europe's "Links to Constitutional Courts and Equivalent Bodies," is maintained by the Venice Commission.

www.worldlii.org/. The World Legal Information Institute Web site lists an international directory of legal resources.

CHAPTER 10

Not Quite Right, but Still Good
The Democratic Ideal in Modern Politics

Clearly, *Why Not Me?* should have won multiple Pulitzer prizes.[1] In this hard-hitting expose Al Franken chronicles his fictional candidacy, victory, and eventual disgrace in the 2000 U.S. presidential election. Funding his run with the proceeds from a phone sex line, Franken supposedly does everything wrong and breaks pretty much every election law there is. The other candidates do make desperate attempts to debate issues of importance, but Franken's campaign theme— that ATM fees are too high—captures the voters' attention even though he offers no solution for the problem. The ATM issue, combined with some timely smacking of people in the head, ultimately propels Franken to the presidency. Given the tremendous social, economic, and musical crises facing the real world today, why is it still so believable that a fully unqualified candidate— and a complete moron at that—could win the U.S. presidential election by running on the platform that ATM fees are too high?

It does not take much of a look at the imperfections of real democracies and real elections to realize that Franken's book is humorous precisely because the insanity it depicts comes so close to absurdities of the real elections that take place around the world. The 2000 U.S. presidential election provides more than enough compelling examples of the sometimes ridiculous imperfections of modern electoral democracies. Although Al Gore hypnotized enough of the suburban electorate to win the most votes overall, George W. Bush easily carried vast stretches of barren land in the West and squeaked through with Florida to win the electoral vote and, consequently, take the presidency. In the critical swing state of Florida—where swing usually refers to the big band music your great grandmother thought was risqué—thousands of elderly, lifelong

Democratic voters "accidentally" voted for Pat Buchanan (running as a candidate on the Reform ticket) when they were confused by the poorly laid out ballots.*

Had Buchanan not benefited from ballot confusion, Gore would have been living in the White House. Had it stopped there, that would have been noteworthy enough. Yet, there was also Ralph Nader, the Green Party candidate with the ongoing pledge to "protect everyone from everything everywhere by getting government out of everything except protecting people from everything everywhere." Had Nader not been in the race or if even a modest majority of the Floridian Naderites voted along with Gore's sleepy minions, Al Gore would have won the part of the election that actually counted. While some undoubtedly shudder at the fact that such a tiny vote difference kept the critical selection of White House dinnerware out of the hands of Tipper Gore, the practical differences for most of us are even more profound. Putting Big Al in the White House would have changed the entire course of late night TV, political cartoons, and other forms of satire for four years. Satirizing a guy named Gore is funny, but could it have ever really surpassed the truckloads of jokes that have been made about George Bush Junior?

Somehow through all of the 2000 election nonsense, most Americans still consider the country a democracy. Clearly, democracy—at least as mere mortals currently practice it—is not perfect. It is the imperfections of democracy that make the absurdity in Franken's book—which we believe should at least have won a People's Choice Award—seem just a little too realistic.

ARROW'S THEOREM

Alas, the American democracy is not so different than any of the world's other democracies. As it turns out, all democracies are fraught with problems. In fact, we just happen to have mathematical, scientific, absolute, geological proof that elections everywhere are imperfect. Using some serious math, an economist called Kenneth Arrow[†] demonstrated that the use of elections does not ensure that the majority's preference will be selected.[‡] How can this be? You would think that if everybody gets to vote, if all the votes are equal, and if all the votes are counted fairly then you would clearly get the outcome preferred by the majority. After all, that is the whole democracy thing we learned in grade school and now that we are all grown-up we put a great deal of faith in election results, right? Unfortunately for those who are easily thrown into a crisis of faith, it turns out that whenever there are more than two choices

---

*There are several good jokes we could have put in this paragraph, from some kind of self-exposure or flasher jokes in regards to Al Franken writing an expose about himself to Buchanan's claim that those elderly democratic voters did really, deep down, want to vote for a loud and aggressive person who was too right-wing to run as a Republican, but sometimes one must pause to simply reflect on the rich humor inherent in life itself. Take thirty-seven seconds to contemplate the nature of irony.

[†]Most people seem to have called him Kenneth Arrow because it was his name.

[‡]This is true even in places other than Florida.

in an election—even if you assume that every vote is counted and all votes are equal—the method used to add up all the votes has a tremendous impact on who is the winner.

What? Addition is addition, right? It does not matter if you add the three to the four or the four to the three, it still comes out a seven, and that means you have "crapped out." The casino will now take your money, please pass the dice to the next person at the table.

Well, not quite. Count on a professor* to figure out that when it comes to elections, addition is not that simple. Arrow found that different methods of counting votes lead to very different election outcomes. Moreover, he also demonstrated that we could never be certain that any one method of counting votes would lead to the majority's single preferred option. Thus, even elections that most of us would consider perfectly fair may be imperfect because we cannot ever be certain the outcome is truly the one desired by the majority of the voting population.

Fortunately, we can demonstrate the idea behind Arrow's argument without resorting to anything beyond street level math. Imagine we are all going to elect the king of the ice cream social. We have five candidates, cleverly named A, B, C, D, and Bruce, the singing wallaby,† who are artfully depicted in Figure 10.1. The most conservative candidate is on the right, advocating the imposition of vanilla for all and all for vanilla, and the extreme liberal is on the left, demanding that we must sample each of the thirty-one flavors between Fiona Apple Crunch Nonpatriarchal Ice Cream and Rage Against the Praline Socialist Ice Cream.[2] In the middle are the moderates, who generally think that something in addition to just vanilla would be nice, but these three candidates are deeply divided over the chocolate, strawberry, or orange sherbet issue. The figure also shows the percentage of the voters who prefer each candidate.

Now if you go with a typical method of counting votes—everyone gets one vote and the candidate with the most votes wins—Bruce, the conservative, wins the election with a mere 27 percent of the votes. This is a fair and simple way to count the votes and it is the method we are most accustomed to. However, if you were to actually ask the voters, it turns out that the vast majority would rather have anyone other than that squawking marsupial as their duly elected monarch of frozen dairy. Despite the fact that every vote was counted and every vote was equal, does such a vote actually represent the will of the majority? How can it be if the majority of people are unsatisfied with the outcome? In Robert Penn Warren's novel, *All the King's Men*, Willie Stark—whose later career is remarkably similar to the real-life Louisiana governor and U.S. senator Huey Long—as a relatively young and naïve politician is supported in a bid for governor. Stark's real world political education begins as he realizes that his support is

---

*Or, better yet, an economist.

†We are not sure if it is a law or something, but it seems that all Australians are either named Bruce or Sheila. For the official, legally binding reference, see Monty Python's *The Bruces* skit.

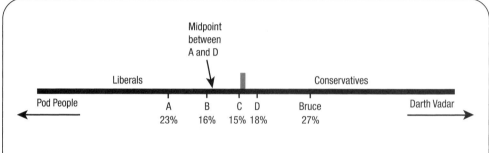

Figure 10.1 Testing the Outcomes of Different Voting Methods

mainly coming from another candidate in the campaign who is just using Stark to divide his opponent's vote.

It may not shock you to learn that this sort of electoral result, where someone with far less than half the votes won, has actually happened several times in the United States. One of the more interesting recent examples is Evan Mecham's election as governor of Arizona with far less than a majority of the votes. The result can only be called a political disaster. Not only did Mecham openly and quite seriously discuss alien landing sites in Arizona, he drove the Super Bowl and all of the money associated with it to California by using an executive order to eliminate the Martin Luther King holiday in the state.

Mecham was quickly kicked out of office, but because of the chaos, insanity, dissatisfaction, and controversy that followed his ascent to the governorship, Arizona, like a few other states, adopted an alternative method of adding up the votes in an election to ensure that a large number of candidates will not lead to the election of someone with a very small percentage of the overall vote. For example, Louisiana and Arizona both now require a candidate to receive the majority of all votes cast before they can be declared the winner of an election. If there are more than two candidates in a race and no candidate wins more than half the votes, the two candidates with the highest pluralities—the most votes—must face each other in a winner-take-all runoff election.

If this system were in place in our fictional—but still highly believable—election of the king of the ice cream social,* the outcome would have been much different. Conservative Bruce and liberal candidate A received the most votes in the first round, with 27 percent of the votes for Bruce and 23 percent for A. Then the two of them would have to face each other in a second round. If you look at the people who voted for the three eliminated candidates, most of them are closer to A on the ideological spectrum in our little figure than to that extremist honky-tonk Aussie, so the vast majority of them would probably prefer Candidate A over Bruce. Thus, in the second round of this different—but still fair—method of holding an election, candidate A would add B's 16 percent, C's 15 percent and maybe even a few of D's supporters to the 23 percent she already had, and pull about 55 percent of the vote, beating Bruce. However, does this method ensure that the election selects the candidate actually preferred by the majority of the population?

---

*Some may question the use of an ice cream social as an example. They may even say it trivializes the deeply held democratic ideal of elections. Obviously, these people haven't read the first nine chapters of this book if they are worried about that kind of irreverence at this point.

It might be tempting to say yes, this method of counting the vote gets you the will of the majority because it eliminated the undesirable outcome of electing a candidate that most of the voters disliked, but you should also realize that the single-vote system that elected Bruce and the runoff system that elected Candidate A are both fair ways to add up the votes to determine the winner of an election. Further, there are other fair ways of adding up votes that can produce outcomes different from either of these two methods. For example, what would happen if you go for reality TV democracy and start voting candidates off the island? Instead of voting *for* the candidate you prefer the most, you vote *against* the candidate you hate the most.* You do this round after round until just one candidate is left. With this method of counting the vote, in each round you vote against the candidate that is farthest from you on the ideological spectrum in Figure 10.1. Unsurprisingly, since so many people disliked him, the winner of the simple vote count that we first started with—Bruce—is the first one voted off the island. If you find the halfway point between the two most extreme candidates, it will be the point that marks the dividing line between the voters farthest from the candidate on the right and those farthest from the candidate on the left. If you are right of that line, A has to be the farthest away, and if you are on the left, Bruce has to be the farthest away. It can't be any of the candidates in the middle. No matter where you are on the line, either A or Bruce has to be the most distant candidate. You do not have to believe us, you can check it out for yourself. No, seriously, go get the little pink plastic ruler out of your Hello Kitty pencil case, find the halfway point, pick some spots on the line and start measuring the distances from those points to each of the candidates and see who is the farthest away. Go ahead, we will wait.

Convinced yet? Not quite? Take a couple more minutes. We are very patient.

Look, just measure a few spots.

Seriously, all the other readers are ready to move on, and it is hard enough keeping their attention as it is.

Fine, but when we get back from the espresso stand, we are moving on with or without you.

Now that everyone is happily caffeinated, take a look at the halfway point between the two most extreme candidates A and Bruce, marked by the thick gray vertical line, and look at how many people fall on each side of that point. All of A's, B's, and C's supporters, and roughly half of people who should be D's supporters will probably vote against Bruce. That's about 63 percent against the caterwauling Australian, and Bruce is off the island before he can win immunity in one of those silly games. However, once Bruce is off the island—safely shipped back to the outback where he is using every last millisecond of his fifteen minutes of fame to cut an album and crank out a video—who

---

*Many people already do this, voting for a candidate not because they like or support him or her, but because they think it would be worse if his or her opponent won. We predict that this sort of voting will define the 2008 U.S. presidential election. If it doesn't, we can just edit this footnote out of future editions of this text and pretend like we never said it.

is the next to get voted out? Assuming that voters will then turn against the remaining candidate who is most distant from them on our fancy graphic, you can again mark the midpoint between the most extreme candidates—this time it is A and D. In order to avoid any more unfortunate delays, we measured it ourselves and marked it on the figure for you. Even for those who cannot manage to operate a ruler, it should be obvious that Candidate A is the next one voted off the island. Bruce's supporters (27 percent), D's supporters (18 percent), C's (15 percent) and probably half of B's supporters (8 percent) all turn against the hapless Candidate A, and she is sent packing for her two-week publicity tour on every cable TV talk show with low enough standards to want her as a guest. Clearly, if Bruce and Candidate A are the first two kicked off the island, the winner of this election will not be same as the winner of either of the previous two elections. In fact, assuming that people keep voting against the candidate that is farthest from them on the figure, the last candidate standing is probably going to be Candidate C, the tall girl standing right in the middle.

In another variation, let's see what happens if you keep the reality TV style round-by-round voting system, but you do it *New Zealand Idol* style.* You vote *for* the candidate you like most and the candidate with the least votes in each round gets kicked off the island? In that case the first one off the island is Candidate C, who was the winner of our third method of counting the votes. If you then split C's supporters evenly between B and D, B moves up to 23.5 percent and D gets 25.5 percent. Thus A's measly 23 percent gets her kicked off. In the third round all of A's supporters go to their next closest candidate, giving B 46.5 percent and leaving D's 25.5 percent to lose to Bruce's 27 percent. In the final round at least half of D's supporters jump to B rather than Bruce, and you have your fourth different winner—Candidate B—in this fourth way of counting the votes.

What if you use ranked votes? That is, what if you used the method the sports writers use to give the wrong U.S. college football team the national championship? Which candidate wins then? What if you have party-based primaries followed by a runoff election? Then A, B, and C have one election among just Democrats and D and Bruce have one among just Republicans, and those primaries are followed by the main event. What if you have party primaries, but allow everybody to vote in both primaries? Then you have the possibility of strategic voting, where somebody can cast a vote in the other party's primary with the intention of selecting a candidate from the other party that her party can beat in the finals. Just try figuring that one out. We have not even gone into all of the strategies about nominations and all of the other stuff that goes on before the vote itself.

At the very least, we have four different, but fair, sets of rules for tallying the votes, and each of those four accounting procedures produces a different outcome. How can you know which outcome is the will of the majority? It is true that we set up this dis-

---

*New Zealand Idol is just like American Idol or Australian Idol, it is just far, far more painful to watch.

tribution of candidates and votes to make it easy to come up with different winners when we used different methods of counting.* However, it is also true that we assumed that the process of conducting the election was perfect. Hanging chads, misprinted ballots, absentee votes from people who were never born, the mysterious voting habits of dead people, voting machine failures, and all of the other things that might make the outcome of a real vote even more uncertain were not included in our example. Is the person who really "won" the 2000 U.S. presidential election the one who moved into the White House? Both the yes and no arguments have merit.

What **Arrow's Theorem**[3] shows us is that elections cannot be the perfect means of making decisions because part of the process—the way you tally the votes—can significantly alter the outcome, even when it is done perfectly and fairly. Since you have no way of being certain that any one of the various fair methods of counting is the correct one, you also have no way to guarantee that the outcome reflects the true will of the majority. Rather than sending us screaming in panic, the imperfect reality of using an election to achieve the ideal of democracy should serve as a reminder of our distinction between the ideal and the real and how that distinction affects politics.

We opened this chapter spending a little quality time beating on your faith in democracy because it is important to get you to think about the distinction between the ideal of democracy and the reality. You have probably never been asked to make this distinction. You have probably never even thought about it enough to realize there was much of a distinction, but doing so—delving into the good, the bad, and the ugly aspects of democracy—is necessary to understand the critical role that elections and other democratic structures play in modern politics.

DEMOCRACY AND THE LIBERAL IDEAL

So far in this chapter we have not really spoken about the concept of democracy at all. Instead, we have been talking about elections, which is what most people probably think of first when they hear the word democracy. Given a more extended opportunity to speak about the concept, people might also mention presidents, prime ministers, legislatures, parliaments, and other aspects of modern democratic governments. However, in the modern world, pure democracy is not actually a viable form of government. Instead, democracy is an ideal, dreamt up by long-dead, slaveholding, wine-guzzling Greek men with lead-poisoning-induced sanity problems. And like all of the other ideals we have discussed, democracy is probably unattainable in practice. The various forms of modern democratic governments are merely efforts to approximate that ideal, and an emphasis should be placed on *approximate*.

Democracy quite literally means "rule by the people," and it reflects the ideal of people governing themselves, which may have been more feasible in the ancient Greek

---

*We can do that. We're the authors.

city-state of Athens. Because Athens was small enough, all Athenian citizens could gather together to share perspectives, debate, and actually vote on policies, in what we would call **direct democracy**. In reality, of course, Athenian citizens had time and space enough to personally engage in politics because they had slaves to do much of their work for them. Only true Athenians could be citizens and that distinction did not include a lot of people—women, slaves, and the poor, for example. Other than that, everything was rosy. Still, the notion of people actually ruling themselves has a certain element of quirky charm to it. The idea was that democracy was more than a means of reaching a fair decision. Democracy also was seen as a means of improving the society. By having people share perspectives, empathize with each other and work out compromises, people created a community that worked to improve themselves and their city-states.

All of this seems quite admirable, that is, at least, until you ponder the trial of the great philosopher Socrates. It was that very same Athenian democracy that gave Socrates a hemlock cocktail for challenging the Athenian democracy's accepted truths and for purportedly corrupting its youth.* Socrates's jury was comprised of the citizens of Athens seated as one group, and it was they who voted to put him to death. That brings up a big problem associated with direct democracy. There is lots and lots of room for participation for those recognized as citizens, but there is often no tolerance for difference and dissent. A democracy in this sense is often associated with the **tyranny of the majority**, where an unrestrained majority bands together to rule a society with a ferocity and cruelty that can be every bit as arbitrary and dictatorial as *Nineteen Eighty-Four*'s Big Brother.

Remember that Plato was not a fan of democracy, and Aristotle listed it among the bad forms of government. Quite possibly motivated by the death of Socrates, Plato believed that simply because a majority of people had an opinion, it did not make them or their opinion correct. Aristotle believed that democracies amounted to mob rule where self-interested factions fought for those things that suited them with no regard for the good of the larger collective. In fact, the framers of the U.S. Constitution† shared this Aristotelian negative view of democracy. In fact, they would never have used the term democracy to describe the American government they created; they preferred the term **republic**,‡ a government in which decisions are made by representatives of the citizens rather than the citizens themselves. One need only think of the many undemo-

---

*Hemlock is a seriously deadly poison, and that is probably the reason Socrates's famous last words were, "I just drank what. . . ?" Also, we stole this joke from Val Kilmer's best movie ever, *Real Genius*.

†Long, long ago in a chapter far, far away—chapter 2—this material was covered. The guys who wrote it, not the ones who put it in that Plexiglas box in the National Archives. Not that there is anything wrong with the Plexiglas box. Seriously, it's a nice box, all clear and bulletproof and everything.

‡No, you are not hallucinating—at least we don't think so. In chapter 6 we told you that according to one definition, a republic was a country without a single authoritative leader. However, this definition is the more common one.

> **With all of its faults, there remains an appeal to democracy that seems unflappable. The idea that ordinary citizens should control their own destinies is one that has had a tremendous appeal.**

cratic features of the Constitution to get the point, for example, the Supreme Court with its members appointed for life terms, a senate that would be chosen by the state legislatures, two votes for every state in the senate regardless of size, the electoral college. Remember that while we ultimately wind up rooting for Jefferson Smith in *Mr. Smith Goes to Washington,* the filibuster he uses to win thwarts the will of the majority and is hardly democratic.

Yet, with all of its faults, there remains an appeal to democracy that seems unflappable. The idea that ordinary citizens should control their own destinies is one that has had a tremendous appeal. The idea that democracy can promote moral values remains with us. Furthermore, it fits in well with the liberal ideal of limited government. In democracies the people ultimately rule and government by the people should minimize the ability of a few powerful elites to extend government into the details of people's lives. Thus, democracy remains a powerful idea and an even more powerful ideal.

Direct Democracy

Exactly how you go about approximating the liberal democratic ideal of a government by the people is, in itself, an interesting question. If democracy had problems in ancient Athens, it is riddled with even more problems when it comes to modern nation-states. To distinguish the dead-Greek-men version from modern forms of democracy, we often refer to the Athenian model as direct democracy. As we have noted, direct democracy can devolve into little more than a polite mob that votes on whom they will lynch—or in the case of Socrates, poison. Furthermore, because in a true direct democracy, everyone votes on every question of government, we can immediately think of several problems that will inevitably arise. How can more than a few people all get together in one place? How will there be time for everyone to deal with every issue? How do we guarantee everyone an opportunity to participate? How will people find the time to participate? Except for perhaps the smallest of groups in the most simple of contexts, true direct democracy, as a system of government, simply cannot function efficiently or effectively.

Elements of direct democracy, however, can be a valuable part of a modern democracy. The closest we probably get to direct democracy in the modern world is the *referendum* or *initiative* process employed by many, but not all, of the U.S. state governments. **Referenda*** are questions that legislatures put on the ballot for the people to vote on, while **initiatives** are questions that are put on the ballot by citizens, usually after some kind of qualification process like collecting a significant number of signatures on a petition. These processes provide mechanisms to circumvent legislatures and other representative governing bodies to allow the public to vote directly

---

*Referendum is singular, referenda is plural. Also, the kiwi fruit is actually neither a native New Zealand plant nor is it really what most would call a fruit. It is actually a berry, the Chinese gooseberry to be exact.

upon policies, laws, or other actions that would normally be taken up by legislatures. Recent examples provide indications of both the difficulties and the values of this limited form of direct democracy.

Initiatives have been a particularly salient part of recent politics in the state of Washington. Washington is the highly caffeinated state right next to Idaho that is not Montana. In 1999, Tim Eyman took some time away from the unlicensed, possibly illegal mail-order business he ran out of his home—a lucrative career selling customized novelty watches to fraternities and sororities—and started an initiative campaign against car licensing fees. At the time, the fees for license tabs* in the state of Washington were based upon a formula derived from the initial sticker price of the vehicle and the alignment of the planets during its last oil change. The annual trauma of forking over several hundred dollars to keep mom's new SUV legal, made the January 13, 1999, *Seattle Times* headline, "New initiative would set $30 fee for all vehicle licenses,"[4] an instant hit and an easy sell at the ballot box.

Anyone reminded of Al Franken and ATM fees?

Mr. Eyman was remarkably successful at tapping into an issue of widespread public discontent. Nobody wants to pay taxes. That has always been an absolute and unshakable truth. Mr. Eyman's greatest talent, politically at least, was his ability to connect that discontent to a simple alternative that was extremely appealing to the average voter. Mr. Eyman seemed to understand how to connect to people whose political interest, involvement, and attention span tended to be severely limited. Drunk on the heady popularity of the car tab initiative with voters, Mr. Eyman offered initiative after initiative: to reduce property taxes, to limit property tax increases to 1 percent annually, to repeal a tax to build mass transit in Seattle, to use 90 percent of transportation funds for building and maintaining roads, to eliminate Seattle's light rail project, to open carpool lanes to all traffic during off-peak hours, to repeal the 5 cent per gallon tax increase the state legislature passed to fund transportation projects in the wake of the massive revenue losses from the $30 vehicle licensing initiative that started it all. Eight years after he started, it does not appear that any single one of Eyman's initiatives has actually become the law in the State of Washington. The Washington State Supreme Court eviscerated them all. In fact, the consistent failures in the face of legal challenges even prompted some critics to argue that Eyman purposely writes illegally worded initiatives. The logic of why he would do that is a little shaky, and his critics have never managed to provide a good reason to believe this interesting conspiracy theory is the truth, but it is clear that the success of these initiatives at election time is not matched in subsequent legal fights.

---

*And you thought you found a spelling error. We don't mean tags as in pet license tags you put on your dog's collar, nor do we mean license plates. Tabs are what the good people of Washington—as well as the naughty ones—call the little stickers you put on the license plate to show that you have paid your licensing taxes for the year.

Not Quite Right, but Still Good

To understate things considerably, Mr. Eyman and his initiatives have been controversial. The debates have been furious and often personal. Critics raged about Mr. Eyman's questionable diversion of initiative campaign funds to pay himself a salary. Other reactions have included an initiative (Washington State Initiative I-831) to have voters officially designate Tim Eyman as "A horse's ass." A judge forced a revision in the official language of the initiative, changing "A horse's ass" to "A vernacular term to denote the back end of a horse."[5] The courts later threw out the horse's ass initiative on technical grounds. Beyond giving us a few laughs, and the chance to use "horse's ass" five times in a single paragraph, the horse's ass initiative does highlight the intensity of the debate. Browsing through the *Seattle Times*'s coverage of the initiatives reads like a saga of old, with venomous editorials, personal attacks, harsh debates, court challenges, and a whole lot of old-fashioned arguing. Still, despite all of this side drama, recent news coverage suggests that there is little reason to expect any kind of reduction in Eyman's effort to push initiatives onto the ballot. Why should he? Even though the courts have struck all of his initiatives down, his foray into direct democracy has changed the nature of taxation in the state of Washington. In 2006 he was still busy, pushing an initiative focused on overturning the state's gay rights legislation.*

The recent changes in taxation in the state of Washington highlight what Eyman and his supporters might argue is the true value of direct democracy. Even in his failure to actually get an initiative enacted as law, Mr. Eyman's use of the initiative process has had tremendous effects. The cost of licensing a car for a year may not be exactly $30, but the Washington State Legislature changed it to a flat fee with limited local additions. At most it costs about $50—far below the several hundred dollars it could run before Eyman's first initiative. The initiatives injected the idea of a tax revolt into every political discussion and every action of the Washington State Legislature. You could also argue that the awareness of the threat of these kinds of initiatives, even when they are not used, has made every legislator in the state of Washington more sensitive to what the public wants and how the public will respond to taxes and spending on transportation.

You could also argue, as many critics do, that these initiatives represent exactly what is wrong with direct democracy. The public's knowledge of the intricacies of politics, particularly in terms of taxes and economics, is limited, and the quality of decisions made by the fleeting involvement of the public tend not to be of the highest quality. People are more interested in the daily challenges of dating, home, career, and figuring out the air date of the "they-used-to-be-celebrities" version of the latest reality TV show. Limiting car licenses to $30 is simple and appealing. In reality, however, what seems like a tax break for many is really a tax break that is limited to the owners of

---

*This raises another point about this type of direct democracy; because the author of the ballot question can make such a difference, is it democratic for only one person to set the agenda for an entire state?

very expensive cars. The owner of a Hummer received an annual tax break of over $700, while the vast majority of car owners—particularly the professor who is still driving the rusted out 1973 Dodge Dart that his parents tried to abandon by the side of the freeway—received absolutely no reduction in their annual licensing costs.

Direct democracy can seem quite appealing to anyone who has struggled with, or just whined about, the inefficiencies, idiocies, and improprieties of a government that pays $200 for a toilet seat and gives subsidies to tobacco farmers while simultaneously suing the tobacco industry and making it illegal to smoke anywhere except designated parking lots in South Dakota. However, the reality is that direct democracy usually does not work in the way that it might have worked as a system of governing for the ancient Greeks. There are several reasons, but two simple and obvious ones stand out.

First, most people have neither expertise nor the time to evaluate and consider all of the details of running a town, county, state, or country. Thirty dollars for an annual license: Does that include the fee for safety and emissions inspections? Does it apply to cement trucks, buses, pickups, motorhomes, motorcycles, ATVs, snowmobiles, parade floats, or that great big tractor thing they use to haul the space shuttle out to the launch pad? If you cut the licensing fee, where does the money for roads come from? Should the fee increase with inflation? What about those license plates with people's initials, cute seven-letter sayings, and tigers saying, "Save the rainforest," which used to cost extra every year? Are they now $30? All of those questions and countless other details must be dealt with by those who govern. In a true direct democracy, the public would have to deal with all of those details as they met together for discussion and debate. We often do not have the expertise and most of us do not have the time to go beyond the most basic aspect of $30 car tabs. Given the massive complexity of governing, it would be impossible for everyone to participate in every decision.

Second, most of the population does not want to. One thing that politicians, philosophers, and political scientists often forget is that many people would be perfectly thrilled if they could just ignore politics and still get a reasonably tolerable government. Most people believe they have better things to do. For most students this involves the frantic quest to locate a significant other with sufficiently low standards to consider dating said student—but that is far from the only thing that most students believe is more important than engaging in political debates. In fact, in terms of the things the average student has decided are worth panicking about, there are exactly 1,384 priorities above the politics of residential zoning laws. In other words, there is no better way to quiet a classroom than to ask a question like, "so what do you think of the debate over the prime minister's new ministerial appointments?"

For the vast majority of us, putting food on the table, having a breakfast nook to put the table in, and all the little things it takes to someday buy and assemble IKEA chairs for the three-legged table found abandoned by the side of the road are the things that consume most of our lives. Politics and governing ourselves has to fit in what little time and energy we have left over, and then it has to compete with all the other things we would like to do such as recovering from hangovers, learning how to program the clock on the DVD player, keeping mom, dad and/or the significant other happy, setting the world record for continuous viewing of the Golf Channel, finding enough money in the couch cushions to get one of those fancy foamed-up coffees, clipping toenails, and, of course, writing a best-selling novel about a goat, a robot, and the clone of Simon Bolivar getting stranded on the third moon of Saturn. Most of us do not want to govern ourselves because we have better things to do and as long as the government does not get too far out of line or interfere too much with those other priorities, most of us are willing to leave most of the mundane governing tasks to others.

Still doubting? Well, stop to think about how close we actually are to being capable of instituting a system of electronic democracy that could closely approximate a direct democracy. Assuming that we can get over some serious problems with computer security, we should soon be able to give everyone a password and ID that will allow them to vote on the Internet. But, why stop there? Why not allow everyone to vote on every issue of concern? Every Saturday night can be voting night. Forget dating and finding the aforementioned significant other, from now on from 5:00 to 7:00 p.m. we can all discuss and debate the issues in one big national chat room. At 9:00 p.m. the vote can take place. Hone up on your knowledge of banking laws. Break out the books on issues of national security. Get ready to parse the specifics of energy policy. When you start really thinking about it, that pain you are feeling in your gut is our point. Most people just do not want the responsibility. Even those who still may be tempted are often dissuaded by the fact that their voice of reason may not win the debate. Consider those neighbors with the swastika tattoos, the families with small-scale hemp farms, the hoarder with 300 cats, or the former figure skating champion with a collection of irreparable cars she uses for lawn ornaments. Each of them would have the same ability as you to vote on issues of national importance.

There is a relatively simple solution. Pay someone else to do it. Whether it is governing society or fixing a toilet, when you have something that needs to be done and you lack the ability, the know-how, or the gumption to do it yourself, you hire someone who can and will do it for you. This has several advantages, the most obvious of which is efficiency. It allows you focus on what you do best, say the farming of a perfectly legal hydroponically grown crop, rather than fixing the toilet. This allows you to become the best farmer you can be and it allows those who fix the toilets, or govern, to become experts who can fix or regulate any part of the waste relocation system in a fraction of the time it would take the average farmer. As any good capitalist would tell you, by specializing, we are all more efficient, and that efficiency principle applies to governing as well as it does to any other task.

On the other hand, we do not want to completely surrender the role of governing to others. Think of Hitler, Stalin, Genghis Khan, Martha Stewart, George Steinbrenner—

history makes it clear that surrendering absolute power to others is not a good thing. So if we do not want to govern ourselves, and we know better than to completely trust others to do it for us, what do we do?

Representative Democracy

It is debatable whether or not the U.S. government was the very first modern democracy. The Swiss and a few others can make a reasonable claim. However, it is clear that many of the structures and processes that Ben Franklin, and the other white wig boys created to approximate government by the people have served as a model to an increasingly democratic world. Even the North Vietnamese communist government of Ho-Chi Minh modeled significant parts of its constitution on the U.S. document. Whether or not the United States was the first modern democracy is less important than the fact that the framers of its constitution* consciously and rationally designed it from nearly a blank slate. Without too many historical constraints or ongoing commitments, the framers were able to invent and adapt structures, processes, and methods to create a functional government that could approximate the ideal of government by the people.

Four factors are critical to the effectiveness and the remarkable endurance of the U.S. system. First, its designers used representatives as a way to create a democratic government of specialists. While the framers did not originate the idea of representatives, they understood those representatives to be servants of the districts they represented and they apportioned the districts so that the representatives could stay close to the people they represent. The second factor is the institutionalization of revolt, in the form of the frequent elections to select those representatives. Frequent elections— two years for members of the House of Representatives—are intended to keep those political experts focused on the demands, wishes, and desires of the people they represent. Third, the framers of the U.S. Constitution recognized the potential downside of democracy—they specifically acted to prevent people from voting to lynch others and otherwise imposing a tyranny of the majority, by limiting the power of government. Article I, section 8 of the Constitution lays out Congress's powers, and the Tenth Amendment specifically reserves all other power to the states and to the people. Further, as chapter 6 mentions, through the use of "separation of powers" and "checks and balances," the framers deliberately made it very difficult for the government to do much of anything at all. Fourth, as noted earlier, the framers further recognized the limits of democracy by specifically adding a few, carefully chosen, undemocratic features. The most notable of these undemocratic features can be seen in the way that minorities and losers[†] are given specific guarantees of protection by the Bill of Rights. These protect dissent and difference and prevent the majority from exploiting minorities or killing a

---

*Again, not the guys who put it in the box.

†The framers meant losers in the political forum, but this idea can be applied to losers more generally.

Not Quite Right, but Still Good

Socrates even if they voted to do so. Thus, the U.S. Constitution really encapsulates the battle of the real versus the ideal when it comes to democracy. The framers were able to promote government by the people by creating institutions that specifically limit the actual role that the people play.

For legal reasons, we are required to inform our readers that this was the point where an argument broke out. The argument was not among the framers of the constitution, but between the authors, our fourth editor (the one who mysteriously vanished during a Dungeons and Dragons tournament), and a student named Larry. Our now missing editor suggested that we use this as an opportunity to connect the discussion back to the theories of politics we discussed in chapter 2, and one of the authors used a crass word when he asked the seventh level, half-elf magic user if he was referring to the Plato "stuff" on good and bad forms of government. Larry—one of "those" kinds of honor students—was standing in the hall and promptly reminded the occasionally politically incorrect professor that the good and bad forms of government discussion was Aristotle's "stuff." A clerical "error" quickly followed, and after Larry discovered that his summer internship had somehow shifted from Boston to Botswana, a debate ensued. There are, indeed, many ways that a discussion of the creation of the U.S. Constitution could be connected back to our initial discussion of theory. Aristotle's good versus bad forms of government does fit here, but also how about Hobbes and the Constitution as an explicit articulation of a social contract? How about Locke's idea of limited government, civil society, and the Bill of Rights? How about Machiavelli's discussion of power and the implementation of checks and balances as a means of using the lust for power to limit the power of leaders? How about Rousseau's argument about "forcing people to be free" and the social responsibilities that go with the rights being articulated? There are plenty of opportunities here, but with the "unfortunate" disappearance of editor number four,* there was no-one all that interested in pressing the issue, so we just decided to finish up the discussion of direct democracy.

Basically, direct democracy in the U.S. system is limited to choosing who will represent your interests in government and your personal involvement in politics is usually limited to deciding who you want to vote for. Not an ideal solution, but this imperfect compromise does attempt to address the most significant difficulty with direct democracy—at least much of the time. Of course, it doesn't take a rocket scientist to recognize that the U.S. system has, at critical times, failed to protect dissenters and minorities. Examples are abundant—slavery, Jim Crow laws, the long-lasting failure to give women suffrage, the internment of the Japanese, the squelching of dissent through the Alien and Sedition Acts, the stifling of protests during major wars, laws aimed at Jehovah's Witnesses, and so on. The point is not that the United States is ideal; it is not. Rather, the point is that the U.S. system is an attempt—especially as it

---

*We did hire a Non-Player Character to search for him.

> **The point is that the U.S. system is an attempt—especially as it has been amended—to find a compromise between the real and the ideal when it comes to democracy.**

has been amended—to find a compromise between the real and the ideal when it comes to democracy.

AN ECONOMIC THEORY OF DEMOCRACY

The surgeon general of the United States has asked us to warn you that the next section of the text will discuss spatial distributions of voter preferences and the mechanisms through which the contours of opinion dispersal place practical constraints on the electoral system's political party structures through its effect on the electability of candidates of given ideological ontologisms.* There are two reasons, however, that you should not panic. First, this methodology is mostly harmless.† Side effects are mild and mostly self-inflicted, but are known to include acute disorientation, sobbing, and the loss of control of certain bodily functions. Second—surprise—we already used this methodology in the discussion of the election for king of the ice cream social and most of you survived probably because we left out the big scary words.

When we discussed how the different methods of counting the votes in the election for king of the ice cream social altered the outcome, we put the conservative candidates on the right, the liberals on the left, and repeatedly said that people would vote for the candidate that was closest to them on the spectrum shown in the figure or that they would vote against the candidate that was farthest away. This is the spatial distribution of voter preferences and this is essentially what Anthony Downs did in *An Economic Theory of Democracy*.[6] This method of thinking about voters, voting, and elections is so effective that even after a half-century Downs's theory remains the best way to discuss much of the *why* behind what we see in modern representative democracies. In fact, it may be the most elegant work of political theory produced by a scholar other than the authors of this text.

Figure 10.2 is roughly the same as Figure 10.1, with the same candidates competing for the same office. The one difference is that we have also graphed the concentration of voters along the line stretching from the liberals on the left to the conservatives on the right. The height of the curve indicates the number of voters holding a particular ideological preference. Notice that the curve is lowest at the ends and highest in the center. This represents the fact that most voters are concentrated near the middle of the political spectrum; they are moderate. While it often seems the opposite in the real world, public opinion polls, particularly in the United States but also in most of Europe and other developed countries, suggest that most people are in the middle. We all tend to notice extremists more because they have the motive to be more vocal and visible

---

*Gotcha! Don't let the jokes and asides fool you. We really can talk and write like professors when we want. We don't do it often, but every once in a while it does pay to keep students honest.

†Thank you, Douglas Adams.

Not Quite Right, but Still Good

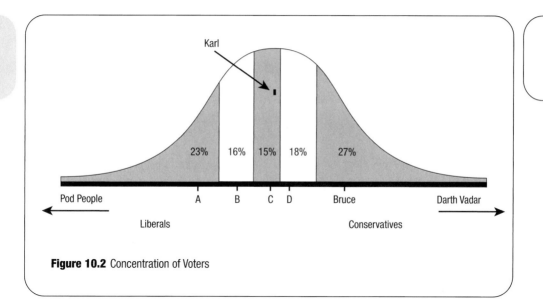

Figure 10.2 Concentration of Voters

than the average person. Furthermore, extremists tend to be less satisfied with the current state of affairs so they scream about it more than the average person. However, extremists are few in number, and there are far more average people than there are goose-stepping militaristic fascists on the right or communal, free-love tofu sculptors on the left.

We are assuming two things that may seem obvious: 1) people will vote for the candidate that is as ideologically similar to themselves as possible and 2) candidates wish to get enough votes to win the election. With these assumptions, we can use the spatial approach to make some interesting arguments regarding the likely ideological position of successful candidates, the most effective ideological position of political parties, and even the number of parties a democratic structure is likely to host depending on how its rules are structured.

Winner Take All

Downs used graphs similar to this one to explain why the United States has, and will probably always have, a two-party system. He was also able to argue that those two parties would always remain close to the nation's ideological center. The United States uses a **winner-take-all** (no proportional representation), **first-past-the-post** (no runoff elections), single-member district system. In other words, each election has one winner, that winner is the sole representative of a given location, and winning is a simple matter of receiving the plurality (most) of the votes cast in the election.[7]

To get at these ideas, we go back to the musical marsupial Bruce and the other characters in our beloved election example. Including the spatial depiction of voters in the discussion explains why some of the things happened in the ice cream social example. Specifically, in Figure 10.2 we can see how an extremist, representing the ideological preferences of only a small portion of a society, can manage to win an election when a large number of candidates are running. Most of the voters are in the middle of the political spectrum, but there are three candidates competing over this slice of the electoral pie. By dividing up the votes of the majority in the middle, it was possible for a representative of a more extreme position to win. Fewer voters overall were near Bruce, but he did not have to share those votes with any other candidate.

To identify the percentage of voters casting a ballot for each candidate you draw a vertical line halfway between the candidate and the opponent nearest him on the ideological spectrum. We have put these lines in Figure 10.2, and the line between any two candidates represents the point where voters go from being closer to one candidate to another. Thus, those on the left side of the line between A and B are closer to A, and they will vote for A. Those on the right of that line are closer to B, and they will vote for B. The number of people voting for each candidate is represented by all of the voters that are closer to that candidate than they are to any other. Thus, the number of votes for B includes everyone between the first voter to the right of the halfway line between A and B, all the way over to the last voter on the left of the line between B and C. Because the height of the curve represents the concentration of voters along the political spectrum, the area under the curve that is bounded by these two lines represents the total number of votes a candidate receives. Thus, the candidates in the middle get a narrower slice of the political spectrum, but that slice is taller and the candidates at the extreme get a wider, but shorter slice of the vote.

In most elections, the middle is where you want to be. Notice that in any scenario where one or more of the middle-of-the-road candidates is removed, the extremists lose. In fact, pick any two of the five candidates and run them against each other, and the one closest to the center will always win. In a two-candidate election, the midpoint of this curve is critical. The area under either half of the curve is the same. Thus, if you can push the dividing line between yourself and the other candidate just one voter onto the other side of the center you will have 50 percent + 1 votes. That one vote in the exact center is called the **median voter**. His name is Karl; he likes muscle cars, football, and the *Sports Illustrated* calendars and his vote gives you the majority needed to win. This fight over the median voter is why Downs argued that the United States has, and will always have, two political parties that are both very close to the political center.

The more generic version of the diagram offered in Figure 10.3 makes it easier to explain Downs's point. Consider a two-party system with one party on the right and the other on the left. To win the general election, which involves the final vote among the whole voting population for who will hold the office, a party must run a candidate who can capture the median voter of the overall population. So, the obvious strategy is to try to get a candidate as close to the ideological middle as possible. The party that runs the candidate that is closest to the center—position 5 in Figure 10.3—will win. However, because the parties represent different sides of the political spectrum, the parties cannot rush all the way to the center. Within the context of a two-party system, with each party staking out one side or the other of the political spectrum, the candidate exactly in the center of the overall population is on the very edge of the political spectrum rep-

Not Quite Right, but Still Good

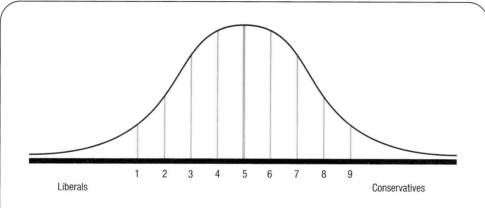

1 2 3 4 5 6 7 8 9

Liberals   Conservatives

Figure 10.3 Spatial Distribution of Voters and Candidates in a Winner-Take-All System

resented by either of the two parties. This, in part, explains why people can complain, with some justification, that presidential candidates tend to sound the same. In order to win the general election, presidential candidates must try to move toward the center, and this inevitably gets you fairly similar candidates.

However, the candidates cannot be exactly the same. There has to be some difference between the candidates of the two parties because within the context of either party, the candidate who is exactly in the middle of the overall population is a bit of an extremist within the party and is some distance from the center of the party's ideological spectrum. With regard to the primary election, the election within the party to select the party's candidate for the general election, the candidate who wins the primary will have to capture the median voter within the political spectrum represented by the party. This requires candidates to always be on the party's side of the overall center. Thus, in a primary election, the candidates usually seem more ideological; Democrats tend to sound more liberal and Republicans tend to sound more conservative.

The result is a balance between these two electoral demands. The need to win the overall election drives the parties to run candidates near the median voter at the overall center. The need to win the primary drives candidates away from the overall center and toward the median voter of the party. Thus, you get parties that claim ideological ground just to the right and left of center, roughly locations 4 and 6 in Figure 10.3.

Once these two parties are established, it is all but impossible to add a third party. The most obvious motivation to create a new party is to serve a portion of the population that is dissatisfied with the candidates offered by the existing parties. Because the bulk of the overall population is scrunched toward the overall ideological center, the median voter within the existing two parties will be skewed toward the overall center. This means that the most dissatisfied voters will be out at the extremes. They have the greatest motivation to try to start a new party and to run candidates that address their interests better than the existing parties. The problem is that those candidates will be further from the center than the candidates of the existing two parties, and rather than helping the dissatisfied voters get a representative that is closer to them ideologically, the new party will actually do the opposite.

If you start with candidates at positions 4 and 6 and add a candidate representing the more extreme ideological position of a new conservative party, say at position 8, then you end up guaranteeing the election of the middle-of-the-road candidate that is farthest from your ideology. By running a candidate at position 8, the new conservative party steals the most conservative voters from the more moderately conservative candidate at position 6 and by doing so guarantees that the more liberal candidate at position 4 will win the overall election. Thus, instead of a reasonable chance of getting a representative on their own side of the median voter, the new party has made the outcome of the election worse for themselves by running a candidate that more closely represents their ideals. This is not just conjecture. Something like this scenario has happened several times in the history of U.S. presidential elections. Whenever an independent or third-party candidate captured a significant share of the vote, the candidate from the established party that was ideologically closest to the added candidate lost the election. Many argue that Ross Perot cost George H. W. Bush a second term as president. While it would be a bit dangerous to assume that this is true, the real world being so untidy and unpredictable, it is a fact that if you were to add the votes for Perot to those of Bush Senior, Bush wins a second term in a landslide and Bill Clinton is never elected president.

As long as you have a winner-take-all, single-member district system like the United States, this will always be the case. Only the candidates that can win the overall vote in any election get the opportunity to actually participate in government. If you lose by even one vote, your party is shut out. Think about how frustrating this could be for a political party that is challenging the status quo. There are 435 seats in the United States House of Representatives. Imagine that the new political party wins 15 percent of the vote across the country, a remarkable start for a new political party. Yet, it is likely that this new political party will actually gain *zero* seats in the House of Representatives. Remember, to win an election in a winner-take-all, single-member district system like the United States, the winning candidate must be able to achieve a plurality to win anything at all. Running candidates for political office is a costly, time-consuming, and exhausting task. It is little wonder that parties that can never get themselves up to a majority in a significant number of locations quickly tire of trying. To add insult to injury, to the degree that a new party has ideas that may appeal to the center, the centrist parties will quickly absorb those ideas. Thus, the only viable parties are those that can win a majority reasonably often, and since the median voter is the key to winning, only the most centrist of parties will succeed and survive.

A big reason that Ross Perot's effort to build a new U.S. political party collapsed was because it failed to win more than a tiny number of political offices, but possibly more problematic was that it also helped Democrats take offices from the Republicans. The Republicans were closer to the conservative political base to which Perot was trying to appeal, thus his party tended to take votes that would have otherwise gone to the Republicans. Meanwhile, both the Democrats and the Republicans began to absorb

Perot's deficit reduction message because it appealed to centrist voters. It is also true that the upstart Green Party in the United States did not endorse Ralph Nader in the 2004 presidential elections despite the fact that Nader is right with them on so many issues. The Greens recognized that Nader would be siphoning votes away from John Kerry and the Greens would not support him because they wanted to be sure that those votes went to the Democrats. The Democrats were closer to the progressive liberal base to which the Greens were trying to appeal than the Republicans, so the Democrats would be more harmed by a second Nader candidacy.

Fine, but if this is true, how can there be so many democratic countries with more than two political parties? The simple answer is that not all democratic systems have rules like the United States. Modern democracies, unlike ice cream, come in two basic flavors:

1. the single-member district systems used in the United States where one winner represents one location.

2. the proportional representation systems that are common in many parliamentary democracies around the world.

The differences between these two basic methods of selecting representatives have effects that permeate the political system all of the way down to the stability of the government.

Winner Takes Their Share

One of the most significant ways in which modern democracies can differ is in the way they translate the votes of the public into the people selected to actually govern in the name of the voters. The United States provides what may be the clearest example of a winner-take-all, single-member district system, but most democracies use a completely different system for using votes to select leaders.

The most common alternative to a winner-take-all system is a proportional representation system (PR). Proportional systems are focused on political parties instead of candidates. At election time, voters across the entire country cast their ballots not for specific candidates but for political parties. There are candidates—the parties offer long lists of candidates—but the transition from candidate to governing representative does not come from achieving a plurality of the vote. The seats in the parliament, Knesset, Diet, or whatever else the legislative body might be called, are divided among the parties based upon the votes they receive. All of the parties that pass the qualifying threshold and get more than a certain minimum percentage of the vote (for example, at least 5 percent of the vote) win seats in the elected body. The number of people taken from each party's list of candidates is based upon the proportion of the vote the party receives; thus it is a proportional system.

Returning to the astoundingly wonderful figure we have been using throughout this most excellent chapter, we can use the spatial depiction of voters in Figure 10.4 to see why political parties in proportional systems tend to proliferate like rabbits.

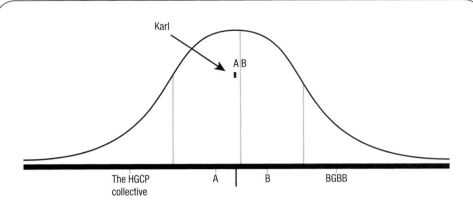

Figure 10.4 Spatial Representation of Voters in a Proportional Representation System

For the sake of the discussion, let's start out with two parties, A and B, fighting over the large number of voters near the center of the political spectrum. We could have started with a billion parties, or thirty-seven parties, and still have ended up in roughly the same place. However, starting with two makes it easier to make comparisons to the two we ended up with when we looked at the dynamics of a winner-take-all, single-member district system like that of the United States.

If you start out with two parties, each striving to dominate the political system by winning the most votes, both parties have the motivation to move toward the ideological center. People will vote for the party that is closest to them on the great horizontal line of ideology that defines all political beings. That means that moderately liberal Party A will get the votes from the vertical line of political division separating it from moderately conservative Party B along with all the votes out to the extreme left-hand edge of the spectrum. Since Party A is slightly closer to the center than B, the dividing line between them is on the right-hand side of the middle, and Party A will capture the greatest percentage of the votes. It is also true that since the seats in the parliament are divvied up to match that percentage, they will also win the greatest number of seats in parliament, and Party A will have the majority it needs to win all the important votes. Specifically, this means that Parliamentary bill 56448 will pass, and all the members of Party B have to sit on the old wobbly folding chairs at lunch.

The problem with that strategy of capturing the middle is that it moves moderately liberal Party A away from the people out on the extreme left. Those people are quite dissatisfied with the arrangement and they want representatives that better reflect their preference for beanbag chairs sewn out of the hemp cloth that is too scratchy to use for underwear. Any rational political entrepreneur will quickly capitalize on the opportunity presented by this dissatisfaction by forming a party to specifically address the interests of this disenfranchised community. Thus, the Hemp Grower's Cooperative People's (HGCP) Collective is born. It assimilates the votes all the way in to the midpoint between it and Party A, thus capturing all the votes from the extreme left. In the example for the winner-take-all system, this leads to disastrous results for the interests of those supporting the new party. In each of the single-member local districts the

Not Quite Right, but Still Good

extremely liberal Collective steals votes from the party closest to them, moderately liberal Party A, and the Collective actually helps moderately conservative Party B's candidates, the party furthest from them ideologically, to win a majority of votes in districts where Party A might have had a slight edge.

In a PR system, however, the result is notably different. Voting is national, not local, and the key to success is the overall percentage of votes that the new party can get over the whole nation. If the Collective can capture more than the minimum percentage of votes, the qualifying percentage, they win seats and win the right to vote in the legislature. In fact, if the Collective can win just enough seats to prevent either Party A or Party B from holding more than 50 percent of the seats in the legislature, then they suddenly hold a power far beyond the number of voters they actually represent. Recall our example from chapter 8 where the religious Party C, a marginal party, could force concessions from the two other parties to wield influence beyond its proportion in the electorate. In a PR system the Collective suffers none of the frustration it would in a winner-take-all system, as it can immediately become an essential actor. It is essential because it controls the votes that either of the other parties needs to get any bill passed in the parliament. Therefore, the Collective must be included if either party wants to get anything done. In any conflict or dispute between Party A and Party B, the support of the Collective is necessary in order to win. Thus, both of the other parties have to cater to the needs of the Collective and scratchy hemp beanbag chairs fill the lunchroom. Resistance is futile.

The dramatic gains in influence by the Collective do not go unnoticed and nobody in their right mind wants to try to eat a tofu chilidog while sitting in a beanbag chair.* Thus a new party springs up on the right, and the Beer Guzzling Bambi Butchers (BGBB) stagger in from their hunting lodges to offer a new alternative to this horrible state of affairs. Beyond an affection for bazookas, the new party hopes to capture enough seats to become an essential actor and redecorate the lunchroom with Barcaloungers and antlers. The proliferation of parties has begun. Any dissatisfied group, regardless of what kind of chair they have an unnatural obsession for, can offer up their own party. The only limiting factors are the percentage of votes needed to pass the qualifying threshold and gain at least one seat, and the strategic need to capture enough seats to either dominate, or to be big enough that one or more of the other parties need you to win votes in the parliament. Typically, this results in one or two large parties near the middle of the political spectrum and a large number of smaller parties vying to become just big enough to tip the scales for one of the larger parties. The lower the qualifying threshold, the easier it is to get a seat and the greater the number of smaller parties you tend to have.

Israel provides what may be the best example of the proliferation of parties in a proportional representation system. With a qualifying threshold set at only 2 percent of the

---

*Be careful, or you'll stain your Phish t-shirt.

On 17 September 2005, during the breaks between that weekend's National Provincial Championship rugby matches, New Zealanders voted. Other than the way political careers in the southern hemisphere swirl in the other direction when election results send them down the drain, the election seemed quite typical, except perhaps for that a heck of a lot of people voted twice, and it was legal. When New Zealanders vote, they cast a vote for both their party preference, as you would in a proportional system, and a vote for a local representative, as you would in a single-member district system. It seems that when it came to the question of using proportional representation versus single-member-districts, Kiwis formed a committee, which took the sensible route of choosing neither and both. We know a committee made this choice because the resulting system is something that only a committee or an insane mathematician could have created. Or perhaps it was a committee of insane mathematicians

There are many sane and simple ways that such a dual system could function. You could have two legislative houses, one filled through the proportional party vote and one filled through the election of the district representatives. Or, you could have a single house with some proportion of the MPs (Ministers of Parliament) selected through the party vote and the rest chosen to represent a specific district. Of course, if you are a committee, you will choose neither of these

reasonable options. Instead, the Kiwi system is a little more complex and provides plenty of jobs for mathematicians. That is why we suspect the original committee was populated by insane mathematicians.

A party that gets at least 5 percent of the party vote *or* has a candidate win an electoral district qualifies for parliament. Thus, in 2005, eight parties qualified. Labour and National parties won large percentages of the party vote and won several electoral seats, New Zealand First and the Green Party won no electoral districts but each received just over 5 percent of the vote, and four parties won an electoral district but far less than 5 percent of the party vote.

Now follow carefully, this is where it gets a bit bumpy.

Once a party qualifies, its percentage of the party vote is used to determine the number of places it gets in the 120-seat parliament. The important detail that makes it insane is that the proportional distribution of seats according to party vote is applied to the entirety of the 120 seats in Parliament. Kiwis do not allocate 69 electoral seats to the winners of the 69 electoral districts and then allocate the rest proportionally. Instead, they allocate all 120 seats according to the percentage of the party vote won, *and* the candidates who won electoral districts both count against a party's total number of seats won with the party vote and they must be seated first. Thus, in 2005, the thirty-one Labour

vote, Israel's 2006 election saw the seats in its Knesset split among ten parties as it only took 62,000 votes for a party to pass the 2 percent qualifying threshold and win a place in the Israeli parliamentary government. This number is down from 2003 when the threshold was only 1.5 percent, or 47,000 votes, and there were thirteen parties that won seats. This is probably the extreme example of both a low qualifying threshold and the number of parties with seats.

The type of election used to create a modern democracy is not an either-or proposition. Mixed forms are abundant. France has a proportional representation system to select its legislature, but a popularly elected president that is selected in a winner-take-all national election. As the Politics in Practice box shows, New Zealand elects some of its parliamentarians in a national proportional representative election

Party candidates that won electoral districts were seated in Parliament, and they were subtracted from the fifty seats that Labour won with their percentage of the party vote. This left nineteen seats to be filled from the Labour Party candidate list.

At first, that system seems to nullify much of the motive for campaigning to win individual electoral districts (called electorates in New Zealand). However, if you go back to the "or" in the definition of the qualifying threshold it is possible to see how—unlike the United States, where single-member electoral districts serve to exclude smaller parties—in New Zealand, these electorates provide a mechanism for the smallest parties to establish or sustain a foothold in parliament. Any MP with solid support in his or her electoral district can keep a party alive as long as he or she can win that district and qualify the party. Once the party is qualified, it takes only a tiny percentage of the party vote to bring another party member into parliament to join the winner of the district. Thus, in 2005, when a policy shift by the large National Party subsumed many of the issues championed by the ACT Party and threatened the political survival of the ACT Party, party leader Rodney Hide focused all of his efforts on winning his electorate and was able to keep the party alive by winning it. Even though ACT New Zealand won only 1.5 percent of the party vote, they qualified by winning an electorate and they had just enough of the percentage of the party vote to get a second seat to add the first person on their list. It is still desperate times for ACT, but the party stayed alive because winning a single-member district kept it qualified.

This is in sharp contrast to the Green Party, which won over three times as many party votes as ACT, but won no individual electorates. With just 5.07 percent of the party vote that was counted on election night, the Green Party had to bite its nails until every last absentee ballot was counted to determine if it qualified in the 2005 election. It came down to a matter of a couple thousand votes to determine if it would get six seats in parliament or none and this uncertainty drastically reduced its leverage as a potential coalition partner in the new government. ACT on the other hand, knew for certain it qualified, and even with just two seats it had far more leverage.

This is still not the most interesting aspect of this system. What happens when you win more electoral districts than seats your party vote percentage entitled you to fill? In 2005, the Maori Party won four electorates, but only won enough party votes to earn two seats in Parliament. How does that fit into the scheme where the electorate seats count against a party's total in the proportional system?

For a committee of insane mathematicians the answer is simple. You bring in a couple of folding chairs and seat 122 MPs in a 120-member parliament.

and others as winner-take-all representatives of geographic districts. Neither method of electing representatives is inherently superior to the other, nor has any particular mixture shown itself to be the magic combination to give us a perfect representational democracy.

THE REAL VERSUS THE IDEAL, AGAIN

Democracy in its ideal form holds great promise. The idea of the will of the people is one that has great symbolic and emotional appeal. It is so powerful that the rationale the United States used for entering into World War I was to "make the world safe for democracy." However, in the real world democracy is wrought with problems. Thus, to meet the conditions of the real world the common definition of the term democracy has undergone some change. When we speak of democracy, we no longer necessarily only refer to **majoritarianism**, rule by the majority. In reality we have infused democracy with elements that are really quite undemocratic. After all, freedom of speech, protection of minorities, freedom of the press, and freedom of religion are not democratic in any sense of promoting the majority's will. They are, in fact, limitations on what the majority can do to often unpopular minorities and ideas.

In fact, the modern definition of democracy has really been stripped down to its bare essentials. In his work, *Capitalism, Socialism, and Democracy*, Joseph Schumpeter strips the term of all values. Instead, he sees it merely as a method of reaching decisions, "the democratic method is that institutional arrangement for arriving at political decisions in which individuals acquire the power to decide by means of a competitive struggle for the people's vote." [8] Gone is any attempt to infuse democracy with a notion of improving people's lives. This definition also is broad enough to encompass the many different ways of counting votes. We are left with a method of governance that is clearly not perfect, but has still managed to inspire people to great acts of courage. It is the reality of democracy that led Winston Churchill to assert, "many forms of government have been tried, and will be tried in this world of sin and woe. No one pretends that democracy is perfect or all-wise. Indeed, it has been said that democracy is the worst form of government except all those other forms that have been tried from time to time."

KEY TERMS

Arrow's Theorem / **227**
direct democracy / **228**
first-past-the-post / **237**
initiatives / **229**
majoritarianism / **246**
median voter / **238**
referenda / **229**
republic / **228**
tyranny of the majority / **228**
winner-take-all / **237**

CHAPTER SUMMARY

While most people would argue that democracy is an ideal to which all nations should aspire, in reality, democracy also has its problems. As the 2000 presidential election in the United States demonstrates, even in long-established democracies, there have been problems with figuring out which candidate has actually won. In fact, in any election where there are more than two candidates, the way votes are tallied will affect the outcome. Thus, every democratic system is flawed. When most people refer to democracy, they generally mean that there should be elections, however democracy actually means rule by the people. Giving all people the opportunity to rule can create problems because the majority can overrun the minority. Thus, people have come to expect that democratic countries will protect minority rights. While some democracies make use of the direct democracy mechanisms of referenda and initiatives, most democratic countries are republics. Yet republics also have problems; the type of elections that a nation employs will affect which candidate is elected. For example, winner-take-all systems are likely to produce moderate candidates in a two-party system. Students should learn two very important lessons from this chapter. No nation can claim to perfectly represent its people; all systems, even democratic ones, are inherently flawed. Second, if you ever thought someone was "a vernacular term to denote the back end of a horse" and wanted to mobilize the electorate to do something about it, Seattle just might be the place for you.

STUDY QUESTIONS AND EXERCISES

1. Imagine that it is possible to have "electronic democracy"—that it is possible to have everyone vote via computer each night on the most important issues in the news. Further imagine that we have managed to get rid of any security concerns with electronic voting. Would you want this type of democracy? Why or why not?

2. What is the connection between the type of electoral system a country has and the number of parties it has?

3. Explain Arrow's Theorem and how it is possible that different electoral systems can reach different results.

4. In most modern democracies, a sizable proportion of the people who are eligible to vote do not actually turn out on election day. How might variance in voter turnout among different parts of the population affect the predictions of democratic theory? Can you think of any other pesky real-world factors that might affect the predictions of the idealized theories of democracy discussed in this chapter?

5. What four factors are critical to the effectiveness and the remarkable endurance of the U.S. political system?

6. Do you believe that the use of referenda and initiatives is a good idea? Why or why not? If you were going to propose an initiative or a referendum, what would it be?

WEBSITES TO EXPLORE

cepa.newschool.edu/het/profiles/arrow.htm. The New School's Kenneth J. Arrow Web page, part of the History of Economic Thought Web site, this page provides a biography and links about Kenneth Arrow.

edibleballot.tao.ca/. The Edible Ballot Society, which criticizes elections, promotes people protesting by eating their ballots; recipes are included.

www.ciconline.org/elections/. This Web site contains eLECTIONS, a very basic simulation of presidential elections that also has information about the U.S. electoral system.

www.fairvote.org/. The Web site for Center for Voting and Democracy, an organization dedicated to electoral reform, Fair Vote provides news and information about elections.

www.iandrinstitute.org/. The Initiative and Referendum Institute at the University of Southern California reports about initiatives and referenda and their uses.

www.vote-smart.org/index.htm. Project Vote Smart is a Web site with information about candidates and issues across the United States.

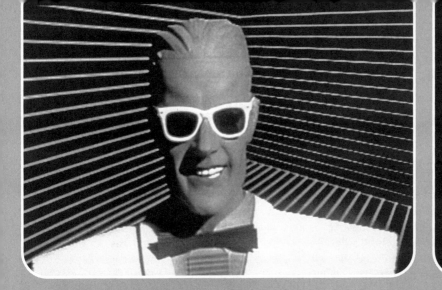

Max Headroom was the artificial star of a short-lived, underrated, and fascinating television series in which the entire world was defined by commercial television providers and their ratings. Unfortunately, it is almost never on TV anymore, and it is almost impossible to find recordings of the episodes.

CHAPTER 11

Media, Politics, and Government
Talking Heads Are Better than None

It is a classic tale. Girl goes on a picnic. Girl chases a rabbit into a hole and falls into a world on the far side of a mirror. Caterpillar gives the girl "magic" mushrooms. Girl attends insane tea party. Girl plays croquet with the Queen using flamingos and hedgehogs. Reality is not what it seems. While *Alice in Wonderland*[1] has been connected with everything from quantum mechanics to the advocacy of recreational pharmaceuticals, the message about reality is the one we want to go with. Questions about the very nature of reality seem to be common in fiction of all sorts. In *The Matrix* movie trilogy, the whole story centers around the idea that what we call reality is actually a virtual reality designed to keep our minds content as our bodies are harvested for energy. It begs the question of why those responsible for the virtual reality we live in don't make the weather better, which would really make us happy in our slimy little energy pods, but the way *The Matrix*[2] takes on the questionable reality of reality is not all that new. In Ursula K. Le Guin's classic novel, *Lathe of Heaven*,[3] the main character changes reality and changes history through his dreams. In Marge Piercy's *Woman on the Edge of Time*,[4] the possibly insane main character skirts along an indistinct border between fantasy, insanity, and what might be time travel, constantly testing and questioning the definition of reality.

We do not even have to resort to bizarre fantasies where impossibilities are tossed around like a poodle in the dryer. Magic, ghosts, vampires, imagined futures, possible pasts, that perfect family on the sitcom, a sexy spy that never quite dies while thwarting the latest attempt to conquer the world, the movie cowboy saving the town that never actually existed, time travel in any form, fiction of all kinds, fiction of any kind is all about immersing the reader or viewer in an alternative reality for the duration of the story. This act constantly challenges assumptions about the nature of reality if only by saying this could be or that could have been. As a more believable fictional bending of the reality of politics some might point to *Wag the Dog*,[5] where a U.S. president, facing a sexual scandal that was remarkably similar to the one President Clinton bumbled his way through, decides to create an imaginary war to distract the public. For the politicians and the public, this imaginary war is as real as any other. Some might point to that movie to illustrate our point but we will not.* A better movie is *Capricorn One*.[6] Well, it may not actually be a better film, but it is a far more obscure movie—one that you have probably never heard of—which makes the authors sound smart for knowing about it. It also fits better with some of the specific conceptual points we want to make in a chapter about the news media and politics.

The basic plot of *Capricorn One* is that one of the biggest moments in history was a complete fiction. The United States never actually landed on Mars and may not have landed on the moon. Instead, the whole NASA program was faked on a soundstage. In addition to the really nifty 1970s haircuts, it asks whether the moon landings could have been faked. Is all that stuff in the textbooks and at Cape Canaveral just part of an elaborate hoax? The sane person's answer is no, but there are plenty of Web sites out there that argue for the hoax and conspiracy. What is the reality? Or more importantly, how do you know what the reality is? *You* did not personally land on the moon. But you probably believe it happened. You also have beliefs about the reality of politics, but like landing on the moon, most of the things you accept as part of the political reality are things that you have not directly experienced. Political reality is a **mediated reality**. It comes to us through channels of information flow, primarily through the news media, and understanding how information is selected, sorted, and presented to us through the news media is necessary for developing a critical understanding of politics and government.

THE WHOLE CHINA CHARADE

Many people believe China exists. Do not feel bad if you are one of the many who have been duped. The global order of restaurateurs has concocted an impressive conspiracy of deception to sustain the illusion of that country's existence. The depth and extent of the effort is extraordinary, including creating a whole language complete with a system of writing that does not even use an alphabet. Then there was all of the work faking all of those maps in all of those books. They even got supposedly "Chinese" athletes into the Olympics. How many bribes to the Olympic officials did that take? Still, anyone who is willing to do a little research on the Internet knows that "Chinese" food was actually

---

*It is so bad that the only way it would get two thumbs up is if we had a hundred hands. Two on a scale of a hundred still sounds a bit generous for this one, but hey, we're nice guys.

invented in Manhattan's Upper West Side by Rachel Wise's great-granduncle Eli who ran a delivery service but had nothing to sell that people wanted him to deliver.

More seriously, how do you know China exists? If you haven't been to China, if you have not wandered down a Shanghai alley to a restaurant where you eat a bowl of soup that has a fishy, almost licorice taste that makes you truly afraid to ask what the chewy bits are, how can you be sure that China exists? The answer that usually is offered is that there are just too many things, too much evidence that there really is a China for all of it to be faked. Even if you funded the scam with every bit of the profits from the 6.83 billion dollars that New Yorkers spend each year on Chinese takeout, a scam that monumental is just too much to pull off. It is too complex. Language, history, maps, Jackie Chan movies, the diplomats at the UN—why the language thing alone takes way more than it took to make up Klingon.

If China were real—and we are not admitting anything by using that hypothetical—then what else is real? Are you sure? How many other things that you have not directly experienced are actually real? The simple answer is that most things you believe to be real are things that you have never directly experienced and the distinction between the realities you have personally experienced—experiential reality—and the other things you take to be real—**agreement reality**—can be useful for understanding politics.

If you think about it, most of the things you believe to be true, most of your reality consists of things that are outside your direct experience. From men on the moon, to wars in places you never knew existed, to the money that changes hands in an eBay auction, to a date that does not end with a restraining order, how many things, processes, or other aspects of the world do you believe to be part of reality even though you have never personally seen them or experienced them?

This is particularly true in the study of politics. There is almost nothing in government or politics that you experience directly.* It is almost all agreement reality. At most, a few hundred people see anything of the workings of Congress on any one day. When was the last time you had a heart-to-heart talk with the prime minister of Tonga? Does Tonga have a prime minister, or a king, or is that little island in the middle of the Pacific ruled by a magic goat? All of the decisions, all of the wars, all of the votes, all of the meetings, how much of the politics that affect your life do you actually witness or directly participate in? Most of the reality of politics is an agreement reality. We come to believe that one political thing or another is true by putting together bits and pieces of information much like the way many of you have been bamboozled into believing China exists. Moreover, how those bits and pieces of information are brought to you and how you use them to create your view of politics is critical to understanding politics.

---

*With the exception, among some other things, of sales taxes, right-to-work taxes, income taxes, property taxes, social security taxes, speeding tickets, parking tickets, and endless waits at the department of motor vehicles. It's just shocking people don't adore government.

YOUR NEW BRAIN AND THE CREATION OF REALITY

While it is, or should be, obvious how the things we directly experience become part of our reality, the creation of agreement reality is a bit more interesting. Take science, for example. In an often-used textbook on social science research methods, Earl Babbie argues that science is not really about lab coats, test tubes, pocket protectors, and all those other must-have fashion accessories that you just cannot buy at the mall.[7] Science can be thought of as a set of rules developed to help us decide when to accept something as agreement reality. By conducting the experiment according to certain rules, a scientist convinces others to accept his or her fantastic discovery as part of reality. Babbie wants students to learn the rules of science so they can create new bits of reality by conducting research. Thus, science is an intergalactic effort to create agreement reality.

Science is not the only intentional way that people try to convince each other to accept something as reality. Think of education. The professor, instructor, or homeless guy they hired from the bus station to lecture for your class, your teacher is intentionally trying to build a specific reality for you to accept. Beyond the detailed outline of the course and this fabulous textbook, the bus station guy is also using the authority bestowed upon him by the structure of the university—even the structure of the classroom itself—to alter your understanding of the reality of politics. Do not underestimate the effect of small details like the shabby suit coat with the patches on the elbows and that little lectern at the front of the class. After all, if the bus station guy was still standing next to his stolen shopping cart full of returnable aluminum cans, would you sit there for fifty minutes and listen to him babble? Would you read what he told you? Would you try to learn what he was teaching?

There are other ways we add things that we have not directly experienced to our understanding of reality. Naïve science is really fun. As little as an afternoon spent in the company of a toddler is enough to make just about anyone willing to believe that it is part of human nature to consider the world around us in terms of patterns of stimulus and response, causes and effects. Academics have formalized this approach to understanding the world in the various methodologies we call science, but science is still all about the basics of repeatedly poking at bugs in the garden and looking for patterns of action and reaction. The problem is that without the rules we have created for scientific inquiry, this natural instinct can lead us astray. We try so hard to put things together and we want so badly to find causes for things that we often fool ourselves. Superstitions such as the doom brought about by black cats crossing your path, bad luck from breaking a mirror, good fortune from rabbit's feet, the lucky jockstrap, all of those things that we all believe or sort of believe arise from the natural human instinct to find causes for all the effects we see around us. This natural human instinct is a big part of what allows humans to make globe-transforming inventions like belly-button piercing, the beer keg, and eBay, but it also makes us prone to fooling ourselves about reality and it makes us susceptible to having our understanding of reality manipulated by people who want us to believe something.

For example, does a full moon really make people behave like insane wombats? For a significant number of students—lunacy, the insanity that is supposedly caused by a full moon—is an unshakable, unquestionable part of their reality. How else can you explain waking up in the chemistry lab wearing someone else's clothes? However, even a quick search of the Internet* reveals that scientific efforts to find some evidence of this phenomenon consistently demonstrate that there is no such relationship. No matter what concrete thing you might use to measure the effect of a full moon—mental hospital admissions, arrests, injuries, emergency-room traffic, accident reports, overdoses, and alien abduction reports—these events are no more common on nights with a full moon than on other nights. Yet many of you will continue to insist that lunacy is obvious; you have seen it.

The way humans perceive the world around them is significant for the mediated reality of politics. If you think about it, you constantly see, hear, and smell far more than your brain perceives. The last time you walked into a classroom, your eyes saw every person sitting in there, but an instant after one of them points out that you have arrived to take the midterm in your underwear, it would be impossible for you to describe everything your eyes saw. At most, a couple of bits and pieces of that reality might stick in your head, for example, the sweaty rugby player that exceeds the legal weight limit for orange spandex pants, the person(s) you find attractive, the uniform of the police officer waiting to talk to you about the events preceding your overnighter in the chem lab, or the vendor who is selling peanuts to the crowd of students waiting to see if you will—yet again—show up for a test wearing nothing but your worst set of underwear. Your mind uses a set of instinctual and learned filters, **cognitive frameworks**, for sorting the mass of incoming information and selecting which bits it will recognize and pass on to the thinking parts of your brain. Every person has several unique sets of mental filters and you use different ones in different situations: being chased across a football field, driving a car, dating, going to school, hanging out with friends, or when you are doing all of those things simultaneously. The diverse ways that we make sense of the world are amazing, but there are a few predispositions that are common across all approximately sane people.

When you are looking for something, you notice things that fit existing beliefs and often fail to notice things that do not. When you search for something, you look where you expect to see it. If what you are looking for is not in a place you would think it might be or think it should be, you will often fail to find something like a set of keys, even if they are sitting out in the open. More generally, when something fits with what you believe or expect, you are prone to notice or remember it in terms of that cognitive

---

*Try a search on "full moon insanity research." See also http://staff.washington.edu/chudler/moon.html.

framework or understanding. Thus, if you believe in the whole moon and insanity connection, you are very likely to notice that there is a full moon out when you see someone knitting an invisible sweater and arguing with Millard Fillmore's ghost. You will connect the moon and the insane behavior you just witnessed and chalk it up as further proof of your belief. In contrast, the things that do not fit your belief are far less likely to be recognized or remembered in the context of that belief. You are particularly prone to missing the absence of one of the two things. Seeing that same insane person in the afternoon, you are unlikely to notice that the invisible sweater is being knitted when there is no moon to be found in the sky. Similarly, when a night with a full moon is downright boring, you are unlikely to realize that this runs counter to your belief and you are unlikely to think of it in terms of disproving the moon and insanity link.

In essence, you are prone to fooling yourself. Once you think the moon-insanity linkage or any other aspect of reality is true, you will notice the things that fit and reinforce the belief, but you will tend to miss contrary information. The authors knew this all along; that is why we gave you that whole bit at the very beginning of the book about using fiction to understand politics. We wanted you to use fiction to get around the beliefs you already have and the things you already know. We are trying to get you to step outside the cognitive frameworks you have already created and consider other perspectives on politics and society.

Beyond the possibility of fooling yourself about things, the way we perceive things can create situations where others, intentionally or accidentally, can manipulate our reality. By using a speech to provide a cognitive framework for understanding an issue, policy, or candidate, a politician can predispose people to interpret a myriad of facts and snippets in one way rather than another. By carefully choosing and building that framework, the politician can lead the public toward a desired conclusion. Some people call this **spin**, and others call it **framing**. Was the U.S. invasion of Iraq a necessary step in the war on terror? Was it another example of a predatory world power? Was it a personal vendetta against a dictator that made a lame assassination attempt on George W. Bush's father? Was it an excuse for seizing control of oil reserves? Was it a command from the magic goat Donald Rumsfeld borrowed from Tonga's king? Was it a Canadian conspiracy? While we have all seen roughly the same information in the news, the reality the information creates largely depends on the particular framework you initially chose and how that framework has been used to filter which information you paid attention to. That framework provided organization to the overwhelming mass of information and it has shaped your reality.

NEWS MEDIA AND POLITICS

A vast proportion of the information you have on or about politics comes to you through the news. In fact, modern politics is often discussed as mediated politics. We can depict

What about that Insidious Liberal News Media?

When addressing the topic of the news media in pretty much any university classroom it is almost certain that some brave student will offer a passionate comment on the evil ways of a liberal news media establishment bent on turning us all into hemp-wearing druids dancing clockwise around a bonfire, teaching evolution, and worshiping organic produce grown on communal farms. Interestingly enough, in that very same university classroom, there is likely to be at least one student who—after pointing out that druids actually dance counterclockwise around the bonfires—will go on to decry how all the multinational conglomerates that own the news media outlets are constantly killing all of the stories that might expose the true extent of their evil and very conservative big-business agendas. If the professor is foolish enough to allow the argument to play all the way out to its furious destiny, it usually ends up with commandos in Kevlar crashing in through the windows and forcibly separating the combatants.

For the students who are not hauled off in handcuffs, the argument will provide an amusing break from the professor's usual sleep-inducing lecture, but it should also instigate a few questions. If the media is so bent against conservatives, how is it that conservative talk-show hosts can use that media to get their message out far more effectively than liberal talk shows? If the media is so biased toward liberal political agendas, how can you explain the fact that they gave massive coverage to the charge that President Bill Clinton lied about his extramarital affair, but did not give nearly the same coverage to the charge that President George W. Bush lied about the reasons for going to war in Iraq? And, of course, if the outspoken druid in the hemp dress bit off someone's ear during the fight, is she still a vegan?

While the last question might be the most interesting, the one we need to focus on to make this point about bias in the news media is: How can both conservatives and liberals believe the media is biased toward the other?

the very nature of politics as a process of strategic communication and social coordination that occurs through the content of the news media.

The news media provide an accessible, inexpensive, communal, and reliable source of information to form agreement reality about politics and government. As a result, the way the news media filters and selects the information it prints or broadcasts, the way it presents the news as a story, can favor certain cognitive frameworks over others. The processes and imperatives that operate in the news media can have a tremendous influence on how you understand the reality of politics.

Notice, however, that we have carefully avoided saying or implying that the news media presented an accurate reflection of political reality. Ideally, news media would provide us with a perfect reflection of political reality. Ideally, it would be full of reliable and accurate information upon which we could make judgments and decisions. As with so much else about politics, however, the real is far from the ideal. The image of politics presented to us by the media is distorted—dramatically distorted—but not in the ways you might think. The whining about a liberal bias in the news, the claims of any kind of conspiracy, most of the gripes about evil corporations brainwashing us with the news, and all those similar things almost never stand up to any kind of systematic scrutiny. They are a lot like the full moon connection with insanity. If you believe in them, you see examples everywhere, but you also fail to notice the evidence that does

Continued from previous page

The bulk of the academic research suggests that the media is actually biased toward the middle. Since the middle is more liberal than the extreme conservative, this makes it look biased toward the liberal side and since the middle is more conservative than the extreme liberal viewpoint, that looks biased as well.

While that may not fit your prior belief, realize that there is a logical, economic reason to expect that this is what research would find. Most people, on most issues, are near the middle of the political spectrum and if you are a news outlet striving to find a nice big audience to sell to advertisers, you want to pitch yourself to where most of the people are. Neither a liberal nor a conservative bias will help if you are trying to attract as much of that middle of the road audience as possible. The middle may not be the same everywhere. You will get regional variations because local newspapers will tend toward the middle of the local political spectrum, thus Utah papers tend to be slightly more conservative than Vermont papers, but note how the logic still holds. If you are trying to capture the largest possible audience in a given location, you will strive to match the conservative/liberal balance in coverage to the bulk of the targeted audience. It is the same logic behind Downs's economic theory of democracy.

The key is the audience, and if low costs of production and distribution make it possible to make money by selling a small portion of an audience to advertisers, some news outlets can move away from the middle and pursue a niche market, be that conservative, liberal, or left-handed. Thus, in a large city you can often find a liberal and conservative paper to go with the mainstream one. When cable TV made it cheaper to distribute news, FOX news leapt to take advantage of the conservative niche market. It is a reasonably large niche market, but it is still smaller than the bulk of the population in the middle of the political spectrum who predominantly watch network television news even though they have access to cable.

not fit with that expectation. Still, the news media does not present a perfect representation of reality, and one must examine the ways in which the news distorts, overemphasizes, or ignores information in order to fully appreciate how it might best be utilized to understand politics. Once you know what the distortions are, you will be better prepared to deal with them in understanding politics or even acting politically.

The Business of the News

While movies and TV shows about newsrooms are less common than they used to be, there is still enough out there that you have probably seen at least a few here or there. Reruns of *WKRP in Cincinnati*,[8] *Murphy Brown*,[9] or even *The Mary Tyler Moore Show*[10] can be found in the wee hours of the morning on many cable networks. Movies like *Broadcast News*,[11] *Network*,[12] *The Paper*,[13] and *Fletch*[14]—we especially recommend *Fletch*—all have some element of the business of the news as part of the plot. The editor or producer is always screaming about deadlines and trying to cut costs at every turn. The harried reporter is always trying to survive the pressure and fighting the constant demand to produce news. Everybody wants to grab the huge story that will blow everyone away. There is always some larger force like a corporation or politician trying to use power or money to stop a story or to get the dogged reporter off the case.

News is a business, a big business. No surprise there, and the truth about the business of the news is that the demands and limitations that arise from the drive to make money have a tremendous, predictable, and consistent effect on the content of the news. It is not usually so dramatic or blatant as the movies would have us believe, but it is there. In fact, the subtle ways in which the demands of the business side of the news shape its content may be more important than the dramatic bits in stories of the news.

First, a trick question: If the news is a business, it must sell a product. What is the product being sold by news outlets? The obvious answer is the news—the stories and pictures we see in papers, magazines, and on TV.

Since this is a trick question, however, the obvious answer is not going to be the correct one. Of course, if we wanted to make it a really tricky question, we could have told you it is a trick question, then made it a question where the obvious answer is the correct answer. Sort of a trick, trick question.

The answer to this relatively mundane and normal trick question is that the news outlets are not selling the news, they are selling *you,* or more accurately your attention.

Newspapers and magazines can be kind of tough to steal, so you might hand over a dollar or two here or there for that particularly important news package you have been eyeballing. However, what you pay is a pittance compared to the cost of producing something like a newspaper and often, most or even all of what you pay for the paper goes to the person who delivers the paper to that puddle in your front garden or sells it to you from the newsstand. Even if every cent of the $1.50 or so you might spend on the paper went to the publisher, it would not begin to cover the cost of producing the paper. A daily paper for even a modest-sized city has more text in it than a novel, and the Sunday edition of the *New York Times* is longer than all three volumes of the *Lord of the Rings* together plus one of those bodice-ripping romances with Fabio on the cover. In the United States, a paperback novel costs five or six times what a newspaper costs, and outside the United States, it is more like ten to twenty times. In New Zealand, a paperback book sells for twenty-five dollars and a daily paper costs just one little New Zealand dollar, about thirty pence, half a euro, sixty U.S. cents, a hundred yen. There is no way a dollar or two is going to cover the hundreds, sometimes thousands of people working to create that paper you read while you eat your Cap'n Crunch cereal.

Not convinced yet? Think about this one: TV news is *free.*

What the news sells is your attention. Advertisers, with all the things they want to sell to you, pay good money for even a brief moment in front of your eyes, and the more eyes, the more the news outlet can charge for the space or time advertisers want. The audience is the primary product being sold by a news outlet and the actual news is only the means by which that audience is created. Everything about the business side of the news is focused on the audience as a product and the cost of creating the audience must constantly be balanced against the size and value of that audience. Thus, news outlets are constantly trying to find the story that will keep your eyes glued to the screen, but they want to do so as cheaply as possible.* Much of the politics of the media build from the tension between these two business imperatives of the news.

The news itself may not be the product the news media is selling, but it is still the key to the commercial news industry. Everything about the news, down to the very structure of news story, is focused on attracting an audience that can be sold to advertisers. The simple fact that we apply the word story to the presentation of the news is telling. All stories have a structure based upon a conflict-driven interaction of protagonists, antagonists, heroes, villains, and ninja robots. The conflicts in news stories always have an introduction, a climax, and a resolution. News stories also have theme music. It is obvious on TV, where you can actually hear the theme music at the beginning of the broadcast, but even newspaper stories have theme music. It is just that most people do not realize you are supposed to hum the theme music for the news you read in the paper. Hum the intro music from *Raiders of the Lost Ark*[15] for a story about whatever country the United States happens to be invading; Britney Spears's "Whoops, I Did it Again" for all those stories about kids falling in wells; and, of course, circus music for stories about the British Parliament. A full listing, along with the sheet music, is available on Looklikeanidiot.com.[†]

The Political Soap Opera

The point is that reporters write news items into the dramatic structure of a story, whether or not the news actually fits it. Thus, the complex and often interactive dance of a bill debated in the Israeli Knesset is discussed in terms of a simple conflict, a fight between its supporters and detractors, the struggle to pass or defeat the legislation. Even when a news event stretches out over days or weeks, every report still must be a story, and the conflict in each story must conclude with one side winning and the other losing some small battle within the larger war. A news story can be an episode within a larger story arc, but just like a television series, every episode must contain within it a whole story that carries the larger plot forward. Thus, the coverage of a war, a large piece of legislation, an electoral campaign, a scandal, a debate, all take on the basic form of a television soap opera, with continuing episodes and large casts of characters. Television soap operas are much better than elections at getting attractive people to play all the important parts, but they are still presented in much the same way.

Actually, soap operas provide some reasonably good examples to help make sense of what makes one thing a better news story than another. The same things that are ridiculously overdone in the hyperdramatic afternoon shows that most people do not admit they watch are essentially the same elements that guide the selection of news stories and get overemphasized in the effort to fit news into the dramatic story structure.

---

*This explains all the stories about those newborn baby zoo animals. Aren't they just adorable?

†Yes, the authors own this domain name and check its usage stats regularly to see how many of you actually go there.

> **Thus, war is a better news story than peace, conflict on the campaign trail is sexier than covering how candidates stand on the issues, the trade dispute is more newsworthy than the thousands of other items that get sold trouble-free from one place to another.**

Conflict Makes the World Go 'Round

The first intergalactic law of the soap opera is that everybody is always fighting over pretty much everything. Wealth, power, love, sex, good, evil, the secret decoder ring at the bottom of the Cap'n Crunch cereal box, it doesn't really matter what the entire make-believe town is fighting over, it is always on the verge of Microsoft World War 3.7 beta. The wealthy bad guy, the nasty and aggressive woman, the confused young girl, the noble young man, the crazy lady who walks around with a puppet that comes to life when no one is looking, the desperately thin, aerobics-addicted housewives of Wisteria Lane, mix and match, there is always a web of conflict and a war where everyone eventually ends up fighting with everyone else at one time or another. The conflicts in soap operas, like everything else in the soaps, are ridiculously overdone, but it is only an exaggeration of the most basic element of the dramatic story structure.

The very premise of the dramatic story structure is that of action and change driven by conflict. Antagonist and protagonist are locked in a death-struggle that must be resolved. Thus, war is a better news story than peace, conflict on the campaign trail is sexier than covering how candidates stand on the issues, the trade dispute is more newsworthy than the thousands of other items that get sold trouble-free from one place to another. This emphasis on conflict even extends to the norms of fairness and objectivity that journalists swear by. These norms exaggerate the emphasis on conflict even further. In order to be "objective" reporters will often provide equal coverage of the arguments of opposing sides in a story even if one side represents a near consensus. This exaggerates the conflict by making it look like the disputants are locked in a debate, even if it is just one crackpot shouting about how real China is.

There is tremendous emphasis on conflict, but it is not just a fight that makes something newsworthy. More generally, newsworthiness has to do with the presumptions of what will entertain the audience enough to keep them tuned in or turning the pages long enough to see the ads. What characteristics of an event or issue contribute to its ability to capture the attention of an audience?

Sex in the City

The second universal law of the soap opera is that sex sells. In every soap opera around the world just about every cast member is beautiful. It is hard to miss. In fact, just to make sure that the viewers realize that the actors are beautiful, all the women and about half the men in Mexican soap operas are forced to wear spandex pants and halter tops all the time. It is the law. The lone exception is New Zealand, where the biggest soap opera—*Shortland Street*[16]—is filled with some very bad actors whose limited acting ability actually shines in comparison to their personal appearance. Further, promiscuity is so rampant in these imaginary little soap opera towns that any character might be pregnant at any time and the paternity—sometimes even the maternity—of every baby is a mystery worthy of dramatic music at the end of episodes.

Sex gets people's attention, and this obvious fact is not lost on the editors, reporters, and producers responsible for creating a news product that will capture an audience for advertisers. While not all papers go so far as *The Sun* (London), which is famous for putting a full-page picture of a topless woman on page 3, you can still see the evidence everywhere. Look at any news rack in any store in any country. At least half of the magazine covers will feature an impossibly beautiful woman: a woman made up, dressed up, lighted up, photographed, touched up, and airbrushed to unattainable perfection. It doesn't even matter what type of news or information is under the cover. Fashion, personal advice, housekeeping tips, sports, photography, architecture, boating, motorcycles, cars, it does not seem to matter what the subject is or who the desired audience is, impossibly pretty women are the norm for magazine covers.

This has ramifications beyond the fact that it effectively prevents the authors of this text from ever looking out at you from the cover of a magazine. It also influences the content of newspaper and television news by shaping the very idea of what stories should be covered. A sexual element adds to the presumed newsworthiness of a story, sometimes to the point that the media obsess over stories that are about little or nothing. President Clinton's affair with Monica Lewinsky had almost no substance, and it took a valiant effort on the part of his political opponents to even come close to connecting it to his ability to lead the country. In the end it was not the affair that had political repercussions, but the fact that Clinton lied about having an affair.

While the president's choice to have a relationship with an intern might be slightly newsworthy, the real story was about little more than infidelity in the White House; yet it was all over the news for just less than three centuries. Sex, especially when it comes with a bunch of scandalous little details, such as the infamous stain on the blue Gap dress, gets people's attention. Thus, it is newsworthy. More generally, think about all the news about the private lives of celebrities. Divorces, affairs, dates, and marriages of movie stars and athletes—why is any of that news? It is the adventure of the soap opera, where the masses vicariously live the sexual lives of impossibly pretty people.

Honey, the Dingo Stole Another Baby

The third interstellar law of the soap opera is that there is no such thing as a normal day. When is the last time a character on a soap opera got a cold? Ebola, leprosy, amnesia, spinal gingivitis, hysterical blindness, Bolivian brain fever, rabies—those are ailments you will see on the afternoon shows, but never a common cold. You can't just have a baby of indeterminate parentage, that baby has to be stolen by a dingo. Wild dogs carrying off children is a surprisingly common occurrence on Australian soaps; you would think after a few dozen attacks the impossibly beautiful residents of the fictional outback outposts would put up a fence or at least make a point of keeping their babies up and out of the dingoes' reach. Pick any long-running U.S. soap and ask how many of the people have been kidnapped in that little town or been jailed for a bizarre crime they did not commit. The unusual is dramatic. Would you watch a show about a guy who rode the bus to work, shuffled paper for eight hours, rode the bus home, treated his hemorrhoids, nuked his dinner, and watched TV until he fell asleep and then got up the next day to start it all over again? Unless something unusual or dramatic happened to that little bureaucratic troll, why would you want to watch?

Newsworthiness is related to unusualness, or the degree that an event deviates from the norm. No one wants to read about the routine functions of government or the commonplace occurrences we all expect to happen. The classic and quite snappy summation, dog bites man, is not newsworthy; man bites dog, now that is something to write about. The more common something is the less newsworthy it is. Even if it is important, if it is commonplace it is not news. In Washington, D.C., murders are unfortunately common, sometimes numbering in the hundreds a year. Despite the other things that might make a murder newsworthy, most of those murders do not make the front page of the paper or the TV news. They are just too common. In New Zealand, where violent crime is rare, any murder is a national story even if it occurs more than one thousand miles from Auckland. Can you imagine New York newspapers covering every murder in Chicago? In North Dakota, an average blizzard seldom makes it beyond the weather report. It takes a monstrous snowstorm before anyone other than the weather girl mentions it. In Florida, the threat of frost is a lead story and can cause panic buying of antifreeze, bottled water, canned goods, and electric blankets.

The Tragically Hip

The final hyperspatial law of the soap opera is that all of the sexy, unusual conflict is nothing unless it somehow is or could be tragic. The evil plot in Bay City is kind of boring unless it could destroy someone's life. The rare disease is no big deal unless it will spread to the whole town or kill the psychic half-alien baby that the dingo stole from the unknown father. The affair only matters if it will break up Bo and Hope. It just is not drama unless it has an impact on "real" people. If a tree falls in the woods and no one pretty is there to get crushed, who cares?

Human impact is one more aspect of newsworthiness. A small fire that destroys the home of a family is far more newsworthy than a huge fire out in the woods. Even when a wildfire hits the news it is usually because it begins to have a human impact, burning through another Sydney suburb, killing firefighters, or blanketing a city in smoke.

As a result, when we turn to the news, we see a world of war, death, and disaster. We see the rare and unusual events that have a tremendous impact on people. War is always newsworthy, peace seldom so. When we read the paper it seems like the whole world is at war all the time, but peaceful interaction between countries is the norm; war is the exception. The **dramatic imperative** of a commercial news outlet distorts the news. Since we build much of our understanding of the reality of politics from this distorted image, awareness of this imperative is critical to our understanding of politics. It surprises most people to discover that cooperation runs rampant among the gladiators we elect to rampage around the political capitals of the world. Politicians often agree on things and a great deal of stuff gets done, but it is lost behind the bickering we see on TV.

Will He Bring Balance to the Force?

As noted earlier, journalistic norms of objectivity and fairness actually make the distortions caused by the dramatic imperative, particularly the overemphasis on conflict, even more problematic. How can the effort to be fair and objective possibly distort things even further? Glad you asked. If you are trying to be fair, it would not be objective to take a side in a conflict. The best way to objectively cover a conflict, even if it is a conflict that the reporter had to search hard to find amongst all that cooperation, is to present both sides of an issue on an equal and fair basis. The problem is that not all conflicts are made up of two reasonably equal sides. This can cause tremendous distortions when a journalist tries to be objective by presenting a small but vocal minority on the same terms as a much larger majority. In the news, it appears that you almost always have two roughly equal sides, but that is often not the case.

Nowhere is this more apparent, and more misleading, than in the coverage of policies and politics related to science education. Take, for example, the issue of teaching evolution in U.S. classrooms. It is a simple debate. In the blue corner, wearing a white lab coat and glasses, is the "We-evolved-from-pond-scum" team, offering explanations for less evolved creatures like politicians and lawyers. In the white corner, wearing fancy robes and a tall mitre hat, the "God-did-it-in-a-week" team, offering explanations for the completely illogical animals that could not have possibly evolved, like the platypus and guests on Jerry Springer.

If you were to follow the debate over evolution in the news, the clear conclusion you would reach is that Darwin versus God is a point of controversy and uncertainty in the scientific community. For every quote from a guy in a lab coat there is an equal and opposite quote from the universe-in-a-week team. The story about evolution is often presented as two sides in dispute and both sides are presented fairly, which on the news means equally. This creates the image of scientific division over this subject and because both sides are presented equally and the differences between them are emphasized, you would be forgiven for concluding that Darwin's theory of evolution is a hotly disputed topic among scientists. You would be wrong, but still forgiven. While the assertion offends those who would rather not see evolution taught in the classroom, scientists of all stripes overwhelmingly agree—and we mean overwhelmingly agree—that the general framework of ideas that Darwin offered about the evolutionary process is the best conceptual framework for explaining critical aspects of the natural world. It is a tiny minority of scientists—most of them at small religious universities—who disagree. It is literally a dozen or so people disputing the scientific consensus supported by tens of thousands of scientists, but because of the news media's emphasis on conflict and fairness, that tiny minority of scientists is covered on equal terms with the overwhelming consensus.

The political or religious aspects of the debate may be more reasonably depicted on equivalent terms. There is a clear division and the political conflict is significant, with substantial numbers on both sides. Judging by public-opinion polls, presenting the political debate over teaching evolution as two roughly equal sides does not distort reality too much, if at all. However, this is simply not true for the scientists and the science of evolution. The scientists agree, but the scientific consensus is ignored. Actually it is more distorted than that. The fact that there is an overwhelming consensus among scientists is almost completely buried by the media's business emphasis on conflict and the journalistic ideal of impartiality and fairness.

Elite Dominance of the Sources of News

Beyond the exaggeration of conflict and an obsession with odd or unusual things that impact people, another way the journalistic presumptions of newsworthiness influence the content of coverage, particularly the coverage of politics, is by supporting a preponderance of elite voices in the news media. Elites, whether they rose to social prominence through politics, business, religion, athletics, entertainment, inheriting the fortune her daddy made with his hotel chain, painting a soup can, or some other means, dominate the news. The latest matrimonial disaster of the aging rock star is all over the news, while your neighbor's divorce, despite the thrown dishes and juicy details, is not. The opinion of the pope is news, not so for the local minister/waiter at Bob's Temple of Heavenly Pancakes. The president's musings on just about anything are global news, yours are not. George H. W. Bush made news all over the world for saying he hated broccoli. You have been saying that since the third week of second grade when you finally learned to talk, and no one cares, least of all the news media. Even the all-star athlete who cannot spell "environment" is likely to get his expert opinion on that "globe warm'n thang" reported rather than the student who has spent her entire junior year obsessing about it from beneath a cloud of purple smoke.

The presumption among journalists is that elites, because they are already prominent focal points for society, are newsworthy. The actions or words of the president, pope, aging rock star, or steroid-using athlete are going to capture or hold people's attention; they are going to contribute to an audience that can be sold to advertisers. Elites are, by definition, unusual, and through their status they can often have tremendous effects on people's lives. Elites that fight with one another are even more newsworthy. Thus, when the aging rock star divorce devolves into a fight over custody of the naughty home videos, the news media coverage is relentless.

A VAST CONSPIRACY?

Elites also have the motivation and the resources to actively try to gain beneficial news coverage. Actors might complain about the invasive paparazzi, but being the object of the public's attention is a big part of why producers pay $20 million for the star who can bring people to see a wretched movie. Talent is often a secondary concern. How else can you explain Madonna starring in movies or the careers of any of the Baldwins other than Steven? Name recognition is perhaps the biggest factor in democratic elections and it often does not matter where that public recognition came from. Ronald Reagan, Jessie Ventura, Arnold Schwarzenegger, Steve Largent, and Fred Grandy (Gopher from the *Love Boat* for the rerun deficient) did not win their first elections because the voters all recognized their lifelong commitment to political service. A big part of why they won elections is because the voters recognized who they were. In democratic nations, the ability to gain coverage in the news media is tremendously valuable. It gets people into the theater, into the voting booth, or even out marching in the street. That attention can be used to create wealth or influence politics. Continued attention is usually necessary to remain an elite public figure and news media coverage can help you sustain that attention.

Given a reasonable motivation to seek coverage, it should be no surprise that members of the elite do things to actively encourage coverage by the news. Think of the red carpet at a movie premiere. What is that but a big, orchestrated event to get pictures taken of the stars and, by association, public exposure for the movie? Statements by publicity secretaries—elites often have employees they have hired just to get the media's attention. Or how about ridiculous stunts? Do you think Britney Spears and her first, twenty-four-hour "accidental" marriage might have anything to do with a shortage of musical talent? Or how about Billy Connelly? As the waning of his comedic career became painfully obvious, he bungee-jumped naked to get some news media attention for his tour of New Zealand. That's a lot of work to get the attention of a country with fewer people, but more sheep, than the state of Alabama.

For political elites, news coverage is even more of a consideration. In addition to being the focus of a great deal of public interest, political elites make decisions and take actions that have tremendous impact on people's lives. Except for an occasional stalker or celebrity impersonator, the aging rock star does not have such a regular or substantial impact on people's lives. A vote in Parliament or the decisions of a president can quite literally have life and death consequences when the bombs start falling. And for the politician, the ability to keep his job, the ability to get reelected, is often dependent upon attaining and sustaining a favorable image in the news that most people rely on for their understanding of the reality of politics.

Elites want to get coverage and the media wants to cover elites; it sounds like a conspiracy. In fact, the way that the news media feature political elites so prominently, combined with the value political elites place upon generating favorable media coverage, makes the conspiracy obvious. Clearly newspaper reporters are just zombified stooges of the rich and politically powerful. Every day an e-mail arrives from The Man's office and outlines exactly what the day's news will look like. Reporters are not completely controlled, however. They get to choose every third adjective.

There is no conspiracy!

The prominence of conspiracies in discussions of the news and the degree to which people truly believe conspiracy to define the news media is hard to describe and even harder to explain. There are far too many people involved in the news media for any kind of conspiracy to ever be possible. It only takes one person—the weakest link—to blow the cover off of a conspiracy and there are hundreds of thousands of very weak links in the chain between politics and the newspaper that gets thrown into your rose garden every morning. You are talking about a conspiracy encompassing thousands of people. Think about how hard it is to get your buddy to shut up about the moderately illegal string of events that led to your overnighter wearing someone else's ball gown in the chem lab, and ask how hard it would be to keep up a conspiracy among thousands. As we discussed before, in any decent-sized college classroom it is almost certain that there will be at least one person ready to enlighten the class with the juicy details about how liberal reporters and editors conspire to attack and defame any politician who dares represent the red-blooded American conservative majority while hiding the indiscretions of their liberal political brethren. In that same classroom will be a student— probably not the same student—arguing that the wealthy and conservative business elites that own media outlets conspire with editors and reporters and use their money to kill any story or report that might bring the "truth" to the public about cars that run on weeds or other things that could save the environment or end poverty.

There is no conspiracy. Conspiracies have to be limited to three people, two of which must be dead. People just will not keep their mouths shut.

The conservatives wailing and gnashing their teeth about the liberal news media have a hard time explaining the media's obsession with Bill Clinton and Monica Lewinsky or any of the other times the media has feasted on the carcass of a liberal politician. The liberals that are horrified that there are conservative big-business owners of the media have a hard time explaining the coverage of Watergate, Martha

Stewart, or any other time the media has eviscerated a conservative politician or wealthy media figure. It is that whole moon and insanity thing again.

There is no conspiracy!

The Mutual Exploitation Model

The reality—if we dare refer to reality in a chapter on mediated politics—is that there is a tremendous coincidence of interests between the news media and elites. The result of this shared interest is not a conspiracy, but what is commonly referred to as a **mutual exploitation model** of the news-elite relationship. The news media exploit elites by using them for cheap sources of news that they know will interest the public. At the same time, the elites exploit the news media by using them to communicate with the public and present a public image that will help their political, economic, or social ambitions. The reason there is no conspiracy is that there is no need for a conspiracy. For the most part, economic forces and self-interest will drive the media and elites to choose to cater to each other's needs. You do not need mysterious men in trench coats causing "accidents" to befall those who stray. Reporters and editors will choose to cover elites, and because they want to preserve access to those newsworthy individuals reporters will tend to cater to the image those entertainers and politicians wish to present. Elites will cater to the reporters' and editors' business needs and will give them the resources for newsworthy copy whenever possible so that they can get their images, ideas, and words to the public. Why in the world would you try to organize a conspiracy to do something that everyone is already doing?

Still, the biggest reason we feel comfortable arguing that there is no conspiracy is that, if given sufficient incentive, either side will turn on the other. Elites that use the media for their own political and personal ends will turn against the media and attack individuals or the entire system if there is enough benefit or if they are sufficiently angered. Richard Nixon used the news media's interest in him as a political elite to save his career. In the infamous "Checkers Speech," [17] Nixon used his pet dog to create the image of a real human being behind his political ambition and showed that he knew how, and was willing, to use the media. Yet later, as president, Nixon viciously attacked the media. He threatened reporters and news outlets, trying to intimidate editors with threats of FBI and IRS investigations and generally being more unpleasant than a rabid walrus at a dinner party. A decade after Nixon used the media to salvage his career, he turned against it because he could gain politically. By arguing that the liberal media was creating a distorted image of his policies and the Vietnam War, Nixon managed to convince much of the public that the war looked worse than it actually was and the media, not the president or his policies, were responsible for how bad it appeared. Did you ever think it was ironic that Rush Limbaugh attacks the liberal media establishment from the platform of his syndicated radio show, a radio show that is broadcast on the stations of that same liberal media establishment? Rush attacks the media because it gives him a saleable point that a conservative audience wants to hear.

There is no better example of the political power of the press than Watergate. Not the Watergate Hotel, the Watergate scandal. It is a perfectly nice hotel and all, with curvy hallways, mints on the pillows, and freshly vacuumed carpets, but it is the political scandal associated with the hotel that every professor will point to when introducing the political role of the free press in a democratic society.

Even after several movies and books on the subject, some of the facts are still a little unclear, but roughly what happened was that Robert Redford and Dustin Hoffman were doing something in a parking garage and Hal Holbrook told them something naughty and the *Washington Post* fired President Nixon. Okay, that is not really even close to what happened, but you can always just go and watch one of the Watergate movies yourself.

What really happened is that during the 1972 U.S. presidential election campaign, the Democratic election headquarters, which were housed just off one of those curvy halls in an office suite in the Watergate Hotel, were burglarized. Nothing much was stolen and it never would have been much of an issue, except for the fact that two reporters, Bob Woodward and Carl Bernstein investigated and exposed a connection back to President Nixon. Once the sordid details of Nixon's illegal and unethical campaign tactics were reported by the *Washington Post,* it became impossible to bury, hide, or ignore the news story and it eventually led to Nixon's resignation.

The real key to the Watergate scandal was the role that the press played throughout. The official law enforcement mechanisms of the U.S. government failed to expose the connection back to President Nixon—the reporters did. The official mechanisms of government also did not remove Nixon from office. They may have, if given enough time, but it was the public pressure created by the relentless press coverage that forced Nixon to resign from office. You can go further and argue that it was the public nature of the scandal that forced many of the official government agencies and processes to engage the scandal and that engagement was critical to exposing the full extent of the criminal activities and keeping the scandal at the forefront of the public's agenda.

Even though Deep Throat is an awesome code name for a secret informant, some have vilified the man that tipped off Woodward and Bernstein, and others will argue that the news media should not have the political power that it demonstrated during the scandal. Still, what is made absolutely clear by Watergate is that the media play a huge role in modern democratic politics and knowing something about the details of the Watergate scandal is an absolute necessity for anyone interested in the role of media in politics. Fortunately, it has been fictionalized for your protection. There is a book about the actual events, Bob Woodward's *All the President's Men,* but it is also the center of several films so you do not even have to learn to read. It is in *All the President's Men* (1976), *Secret Honor* (1984), *Nixon* (1995), *Dick* (1999), and you can find hints of it all over the place, from *Forrest Gump* to reruns of the *X-Files.*

The way that politicians turn against the media, however, is nothing compared to the way that the media will turn against a member of the elite if the story is sufficiently newsworthy, as the text box on the Watergate scandal shows.

The Watergate scandal may be the most obvious example of how the media will turn against even the most powerful of elites if the story is good enough. The relentless coverage of the issue was the prominent story across the news media for months and the subject of significant coverage for years. Watergate also shows that this kind of coverage has tremendous costs for elites that are at the center of a storm. Entertainment elites, political elites, any kind of elite always faces the reality that any kind of scandal or conflict they might get caught up in will be newsworthy and will get reported by a news media obsessed with drama, regardless of the impact that coverage has on the elite individual.

Watergate also gives us a bit of insight in the democratic role of the press. Journalism not only exposed the illegal activities that cost Richard Nixon the U.S. presidency, the simple fact that every bit of that political catastrophe was so heavily and thoroughly covered was a significant factor in what made it impossible for Nixon to remain in office. Media coverage was key to the end of his presidential career.*

Watergate is not the only example of a political career flushed down the toilet by a flood of news coverage. Because of media coverage, many democratic leaders have lost their offices or their standing over far less substantial scandals. In fact, the effect of scandal goes beyond just demonstrating that the media will turn on the elites it is so fond of covering. The fear that a career-ending scandal creates in politicians may be the biggest part of how the news media keeps democratic leaders from doing the things for which the public will punish them. It only takes an occasional Gary Hart or Gary Condit to convince other politicians that they should not change their name to Gary and to remind them that getting on the wrong side of a media scandal can cost them their entire career. Gary Hart had a fair chance of becoming the Democratic presidential nominee until a picture of him wearing a blonde on his lap was sold to the tabloids. In a fit of unbelievable stupidity that transcends Bill Clinton waving his finger and saying that he did not have sexual relations with that woman, Gary Hart had actually dared the media to follow him when rumors of an affair emerged in the media. A few days later, he was caught sitting under a young blonde, on a yacht named "Monkey Business" of all things. Gary Condit's political demise is even more telling. After the disappearance of an intern that was both young and female, suggestions that he might have at one time or another smiled at her in the office spun into rumors of an affair, which led to stories about a murder conspiracy. There was no evidence or anything of that sort, but the relentless media coverage drove him from office. While many people will recall that part of the saga, few know about the evidence that later indicated that it was almost certainly a random attack in a Washington, D.C., park that led to the disappearance of the intern. That a politician might possibly, maybe, perhaps be involved was newsworthy. Over a year later, the fact that he was almost certainly not involved was not all that newsworthy.

Of Cockroaches and Politicians

These media-induced political vivisections are significant in not just the way they remove a misbehaving or unfortunate politician from office, but also in how they influence the activities of other political actors or politics in general. The greatest fear of any

---

*Years after leaving office, however, Nixon enjoyed a resurgence as a domestic and international political elder statesman and analyst.

modern democratic politician is to get caught in the middle of a media feeding frenzy over a scandal or disastrous policy. In fact, we can argue that the way the media can turn on a politician is the most important role that the news plays in democratic politics. Call it the **cockroach theory of politics**.* Like the beloved insects, politicians do not want to be spotted anyplace where they can be stomped on. When the media rips the liver out of a politician caught in a scandal, it tells all the other politicians they had better not do the same stupid thing, and you often see evidence of a scramble among other politicians or officials to avoid getting noticed for a similar indiscretion.

As an anecdotal example, consider the case of the parking enforcement division of the police in an unnamed city that used to be in the middle of the swamps at the very end of the Mississippi River just south of Baton Rouge. The parking police were well known for their extremely aggressive enforcement of the city's bewildering codex of parking regulations. Some even carried rulers with them to measure the exact distance of tires from curbs, writing citations for cars that had one wheel as little as one quarter-inch over the maximum distance from the curb. Further complicating things, there often were no curbs, in which case, the measurement was made in relation to the imaginary place where a curb might go.

Surprisingly enough, these valiant defenders of automotive order refused to confront the egregious activities of the most blatant and persistent parking renegades in the city. A facility that provided services to senior citizens was experiencing tremendous difficulties with people parking in a passenger-loading zone. Located on Canal Street, a six-lane parkway that served as a major thoroughfare into the city, the curb in front of the facility was designated as a passenger-loading zone. At stake was the safety of the hundreds of senior citizens who were brought in daily from around the city for services ranging from physical therapy to small social events. This loading zone, however, was always full of cars that didn't just exceed the fifteen-minute limit, they parked there for the entire day, forcing the senior citizens to use the traffic lanes for getting in and out of cars and shuttle buses. Even though the police station was just across the street, the parking enforcement officers never ticketed the illegally parked cars and refused to respond to repeated calls and letters from the director of the services agency.

In the end, it was the television report of an investigative journalist, Richard Angelico, that resolved the issue. The illegally parked cars were the cars of the parking enforcement officers. They were using the loading zone as their own private parking lot. The story played out on the news. The mayor expressed dismay. The police chief acted outraged and police supervisors ritually sacrificed underlings, and to no one's surprise, that loading zone suddenly became the most fastidiously policed parking location in the city.

What is even more significant for the argument that media coverage is an important part of keeping democracies democratic is not the immediate and obvious response to

---

*Yes, this is pretty much the same thing as the cockroach theory of bureaucracy we talked about in chapter 8.

the coverage of such scandalous behavior by the parking enforcement bureau. Only one person, the immediate supervisor of the parking banditos, was fired. Only the handful of parking officials actually caught on tape were reprimanded. What is significant is that those who were not directly the subject of coverage or the recipient of punishments also changed their behaviors.* Much like the way that a public flogging is intended to keep others from committing the same crime, everyone policed their behavior. Without any official decree, demand, or institution of any official mechanism, the behavior of all parking officials and even some patrol officers changed. Nor was the change limited to the loading zone that was the subject of media attention. Several no-parking zones near police stations around the city were suddenly free of illegally parked cars and all short-term parking locations throughout the city became subject to scrupulous enforcement. In the same way that a huge number of Wall Street firms scrambled to review and adjust their accounting practices in the wake of the Enron scandal, the behavior of police and government officials in that forlorn swamp city changed, sometimes drastically, even though they were not directly the subject of media scrutiny and related punishment.

Still want to argue for a conspiracy?

Protest and the Disadvantaged Voice

Another way of addressing the idea of a conspiracy between the media and whatever elite allegedly manipulates it, is to take a look at the things that get into the news despite the preferences of the elite. Scandals and the intense coverage of failed policies are good examples, but there are plenty of other examples that demonstrate that if there is a conspiracy, it is a pretty lame and ineffectual one. Elites are prominent, if not dominant sources of news coverage but they cannot shut out others. Consider protests. Protests are one way that non-elites can get their voices and opinions inserted into the content of the news media. Protests, en masse or the occasional dramatic individual action, get coverage, and by getting coverage they provide an opportunity to insert a non-elite opinion, demand, or issue into the mediated political world.

The reality of protests is that even the biggest protests involve only a tiny portion of the public. A protest involving thousands is huge, but the world is populated by billions. The proportion of people protesting anything is miniscule, but when those thousands get on TV or get on the front page of the paper, the media creates a separate political reality. There becomes a perception that the protests involve or represent a significant portion of the public and the politicians often treat that tiny minority that are protesting as if they do indeed represent a significant number of people. Before any of the other factors relevant to the political success of a protest can even be considered, the

---

*Think of how this creates a Pan-Optic mechanism for controlling the behavior of these and other officials. Even though they are seldom if ever caught on tape, the minute they think it is possible, they choose to change their activities to avoid the potential punishments.

Politically Effective Protest

Political protest has been around for quite some time. The most famous of which might have been that tea party in Boston where a bunch of Yankees protested their $200 million payroll by throwing four straight playoff games into Boston Harbor so the Red Sox could come back from three down and win the series. However, you can find plenty of other really, really, really important protests, if you really look, like that whole Protestant church fracas. In fact, in most of the countries where they frown on chopping off heads or otherwise ban being really, really mean to people who protest, there is plenty of protest all the time. However, most of these protests—including a lot of the big ones—fail to accomplish anything. Why?

While there is no transuniversally agreed upon answer to this question, based upon some of the ideas offered in this textbook and from various studies of protests, it is possible to offer a list of four necessary criteria that must be met before a protest has any chance of success.

1. **Media Coverage is a Must.** Protest is usually, if not always, a way that those who are not in power attempt to get a desired response from those who are in power. In order to accomplish this, the issue or demand must be placed upon the political agenda, it must be brought to the attention of those in power—hereafter referred to as "The Man" regardless of actual or approximated gender—and media coverage is the key to getting The Man to pay attention. Media coverage, however, is not all it takes. There are plenty of protests, such as the anti-globalization protests, that get plenty of media attention but still fail to get The Man to behave.

2. **Demand a Clear and Simple Response.** The Man is not psychic. If it is not clear what The Man must do to appease the protesters, how can The Man ever do it? It is also tough for The Man to handle complex tasks. The non-male portion of those reading this book may feel free to interject a snide and crass comment at this time, but the point is that a lot of protests fail because nobody has any idea what could be done on behalf of the protesters. This is where the anti-globalization protests fail. Other than whacking off a few chunks of the planet and turning the whole thing into a nice cube or a dodecahedron, how exactly might The Man go about unglobalizing the world? Further, even if you could define how, do you really think it is even possible to dismantle the world's economic system? And how many people would starve while you were trying to figure out a new economic system? Even meeting these first two conditions, however, does not guarantee success.

3. **Appeal to Self-Interest.** Even when a simple request is made abundantly clear to The Man, The Man is not going to react unless there is a clear political motivation for doing so. Big protests that get lots of media coverage and make a simple demand, still often fail. What could be clearer than hundreds of thousands of people making the clear and simple demand that the United States not invade Iraq? Yet this protest failed. While the authors reserve the right not to refer to George W. Bush as The Man, it is still pretty clear that the antiwar protests failed primarily because the protesters were unable to demonstrate to the president that there would be sufficient political punishment or reward related to their demand.

4. **It Seems to Take a Bit of Luck.** The three conditions above are necessary to successful protest—they all must occur for a chance of success—but they are not sufficient to ensure success. There are all kinds of little things that can cause a protest to fail. Sometimes, even if The Man wants to act, something may derail the process, or something more urgent may arise, like a good rugby game on TV.

protest must gain a significant amount of media coverage, as the text box on politically effective protest shows. It must insert itself into the political reality of the majority of the population and the majority of political elites, few of whom saw, heard, or otherwise experienced the protest directly.

UNDERSTANDING THE DISTORTIONS IS THE KEY

The most important aspect of understanding the role of the news media in politics is understanding the consistent distortions created by the media, but that is clearly not the only aspect of the news that is important. Like many of the other aspects of politics that we have introduced in the text, we could fill not just one, but several books on the topic at hand. The role of political commercials in elections, the coverage of war, the role of investigative journalism, how media creates our understanding of other places, how leaders act to manipulate their media image, how the media influences the public and political agenda, any or all of these topics could easily be worth an entire undergraduate course worthy of study. What we have tried to do here is provide the first step into the subject, acquaint you with the fundamental ideas, and help you understand enough about the topic so you can look less stupid when your parents ask what their tuition checks have bought. It is also here to help you decide if you want to learn more.

For the role of the media in politics, most of the other topics we could introduce in this chapter, or in a ten-volume set of textbooks, build on the idea of how news media distorts the reality it creates. For students, we suggest thinking of it all in terms of astronomy and great big telescopes. When the Hubble Telescope was launched, a skinny guy in a white lab coat with plastic pocket protectors discovered that some idiot (no relation to the authors) had screwed up the math and the billion-dollar telescope was nearsighted. In other words, it was presenting a distorted image of the universe. Once scientists knew that distortion was there, they could make adjustments and use big expensive tools and fancy math to correct what they saw. They could still get tremendous benefits from an imperfect image.*

The practical side of understanding the basics of how the news media distorts the political reality that you and everyone else works from is that you now have the tools to begin peering beyond what is presented to you on the screen or on the page. You have an idea of the biggest and most important ways in which the news has exaggerated, distorted, or ignored aspects of a political issue and you can apply your own image correction routines. Further, we hope you are also at least willing to consider the

---

*Once the specifics of the distortion were known, computer corrections sharpened many images. Certain studies, which needed to be above the atmosphere, which blocks out several scientifically important wavelengths of light, but did not need the full resolution the telescope had been designed for were given priority until the problem could be fixed.

distortions your own cognitive frameworks are creating and make adjustments for them as well. Remember, whether you are liberal or conservative, superhero or mere human, the more strongly you feel about something, the more steadfast your beliefs, the more likely it is that you are missing the information that does not fit with the world you expect to see or want to believe in.

KEY TERMS

agreement reality / **251**
cockroach theory of politics / **269**
cognitive frameworks / **253**
dramatic imperative / **262**
framing / **254**
mediated reality / **250**
mutual exploitation model / **266**
spin / **254**

CHAPTER SUMMARY

Nobody would deny that the news media plays a crucial role in politics. However, the importance of news media becomes even more apparent when we consider that our political reality is crafted by the flow of information. Thus, understanding how the media selects, sorts, and presents information is critical for understanding politics and government. Further, it is crucial to realize that not everyone interprets information in the same way; we all have several unique sets of mental filters that we use to make sense of the world. These filters can distort our understanding of the world, and politicians attempt to manipulate these predispositions to make us interpret the news in a manner that works to their benefit. The majority of the news media is commercial, and the need to attract an audience affects which stories the media selects to present and how it portrays political information. The journalistic ethic of objectivity even further warps the media's presentation of political information. All of these factors work to create a mutually beneficial relationship between elites and the media. Elites benefit from the exposure they receive, while the media gets marketable stories. However, this relationship is unstable. The media will quickly turn on elites if the story is good enough. Students should learn two important lessons from this chapter. First, to be critical consumers of information, we must appreciate how the media presents the news. Further, we must also be cognizant of our predispositions and how we use them to make sense of the world. We must also be on guard for those who would manipulate our predilections for their own benefit. Second, if dingoes keep stealing your babies, it is probably time to invest in a quality fence.

STUDY QUESTIONS AND EXERCISES

1. Bearing the concept of cognitive frameworks in mind, watch a story on the news or read a story in the newspaper. Consider how someone with different cognitive frameworks might interpret the story differently. Try this approach for both national and international news items.

2. Think of an example of how a politician has framed a news story so that the public reached a conclusion that the politician desired. What skills are necessary to be a critical consumer of the news? Do you have these skills?

3. Considering that most news outlets are commercial enterprises, what makes one news story preferable to another?

4. How can the journalistic norm of objectivity and the dramatic imperative lead to distortions of the news?

5. What is the mutual exploitation model, and how do economic forces and self-interest drive the media and elites to choose to cater to each other's needs?

WEBSITES TO EXPLORE

http://mediamatters.org. Media Matters for America is a Web site devoted to exposing conservative bias in the news.

www.americanpressinstitute.org. The American Press Institute is a Web site created by newspaper publishers for the training and development of journalists and news outlets.

www.comedycentral.com/shows/the_daily_show/index.jhtml. This is the Web site for "The Daily Show with Jon Stewart," a parody of the day's political news.

www.comedycentral.com/shows/the_colbert_report/index.jhtml. This is the Web site for "The Colbert Report," a parody of political news pundits.

www.lib.umich.edu/govdocs/psnews.html. "Political Science Resources: News Media" is the University of Michigan Library Document Center's list of links related to the news media.

www.mediaresearch.org. Media Research Center is a Web site devoted to exposing liberal bias in the news.

If one guy trips, would it be like a bunch of dominoes?

CHAPTER 12

International Politics
Apocalypse Now and Then

As everyone knows, the best way to conquer the world is to start with all your armies on Madagascar and then take Africa. You hold Africa for a while and save up all the extra armies for holding a continent, then you bust out, jump over to Brazil and take South America. Once you have both Africa and South America, then it's just a matter of time before you get the rest of the world in your greedy little hands. That is the way world politics works, as every kid learns early in his or her Risk™ career. Of course, the simple fact that none of the leaders of Madagascar have ever managed to conquer the world throws some doubt on the Risk model of international politics, but then again, the fact that we have global conquest games designed for ten-year-olds says something about war and politics.

International politics is about far more than war, but war is the part we notice. That should not be surprising. War is, by its very nature, the quintessential example of the newsworthiness concept we discussed in chapter 11. War is conflict with a tremendous human impact. It deviates from our normal lives in both its scope and its violence. It embodies the dramatic story structure of Us versus Them and creates a context for both extreme heroics and extreme villainy. Most of history you will read is the story of war and it is impossible to count or categorize the number of novels, films, television miniseries, and children's cartoons that are about war. Quick, name a John Wayne movie that is not about war. For our less gifted readers, quick, name John Wayne. Even Disney makes cartoons about war. *Mulan*[1] was pretty lame for a Disney flick, but it was about a very real war.

BOARD GAMES AND WORLD POLITICS, NOT SO RIDICULOUS

Checkers, chess, Stratego, Risk, Go, Barbie Dream Date—even before we get to the bloodthirsty first-person computer games or all the contact sports played by big hairy guys running around in a stadium, it sometimes seems as if every game is about war. And many people say we should take these games seriously. Playing war warps the minds of the vulnerable, like children, the mentally incompetent, and professors. Some even believe we should run around and panic before these insidious games bring society crashing down around our ears. We will leave it up to you, though, to choose which threat to the foundations of society you wish to panic over.

Aside from training kids for all those career paths that are dependent on frantically pushing buttons with your thumbs, these combat and conflict games can provide valuable insights into the politics of international relations. The board game Diplomacy provides a near-perfect representation of the realist theoretical perspective on international relations and has been used by political scientists to test theories on balances of power, stability in the international system, the effects of leadership change, and the possibility that human innovation will prevent effective forecasting of international politics. The ICONNS simulation at the University of Maryland and the decision board at Texas A&M University have been used to explore the dynamics of decision making regarding war, peace, and foreign policy. Online gaming environments are now used to study everything from the nature of personal identity to the formation of communities around conflicts.

So maybe there is some value in all those war games.

Still, despite all the attention it gets, war is rare. If you consider all of the combinations of countries in the world that could be shooting at each other on any given day, the number that are actually dropping bombs and launching missiles is almost zero. War is so rare that the political scientists trying to find out what factors are associated with war actually had to develop, borrow, and steal new statistical techniques to try to distinguish the characteristics of that tiny fraction of countries that are fighting from the vast pool of countries that are at peace. Most of international politics is actually about cooperation; trade, travel, mail delivery, telephone service, environmental regulation, and the brutal suppression of guys inventing cars that run on switch grass.* These cooperative aspects of international politics are all far more common than war. We all know someone like that guy, Larry, who lives down the street. One day he is filling his Hummer's gas tank with lawn mower clippings and the next day Exxon's international commandos are flying the UN's black Stealth helicopters into town. They haul Larry off to an asylum in Tonga and his vehicle has to be towed away because it "doesn't run" anymore. We all have, or had, neighbors like that. It happens all the time. While it may be extreme to claim that impossible international conspiracies are far more common than war, it is difficult to emphasize how rare war actually is in the international scheme of things. Still, when it comes to international politics, most of the history, news, movies, books, and computer games are about war, so war seems like a good place to start the discussion of international politics. Remember, however, war is only the starting place.

---

*What exactly is switch grass anyway?

CAUSES OF WAR

With all the film and fiction about war, you would think that the fiction examples in this chapter would rain down on you like beer cans after a tornado hits a NASCAR race. The problem is, the fiction about war seldom addresses the international politics related to war. The novels and films are usually about the people caught up in the war, or about the strategy of war. *Saving Private Ryan*[2] tells us about the personal struggles of some of the men caught up in and ultimately killed in the Allied invasion of Normandy but it says almost nothing about the decades of political dynamics that drove the Allies to choose a costly invasion over a negotiated end to World War II. Consider *Full Metal Jacket*,[3] *Catch-22*,[4] *The Forever War*,[5] *Tora! Tora! Tora!*,[6] *All Quiet on the Western Front*,[7] *Apocalypse Now*,[8] *M.A.S.H.*,[9] and *The Guns of Navarone*[10]; the stories are either about the people caught up in the conflict or they are about the interplay of opposing military strategies. While combinations of these two themes make for much better stories than the politics that led to the war, they do not help much in our effort to get at the how and why of war.

In fact, when fiction does address the causes of war, it does more harm than good to our understanding of international politics. The only consistent theme you are likely to find in fiction about the causes of war is that war is largely accidental. In *Dr. Strangelove*,[11] a comedy of errors and insanity causes world-ending nuclear war when an insane general and a string of accidents prevent the leaders of the United States from stopping Slim Pickens from riding a nuke down into Moscow. In *War Games*[12] a military computer is accidentally set loose in what it thinks is a game scenario and that mistake threatens the same nuclear end of the world. In Joe Haldeman's *The Forever War*, a centuries-long war with the alien Taurans is flippantly dismissed at the conclusion of the book as a misunderstanding. Similarly, the *Ender*[13] series by Orson Scott Card pins the cause of a war that eliminates an entire species on a misunderstanding between cultures that not only triggered the fight, but also prevented them from finding an end short of genocide. The impression you might reasonably glean from fiction is that war is so horrible that only an accident or misunderstanding could explain it. The obvious solution is to understand each other better, communicate more effectively, and send folk dancers on world tours.

The problem with the whole wars-are-accidents theory is that it is about as plausible as the Dallas Cowboys winning the World Series. Seriously, it only takes a quick look at the reality of politics to argue that it is ridiculous to think that wars are all accidents. After George W. Bush spent well over a year campaigning for support for his invasion of Iraq, no one could seriously argue that the Second Gulf War was an accident or a cultural misunderstanding. More generally, wars usually occur between neighboring countries, countries that know each other quite well and have more in common than they have differences. And even if the causes of war were all just a matter of cultural differences, will cultural understanding and exchanges actually help? After an hour of Bulgarian folk disco, most of the audience will be screaming for a tank or a bomb, anything to make it stop. Soccer, which many Europeans consider to be the pinnacle of modern cultural exchange, actually triggered a war in Central America.[14] Wars as a clash of cultures may be a catchy thing to say and an easy thing to believe—after all, Canadians are just so, well, Canadian—but ultimately the idea is like connecting increased outbreaks of insanity with the full moon. When there is a war, cultural differences are the noticeable things that our minds latch on to and we fail to notice all the cultural differences that exist between countries that do not go to war. And while the fear of an accidental nuclear war was—and to some degree still is—very real, war is no accident.

The choice to go to war is consciously and rationally made by at least one of the participants and even when a war appears to be an accidental cascade of events triggered by a minor incident or a gross miscalculation, those appearances are usually deceiving. To say that the assassination of a minor archduke from a fading imperial power explains why World War I started is like saying that the second cigarette on June 5, 1998, caused Aunt Lulu's lung cancer. Even if you could pin down the moment that that first one of Lulu's lung cells became cancerous, even if you could figure out which puff of smoke did it, was that single thing really the cause? What about all the cartons of cigarettes before that one drag, or the countless Virginia Slims that followed that one puff? What about all those asbestos sculptures she made for the local grade school art fairs? The causes of cancer are complex, often subtle, and often the result of things that accumulate over time.

War is often the same way. We can often spot a visible, often dramatic, initial event. Wars start with the blitzkrieg of Poland, a declaration of independence, or John Wayne saying something like "to hell with the border, they stole my beer," but are any of those the actual reasons why the war occurred? The dynamics that actually cause the war are far more intricate and complex than the event that sparked the conflagration.

BACK TO ANARCHY

With all the killing and primitive, savage brutality we see in battle, it is easy to think of war in terms of cavemen crushing each other's skulls with clubs. To the relief of everyone who has to study this chapter for a test, the easy way of approaching the subject is also the best way. The predominant theoretical framework that underlies most studies of war and international politics is essentially the academic version of the caveman stories we used back in chapter 3 to talk about anarchy and the reasons for government. The effects of an anarchical environment on behavior, the security dilemma, alliances, the tragedy of the commons—remember all those concepts? We could almost build this section by repeating the beginning of the book and referring to a few good flicks. Take *Mad Max*[15] and *The Road Warrior*[16]—replace the barbarian motorcycle gang with the Visigoths sacking the corpse of the Roman Empire and you could be in a history class.* Take *Lord of the Flies* replace Ralph, Piggy, and Jack with Britain, France, and Germany, and we could be talking about any number of wars in European history. There are several alternative conceptual frameworks for looking at international politics, some of which we will discuss, but to state it simply, humans have never managed to establish a formal, hierarchical political structure that encompasses enough of the world to create a global governed environment. As a result, anarchy is most commonly assumed to be the underlying dynamic of international politics. The theoretical construct of **realism**[†] provides the best example of how international politics operates in an anarchical environment. Interestingly enough, even though realism refers to a specific theory of international politics and is distinct from our "real versus ideal" theme in this text, the realist theoretical perspective was developed in reaction to what is often called a period of idealism in the study of international politics.

WORLD WAR I WAS UNPLEASANT

If we look into the archaeology of the study of war, we can see that the wars-are-accidents theme found in literature has a parallel in the early study of international politics and, further, we can explain why. As is the case for just about everything—other than the horrible grade you got on the last exam—there is a reason.[‡] In short, the whole idea that war must be an accident arose from the fact that World War I was unpleasant.

The Horror, the Horror

In fact, we can blame World War I for a lot. The concerted academic effort to come to grips with international politics and part of the reason the study of international politics is so focused on war were both initiated by the horrific experiences that the soldiers and societies suffered in World War I. It probably is not possible to overstate the impact that "the war to end all wars" had on the societies involved, particularly in how it affected the scholars who studied conflict and politics. The war was such a hellish experience that it is nearly impossible to fully describe it. However, to set the proper mood, we will crank up the surround sound and try to paint a gruesome picture for you.

Imagine you are fighting in a war. Now, wars are bad enough. People are getting killed and wounded in the most unsettling ways; blood, guts, and gore are flying everywhere; heads are getting blown off and so forth, but the carnage in World War I was exceedingly gruesome. For this, you can blame the machine gun. Unlike previous wars where the battles were brief and the dynamics of the fronts and lines shifted rapidly, war in the age of the machine gun was a static slaughterhouse. In battle, soldiers used

---

*The clothes are even the same.

[†]Realism is a specific theory of international politics and is different from a common-language understanding of the word.

[‡]We all understand that your horrible grade must have had something to do with the random whims that churn through what is left of your professor's alien brain.

to be able to march towards each other, fight in the open, have some hope of winning when they attacked and then retreat back to a camp after a day or, at most, a few days of fighting. War used to consist primarily of lots of marching and camping, with a few frantic moments of blood and death mixed in, but in World War I, the battle became constant. Machine guns were so effective at defending territory that generals dared not give up any ground on the battlefield. If they let the troops retreat out of machine-gun range even just for the night, they might never recover that lost acreage. As a result, the commanders had to keep their men out on the field, defending the front line all the time. The battle became constant. The war devolved into a defensive stalemate where the armies fought, pretty much around the clock, for years on end.

The technological advance of the machine gun was key, but there were several other factors that, when combined with the new guns, made World War I the most hellish war ever fought. Machine guns killed at an astounding rate. They poured out ammunition so fast that the only way soldiers could even hope to survive in battle was to dig in, and to stay down in a trench. So the soldiers fought around the clock from huge trenches. These trenches were twenty feet or more deep and after the first couple months of the war they zigzagged their way across a good chunk of Europe. Now, as any wino can tell you, living in a ditch is miserable enough, but the climate of Western Europe made life in the trenches absolutely unbearable. It was bitterly cold and wet, and that was in the summer. It does not take much thought to figure out what happens when you live in deep trenches exposed to constant, cold rain. You are knee deep in icy mud. Your leather boots rot from your feet and your feet themselves are rotting. Further, it is hard to control sewage. Those horrible conditions and the infections they foster, combined with primitive medical treatments, meant that the slightest wound was likely to be fatal. In fact, more soldiers died from disease and infection than were killed directly from enemy fire, and that statistic is made all the more remarkable by the sheer number of men killed by bullets.

Still, as miserable as a cold, muddy, sewage-filled ditch sounds, if you are a soldier, down in that trench is where you want to be and where you want to stay. The enemy's machine guns are always waiting, waiting for your leaders to issue that order to climb over the top and attack. Compounding the lethality of the machine gun was the lack of any kind of tactical understanding of how the new weapon had changed the very nature of battle. In World War I, what little understanding of war the leaders of either side had dated from an earlier era, where guns were slow to fire and, as often as not, the guns were most deadly when the pointy bayonet on the end was used like a spear. The commanders, particularly the British generals, used nineteenth-century tactics, repeatedly ordering their troops to charge into the meat-grinding maw of those machine guns. Soldiers were sent climbing over barbed wire and dead bodies, running at the enemy while the machine guns just fired away. If a soldier was lucky enough to survive the charge, then he got to jump into the enemy's trench and fight hand-to-hand. Most histories of World War I will emphasize how many soldiers died because their commanders simply did not appreciate that the nature of war had changed.

There is yet another aspect of World War I that should drive home just how gruesome the experience was for the soldier. Even hunkered down in the sewage-filled trench, out of sight of the machine guns, you were not safe. There was the constant barrage from long-range mortars, which at any time could drop an explosive shell into your trench. But troops could build sandbag shelters to deal with the explosives. The absolute worst aspect of fighting in World War I was when those mortar shells were filled with mustard gas instead of explosives. Mustard gas, not actually poisonous, is highly caustic. It is heavier than air and when it settled down into the trenches it was essentially like inhaling drain cleaner. It killed by eating away the lining of your lungs, slowly drowning you as the fluid from your blood seeped into your lungs. It would often take hours to slowly suffocate, as you writhed in agony from the chemical burns inside your chest. Even if you managed to get your gas mask on in time, imagine sitting in one of those trenches next to someone who did not. Imagine sitting through the night while a friend of yours died like that.

All Quiet on the Western Front?

There is little doubt that World War I was a horrible experience for the soldiers, but it was also socially traumatic. Few events in history have had so profound an effect on the social and political structures of the world. The primary reason the war had such an impact on the modern study of war and international politics was its effect on the British, the predominant academics of the time. The officers in the British army—particularly the field officers down in the trenches—were elites who had been drafted into the war. These men were the educated sons of wealthy or otherwise important people, and after the war, those who survived became professors, politicians, and artists. They also had what may have been the most traumatic of experiences.

For the field officers, the hell of the World War I battlefield was so close to the normalcy of London omnibuses and afternoon tea that it was unbearable. An officer could get a four-day pass—often as frequently as every month—and hitch a ride from the front to the coast, ride a ferry across the English Channel, catch the train from Dover, and be in London for supper. In a matter of hours, you could leave the mustard gas and the sewage-filled ditches behind and be back home where everyone was carrying on like normal. A few days later you were back on the train to that cold, wet, deadly hell on the continent. If you were one of the lucky few who managed to survive through the next month, you might get another four-day pass, but even while you were sipping tea with Mum, you knew that it was probably the last time you would see her. Surviving in the trenches for more than a few months was not at all likely. It was not unheard of for a single day's battle to slaughter tens of thousands of soldiers. It was not unusual to have to climb over the bodies of the people you had just been standing next to in the trenches. It was commonplace for entire regiments to be wiped out when charging at the enemy trenches. Yet with a four-day pass, you could all of the sudden be back home. This cycling back and forth between normalcy and what was perhaps the most miserable wartime experience ever. It was almost worse than being thrown into the trenches for the duration. Humans have the ability to hunker down and endure misery. Prisoners of war, concentration camps, and slavery all offer examples of people's ability to become numb to horrendous circumstances and adjust to endure the worst of conditions. The problem for the British officers was that right about the time their minds and spirits managed to grow numb to the horrors of war, a four-day pass and a quick trip home brought back for them what was supposed to be normal and reminded them all over again just how horrific the trenches were before throwing them back in. Then, next month, just as they were getting numb to the horrors, they went home again, if they were still alive.

This trauma influenced English literature between the wars. From about 1920 through the start of World War II, these experiences permeate most British novels. World War I traumatized British society as a whole. The officers came back to their positions in the elite social circles of British society. They became authors and scholars. They researched social phenomena and political history and the experience of the war gave them a mission. With an almost religious conviction, they were determined that such a hellish war would never happen again. They attacked the disease of war with evangelical determination. The modern study of international politics was born during the interwar period and the scholars, even the diplomats of this period, were obsessed with the quest to find a peaceful world. This quest shaped the study of international politics to this very day.

One result of the obsession with preventing another world war was a body of academic study and theory that is often referred to as **idealism**. Beyond the quest for peace, there are two clear aspects to this experience and obsession that show up in the early study of international politics. The first is the belief that conflict of any sort is bad. Conflict is treated as you would treat a disease, and this is part of what sociologist Lewis Coser was reacting to when he wrote *Functions of Social Conflict*.[17] The second is the belief that no rational leader would choose to endure the massive destruction caused by war. Thus, war must result from an accident, insanity, or a gross miscalculation of some kind. You see an antiwar strain in much of the fiction about war, but you can also still see the idealist drive to end war in the titles of the two most prominent academic journals specifically focused on the study of war—*The Journal of Peace Research* and *The Journal of Conflict Resolution*.

REALISM AND WAR

The big problem with idealism and the obsessive quest for peace was that it did not work. Two decades worth of theorizing about perfect worlds and the countless political

> **Some of the effort to find peace at any cost may have even helped bring about the World War II, a world war that was bigger than the first.**

actions taken to create a world free of conflict all failed, and failed miserably. Some of the effort to find peace at any cost may have even helped bring about World War II, a world war that was bigger than the first. European leaders wanted peace so badly that they were unwilling even to contemplate using force against Hitler as he rose to power, broke agreements, rearmed Germany, annexed Austria, and took over Czechoslovakia. Just before German tanks rolled across the Polish border, E. H. Carr, a British scholar studying international politics and war, published a small, but radical book that changed the study of world politics. *The Twenty-Years' Crisis*[18] examined why the Nazis were able to take power in Germany and why they were able to grow so quickly into an international threat. Most notably this book was built upon the explicit premise that international politics could only be understood if we set aside the idealistic perspective and looked at the reality of politics. Carr argued that the reality of international politics was all about rational choices made in the pursuit of power in an anarchical international environment. Later, the theoretical approach built from this argument would be called realism, a term most often associated with another classic scholar, Hans J. Morganthau.[19]

Essentially, realism gets us back to the Risk model of international politics, or war as a strategy game. There is a great deal of diversity in realist theories and conceptual perspectives that build on a realist foundation, but they all are based upon three key assumptions.

1. **States are rational unitary actors.** Thus, we can talk about countries as if they were people making choices in their own best interests. Botswana makes a decision. Indonesia takes a certain position in international negotiations. China takes advantage of a trade relationship. Or, the United States is annoyed with France, again. While the early realist scholars were careful to point out that the different political and social structures within governments are important, the constraints and imperatives of the international system are predominant and those forces act the same on all states. This line of thinking limits the effect that domestic politics can have on international relations to the point where most phenomena can be explained entirely by dynamics external to the state.

2. **These unitary rational states interact in an anarchical environment.** Thus, the dynamics we talked about with individuals in an anarchic situation, such as the security dilemma, can be applied to states in international politics as well. States seek security in a world where there is no overarching authority to which to turn for protection. There are no courts or police to enforce agreements. It is a self-help environment, *Lord of the Flies* but with tanks and guns. Realism is often described as a systemic theory because the nature of the anarchical system defines the dynamics of how international politics will work. Everything builds from

the dynamics of anarchy. Every realist theory of why things happen starts with "we have an anarchical environment, therefore. . . ."

3. Power is the fundamental resource to be pursued. While we are treating the pursuit of power as a separate assumption of realist theory, you could also argue that it is a result of the anarchy assumption. In the anarchical environment, power, or the ability to do something, is all that is required to do whatever it is that the unitary rational state thinks needs doing. All other needs, wants, or desires, particularly the most important and primary concern of security, can then be attained with power.

The result is a simplified image of international politics that is remarkably similar to teenage kids at a card table moving plastic armies around a cardboard map. Each individual player is a country and the goal is always to gain more power, usually represented by more territory, for which you need more armies. Within the rules of how armies move and conquer, there is no referee to force the players to keep agreements they make with one another. If you have the power to take out someone and grab all of his stuff, there is nothing to stop you even if you double-promised you would not annihilate him. Thus, Nazi Germany can sign a statement of eternal peace and promise to have a sleepover with fuzzy slippers with the Soviet Union, and then turn around and attack them a few months later without any referee stepping in. The only repercussions are those the Soviet Union can find the power to inflict on Germany. Hitler had the tanks to attack, and in the end, the only thing that stopped German troops short of the Urals was the fact that Stalin had enough men with guns to stop the Panzers.

As an example of how something this simple can explain a great deal about international politics, let's look at how realism gives us two motives and two strategies for forming alliances that help understand how the choice to go to war might be rational.

Opportunity

If you think back to our stories about the bullies and geeks fighting over fish on the deserted isle, there is one obvious reason why someone in an anarchical environment would choose to go berserk and take out someone else—opportunity. The bully beats up the geek because the half-evolved brute has the opportunity to use his power and take the fish. The third assumption of realism, the assumption that power is the primary resource to be pursued includes this idea of going after gains when the opportunity arises. You can repeatedly see this in both the explanations offered for the start of wars and in the way they play out. Take for example the whole idea of *lebensraum*, which translated from German literally means "living space." The expansion of Nazi Germany was often discussed or justified by the Germans as the need to find this living space for their growing population and they used their military power to take advantage of opportunities to accomplish it. Czechoslovakia, which had almost no army in comparison to the Nazis, was bullied into ceding territory—the Sudetenland—without a fight, then that territory was used as a staging ground to take the rest of the country by force of arms. Poland was still fielding horse-mounted cavalry when Germany took advantage of their weakness and the Panzers rolled over the border in the first example of the tactic now known as blitzkrieg or "lightning war." Holland, Belgium, Denmark, and then France—Germany's conquest of Europe is a story of a huge military power taking advantage of its strong and well-equipped army to take what it wanted.

Whether it is the United States seizing the customs house of a small banana republic to assure that the United Fruit Company gets the money it claims it is owed, or it is Iraq rolling over the border of Kuwait, we can point to any number of wars and talk about them in terms of a powerful country seizing an opportunity to use its power to get something it wants. Countries can do this because it is an anarchical environment out there and there is no world government to stop them or punish them. There are, however, several wars that cannot be explained this way.

Fear This

In 1967, a single week of fighting defined one of the most stunning wars in modern history. Outgunned and outnumbered, Israel used better training, better equipment, and a masterful combination of tactics to simultaneously attack Egypt, Syria, Jordan, Iraq, Saudi Arabia, and Lebanon, defeating the whole lot in six days. The truly curious thing about the war is the simple fact that Israel attacked. Israel initiated the fighting even though any measure of power would have put them at a massive disadvantage. Further, the Israelis knew they were massively outgunned, and that was a big part of why they chose to attack.

Why on earth would a weaker power attack several larger powers?

The simple answer is fear. Israel feared an attack. Its leaders were convinced that war would come and every additional day the Arab powers would have to maneuver and prepare just made the odds worse. Beyond the usual threats and bombastic statements that have been elevated to an art form in Middle Eastern politics, the actions of the countries around Israel—Egypt in particular—gave the Israelis good reason to believe that they were about to be attacked, whether they liked it or not. Egypt asked United Nations peacekeepers to leave the border area between Egypt and Israel and moved substantial firepower toward that border. Jordan stationed a significant number of tanks at the outskirts of Jerusalem, just a few miles from cutting Israel in two with an attack. Syria reinforced their ability to strike from the Golan Heights and all of the Arab countries stepped up the level of threats. Israel feared an attack and had no real way to defend itself against the combined might of those three countries.

Given the disadvantage in terms of power, the rational response to that fear was to attack. Still doesn't make sense? Think of the Six Day War as the international version of surprising the big bully with a swift kick to the groin. The Israeli air force timed the

Figure 12.1 Israel and the Disputed Territories

GOLAN HEIGHTS: A mountainous area with peaks high enough to allow skiing in the winter. There is no natural barrier to prevent the holder of the heights from launching a tank assault either into Israel or Syria.

The Jordan River: From the West Bank, a column of tanks can reach Tel Aviv in minutes. However, the Jordan River that defines its eastern edge is large enough to effectively prevent a tank attack from Jordanian territory.

The Suez Canal: Like the Jordan River, the Suez Canal, which defines the edge of the Sinai Peninsula, is a waterway that presents an almost impenetrable barrier to an armored assault.

LEBANON

SYRIA

GOLAN HEIGHTS

Haifa

Sea of Galilee

Nazareth

Jordan River

WEST BANK

TEL AVIV

Amman

Mediterranean Sea

Jericho

Jerusalem

Port Said

Gaza

GAZA STRIP

Suez Canal

Suez

Hebron

Dead Sea

SINAI PENINSULA

Beersheba

EGYPT

ISRAEL

JORDAN

NEGEV

EGYPT

SINAI PENINSULA

Gulf of Aqaba

The defensible borders Israel secured with the territories occupied in 1967.

Source: Stephen W. Hook and John Spanier, *American Foreign Policy Since World War II,* 17th ed. (Washington, D.C.: CQ Press, 2007), 259

initial attack so the first bomb dropped ten minutes after the Arab officers—a classification that included all of the pilots—started their breakfast. At that time of the morning, none of the Egyptian, Syrian, Jordanian, Saudi, Lebanese, or Iraqi planes were in the air and none of the pilots were anywhere close to the planes. In a single, perfectly timed and executed attack, Israel destroyed almost everything that the Arab forces could fly while the machines were still on the ground. By gaining control of the air, Israel effectively reversed the relative balance of power, and by the end of the day, any of the Arab tanks that had not been destroyed from the air were retreating from the similarly well-executed attacks made by the Israeli armored units. A few days later, Israel had conquered three geo-strategically critical territories: the Golan Heights, the West Bank of the Jordan River, and the Sinai Peninsula. Holding those territories gave Israel borders that it could reasonably hope to defend against an attack. That is a big part of why Israel still holds parts of those territories.

Instances when a country attacks out of fear are rarely this obvious and they seldom work out very well. After all, if you fear the greater power of another that means you are the weakling and already at a disadvantage, but we can take a quick look at other responses to fear to see how power and the anarchical system shape the fundamentals of international politics.

Balancing and Bandwagoning

Chances are you have heard the term *balance of power* somewhere along the line. Chances are also pretty good that you do not really know what it means. Do not feel bad; most professors do not either. Some will talk about it as a verb, something countries do. Some will talk about it as a situation, something that does or does not exist. Some will talk about it as a specific historical period where Britain was a dominant world power. Some scholars studying what are known as "power-transition wars" will say that the existence of a balance of power makes it more likely that a challenger will go to war with a dominant power while some will argue that a balance of power will prevent war by keeping countries from believing they have an opportunity to make easy gains off a weakling. In short, it is not that unreasonable for you to be a bit confused about the term.

As confused as the usage of the term may be, **balance of power** might be best described as the way in which the distribution of power across the international system influences the pattern of alliances that tend to form in an anarchical environment. In fact, we have already discussed this understanding of balance of power in the scenario of bullies and geeky kids catching fish. The international version of the story is a little more violent, but it is the same idea of forming an alliance to counter, or balance against the power of others and protect what you consider to be valuable.

The one notable difference between balancing against power in the international-relations version of the story and the bullies-on-the-beach version is that the primary motivation in international politics is presumed to be fear rather than opportunity. When we speak of balance of power we are usually talking about a situation where alliances are formed or alliances shift in response to the perception of threat, or where small countries ally together to protect themselves from the big bully. In what was often referred to as the Balance of Power era, England used a balance of power strategy explicitly in the effort to maintain peace in Europe. As disputes arose and threatened to escalate to war, England would lend support to the weaker side in order to balance the power on both sides and prevent either side from believing it had an opportunity to make gains by war against a weaker opponent. This is also part of the reason why the term is so confused. Balance of power defines an era in international politics, it describes an action and strategy that England used in international relations, and it also signifies a condition that can exist when the power on both sides of a dispute is roughly equal.

Balancing can be thought of as alliance formation driven by the fear that the more powerful side might be pursuing gains, but we can also talk about international alliance dynamics in terms of an opportunistic motive. Instead of siding with the weakling to thwart the bully, you could ally with the bully in order to carve out your own slice of the spoils. You could talk about the Second Gulf War in terms of **bandwagoning**.*

A reasonable argument can be made that the countries that allied with the United States to topple Saddam Hussein were hoping for spoils such as rebuilding contracts and U.S. support in other areas of international politics in return for lending a few troops to the war effort. They pursued opportunity rather than acting out of fear of the United States.

Why?

Before you rush off into claims of the United States' noble motives and moral superiority, or the corporate conspiracies of oil companies as reasons why these countries would join with the United States, think about the question of why in terms of realism, in terms of power. Did any of these bandwagoners have enough power to do anything else? The overwhelming power of the United States compared to Iraq is a significant consideration when it comes to the question of bandwagoning in the Second Gulf War. It is notable that none of the U.S. allies could have thwarted the United States by allying with Iraq. This seems to be relatively typical of instances where you could call alliance formation an act of bandwagoning. One side is so much stronger than the other that victory is all but assured and joining in the alliance is opportunistic or desperate, either currying favor of the stronger power or seeking a share of the spoils from a conflict that they cannot do anything to stop. With so much opposition to the war around the world, it is interesting to consider what would have happened if there had been a country in the world that was powerful enough to protect Iraq with an alliance.

---

*This phenomenon also explains why there are an inordinate number of Yankees fans.

Notice that in both balancing and bandwagoning, the key is power. You balance against a greater, threatening power. You bandwagon against a weaker power to gain part of the spoils. In realism, power and anarchy act to define international politics.

CHALLENGING THE REALIST PARADIGM

In spite of the surprisingly good explanations realism provides for some things, particularly those related to war, there are problems with its simplified image of international politics. Realism, it seems, is, in a number of ways, just not that realistic. At the very least, it has a tough time explaining all of the cooperative international behavior that, by any reasonable measure, is far more common than war.

A tremendous number of refinements or alternate theories can be offered to address the shortcomings and failings of realism. Judging by the latest offerings in introductory international relations textbooks, liberalism and constructivism are the two most popular counterpoints to realism for the classroom. However, how well the demands of the current textbook market accurately reflect the subject is an interesting question. Marxism has fallen almost completely out of introductory international relations texts, yet the *vast* majority of research presented at the last five of the International Studies Association* annual conventions examines international political economy, economic development, the political effects of poverty, sanctions, trade, or foreign aid. While many of these studies do not explicitly work from a Marxist intellectual foundation, almost all presume the Marxist conceit that wealth is the primary factor driving international politics. Yet Marxism, which used to be a mandatory counterpart to realism in any course on international relations, has vanished along with the communist bloc. In addition to running counter to the trends in research, this is particularly ironic when you consider how much Karl Marx would have despised those brutal totalitarian regimes.

Liberalism might reasonably be considered an equal to Marxism as a challenge to realism. It is the primary theoretical construct underlying many significant areas of research, including the idea of the democratic peace, which is highlighted below. However, an examination of the current state of the discipline makes it difficult to make the claim that constructivism is equal to either liberalism or Marxism, and it is impossible to argue that it should displace Marxism from introductory international relations textbooks. That said, there must be a reason why constructivism is so popular in the classroom. Professors do not make those sorts of decisions lightly.[†] And even though we focus on the reasons for a cautious approach to making bold claims about constructivism,

---

*The ISA is the largest organization of scholars studying international relations in the world, and it publishes the top five (in terms of circulation) international relations research journals.

†Regardless of the arguments made about alternatives to realism, there is one thing that is clear, they are *alternatives* to realism. Whether the field is examined from a historical perspective or a survey of its current state, it would be difficult to dismiss realism as the central conceptual perspective on international relations. Thus, for this chapter we work from that foundation, taking small steps away from realism as we try to describe the study of international politics and the specific theories and research programs we discuss are chosen to help students make those small conceptual steps.

that should not be taken as a slight on its value as an approach to international relations.* Rather, it reflects an uncertainty over how it fits into the constellation of theories and hypotheses in international relations.

The Not So Black Box

One of the most obvious ways that the simplifications of realism run afoul of the real world is in the presumption that states behave as if they are rational unitary actors. In essence, from a strict realist perspective, the internal workings of a state do not matter. The leaders, governments, processes, economies, societies, religions, and all the other goings-on inside the state can be put in a black box. Not a real black box—you would never be able to build one that was big enough—but a figurative black box where what goes on inside can be ignored. The idea is that for a given input from the international system, the output of all domestic governments and societies must be the same regardless of how things are done inside. That strict interpretation of realism, however, is a bit troubling because it seems pretty obvious that process, structure, and particularly leaders make a big difference. Would the cold war have ended peacefully if Gorbachev were replaced with a hard-line militant Stalinist? If Gore, not Bush were in the White House, would the Second Gulf War have happened? Replace Hitler, Tojo, Qaddafi, Stalin, Roosevelt, any of England's King Edwards, Genghis Khan, or Millard Fillmore and the politics of the world would probably be radically changed. If leaders do not matter, how is that we can have great or horrible leaders?

One of the theoretical perspectives that directly challenges the realist presumption of the state as a unitary rational actor is Foreign Policy Analysis.[†] In short, Foreign Policy Analysis argues that states do not make decisions, individuals make decisions and understanding how those decisions are made within the structure, process, and context of domestic politics is essential for understanding international politics. From the effects of bureaucracies to the psychological profiles of leaders, Foreign Policy Analysis is all about what goes on inside the black box and how that defines or alters the interactions of states. Most Foreign Policy Analysis theories and studies do not challenge the idea of an anarchical international system, but they do place less emphasis on the influence of anarchy, structure, the international system, or power. Rather than determining specific actions and events, Foreign Policy Analysis scholars argue that the system defines or limits the menu of choices available to leaders. After all, there are plenty of countries the United States has the power to invade, but which ones get an olive green calling card, now that is the question. Another way to think of this is

---

*It should be noted that one of the authors of this text studies the effect of news media on international politics and almost all of his work relies on, and can be fit within a broad conceptualization of constructivism. Clearly, the approach to constructivism used in this chapter does not reflect any kind of disregard for its intellectual value; just the questionable claim that it should displace Marxism.

†Do note that while we do not capitalize realism, we capitalize Foreign Policy Analysis in order to differentiate the theoretical approach from the research activity the words could also denote. It also annoys realist theorists, which is fun.

the idea of foreign policy substitutability. Roughly put, for any one input from the anarchical international system, there is usually a whole set of options that might reasonably be chosen in response. From the context of an anarchic international system the 1991 Persian Gulf War, the First Gulf War, is particularly interesting. The U.S. response to Saddam Hussein's 1991 invasion of Kuwait could have reasonably stretched from ignoring it entirely to launching an all-out war. Those extreme options and all the options in between have advantages and disadvantages, costs and benefits, risks and rewards, short-term and long-term consequences. All of those factors have both domestic components and international components. How all those nonsystemic factors sort themselves out into a decision and an action is a function of the processes and structures that, from a realist perspective, supposedly do not matter—all of the things in the black box of domestic government.

While this makes sense, the difficulty with looking inside the black box is that it makes a complicated mess of things. No two governments are the same, no two leaders are the same, and with any kind of study you quickly run into difficulties separating the more theoretically interesting general reasons why things happen from the unique aspects within the country or countries in question. When a scholar chooses to open the black box, getting buried by the details is always a danger. There are rewards, but they are coupled with difficulties. One reward that we want to highlight might be a hint at how to get closer to the elusive peace that idealists dreamt about in the aftermath of World War I.

Why Kant Democracies Fight?*

Opening the black box of government has made possible the simple discovery that the basic type of government structure can have a significant effect on the choice to go to war. Long, long ago, in a university far, far away, Immanuel Kant argued that democracies, such as the fledgling United States, would be less prone to go to war than the kingdoms and empires of Europe.[20] Kant's logic was simple: Wars placed tremendous burdens on the average person—the taxpayer and the soldier—and since the leaders of democracies were held accountable by those average people, democratic leaders would only choose to go to war if they could justify the loss of life and money to the people who vote. This need for accountability would eliminate many of the frivolous wars entered into by kings and princes, and thus make democracies more peaceful.

The logic makes sense, but a couple of centuries later, when political scientists had gathered the data needed to check and see if democracies were indeed more peaceful, Kant's prediction did not exactly prove to be true. Democracies did not seem to be any less prone to go to war than other forms of government. As a bit of a curious aside, however, one of the studies noted that democracies did not seem to fight one another.

---

*We apologize to Cliff Morgan and Sally Howard Campbell for stealing the title from one of their research articles, but it is catchy and makes for a great section title. T. Clifton Morgan and Sally Howard Campbell, "Domestic Structure, Decisional Constraints, and War—So Why Kant Democracies Fight?" *Journal of Conflict Resolution* 35 (1991): 187–211.

This observation turned out to be a big thing. Time and time again, studies have repeatedly demonstrated that liberal democratic political regimes do not fight one another. There has been a great deal of bickering over the specifics of statistical methods used in analyses, what defines a democracy, what defines a war, and so forth, but this idea of **democratic peace**—a peace between democracies or between countries sharing a characteristic closely associated with modern democracy—is about as close as political scientists ever get to agreeing on anything. It seems that there is something about the way democracies work, something within the mess that realists would stuff inside the black box, that is having a clear and consistent influence on war and peace.

Unfortunately, this agreement over the presence of a democratic peace is not matched by anything close to a consensus on why democracies might choose not to fight one another. How shared democracy creates peace is not at all clear. Explanations from economics and trade, to shared culture, to news flows, to the influence of McDonald's and other international corporations have been offered, but even after several hundred research articles and several dozen books devoted to the subject, it is not clear exactly what is happening. What is clear, however, is that what goes on inside the black box matters. If something as simple as the basic type of government can have such a clear effect, then other aspects of process and domestic politics must also be important to the conduct of international politics.

Another important point is that the democratic peace is a specific area of research and is not a theory of international politics. While some might plausibly argue that Foreign Policy Analysis is a theory of international politics that fits within the liberalism conceptualization of the world* no one would argue that the democratic peace is. The democratic peace is a research topic that fits within the commitment of Foreign Policy Analysis to opening the black box of domestic politics and, perhaps more importantly, is one of the best examples of research conducted from the liberal theoretical perspective. Liberalism is harder to define than either realism or Marxism, but one way to describe it is as the cooperative counterpart of realism, or perhaps an embodiment of the Western ideal of the enlightened individual. It is a collection of theories that presume that human beings are generally cooperative, cooperation provides greater overall benefit for everyone, and that the closer you get to the democratic ideal of informed individuals participating in policy, the more cooperative politics will become. The democratic peace fits that bill perfectly.

The Shadow of the Hegemon[†]

Another way that realism can be challenged is by questioning the assertion that the world is anarchic. Even in our simplified stories of kids on a deserted isle, anarchy was

---

*They would probably lose the argument, but they could still make it without being too horribly embarrassed later.

[†]If you recognize that title, you are a true and certified geek. Congratulations, you can now wear a gold shirt instead of a red shirt when you beam down to Planet Doom and you can pick up your membership certificate from Orson Scott Card at the next World Science Fiction Convention.

> **Trade is common; war is rare. War may be dramatic but trade is pervasive, and half the time, wars are fought over trade or economics anyway.**

fleeting when it existed. In *Lord of the Flies*, look at how quickly the boys try to take themselves out of anarchy, how quickly they act to reestablish social structures for interactions. From the minute Piggy starts talking to Ralph, the exchange can be viewed in terms of the two of them trying to establish a hierarchy, a social structure to manage their interaction. Within a few pages, the boys are gathered at the little meeting, with big kids in charge and the conch shell being used to regulate behavior. Is it any less likely that states in the international system would try to establish some form of international social and political structure? After all, trade, exchange, and diplomacy are ancient and persistent activities. In fact, many international relations scholars would be willing to agree with the statement that international economic activity is far more important than war when it comes to the relationships between countries. Trade is common; war is rare. War may be dramatic but trade is pervasive, and half the time, wars are fought over trade or economics anyway.

One of the simplest ways to challenge the realist presumption of an anarchic international environment is to talk about international hegemony. A **hegemon** is simply a dominant power, either some individual or, in the case of international politics, some country that is powerful enough to dominate all others. Through this domination, the hegemon can impose a structure on the anarchical system. Further, many countries will willingly accept this domination. They might even seek it.

Think of it in terms of Mafia movies, where one crime boss, the don, becomes so powerful he can dominate all the criminals in town and impose a form of order and structure on their activities. The don creates rules that disproportionately benefit his bank account and the system is nowhere near fair or just, but it does create a hierarchy that can enforce rules and agreements and it takes the majority of criminals out of anarchy. The typical criminals in this crime-boss governed environment can confidently create numbers rackets, loan sharking operations, prostitution rings, drug distribution cartels, and other forms of criminal investment because they know that if they follow the rules laid down by the don and pay the proper percentage, the Mafia boss will protect them from other criminal bullies who could use their power to take all the fruit of those investments and labor. The criminal version of an economy can work within the rules of the hierarchy imposed by the dominant power.

Something similar can be seen in the international system as well. The underlying dynamic of the international system may be anarchic, but there is seldom if ever any real anarchy. History is in many ways defined by the waxing and waning of dominant powers, or hegemons, which can impose order and a hierarchy on the system. The Mongols, Persians, Egyptians, Greeks, Romans, Spanish, Dutch, British, and Americans— while it is arguable whether these or any other powers were truly hegemonic—in one way or another, each was able to impose some degree of structure on trade and often other aspects of the interactions between the world's independent political entities. A hegemon creates and enforces rules that allow the weak to invest and trade. In the modern world, these facilitating structures are everywhere; think of the World Bank, the post office, duty-free stores, and the international rugby union. One of the first things you might notice if you travel around the world is how much things are the same and how easy it is to spend your money just about anywhere. A great deal of this ease of exchange is a result of the United States and, earlier, Britain using their power to create and sustain a structure for trade and currency exchange.

While there are examples of brute force being used, particularly in Latin America in the middle of the twentieth century, most of the structures you see formed as part of the U.S. turn as hegemon are reasonably voluntary, or at least nonviolent. As far as we can tell, the United States has not yet sent the marines into any country to force them to adopt the standards that allow computers to link to the Internet or make it possible to place international phone calls, yet these standards are quite common. Putting aside, but not dismissing, the philosophical argument that the very existence of an international hierarchy of dominance relationships precludes anything being truly voluntary, we can ask why any nation might choose to accept U.S. hegemony and its rules for trade.

Consider a Japanese car, built for the Japanese market. It can be sold, used in Australia, then shipped to England when your band becomes famous and you move to Liverpool. Why is this possible? Because Japanese carmakers make most if not all of their cars to meet U.S. safety standards. Why does this matter if we are not even talking about the United States in this example? Well, Australia, Great Britain, and most other developed countries demand safety standards that roughly match those in the United States. Why would they do that? Why would they not set their own standards? It is simple, economics. The U.S. market for cars is huge, most manufacturers want to ship their products to that huge market, and meeting the U.S. standards is required before the product can be sold in Chicago. Since design is such a huge part of the cost of a car, manufacturers use the same design for all or most of their cars, and build all of their cars to meet U.S. standards.

Imagine you are a small country enacting car safety standards. For countries that import cars from Japan, adopting U.S. standards is an easy way to get the cheapest possible new cars for your insane taxi drivers. All the big car companies are already set up to meet the U.S. standards. The whole idea of economies of scale says it is easy and cheap for those companies to just build a few thousand extra of those same cars and ship them to Bulgaria. Even if you have legal standards that are lower than the U.S. standards, if you are a smaller country it would be so expensive to make any kind of significant changes to the assembly of cars that it is unlikely to be worth any savings that might be found in building down to your lower standards. Thus, except for expensive and easily removed items such as air bags, you may as well just say, give us the same standards as the United States. Lowering your standards is unlikely to get you cheaper cars.

In the other direction, unless you are a huge country or a huge common market of cooperating countries like the European Union, setting higher standards than the United States is even more difficult. An import market of a few million people, such as New Zealand, would find it impossibly expensive to unilaterally set higher safety standards than the United States. What manufacturer will make a significant change in the car design to meet the demand of 4 million people when you have billions of people out there ready to buy the U.S. standard? Simply by setting rules for access to the U.S. market, the United States can set the trade rules for a significant portion of the world. To be traded on the New York stock exchange, foreign countries have to meet U.S. accounting standards. To ship carcass pucks to burger joints in Sioux Falls, the cow grinding plants in Brazil have to meet U.S. health standards and in most cases they have to be inspected by U.S. health officials. Other countries wishing to protect the health of their citizens can then take advantage of that and insist that their imports from Brazil be U.S. certified as well. In that way, smaller countries get the United States to do all of the work in assuring safety, and producers get the benefit of a consistent set of standards.

Predictably, the rules that the hegemon sets up are biased to benefit the hegemon. For example, the specifics of a U.S. manufacturer's product are often used as the legal standard and competitors that want to import are forced to adapt, giving the U.S. firm a head start. International banking regulations are set up to match those already existing in the United States and foreign banks are forced to change, while domestic banks get an advantage by already having the system in place. However, hegemony is a double-edged sword. The hegemon has to invest a great deal to keep the system in place. In the eighteenth and nineteenth centuries, Great Britain had to take on most of the cost of keeping the seas free of piracy so that the global trading system it had set up between its colonies could continue functioning. This required a huge navy that could patrol the entire world. The cost of the ships and sailors was a tremendous drain on the Royal piggy bank. A global naval presence also required ports and bases and colonies spread out all over everywhere, including the Falklands, Zanzibar, Belize, Gibraltar, and all kinds of other places that most Americans have never heard of, like Canada. Some of these colonies and far-flung outposts of empire, like Hong Kong, were profitable, but many—if not most—were not and Britain had to bear this economic burden as part of being hegemon. Other countries could then take advantage of the pirate-free oceans and conduct trade without having to do much if any of the work chasing the pirates away. This was just like letting the United States spend the money to verify health standards, develop and approve drugs, or do all the testing to establish car safety standards. In the eighteenth century, countries could take advantage of the British provision of seas safe for trade without contributing to that security.

Eventually, the costs of being the hegemon and sustaining the system outweigh the benefits, and the dominance of a hegemon begins to fade. Fading hegemonic powers

THE MERCHANT OF VENICE

While many students find Shakespeare's play, *The Merchant of Venice* to be shockingly antisemitic, when forced to look past the Jewish moneylender's demand that a metaphor in the contract be taken literally so that Antonio must surrender an actual pound of flesh when he cannot repay his debt to Shylock, the moneylender, what is most interesting is that the play is set in Venice. Why Venice? In fact, if you ever visit Venice, one of the first questions you might ask is, "Where is the insect-infested-hostel-for-impoverished-college-students?" Once you check in and introduce yourself to your fifty-three thousand roommates, you might reasonably ask, "Why is Venice even here?"

The answer to that second question, as well as the explanation for why the play is called *The Merchant of Venice* and not *The Merchant of Manchester* is simple—it comes down to international politics.

From a construction standpoint, a swampy, sinking island out in the middle of a lagoon is a pretty lousy place to build a city. In fact, the architectural history of Venice is largely a story of abandoning lower floors, filling them in, and building more on top as it all gradually sinks. However, in terms of international politics, that swampy bit of land is the perfect location, and it allowed the tiny little city of Venice to dominate a large portion of the world for generations.

First, the water surrounding the little group of islands kept Venice secure against the armies of the continent. Wealthy people who wanted to protect themselves from looting and pillaging really liked the security provided by that natural moat and they moved there in droves. Further, that moat made it easier for the rulers of Venice to defy the latest Italian prince who had assembled a powerful army and was trying to unify the peninsula. It made it easier for Venice to keep consistent tax, trade, and banking rules that encouraged wealth to migrate to and accumulate in Venice.

Second, Venice occupied a key location for trade. Like Amsterdam, London, and New York in the centuries to follow, Venice was in the perfect spot for getting trade goods into and out of Europe. The ports and warehouses in this secure little city provided the perfect location for exchanging and transferring cargo between ships plying the Mediterranean and also to shift cargos from ocean trade routes to overland routes into Europe.

The result was a tiny city that dominated trade to the point that it could set the world standard for contracts, banking, and other laws related to commerce. For fear of being shut out of this most important of ports, no trader would dare defy the laws of Venice. All the most profitable trade routes went through Venice, all of the banks were in Venice, all of the contracts for trade were registered in Venice, and the legal enforcement of those contracts was provided by Venice. Thus, because of the reality of international politics and trade, a sixteenth-century story about a moneylender abusing the courts to inflict serious injury upon a rival had to be set in Venice.

can hold things together for quite a while, but eventually, a rising power will mount a challenge and try to take control of the international system. The result might be referred to as hegemonic war or a system transition war. Several big wars, including the Napoleonic Wars of the early nineteenth century and World War I are talked about in terms of a challenger taking on the hegemon and trying to alter the rules of the game of international trade, sort of like a new crime boss moving into town.

It's the Economy, Stupid: World Systems Theory and Anti-Globalization Sentiment

Another alternative to the classic conceptualization of an anarchic, realist world is to challenge all three assumptions—that unitary states are the primary actors, that the international system is anarchic, and that power is the fundamental resource to be pursued. Instead, we could assume that the core component of global politics is economic, the basis of **world systems theory**. Politics occurs within an economic structure defined by exploitative trade relationships, with corporate, class, and multinational entities defining the units of action. It is all about wealth and economic exploitation on a global scale. If someone in your class thinks that globalization is the root of all evil and protests against the G-8* this is the part of the text where they will get all excited. They will also probably be at least a little bit disappointed by this section. As with all the other theoretical approaches to the study of international or global politics, there are some aspects of world systems theory that seem to just hit the nail on the head, but it falls far short in other areas.

Building from a foundation of Marxist theory, world systems theory is based on an internationalization of the exploitative economic relations between classes.[†] Marx talked about this relationship *within* a country—between the capitalists and the proletariat—and he argued that the exploitation caused by the capitalist imperative to compete for efficiency would doom the system to collapse. When the preordained Thursday afternoon passed and capitalism did not collapse on schedule, Lenin argued that Marx had not considered the externalization of capitalism. By expanding from national economies to globe-spanning colonial empires, the collapse had been delayed. Continual growth had allowed capitalists to buy off the most disgruntled workers with gold, goods, and land from far-flung places, making them nice gruntled workers again. But the inevitable collapse was still on its way. It was just delayed until the world ran out of places for Europe to colonize.

After another half century without the end of history, Johan Galtung rethought the idea of an economically-defined political world and wrote *A Structural Theory of Imperialism.*[21] Extending Lenin's basic idea that capitalism had been internationalized, Galtung described a worldwide capitalist system made up of hierarchical relationships between cores and peripheries, illustrated in Figure 12.1. Cores are economic elites, capitalists that invest in the means of production that transform labor into wealth, the controllers of the factories and corporations. The periphery is the working class, the laborers. The argument is simple and elegant, highlighting economic relationships and exchanges that can explain a great deal about how the world works.

Every country in the world is made up of a core and a periphery, a small capitalist elite core and a large working-class periphery. Further, the countries of the world can be divided up into the same categories, a small core of wealthy, elite, capitalist countries

---

*The G-8 is not a new version of the Xbox. It is the shortened name for the Group of Eight, an informal organization of eight developed countries that meet annually and basically dominate the world's economy—Canada, France, Germany, Italy, Japan, the United Kingdom, the United States, and Russia.

[†]See, we told you we would get back to Marx.

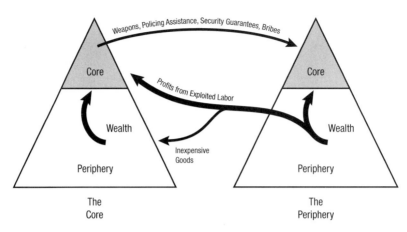

Figure 12.2 The Core and the Periphery in World Systems Theory

Source: An artful and most excellent adaptation from Johan Galtung, "A Structural Theory of Imperialism," *Journal of Peace Research* 8, no. 2 (1971): 81–117

and a much larger periphery of poor, less-developed countries that play a global economic role similar to the worker or proletariat in Marx's analysis of capitalism. The result is a world economic system that replicates the capitalist exploitive relationship on a global scale. What is remarkable is the way that the discussion of a few simple and seemingly obvious aspects of the relationships between these various cores and peripheries can explain a tremendous amount of what we see in early twenty-first century global politics.

The most obvious feature of this global capitalist system is the flow of wealth from peripheries to cores, both within and between countries. The capitalist elite core of every country exploits the labor of its periphery, using control over the means of production to extract wealth from their labor. This is replicated on a global scale by core countries using control of international mechanisms of trade to extract wealth from periphery countries. This extraction of wealth not only enriches the capitalist elite of core countries, it keeps the periphery countries stuck in the periphery by taking the wealth the periphery countries need for investing in their own development. The poor are kept poor so they have to work for the core. Now if this was all there was to the system, it would probably collapse, much as Marx and Lenin expected. The competition among capitalists would push them to extract more and more from the periphery until the poor were pushed to revolt. After all, it would be only a matter of time and education before the periphery population of the core countries and the periphery population of the periphery countries realized their common suffering from exploitation by the core population of the core countries and rebelled against it.

The key to world systems theory and its ability to explain things like dependency and the lack of revolt against the core is in its depiction of how the global system is sustained. The core of the periphery is kept in power because it receives key resources from the core of the core. Weapons and police training are some of the things the core of the core provides to the political and economic elites of the less-developed countries being exploited, but there is also some degree of direct protection offered to the peripheral leaders. Would the leaders of Kuwait be back in power if not for the direct actions of the United States? More important than these direct actions is how the global capitalistic system keeps the periphery of the core and periphery states from sharing a common economic misery. The core of the core prevents a revolt of its own workers and prevents those workers from finding a reason to join with the periphery of the periphery in changing the system by diverting a significant amount of wealth extracted from the periphery states, to the periphery of the core. As a result, the periphery of the core has no interest in changing the system. They also benefit from the exploitation of the periphery of the periphery. They do not share a common economic cause with the downtrodden masses in less-developed countries. In short, the average person in the United States, Europe, or any other developed capitalist country gets paid off with wealth extracted from the less developed.

What's that, you say? You have not gotten your world systems periphery exploitation check? Well, actually, you are wearing it. Inexpensive clothes are one particularly obvious way that the average person in a core country benefits from the economic exploitation of the periphery. Heard about all of that protesting of Nike's Malaysian sweatshops? Well the use of cheap foreign labor goes to more than just corporate profits. It also leads to less expensive, much less expensive, shoes. Forget the super flashy basketball shoes that will never actually get anywhere close to sweaty feet on a court; go into a discount store and look at the price on an average pair of shoes that a normal human would use to play basketball. We can even be generous and avoid the really cheap stuff and only look at the ones that are marked, say, fifty dollars a pair. What would it have cost to make those in the United States or Europe? Well, find another store and see how much cash it takes to buy a pair of Italian designer shoes. Even at a discount store an average pair of Italian-made shoes will cost at least twice what you lay out for the sneakers. The biggest part of that difference is the cost of the labor. Shirts, pants, coats, even your underwear, they are all far cheaper because they are made by the periphery workers of the periphery states. Even if you do not find cash falling in your wallet, your dollar, yen, pound, or euro buys far more stuff because of the exploitation of the periphery. If you united with the periphery of the periphery and overthrew the global economic system, you would also be giving up all that cheap stuff. We like our cheap stuff.

So you are kept happy and nonrevolutionary with your cheap stuff, and that bit of insight is what separates Galtung and world systems theory from other Marxist or economics-first theories of politics. Galtung not only explains why the system keeps poor countries poor, he also demonstrates how the system is sustained and why it does not collapse. This is also what all the noise regarding anti-globalization is about. The anti-globalization demonstrators who can think beyond the catchy slogans and actually understand why they are harassing the G-8 meetings and smashing the windows of Starbucks, are protesting against the fundamental unfairness of this global economic capitalist system. For wealthy countries, the infrastructure of the global system for trade acts much as the ownership of factories did for the early industrial capitalists Marx wrote about. By controlling the World Bank, monetary exchange systems, and access to sources of investment capital, developed nations force less developed nations to play by unfair economic rules. Loans, development grants, foreign aid, and trade agreements are all self-serving actions by the developed countries. These actions build economic infrastructures not for local development, but to facilitate the exploitation by the economies of core countries and they tie developed countries to debts that extract capital at an alarming rate through interest payments.

An entrepreneur in the Republic of the Congo has no realistic hope of becoming the next Bill Gates. The infrastructure of the Congo will not provide him the education, nor will it allow him to develop the products needed to bring wealth to the country. As for computers or communications lines, even if you could get access to reliable electricity in the Congo it is almost impossible to buy a lightbulb. If Einstein's smarter brother was reincarnated in the Congo he would have to go to a developed country to succeed in business. He would have to leave to even be educated enough to understand what his less-gifted, crazy-haired brother said. Developed countries not only keep the wealth flowing home, they keep the opportunities at home and extract everything that less-developed countries would need for building an economy that does anything more than service the dominant, wealthy parts of the world. The core even extracts the people from the periphery. Most of the foreign students you see on campus are the brightest and best their country has to offer. They represent the best resource those countries might have for development, and most of those students will stay in the United States or Europe to work. Except for money sent home to families, those students will contribute to developed economies instead of their lesser-developed homelands; they will pay taxes, create businesses, and contribute to your standard of living instead of going home. In the Congo, there is very little work available for molecular biologists. Thus, the Congo and all the other developing countries have little hope of keeping their best and brightest at home to pull the country up economically. The unfairness of all this is what the anti-globalization demonstrators are really protesting about.

Now we said that the anti-globalization crowd would be displeased with this section, and here is the part they really will not like; there are two big problems inherent with the politics and the reality behind all the anti-globalization protests and window smashing. Pointing these things out never fails to really irritate a few people, but if we were worried about upsetting people then it would be awfully hard to teach about politics.

The first problem is that not everything about globalization is bad and evil. That is not to deny that there are truly wretched things that we can blame on the effects of global capitalism, but if you look at all the ways capitalism has changed the world over the last couple centuries, or even over the last half-century, there are several good things. *Better* or *worse* are value judgments and they depend greatly on what you, personally, value, but there is enough of a variety of good things that we can probably find something you think is good.

You are in college, so maybe you like education. We are not going to make any presumptions on this topic, but if you do like education, it might interest you to know that literacy rates around the world are higher now than they have ever been before and more people have access to basic, advanced, and technical education than ever before in history. Maybe you like being alive. Many people do. In that case consider that access to basic health care, vaccinations, the likelihood of surviving childhood are all now higher in just about every country around the world than they were in *any* country before capitalism became a prominent economic phenomena. What about bananas? Do you like them? Many of the foods you probably enjoy do not natively come from the country you live in, but are available to you through international trade. How about something more esoteric, like human rights? While there are still some notable and ugly exceptions, basic rights for women—almost nonexistent prior to the capitalist economic revolution—now exist in some meaningful form for the vast majority of the better-smelling gender. There are currently more democracies in the world and more people living in democracies than ever before in history. At the very least, before you smash that Starbucks window, you should look at both the good and the bad things that we might reasonably blame on capitalism. For the last half-century, the United Nations has been gathering and publishing data on living conditions around the world. Even a cursory examination of their Web site will show many things that have improved. Some things are worse, some are better, but the balance between the good, the bad, and the ugly is a matter of judgment and personal values. That is a judgment you should make in an informed and considered manner.

The second thing that will displease an anti-globalization protestor is a simple question: What do you think you want? "Stop globalization" may be what you spray paint on the side of the cow you stole and tied to the front door of the McDonald's, but is that possible? Globalization is a phenomena created by advancing technology, increasing worldwide education, and the aggregate economic choices of billions of people around the world, among other things. It is not like the global release of *Gigli,* which somebody could have and very well should have stopped. Is there anyone, any country or any group of countries that could actually stop or reverse globalization? What alternative is there to globalization? The technology is already out there; can we take it away? Certainly there must be things that leaders or countries could do to reduce the negatives and enhance the positives, but can the increasing economic integration of the world be stopped? Can it be reversed? If you cut a country off from all aspects of international trade and international communication, would it really be better off? North Korea suggests the answer might be no, but having an insane dictator might be part of the problem there. Even if you are a leader who wants to give the anti-globalization protesters what they want, what is it that you could give them?

Dude, Think about the Fish

The tragedy of the commons represents another way the study of international politics can mirror the caveman stories from the beginning of the book and yet another way that international politics diverges from the simplistic model of realism. Collapsing fisheries, disappearing forests, transnational pollution, population pressures, and plagues are all issues the world has seen before. The Roman Empire had serious problems with airborne pollution from silver smelting. Historically, deforestation has repeatedly been a problem for naval powers from the Greeks to the British, often sending them to farthest reaches of their trade networks for the timber needed for shipbuilding. Ancient civilizations from Cambodia to Peru appear to have fallen victim to the cumulative effects of intensive agriculture, causing regional, and possibly continental economic and social collapses. Many of these transnational or regional catastrophes, however, occurred in the shadows. The overexploitation and collapse of communal resources left little or no impression in written histories and were usually discovered by archaeologists digging in the dirt rather than historians digging through archives.

Today, the struggle with the forces driving us into the tragedy of the commons has gone global and every year the number of ways that the feeble humans of planet Earth face problems that threaten the global commons increases. From population pressures, to collapsing ocean resources, to ozone depletion, to access to fresh water, to acid rain, to disease control, to reality TV,* a list of global tragedy-of-the-commons issues could grow very long. The length of this list might reasonably be attributed to the forces of globalization. With capitalist pressures becoming ever more universal, the number of ways those economic dynamics drive people to overexploit common resources increase and become all-inclusive. Further, the economic pressure driving overexploitation is now relatively consistent around the world, driving everyone everywhere toward the same tragedies and making it difficult for regional booms and busts to average out.

Fisheries have often been overexploited to the point of collapse. The California anchovy fishery that collapsed right about the time Steinbeck was writing *Cannery Row*,[22] is just one example. Previously, however, an event like that was isolated and when the fish were gone, the world's consumers could go elsewhere for another tin of salty pizza toppings. The fishermen would abandon a commercially unworkable area and essentially leave it to recover while they destroyed someplace else. Now, it is all happening at once. The Canadian Atlantic cod fishery has already collapsed and the Icelandic, North Sea (European), Alaskan, Japanese, Peruvian, and Antarctic fisheries are all under intense commercial pressure. Globally, the levels of exploitation appear to be well beyond what might be sustainable and if driven to collapse, there is nowhere else to fish for something to go with your chips.

---

*Obviously, this is a joke. There is nothing more horrific than reality TV and it should obviously be first on the list of things that threaten the very existence of the human race.

However, part of the increase in attention paid to the exploitation of the commons in international politics might be attributed to an increase in education and awareness. Almost unheard of a half-century ago, environmental and shared resource issues have become such an integral part of education that in 2002, the Europe-Wide Global Education Congress included international environmental cooperation next to literacy, history, and mathematics in the definition of a basic education. Recycling, energy conservation, deforestation, endangered species, acid rain, global warming, the global spread of disease, the French tolerance of body odor—we may not agree on what if anything should be done about these environmental issues, but they are issues on the international political table and they are all new. Fifty years ago, none of them were any part of the mainstream political debate and today they are global issues.

These global tragedy-of-the-commons issues are also well represented in fiction.* The most relevant for today's students might be the movies about a global epidemic, such as *12 Monkeys*. In addition to making it uncomfortably clear that Brad Pitt is just a little too good at playing the part of a lunatic, *12 Monkeys*[23] also shows just how hard it is generate the collective actions needed to protect even the most precious of global commons. It would not take much to stop the release of the virus that is about to destroy the Earth, but convincing anyone to act against an abstract and seemingly distant threat turns out to be an impossible challenge. If it is that hard to convince just a few people to act, how hard must it be to get the massive and coordinated action necessary to combat bird flu as a likely pandemic?

This is, and likely will continue to be, a significant part of global politics, but there is not a tidy theoretical perspective with a catchy name to attach to the study of the political dynamics of a global tragedy of the commons. Still, a few dynamics are becoming apparent. The first is that it is difficult to label this as international relations. Rather than being part of the politics *between* nations, it is more of an issue and a dynamic that extends *across* nations. It is a transnational issue involving nations, but also includes groups and organizations that can't be put in that category. Subnational political units such as cities, political parties, states, and provinces are acting across and beyond national borders. Multinational entities such as the UN, NAFTA, the International Whaling Commission, and the World Bank are involved. Transnational organizations, entities that exist outside and across the geographic definition of states, are involved, such as Greenpeace, the Sierra Club, Doctors Without Borders, and international businesses. Additionally, economic dynamics, political dynamics, and issues of science and research all come into play. How all of these additional factors sort out into a simple model of how the world works is an interesting and complicated question.

---

*David Brin's *Earth*, James P. Hogan's *Thrice Upon a Time*, Kim Stanley Robinson's *Mars* Trilogy, *Soylent Green*, and *Omega Man* are all stories of environmental collapse. Larry Niven's Gil Hamilton stories, and many of his *Known Space* stories are built on themes about population pressures and the limits of the biosphere.

Constructivism

While it can be a challenge to get everyone to agree on a definition of **constructivism**, or even to agree on whether it qualifies as a theory of international relations, it can reasonably be depicted in terms of its fundamental claim that human beings construct the reality around them—the reality upon which decisions and choices are made—through language and communication. The conceptual framework used to describe something enables certain actions and prevents others. The analogy chosen for thinking about something defines the logic by which all current and future information on the subject is interpreted. What is, or more importantly, what is not communicated, drives politics because what we do not hear about, we cannot address. From this perspective, international communication, both in terms of capabilities and in terms of filters on the content, becomes the critical consideration in the study of international relations. With all of the technological, social, and political interest in the recent and rapid advances in communication technology, it should not be surprising that constructivism has garnered a great deal of attention.

In the study of international politics, constructivism is certainly equal to or more significant than many of the perspectives, issues, or ideas highlighted in this chapter, and as a challenge to the realist perspectives, its claim is unquestionable. Arising out of postmodern critiques directly attacking, if not assaulting realism as a theory,* it has an anti-realism pedigree that not even Marxism can match. It would appear that all the factors have aligned for a big and flashy section on constructivism, parade and all. However, in addition to the technical challenge of including a parade in a textbook, there are several reasons for exercising caution in regard to constructivism. Three are particularly troublesome:

1. As a theory, constructivism is new, very new. It has been less than a decade since it first began coalescing as any kind of coherent approach and there simply has not been a lot of time for academic research to thoroughly sort out its strengths and weaknesses. In contrast, realism, Marxism, and liberalism have all been around longer than almost any of the professors currently studying them. There has been plenty of time to sort through their implications and the limits of how much they can explain in international relations.

2. The enthusiasm inherent in many of the earliest studies on constructivism may have distorted assessments of its scope and applicability. The CNN-effect is the primary example. The moment it was suggested that the real-time global news media was driving leaders into actions they would rather avoid, the idea was touted as a revolution in the very nature of international politics even before any

---

*As an example see, Ashley, Richard C., "The poverty of neorealism," in *Neorealism and Its Critics*, ed. Robert O. Keohane (New York: Columbia University Press, 1986).

significant research had been conducted. Subsequent research has shown that the CNN-effect is extremely limited, particularly in terms of how far it can push a leader against the flow of other influences. In fact, the CNN-effect seems to be largely confined to an influence within the limits of policy action defined by either the economic constraints of the world system or the power constraints of a realist political environment.

3. Claims that constructivism represents a new way of understanding a new world are a bit questionable. It may be reasonable to say that it is coalescing into a new way of understanding international politics, but the claim of a new world order is not holding up well in the face of most research. As far back as existing records make it possible to study, the news media have always had a modest but clear influence on international politics. One of the best explanations for choices the United States made in the Vietnam War is media coverage and the use of analogies to conceptualize and debate the issues. Another example is the way in which President Truman's presumptions and beliefs about the Soviet Union, and the way those cognitive frameworks prevented him from even considering cooperative options, appear to have been significant factors in the beginning of the cold war. In short, many of the elements of a constructed reality of politics are not new phenomena that have arisen out of the latest revolution in communication technologies.

However, all of these cautions concern the place of constructivism as equal to liberalism or as supplanting Marxism, not its inherent value as a new and interesting theoretical construct. Research will eventually tell us exactly where it fits; we just have to be patient.

Roaring Mice and Vacation Hotspots

Like everything else in politics, international relations is probably best discussed not in terms of which theoretical approach is correct, but instead in terms of how different ideas help us understand parts of what is going on. To conclude this chapter, we ask a simple question, "Why does Barbados exist?"

No, we are not talking about how the island was formed—by volcanoes—but the mere existence of Barbados as an independent country, which is a very interesting thing to consider. Barbados has absolutely no power in the traditional, international relations sense of the word—no army, no navy, no air force, no Girl Scouts brandishing pointy marshmallow roasting sticks. The United States could conquer the island without mustering any forces beyond the guys hanging around a typical Minnesota hunting lodge. If the world is anarchic and you can only survive if you have the power to protect yourself, how can Barbados exist? Is the answer economic? Is it a moral issue? Is it just something we haven't gotten around to doing? Watch *The Mouse that Roared*[24]—

either the movie or the *Pinky and the Brain* cartoon version—and then ponder how it is that a powerless country like Barbados continues to exist as an independent entity. None of the theories of international politics we have offered here can offer a satisfactory answer.

KEY TERMS

balance of power / **287**
bandwagoning / **288**
constructivism / **304**
democratic peace / **292**
hegemon / **293**

idealism / **282**
realism / **279**
world systems theory / **297**

CHAPTER SUMMARY

When we think about international relations, we most often think about war. Given the horrors, tension, and fear associated with war, this is understandable. However, given the number of countries that exist, war is rare. In fact, most of international politics concerns cooperation. Thus, a truly interesting question is: why do wars happen? The tendency in fiction to explain wars as accidents flies in the face of reality. Wars are not accidents; they are the result of conscious, rational action. Spurred by the horrors of World War I, scholars were motivated to focus on peace. World events ultimately put a damper on idealism, which led scholars to embrace realism as an explanation. Realism, with its presumptions that one can explain international relations in terms of strategy, rational action, and power in an anarchic environment, did not explain every war. Scholars focusing on foreign policy analysis challenged liberalism's presumptions that the internal workings of governments do not matter. There has been a lot of attention paid to the fact that democracies do not fight one another, although scholars do not agree why this is. Other schools of thought have emerged to explain international relations. Among these, one focuses on the dominance of a nation, another focuses on the global economy, and yet another focuses on the global dominance of one country. Students should learn two very important lessons from this chapter. First, there is no one simple theory that explains global interaction; international relations are complex and multifaceted. War, albeit attention grabbing, is only one part of this complex labyrinth. Second, it will, from now on, be difficult to purchase a pair of sneakers without your mind wandering off to consider cores and peripheries.

STUDY QUESTIONS AND EXERCISES

1. This chapter discusses a number of theories that seek to explain international relations. Which of these theories do you believe best explains the current world situation? Why?

2. What are the three key assumptions that underlie the realist perspective on international relations?

3. What are the flaws in the realist perspective? What are the flaws in the other perspectives?

4. What prompted idealism?

5. Find an article or editorial that discusses the issue of globalization. Do you agree with the perspective in the piece you have selected? Why or why not?

6. What is a hegemon? What role does a hegemon play in international relations?

WEBSITES TO EXPLORE

http://europa.eu/index_en.htm. The Europa: Gateway to the European Union Web page includes news and information about the EU.

www.du.edu/~bhughes/ifs.html. Barry B. Hughes' International Futures links to a computer simulation of global systems for classroom and research use.

www.imf.org/. Here is the Web site for the International Monetary Fund (IMF), an organization of 184 countries that aims to foster global monetary cooperation, secure financial stability, facilitate international trade, promote high employment and sustainable economic growth, and reduce poverty.

www.library.gsu.edu/research/pages.asp?ldID=41&guideID=101&ID=560. Georgia State University Library's International Relations Resources Web page includes general resources, gateways, proprietary resources, international law resources, and more.

www.library.yale.edu/ia-resources/polecon.html. Yale University Library's Political Economy & Development Resources Web page provides links to relevant organizations, journals, data, and more.

www.library.yale.edu/ia-resources/resource.html. Yale University Library's International Affairs Resources Web page includes links to international organizations, news, research institutes, and more.

www.un.org/. The United Nations Web page provides information about the UN, its member nations, its policies, and more.

www2.etown.edu/vl/research.html. The World Wide Web Virtual Library: International Affairs Resources contains a list of research institutes focused on international relations.

I BELIEVE IN A BLACK JERSEY.

CHAPTER 13

Political Culture

Sex and Agriculture, Getting Rucked Explains It All

When the gang from Morningside accidentally gives the first fifteen food poisoning, they get thrown into the scrum and they are all that stand between the St. Sylvester Savages and an inglorious rucking from the old boys. The consequences of this latest misadventure could be worse than when the class visited the Marae, found themselves in the middle of a Tangihanga, and Jeff the Maori was mistakenly asked to decide the fate of his Iwi. It could be worse than all the girls left up the duff after the St. Sylvester ball. This disaster could even be worse than when Mack gets the cross-dressing Brother Ken thrown in jail and triggers a paedophile witch hunt that engulfs Morningside in a frenzy driven by their lecherous but hyperconservative minister. Yes, it could be the worst yet. However, in the tradition of all good comedies, in the end we all learn the lesson that it does not matter how well you play the game, you are cool as long as you are severely injured while playing.

The social value of violent injury is a common theme in *Bro'Town;*[1] after all in the very first episode Valea became a genius when he was hit by a bus. However it is the raw ethnic humour in *Bro'Town* that sets it apart from most other satiric cartoons. *Bro'Town* is littered with toilet humour, stuffed with sexual jokes, and it makes a point of skewering religion, even beginning one episode with God playing strip poker with Buddha. Still, it is the casual use of impolitic racial references and crass ethnic jokes that are the most striking. "Jeff's Maori, he can break into anything." Pacific Islanders are referred to as "Taro Eaters." If you want to butcher an old racehorse, you take it to Tommy the Tongan Butcher because Tongans will kill anything for you. Abo is an Australian Aborigine running around in a loincloth and eating grubs. The "fat brown kid" is obviously a good flanker because "those pollywogs have it in their blood" and all the Chinese kids are masters of martial arts who are caught up in organized crime and eat stir-fried puppy-foetus rice. *Bro'Town* is politically incorrect to its core.

What? You have never seen *Bro'Town*? You don't know who the gang from Morningside is? You say that some of those words and a lot of those references look strange? Sort of like it is almost English, but not really. Oh, that's right; you are probably from <u>that</u> side of the world. You are probably misspending the last and best part of your youth at a North American University. You also are probably immersed in U.S., and to a lesser degree, Canadian culture* and that is why you cannot hope to understand half of the references in these opening paragraphs and you will never get any of the jokes.

If you are on that side of the world, it probably means that you do not know that "Sex and Agriculture" actually refers to the best CD since the Bronze Age. You probably do not even know who The Exponents are or why four million people—and roughly sixty million sheep—will instantly associate the chorus from "Why Does Love Do This to Me?" with grown men crashing headlong into each other. If you happen to know what scrums, rucks, and mauls are, then you will know that getting rucked is nothing even remotely close to a sexual reference[†] and you just might know what a *Haka* is, but how about a *Hangi*? What kind of a beast is a *Pakeha,* and what should you do if one gets loose while you are at the zoo? From way over on that side of the world, you probably do not know that Rove wants you to "say hi to your mum" for him, and you almost certainly have no idea what a Logie is, or why you might want an attractive woman in a tight dress to give you one. You probably do not even know where we switched countries in this paragraph.

POLITICAL CULTURE

It probably seems strange that one of the subjects we have barely mentioned in a textbook that uses pop culture to examine politics, is political culture, but *Bro'Town* is the reason. Well, not specifically *Bro'Town*, but rather what it represents in terms of political culture. Put succinctly, culture is a somewhat problematic issue for the study of politics because by providing a seductively simple explanation for just about everything it risks telling us nothing.

One of the most common ways to define **culture**—the set of values that a group shares—is in terms of implicit and explicit beliefs, practices, and expectations. In an ideal world, we would all share enough culture to be able to communicate clearly to one another, and everybody would agree upon common terms for understanding the best solutions to key problems. And except for the toilets, when the 747 dumps a North American student at the Auckland airport, said student will find Kiwi culture to be quite familiar.[‡] Prospects

---

*Yes, Canadians have culture.

[†]Rucking is a rugby term for stomping on someone who is lying on the ground and obstructing the ball. However, there is a rule against rucking someone's head. Rugby players aren't savages, at least not completely.

[‡]Unlike the dainty little water-saving, environmentally friendly low-flow toilets that decorate the bathrooms of North America, New Zealand toilets are notable for generating a thundering rush of water that is powerful enough to flush a buffalo. This is all the more remarkable for the fact that there are neither buffalo nor bison in New Zealand.

look good for communication and understanding. However, what the *Bro'Town* example shows us is that in the real world, even when two societies share most key aspects of culture, the cultural gap between them can still be huge. Even when the two societies are both developed, Western, capitalist, democratic societies that are, for the most part, populated by people who share the same ethnic and religious background, even when they almost speak the same language,* culture can still impede communication and understanding. Even with the briefest of exposures, there is no mistaking the differences—sometimes subtle, sometimes huge—between North American and New Zealand cultures. Humor is particularly good at exposing the width and depth of that gap because humor works by subtly twisting some bit of truth in an unexpected direction. Because of that need for subtlety, until you have spent a good year or more living in New Zealand and have picked up some of those subtle bits of Kiwi culture, you will miss half the jokes in *Bro'Town*. Similarly, in New Zealand, urban humor—particularly the variety of New York humor found in Woody Allen movies—is completely lost on a country with a capital city that is smaller than Toledo, Ohio.

Consequences of Culture

Beyond which jokes do and do not work, there also appear to be some obvious political consequences of culture. Take the regulatory standard for broadcast TV as an example. In New Zealand, sex, religion, and ethnicity are fair targets for a comedy that airs at 7:30 p.m. on broadcast TV. Partial nudity is allowed after 9:30 p.m., so most nonviolent films with a U.S. "R" rating can be shown uncut late in the evening, but many "PG" films that would have to be edited for content to be broadcast at all in the United States can be shown at any time of day in New Zealand. For New Zealand broadcast TV, the rules regarding foul language are also far more liberal, even for TV commercials. In a government-funded public service commercial about drunk driving—a commercial that is shown during afternoon and weekend shows targeting an adolescent audience—one teenager calls his friend a "dick" and the friend retorts, "Well, at least I've got a dick." In the United States, because of that language, that commercial would never be broadcast. Similarly, in the United States, *Bro'Town* would definitely be relegated to cable, if it were shown at all. Even if it were on cable, can you imagine the uproar over a cartoon that spends an entire episode making jokes about a kid getting an erection from watching *Xena: Warrior Princess* putting a condom on a banana? And *Bro'Town* would not fare any better in the Great White North. The crassness of the ethnic humor, particularly with so much of it directed at native peoples, would probably

---

*New Zealand English and U.S. English are *NOT* the same language. Consider the words "bum" and "fanny." In the United States, bum refers to a homeless alcoholic, whereas in New Zealand it refers to a portion of the anatomy used for sitting. In the United States, one way to refer to that part of the anatomy used for sitting is to call it a fanny, but that is definitely not what a fanny is in New Zealand. In New Zealand, a fanny is a part of the female anatomy that you cannot refer to on TV, not even New Zealand TV.

keep *Bro'Town* off Canadian TV altogether. All of this, however, is acceptable in New Zealand. Clearly, New Zealand's more liberal political culture has a profound influence on its broadcast standards.

Or does culture have anything to do with it?

At first glance, it seems obvious that a few small but important cultural differences explain the divergence between what is shown on New Zealand and U.S. broadcast TV. Clearly, New Zealand must be a more liberal country. One only has to look at the arguments in the United States over teaching evolution to see that the political power of the religious right and social conservatives is far more prevalent in U.S. culture than it is in New Zealand. That surely explains why you get some naughty words and an occasional glimpse of naughty bits on New Zealand broadcast TV but not on the U.S. networks.

However, that cultural argument cuts both ways. In comparing the two countries, it also becomes clear that Kiwis as a whole seem to be more sensitive to the value inherent in racial and ethnic diversity than Americans are. Kiwis engage racial and ethnic political issues, particularly those involving indigenous peoples, far more effectively than Americans, or anyone else in the world for that matter. If anything, when it comes to race, Kiwis seem to be far more like Canadians than Americans,* and a cultural explanation for the differences in broadcast television content would lead to the expectation that in New Zealand, ethnic humor—especially when it targets the indigenous Maori— would be treated like ethnic humor in Canada, discouraged to the point of being shunned. However, *Bro'Town* makes it clear that that is not the case.

If Not Culture?

Instead of culture, perhaps one could use a simple market model to explain the differences between U.S. and New Zealand broadcast television standards. In the United States, cable TV has been around for over a quarter century and has been available almost everywhere in the country for the last twenty years or so. This is significant because you have to pay for access to cable TV and that means that the content of U.S. cable TV has always been governed by a different, and far more liberal, set of rules than broadcast TV. The argument that you have to shield those who do not wish to see a few naughty bits does not apply if you have to pay to watch. As a result, in the United States, shows that pushed the boundaries of social acceptability had an outlet other than broadcast TV. That alternate outlet eliminated, or at least severely reduced, most of the social pressure to liberalize broadcast rules and the United States ended up with what, by a global measure, can only be called prudish standards for broadcast television.

---

*While Canadians live in the chilly part of North America—the part that justifies adding North to the continent name and that does make them, technically, Americans—we would rather not insult the Canadians by referring to them with the term most of the world uses as a disparaging reference to the United States.

In contrast, there was no alternative outlet for that boundary-challenging television content in New Zealand. With roughly the population of Connecticut, most of it rural and spread out over a mountainous country that would cover the entire West Coast, from Los Angeles to Seattle, if you laid it over a map of the United States, simple geography prevented New Zealand from experiencing the cable TV boom that hit the United States in the early 1980s. In New Zealand, it was just too expensive to hook everyone up and until the quite recent expansion of satellite TV delivery, most New Zealanders had access to nothing but the two nationally broadcast television channels. As a result, there were no alternate channels available and any demand for content that challenged the limits of social acceptability could only be addressed by adjusting the broadcast standards governing the limited channels that were available. As a result, there was political pressure placed upon those standards and that led to far more liberal broadcast standards in New Zealand.

But then again, maybe it was just culture.

Culture as Explanation

The problem with using culture to explain political phenomena is that culture—political or otherwise—offers a universal explanation. Everything political can be distilled down to some group's shared beliefs, or shared expectations, or shared linguistic referents. Why are the Nordic countries of Europe far closer to the socialist end of the economic spectrum than the rest of Western Europe? You could argue that it is simply a reflection of their culture. If you visit Norway, Denmark, Sweden, or Iceland you will discover that a sense of social responsibility seems to be a very big part of their culture. When you visit, it actually feels very socialist there. Some would argue that this social responsibility arose out of the extreme winters, where not looking out for a neighbor could be deadly, and the Nordic countries do seem to share a belief that community responsibility should be extended and applied to the country as a whole. In the Nordic countries many clearly believe that society has a responsibility to take care of those who fail economically. In fact, saying that a person "fails" economically or in any other way suggesting that an individual is responsible for his or her own poverty is something that really would not fit with Nordic cultural norms, but is that really an explanation for why they are the most socialist of the developed countries in the world? Is it enough to say that the economy is that way because they share the belief that it should be that way? Does that really tell us anything? Isn't it possible that the economy was that way first and after adjusting to it they found they liked it?

If culture is enough of an explanation, then how do we explain change? How do you get from raiding and pillaging Vikings literally slaughtering people to take their wealth, to a Norway that is synonymous with the Nobel Peace Prize and abhors the very idea of people suffering for want of money? Perhaps culture could change that drastically over the course of a few centuries, but gradual change does not explain how culture

> **If culture is enough of an explanation for national economic models, then how do we explain when vastly different things happen in similar cultures or when similar things occur in vastly different cultures?**

could account for both China's embrace of communism and the ferociously competitive, almost predatory capitalism that has evolved there over the last few decades. Could Chinese culture, built upon a historical foundation stretching over several millennia, whipsaw back and forth that quickly? If culture is enough of an explanation for national economic models, then how do we explain when vastly different things happen in similar cultures or when similar things occur in vastly different cultures?

There is no denying that culture is real and it has a significant influence on politics. It is almost certain that the Swedish economic model would never work in Australia. It does not take much research to see that a heavily socialist economic model just does not fit with the rugged-individualist ideal of Australian culture. Crocodile Dundee and Steve Irwin may both be caricatures of Australian culture, but caricatures always have to reflect a fair bit of truth in order to work. However, that very same example also makes it clear that we must be very careful in what we attribute to culture. In addition to what Australians think might be culture,* an explanation of the current nature of the Australian economy would have to address all of the historical, political, geographic, demographic, economic, domestic, and international factors that have shaped all the choices and decisions that have led to their current economic model. The lonely, uninhabitable stretches of desert that dominate most of the country, where the monstrous ranches dwarf those of even the United States, explain a lot about the Australian economic model. It also seems to explain a great deal of the country's culture, but then again how does that rugged, extremely rural explanation fit with the fact that Australia is one of the most urbanized countries in the world?† Culture clearly does matter, since it effectively rules out certain possibilities and probably favors others, but it is also clearly not deterministic. The hard part is figuring out how much culture matters. When does culture matter and how does it matter relative to other forces shaping politics? And what influences culture? Clearly, if a comparison of the Romans and the Tifosi‡ is any indication, culture is not static—so something must influence it.

The short answer is that political scientists really do not have an answer for how to factor culture into the study of politics. Many political scientists ignore culture entirely. Many argue that culture is merely a universal term to cover what otherwise cannot be explained through other factors. Some political theorists argue that culture or some

---

*As a resident of New Zealand, one of the authors is legally required to disparage Australia at any opportunity, but don't worry, Australians don't know what "disparage" means.

†Even with a whole continent at hand, the vast majority of Australia's nineteen million inmates live in cities, with 64 percent of the population living in the capital cities of its states and territories. Any measure of urbanization that takes into account the total space available puts Australia at the very top.

‡Tifosi are the rabid and radical fans of Ferrari's Formula 1 team. Even the non-Italian ones are very Italian.

aspect of culture such as language and the choices of shared cognitive referents are the most important factors in politics and define all but a few details of events.

This unresolved—perhaps irresolvable—issue is a big part of why we have put off addressing the question of political culture. Political culture is an excellent example of a seductively simple explanation that seems to explain everything but in truth it is neither simple nor universal. Wealth, power distributions, geography, gender, cognition, rational choice, social psychology, the structure of the family, religion, the evolution of the human brain, grand conspiracies, and alien interventions are some of the countless, often compelling explanations that have been offered to explain it all, or to at least explain huge swaths of phenomena from Britney Spears' otherwise inexplicable success to the likelihood that a given country can embrace democratic values. The problem is that even though all such universal explanations are problematic, we cannot simply dismiss them. Most do offer some insights. It is hard to believe that war and the global obsession with nuclear missiles can be entirely explained by insecure men compensating for a small . . . uhm . . . for personal shortcomings that threaten their confidence in their masculinity, but it is also hard to deny the conceptual value in many of the more moderate feminist arguments regarding international politics. Wealth may not explain everything, but Marxist theories, such as world systems theory, provide valuable perspectives that show how wealth shapes the nature of the world. Aliens do not control everything, but it is pretty obvious that the Eiffel Tower is a thinly disguised, model number 3FB, transgalactic broadcast station.

In most cases, these grand explanations can neither be simply accepted nor rejected.* Instead, the best approach may be one of informed skepticism—dismissing the universal but assuming that there is some value in there and considering the hows and whys of the idea to try to find that value. The analytical skills that this book was designed to help you develop can be particularly valuable, enabling you to act as an "informed consumer" when it comes to explanations for political phenomena. To provide an exercise of those skills, we discuss two aspects of New Zealand politics that might easily be explained or described in terms of political culture. In addition to highlighting some of the difficulties with the very concept of political culture, this gives you an opportunity to exercise those analytical skills.

APPLYING POLITICAL CULTURE

To start, we take a careful look at how people have defined culture and how it might be applied to politics. Culture has been defined as everything from language to a shared appreciation for a particular body shape.† One constant throughout those definitions is

---

*The exception, of course, being the role of aliens. Resistance is futile.

†Body shape is a surprisingly common referent in discussions of culture. From Renaissance art, to advertising, to African cultures that associate obesity with social and economic success, body shape is in there a lot.

the idea that culture is something shared by a group. It is something that helps individuals identify with the larger group and provides a context for action by and within that group. Thus, for this analysis we are going to think of **political culture** as the shared social context from which people make political choices. Related to that is **political socialization**, the process by which the group teaches the shared context to the members of society. And related to that are **agents of political socialization**—or those from whom the group learns the political culture—which can include schools, parents, the media, politicians, friends, religious leaders, etc. And related to that is the whole success of Britney Spears conundrum. It's sort of a circle of life thing.

One can understand New Zealand political culture in terms of the things that make it a way better culture than Australia's, such as knowing better than to live with poisonous things. You could also add in there factors such as geographic isolation, a largely agricultural economic base, historical and legal inheritances from British colonialism, and the fact that descendants of the precolonial inhabitants, the Maori, make up enough of the population to have a successful political party. Within countries, we often find **subcultures**, which are smaller cultures within the main political culture. Within New Zealand, we could talk about regional political cultures, the most obvious being the noticeable differences between the North and South islands.

From that foundation we can apply the idea of culture as shared social contexts and look at the role of culture in two different ways that it might be related to politics. First, there are the influences culture could have on politics, specifically how a culture of isolation has shaped New Zealand's foreign policy. Second, there is the intentional use of culture as a means of attaining a political end, such as using culture to establish and enhance local and national identities within New Zealand. Finally, we conclude by asking a few questions about the politics of what might be called cultural ownership and cultural preservation.

A Thousand Miles to Nowhere: Isolation and Foreign Policy

From New Zealand, it is quite literally a thousand miles to nowhere. Even if you were to convince Kiwis that Australia was more than just a bunch of louts with surfboards stuck between all that poisonous stuff on the land and the sharks in the ocean, that nearest of neighbors is still a very long way away. A thousand miles in a plane leaves you with 334 miles of swimming before you can rescue Nemo from the dentist in Sydney and the next closest country is on the other side of that quaint little continent full of toxic frogs, poisonous snakes, deadly spiders, and venomous egg-laying mammals.* Los Angeles, Tokyo, and Singapore are all about a twelve-hours flight away, and for most other destinations you have to fly through one of those cities. The mostest totally directest flight to London, not including the three-hour stopover in Los Angeles, will take more

---

*The male platypus has a barb on its hind legs that injects what some consider to be the most painful venom of any animal on the planet.

than twenty-five hours. No matter how you measure it, New Zealand is, without question, the most isolated of all the developed countries and except for perhaps a few very small Pacific island nations, it is the most isolated country in the world.

There are clear cultural effects that seem to follow from that geographic isolation. The "overseas experience," or OE,* is encouraged both socially and officially. Even though the costs of travel from New Zealand are tremendous, a large percentage of Kiwis enhance their education with an extended stay somewhere else, often arranged with the help of schools. Similarly, a trip overseas is unquestionably accepted as a justification for an extended absence from school and families are encouraged to take advantage of those types of travel opportunities no matter when they might arise during the year. This is a stark contrast to most states in the United States where schools are required to fail a student for an extended absence from school, regardless of the justification. As a result, a far higher percentage of Kiwis have traveled overseas than Americans, even though it is far easier to travel from the United States.

New Zealand's isolation also has a practical effect in terms of border-related politics, such as immigration, and that creates some cultural differences as well. New Zealand has extremely strict immigration laws and with all of that ocean for a border, it is probably the second-most effective country in the world at enforcing them.[†]

As a result, all the U.S. and European political conflicts over immigration, particularly illegal immigration, usually lead to a confused shake of the head in New Zealand. In New Zealand there is no question that a country has the absolute right to regulate everything about immigration. There is broad acceptance of strict laws that are overtly crafted to ensure that people moving to New Zealand will contribute significantly to the local economy.[‡]

For all but the most liberal of Kiwis the idea of an obligation to accept or support impoverished or unskilled immigrants, particularly those who arrived illegally, seems bizarre. One of the most telling comments was offered by a student during a classroom discussion of U.S. immigration issues, "What part of 'illegal' makes those immigrants anything but criminals?"

The culture of isolation also affects attitudes toward material possessions. Except for equipment related to raising sheep, New Zealand is a very small market, far too small to support the manufacture of many things, and it costs a lot to ship things to New Zealand. As a result, things such as cars and building materials are expensive. The average car in New Zealand is far older than in most other places around the world.

---

*Not to be confused with *The O.C.* However, even though a moral objection to the entire genre of hyperdramatic primetime soap operas prevents the authors from acknowledging the existence of *The O.C.*, both applaud the fact that the geeky kid somehow managed to charm the pretty girl. Yeah, Seth Cohen!

†North Korea probably gets the nod for number one.

‡In fact, opinion polls suggest that the majority of Kiwis would like the immigration laws to be even stricter and more forcefully implemented.

New cars are rare. In fact, the majority of cars arrive in New Zealand after a full auto-motive lifetime of use in Japan or Britain. Building materials are also expensive and a prominent industry in New Zealand is the building recyclers who buy and resell every-thing from windows to doorknobs. There is a building recycler in every town. This is related to a whole set of norms and shared beliefs regarding the nature of a house. In New Zealand there is more than a little admiration for a bach built out of whatever ran-dom bits and pieces might have fallen into someone's hands.* Even this has political ramifications. Currently this cultural ideal of the bach is clashing with an effort to improve housing quality through the strict regulation of building practices and laws regarding the approval of building materials.

However, of all the cultural aspects of New Zealand that might be attributed to its geographic isolation, the one with the most obvious political ramifications is a sense of political isolation from the rest of the world. In the debates over foreign policy, it is clear that there is little evidence of any kind of geostrategic motive. There is no sense that anyone feels that it is necessary to engage directly most of the major issues that arise in world politics.†

What may be the most obvious reflections of the political effect of a culture of iso-lation is that moral, not geostrategic reasoning, is the primary benchmark for current New Zealand foreign policy. Foreign policy actions based upon a moral obligation to act are common and this was clear even in the decision to send troops to Afghanistan and Iraq after the U.S. invasions. New Zealand refused to participate in the invasions and when it sent troops, its leaders bent over backwards to make it absolutely clear that the Kiwis were in those countries to protect the innocent victims of the conflict and help them rebuild, not to support the U.S. occupation. In fact, some of the strongest reflec-tions of this culture of isolation can be found in the arguments against committing troops to post-invasion Iraq and Afghanistan.

In New Zealand, there is a strong sentiment that there is a moral obligation to defy the United States when the world's most powerful nation acts geostrategically at the expense of democratic and liberal ideals. As a result, far from any interest in trying to win favor from the United States, the arguments for acting in Afghanistan and Iraq had to *overcome* the fact that it would appear that New Zealand supported the U.S. inva-sion. The presumption is that New Zealand will defy any U.S. demands unless a solid moral justification can be made for going along with the United States. Despite long-standing and intense pressure from Washington, New Zealand still refuses to allow

---

*A bach is something like a cabin in the United States. The word comes from the ramshackle bachelor housing that used to be built for miners, loggers, whalers, and farmhands, and are now used as beach and forest retreats. Most have no power or other services, and many are still accessible only by boat or horse.

†There is a clear indication of loyalty to the Crown and with that a need to support the British Commonwealth, and that support does lead to some engagements with the world that would otherwise be hard to explain from a strictly isolationist cultural perspective.

> **In New Zealand, there is a strong sentiment that there is a moral obligation to defy the United States when the world's most powerful nation acts geostrategically at the expense of democratic and liberal ideals.**

nuclear-powered ships or any ship that might carry nuclear weapons to enter its territorial waters. In the most recent elections, the mere suggestion that one of the parties wanted to capitulate to U.S. demands to drop that ban was considered to be an underhanded slur against the party's leader. New Zealand also defied the U.S. attempts to politically isolate Cuba, and later, Vietnam.

Arguably these actions reflect a culture of isolation because Kiwis feel distanced from the security imperatives that drive the foreign policies of most other nations. That ocean is very comforting. Despite being a tiny country, New Zealand can defy the United States because Kiwis neither feel threatened by U.S. military might, nor do they feel a need to seek its protection from the threats of others. Threats are far away and almost never invoke any sense of a need to act to protect the homeland. The dynamics of the foreign policy debates in New Zealand are remarkably similar to those of the United States from a century ago, when the Atlantic Ocean gave Americans a similar sense of isolation from the politics of Europe, despite plenty of evidence of economic engagement. However, it could also be argued that culture has nothing to do with it. Perhaps the physical distance that separates New Zealand from the rest of the world, in and of itself, explains New Zealand foreign policy. Not only does a thousand miles of ocean make New Zealand safe from any plausible direct threat to its physical security, it also makes it pretty much impossible for New Zealand to militarily threaten anyone else. This effectively takes issues of threat, force, and power out of both sides of the foreign policy equation and means that, culture or not, New Zealand foreign policy would have to focus on something else first.

Culture and Social Distance

Perhaps the most interesting aspect of a relationship between culture and isolation is not in how isolation might lead to some aspects of culture, but in the way that culture seems to shrink the reality of distance. Despite the fact that London is twice as far away as Los Angeles, Tokyo, Shanghai, or Singapore, New Zealanders are both far more culturally affiliated with England and far more politically engaged with London than any of those other locations. When Kiwis talk about travel, or trade, or political issues they tend to equate the distance to England with the distance to the United States even though they fly through the United States to get to England. Kiwis think of Japan as being much farther away than England even though Japan is actually half as far away.

More telling is the New Zealand relationship with the island nations of the Pacific. The Maori of Aotearoa* are Polynesians, related to Hawaiians, Samoans, Fijians, and other

---

*Aotearoa is the Maori word for New Zealand. Its literal meaning is the land of the long white cloud, signifying the way that clouds form along the ridge of mountains that define most of the country.

Pacific island communities. This cultural connection serves to shrink the extremely large distances to these small island nations. Thousands of miles away, most of these islands are far closer to Japan than New Zealand, yet Kiwis consider them to be neighbors. By any kind of global measure they are economically insignificant, yet New Zealand puts a priority on economic relations with them, including sending almost all of New Zealand's foreign aid to them. By any global measure these nations have no military might or power, yet New Zealand is intensely concerned with their security and it is the one region in the world where New Zealand will send troops in response to security threats. It is hard to find an explanation other than culture for New Zealand's interest in those island nations.

Culture as Politics

The political aspects of culture extend far beyond the possibility that culture influences politics and policy. Culture can also be applied to the pursuit of political and social goals. During the cold war, the Russian ballet frequently toured the world and served as a means of establishing some nonhostile interactions between countries that were otherwise engaged in the most protracted security crisis the world has ever known. Sporting events, particularly the Olympics, have been intentionally used to serve a similar purpose of bridging the rifts between countries.

Culture is constantly used as a means to define or justify policy. For example, using the story of "The Rape of Kuwait" to explain the need to act in the First Gulf War resonated with an American culture obsessed with stories of selfless heroes riding in from afar to rescue virtuous damsels from the hands of evil and power hungry villains. Not only did the invocation of this cultural framework shape policy by eliminating policy options that contradicted the story structure, it was intentionally used to generate overwhelming domestic support for the First Gulf War. The first Bush administration went so far as to orchestrate events that reinforced this cultural ideal, with the most blatant example being the congressional testimony of an "eyewitness" to the atrocities of the Iraqi occupation. This fifteen-year old girl was later identified as the daughter of Kuwait's ambassador to the United States, and she had not witnessed what she had claimed.[2] However, what she said fit so strongly with what Americans wanted to believe that even after she was exposed, the vast majority of Americans continued to believe her story. The shared knowledge created by U.S. sport was also used to great effect during the invasion, with military officials describing events to the public using football and baseball terms.

From politicians slipping out of their Italian shoes for an afternoon to make a show of hunting or fishing in order to connect with a rural constituency, to American television creating overseas demands for U.S. products by featuring them in sitcoms, the use of culture for political or other ends appears commonplace. However, one of the most interesting ways that culture can be used politically is the way that culture can influence group identity. Not only do the Olympics provide an example of modern sporting culture being used to build bridges between estranged countries, they—and sport in general—also provide an example of how cultural and sporting events can be used to enhance national or other group identities.*

The Soviets invested a great deal in sports such as gymnastics, partly as a demonstration of Russian power to the world, but also to use the Olympics to enhance a sense of national identity in a country that included hundreds of nationalities that had been forcibly incorporated into the Russian Empire. Schools, cities, and regions around the world use athletic teams as a means to generate community identities. The display of jerseys, caps, and posters identify members of the community to one and all and remind the people who see them of that community.

In Liverpool, the red jersey, scarf, or cap means you will never walk alone. In the United States, high school homecomings are annual events that connect a shared identity across generations of students and help bind small towns into communities. It is no accident that colleges and universities in the United States invest a tremendous amount of time, money and effort into not just athletics, but the logos, mascots, school colors, and all of the other signifiers of community associated with them. The sense of ongoing community that keeps wealthy alumni and their donations connected to the university makes that investment perfectly rational. The broader sense of community created among locals who never attended, but still watch the games, bolsters demand for government support of universities and again, makes it rational to invest in the athletic programs and the sporting events that provide the means to create that community.

The Sound of Black

Sport as culture and its role in community building can be applied directly to New Zealand. It is unlikely that there is any other athletic team in the world that is as intimately connected with a nation's identity as the All Blacks are connected to New Zealand. Kiwis find it easier to recognize the All Blacks' flag than they do their national flag. In fact, over the last few years there has been a recurring debate over calls to adopt the All Blacks flag—or a close facsimile—as the national flag and when New Zealand won the right to host the 2011 Rugby World Cup, someone climbed up on top of the parliament building and replaced the New Zealand flag with the All Blacks' flag. The stylized silver fern on a black background not only flew up there all day, but no one complained. That really was not all that surprising. Kiwis are astoundingly passionate about their rugby. How else can you explain the fact that a country of just four million people can produce a team that far larger countries—some of which are fifteen times as large as Aotearoa—strive to match and often struggle to even compete with? The passion for the All Blacks is so all-encompassing that it is hard to find a Kiwi-born

---

*We hope that the discussion of the political aspects of group identity and the sociology of groups is still floating around in your head somewhere.

bearer of a Y-chromosome that does not spend every possible moment running around the schoolyard tackling anything too slow to get out of his way and dreaming of wearing the coveted black jersey.

That however, is not the best example to use. The All Blacks are an indispensable part of the heart of New Zealand,* but it is the All Blacks' *Haka* that provides the more interesting example of culture being used to create a shared identity. Quite literally, *Ka Mate* is a part of a traditional culture being used to create a larger shared culture for a nation.[†]

A *Haka* is a Maori call to battle and *Ka Mate* was created[‡] in the 1820s by Te Rauparaha, the high chief of the Ngati Toa Iwi[§] and it has been a part of the All Blacks' history since the beginning, some one hundred years ago. As old footage shows, for most of that history the *Haka* bore little resemblance to the modern version. Roughly twenty-five years ago, one of the Maori All Blacks decided that the *Haka* needed to be done right and he taught the others the traditional form and how to give it the passion of a warrior's challenge. Now it literally thunders through the stadium and you can see its effect on the opposing players.

A lot could be said about how the *Haka* creates a team unity that transcends what can normally be created in a national all star team, or the way it intimidates opponents, but the social effects of the way the *Haka* resonated with all those Kiwi boys dreaming of a black jersey is more interesting. That piece of Maori culture and heritage that was shared through the All Blacks became accepted as not just Maori culture, but as New Zealand culture. Though there is obviously a mélange of cultural, economic, and political forces at play in New Zealand, the *Haka* appears to be a significant part of the current and growing respect and acceptance of Maori culture as a significant, if not defining, facet of a New Zealand culture.

The relationship between *Pakeha*[§§] and Maori is certainly far from perfect and it would be impossible to argue that any relationship between colonizers and indigenous populations can ever be considered ideal. However, the rest of the world could learn valuable lessons from what New Zealand has accomplished. There are still significant political, economic, and social conflicts, but the average *Pakeha* knows and understands Maori culture to a degree that is far beyond the understanding of native peoples by all

---

*The left ventricle, to be specific.

†There is a link to all kinds of information on the *Haka*, including video clips and a history on the All Black Web site. See www.allblacks.com/.

‡Some suggest it was adapted at this time rather than created.

§*Ka Mate* is of the *ngeri* style, which did not involve weapons. Also, an *Iwi* is a social/political/spiritual Maori group. It shares many characteristics with a Native American tribe, particularly in its legal standing and the way it serves as a social and political entity, but there appears to be far less emphasis on language that is unique to an *Iwi* and a greater emphasis on spiritual matters and local community activities.

§§*Pakeha* are New Zealanders of European heritage and it is notable that these pale and sunburnt Kiwis frequently use the Maori term to refer to themselves.

The *Haka* in Texas

Euless, Texas, might seem like the last place you would expect to see one of the best examples of how the *Haka* creates a shared identity. The most distinguishing characteristic of Euless was the fact that it is close to the Dallas-Fort Worth airport and Euless Trinity High School was known primarily for how kids came and went as airport jobs brought their parents into town and took them away again. However, largely because of the *Ka Mate Haka,* all that changed in the fall of 2005.

As with all great stories, it started on a dark and stormy night. Actually it was a rained-out practice, but that is pretty much the same thing. The coach had caught one of the players showing another the video of the *Haka* from the All Black's Web site, and they were all talking about it. One of the many Tongan players on the team knew it well enough to start teaching the others and by the end of that rained out practice, something magical had started. The *Haka* united the team. The *Haka* united the school. The *Haka* brought alumni back to the stands for the games. It created something that all of the Euless Trinity Trojans shared, something they called their own, something that distinguished them as a group from all of the thousands of other high schools in Texas. In the fall of 2005, they adopted the *Ka Mate* and it carried their football team to the Texas State Championship.

There is a story here about the way this aspect of Maori culture created a sense of group identity for Euless, much as it has done for New Zealand, but there is also a story about cultural ownership here that has yet to play out. *Ka Mate* belongs to the *Ngati Toa Iwi* and is licensed to the All Blacks, which means that every time the Euless Trinity Trojans perform the *Haka,* they are breaking the law. *Ngati Toa* has yet to act, in fact at the time this textbook went to press it is not clear if they are even aware of what is happening in Texas, but in general the Maori of *Aotearoa* have been both aggressive and effective in using Western legal mechanisms to protect their culture and the legal relationships between New Zealand and the United States give the Iwi exactly the mechanisms they would need. Further, there are several aspects of how this high school is using *Ka Mate* that are unlikely to endear them to the *Iwi,* such as raising money by selling "Got Haka?" T-shirts. As it stands, *Ngati Toa Iwi* has every legal right to gut the treasury of the school, the school district, and probably several of the individuals involved.

Will they?

Should they?

but the most informed Americans, Canadians, or Australians. Maori language is taught in grade schools, including grade schools with few Maori students. How many Americans outside of a reservation can offer a greeting in Navaho or Chinook? How many Canadians know any of the First Nations' creation myths? There is also a great deal of respect that accompanies that knowledge. *Kapa Haka* groups, which perform competitively, are also common at all school levels and, to a great deal, irrespective of the ethnic mix in the schools. Many, if not most, of New Zealand's English place names and geographic references have been replaced by the original Maori names. And while it might seem trivial to point out that *all* New Zealanders grumble when they see foreigners sporting a *Ta Moko,* a Maori tattoo, the sense that these cultural referents are shared across ethnic lines goes a long way toward reducing the otherness separating Maori and *Pakeha.*

Is the All Blacks' *Haka* the explanation for the better than average state of relations between Maori and *Pakeha*? Is it why Maori culture and heritage gets more respect from the average New Zealander than the First Nations receive from the average Canadian? Obviously it is impossible to say conclusively, but the fact that every little Kiwi boy learns the words and the movements of the *Haka*, of the first part at least, so he will be ready when he gets that chance to put on the black jersey must help. The fact the *Ngati Toa Iwi* lends that *Haka* to all the people of New Zealand surely must serve as a bridge to help those kids, regardless of the soil under the roots of their family tree, grow up into voters that feel at least some connection to and at least some respect for all things Maori. The fact that every barkeeper in the country turns the TV volume up to full blast for the pre-match *Haka* must help sustain that childhood connection and it must nourish that bit of respect that goes with it.

There is no need to accept the authors' assertion regarding the respect for Maori culture in New Zealand. New Zealand filmmakers are better at making the case anyway. *Whale Rider*,[3] *River Queen, Once Were Warriors*,[4]—pick up any New Zealand film you might find in your local Blockbuster, and if it is a recent film funded and produced by Kiwis, it will almost certainly place Maori culture and society front and center.

Of course, the *Haka* might have nothing to do with it. It could all just be a practical reflection of a liberal political system and the fact that Maori make up enough of the New Zealand population to have some political and economic clout. It could be that in the treaty of Waitangi the Maori managed to retain enough assets to make them, their culture, and their interests a significant factor in New Zealand's future. Perhaps the sharing of the *Haka* explains nothing.

Regardless of what conclusions might be drawn from this or any other discussion of *Ka Mate* and New Zealand national identity, it is also significant in the way it relates to cultural ownership, the concluding topic for this chapter. Despite the role the *Haka* seems to play as a part of New Zealand national identity, it is not in the public domain. Its "ownership" is, in fact, legally protected.

Cultural Ownership

Culture has value. In addition to all of the innate aspects of culture that make it something that is valued, if not treasured, the fact that culture can be used to accomplish things indicates that it has instrumental value and that connects directly to the issue of cultural ownership. When something has instrumental value—when it can be intentionally used as a means of accomplishing something—it is likely, if not inevitable, that someone will attempt to possess it in order to control its application to the pursuit of economic, political, or other ends.

Navigating through this aspect of the relationship between politics and culture is more than difficult. Just referring to cultural ownership in a textbook is fraught with known and hidden hazards because the very idea that something that is part of a group's shared identity can also be owned is antithetical to the foundations of many cultures. However, many, if not all, of the cultures that disagree with the concept of **cultural ownership** must also

Maori and Pakeha perform the Hongi. The ritualistic touching of noses and foreheads symbolizes the uniting of two breaths of life together. Like the distinctive but undefinable pattern of *Ta Moko* facial tattoo, it is another Maori cultural tradition that is widely considered to be a part of a larger New Zealand identity.

contend with the reality of the global reach of the Western economic model that embraces and legally entrenches the ownership of pretty much anything and everything, from a particular shade of purple to the genome of a traditional food plant.* At the very least, ownership of culture must be established in the legal system in order to prevent someone else from doing so. This leads to the problem of having to redefine culture into things: artifacts, patents, trademarks, and other legal entities that can be owned, even when the idea of owning the things that are treasured by the community is foreign to the culture of the group seeking those protections.

In addition to often being contrary to the very nature of the culture that might seek to be protected, forcing groups to engage the Western legal tradition in order to prevent the exploitation of their traditional culture also leads to the problem of the system's inability to handle those aspects of culture that cannot fit into one of those Western legal mechanisms. Consider *Ta Moko,* the traditional Maori tattoo. It is both distinctive and impossible to define in any way that would stand up as a trademark or any other form of copyright, patent, or trademark, but once you have seen one, you can recognize another immediately. You know when you see one coming out of a Swiss tattoo parlor even if you could never legally define what makes all of those patterns of broad swirls *Ta Moko.*

BACK TO THE QUESTION OF "WHAT IS CULTURE?"

When it comes to the politics of cultural ownership, there are really two interrelated questions that one has to consider. First is the question of how you define culture. That question has to come first because even if we all agreed that culture should be protected, it is pretty tough to engage the second question—how you protect culture—until you know what you are including.

Consider some of the names of a few U.S. sports teams: The Florida State Seminoles, Cleveland Indians, Atlanta Braves, Washington Redskins, Minnesota Vikings, Boston Celtics, Kansas City Chiefs, Golden State Warriors, Seattle Thunderbirds. At what point

---

*Cadbury holds a trademark for the shade of purple used for its candy wrappers and the University of Hawaii raised a bit of a stink when it filed for patent protection for the genome of certain varieties of taro.

does the name or the icons associated with the team cross the line and become the exploitation of a group's culture? Is the war paint on the face of the fan in a Tallahassee stadium too much? How about the tomahawk chop in Atlanta? The profile of a Native American chief on a helmet in Washington, D.C.? If any of those cross the line then the horned helmets and furry vests in Minnesota must also, right? Or what about the Harvard lacrosse team? Lacrosse is, after all, a Native American sport.

Where the line is drawn is a tough question. Is it a matter of who makes the money? Is the Tiki God coffee mug—treasured because it holds twenty-two ounces of caffeinated sludge—acceptable since it was made in Hawaii by Hawaiians? Or is it simply a matter of being able to clearly identify the stake-holding group of a specific, definable item, regardless of the money that might be involved, and asking their permission? Applying that logic, the tomahawk chop cannot be protected because it is not clearly associated with any one tribe that might have the legal standing to claim ownership, but something specific, like the hula, can be protected. What then of all the unlicensed non-Hawaiian dance teachers teaching the hula to little girls in their ballet classes?

The various incarnations of a Western legal system seem to have proven reasonably effective at protecting things like dances, icons of cultural mythologies, or spiritual traditions, but what about language and linguistic referents to a culture? When it was discovered that a major tobacco company was selling a Maori-blend cigarette in Israel, New Zealanders were displeased, to say the least, and it did not take much of an expression of that displeasure to get the tobacco company to back down and pull that brand from the shelves. No one in New Zealand was happy that there had been a Maori-blend brand of cigarettes, but everyone seemed to agree that quickly pulling it from the shelves was a reasonable response to the situation. Similarly, when major league baseball was brought to Arizona, there was some suggestion that the team be called the Apaches. That was shot down, quickly, using the argument that no one but the Apache tribe had the right to use that name, but what does that say about the Yakima ski and sport racks that keep half the continent's Volvos securely centered under their mountain bikes? By the logic that got the cigarettes off the shelf and made the baseball team the Arizona Diamondbacks,* only the Yakima tribe should be able to use that name or at least they should get to decide who gets to use it and perhaps get a little cash in return. Tillamook cheese, Snoqualmie vineyards, Motel Puyallup†—it can be a challenge to find the name of a North American Indian tribe that is not used as part of a business name or trademark. How does that fit with the Arizona Apaches or Maori-blend cigarettes examples?

Beyond the fact that many tribal names are also used as place names in the United States, this question of the use of words or names as cultural referents becomes particularly

---

*Do note that no one seemed to care about the cultural rights of the diamondback rattlesnakes.

†"Pyew-al-up" not "Pu-ya-lupp."

difficult to manage in the face of the argument that language is either the key aspect of culture or it is the one and only true representation of culture. When it comes to political efforts to address culture, such as the efforts to preserve indigenous cultures around the world, language always seems to be the first target on any list. Quite a bit of time and effort is put into recording languages and teaching them to kids in order to keep them alive as spoken languages. How does that concrete acknowledgement of language as the central core of culture fit with cultural ownership? If language is the heart and soul of a culture, it seems reasonable that it should be the first, and perhaps most important, thing a group should be able to protect from exploitation, but can you copyright a language? And if you could, how would you charge royalties for the use of language? Maybe you could use something like the swear jar that your mother made you constantly feed your allowance into when you used those certain words; then again, maybe not. And if you could charge for the use of language, would you have to pay the French for all those extra vowels that never get pronounced?

Ultimately, we could spend forever and a day discussing the French vowel fetish and other imponderable questions regarding culture—including what is part of culture, and what should or can be protected against exploitation by others—but in the end, much of it boils down to political questions, political debates, and political attempts at resolution. Politics truly does seem to permeate everything.

KEY TERMS

Agents of political socialization / **315**
Cultural ownership / **323**
Culture / **309**
Political culture / **315**
Political socialization / **315**
Subcultures / **315**

CHAPTER SUMMARY

Political culture causes a great deal of difficulty for political scientists. While it is clear that societies share a context from which they make political choices and that this context is learned, it is not clear how valuable political culture is as an explanation for political phenomena. Political culture does have some explanatory value; however, it cannot explain all differences among nations. In fact, political scientists disagree about whether and how to factor culture into the study of politics. Despite the disagreement about political culture as an explanatory variable, it is clear that it is related to politics in three ways. First, culture can affect a nation's approach to policy choices. For example, a country's shared context can explain how it relates to other nations. Second, politicians can use a nation's culture as a powerful tool to achieve political ends and to establish group identities. Last, culture poses a particular problem as countries struggle over the question of how to deal with cultural ownership. Students should learn two important lessons from this chapter. First, while political culture can be an amorphous topic, it cannot be ignored. On top of the fact that culture resonates strongly with people, it is clear that it can have an effect on politics. However, it is important not to overly generalize the explanatory import of political culture when other factors may provide satisfactory answers. Second, quit asking about Hobbits when you visit New Zealand. It was just a movie. Get over it.

STUDY QUESTIONS AND EXERCISES

1. Consider how political culture can influence policy preferences within a country. What regional political subcultures can you identify?

2. The chapter discusses how culture can be used to build group identity. What examples can you come up with to demonstrate how culture has been used in this way?

3. What is political socialization? Which agents of political socialization have had the greatest effect on your view of the world?

4. Think about the United States' war with Iraq. To what degree, if any, did culture play a role in the decision to go to war, the public's support of the war, and how public officials discussed the war?

5. Why should students be wary of those who explain politics solely in terms of political culture?

6. Explain the concept of cultural ownership. What factors make discussions about cultural ownership complex?

WEBSITES TO EXPLORE

www.brotown.co.nz. Check out *"Bro'Town,"* the Web site for New Zealand's first primetime animated show.

www.civilsoc.org. Civil Society International is an organization that assists organizations that work for democracy and civil society in hostile countries.

www.fowler.ucla.edu. The Web site for UCLA's Fowler Museum of Cultural History explores past and present art and material culture to foster an understanding of cultural diversity.

www.haka.co.nz. The Haka Web site is all about New Zealand rugby.

www.uiowa.edu/policult. "Center for Media Studies and Political Culture," Professor Bruce E. Gronbeck's site at the University of Iowa, seeks to examine how political processes and technologies intersect.

CHAPTER 14

Birth, School, Work, Death
Your Moment of Zen™

In November 1987, the Godfathers played the Ballard Firehouse, a club in . . . Ballard, Washington, of all places. Known for grinding guitar riffs under angry, angst-ridden lyrics, the Godfathers were the perfect contrast to the giddy fascination with electronic everything that had defined the music of the decade. They also wore cool suits and greased their hair back. That cold November night, however, would not be remembered for the music, or even the odd theft from the nearby hardware store, but for the way the show abruptly ended. After the opening act refused to leave the stage and the management had to organize a posse from the audience to force the issue, the Godfathers quickly pushed their way through the crowd to get to the small stage and they launched into the first song even before the opening act's drum set was out of the way. A big-time band playing a small club, they were anxious to get started, worried about having enough time to get through their set before Ballard's 1:00 a.m. curfew for live performances took effect.

Unfortunately, they were too big of a band for too small of a club. Halfway through the first song, they blew out the electrical circuits powering their amps. Circuit breakers were flipped, but to no avail. Those big black banks of speakers just needed too much power. Someone broke into the hardware store across the street and dozens of orange extension cords suddenly appeared, running everywhere, over the bar, into the bathrooms, connecting some of the amps to different circuits. That got them through the first song, but ultimately the jury-rigged fix just made things worse. Halfway through the second song the band blew the main breaker for the whole building, taking out the lights, and everything else.

At this point the lead singer was so incensed that he climbed up on top of a speaker and shouted, "Tear the place apart!"

The response to that irresponsible, but in many ways predictable, incitement of an already riled-up crowd, was swift, immediate. It was the stuff of legends.

No one did anything.

The club was in Ballard after all. Known for the prevalence of "uff da" bumper stickers on cars driving five miles per hour, known for bakeries where old Norwegian men sat around making fun of old Swedish men, Ballard was not really a looting and rioting kind of place. Not even the pale skinny guys sporting purple Mohawks* were interested in actually breaking anything, especially with all the cops across the street investigating the robbery at the hardware store.

The lead singer was a bit confused, but not that easily thwarted. He took charge, pointing to some truly ugly guys in torn-up leather jackets and shouting, "You ugly #$@@&%'s. Throw that %*&ˆ# table through that %*&ˆ# window."

The young, appearance-challenged gentlemen complied. They opened the sliding glass door before carefully tossing the small bar table out onto the patio, but they did throw it out the window as requested.

And with that, the lead singer screamed some very complex, almost literary profanities and the band left the stage, never to return. That was how the show ended. The crowd, soothed by a cute bartender's bold and brilliant decision to open the taps and give away all the beer left in the kegs, elected a representative to negotiate a refund of the cover charge from the club owner. It all ended quite civilly. But then again, it was in Ballard and no matter what unnatural color your hair might be, you just do not riot in Ballard.

HERE'S WHERE THE STORY ENDS

Everything must end, even a textbook that students have grown to love more than beer itself, and we have spent a great deal of effort trying to create just the right ending.

We failed.

Jon Stewart ends the *Daily Show* with the Moment of Zen™, and even after we decided not to write a conclusion that focused on the role of satire in politics we left that in the chapter title. To some degree, we left it there just because we like the show and what better way to show our respect than throwing in another gratuitous reference to it, but we also like the way it ends the show. If we could have figured out a decent ending for the book, it would have been like the *Daily Show*'s Moment of Zen.™ If we could have figured out the perfect way to end the book, it would have been the textbook version of that one imponderable image, that one thought, that one quote that just made the reader stop and think.

We tried lots of things:

- A section on religion and politics that showed the uncomfortably extensive parallels between the Crusades and Bin Laden's Jihad.

---

*Unless someone uncovers photographic evidence, neither of the authors is going to admit anything at all about a purple Mohawk.

Politics is like the weather. It is everywhere. Everyone talks about it. We all think we know something about it but even the experts have trouble predicting what will happen next.

- A short chapter on conspiracy theories and alien abductions.

- A picture of a monkey trying to shove something that looked suspiciously poo-like into a ballot box.

- The reprint of an article claiming The Wizard of Oz was a political statement about abandoning the gold standard for U.S. currency.

- An analysis of one of those letters from Nigerian katrillionaires asking if you will help him recover his money.

- A short story about a robot, a priest, and a farmer, made up entirely out of quotes from the U.S. tax code.

We finally gave up, another one of those instances when the ideal crashes headlong into the real and you have to settle for something less than what you had hoped. The end of The Godfathers' show was close, but not quite it and we will have to settle for an explanation of what we hoped you gleaned from this most excellent of all excellent textbooks.

LIKE THE WEATHER

Politics is like the weather. It is everywhere. Everyone talks about it. We all think we know something about it but even the experts have trouble predicting what will happen next. The dynamics that drive it are complex and it has a tendency to dump unpleasant stuff on people's heads. Also like the weather, by carefully considering the underlying dynamics of politics we can understand how and why things happen even if we cannot predict it or control it.

In the same way that a good introduction to meteorology text tries to help meteorology students develop a basic understanding of how heat transfer, moisture evaporation, topography, and air pressure differentials combine to explain why the rain in Spain falls mainly on the plain, we have tried to provide enough insight into the human and social forces that drive politics so that you can leave the class with the ability to interpret the politics of government and everyday life.

This lofty educational goal, however, has to be balanced against the fact that this textbook is only an introduction to the vast complexities of politics. Most of these chapters could be expanded into textbooks of their own and there would still be huge amounts of material waiting for the next course. There is a lot left to learn, but at this point you can consider yourselves, Certified Minimally Competent.*

---

*No warranties expressed or implied. This certificate is free, but if you are for any reason unsatisfied, return it within ninety days and for a processing fee of only $14.95 it will be replaced, no questions asked. This certification expires upon delivery.

Novel   Film   TV Show

Fiction Appendix

APPENDIX A

Alice in Wonderland
Lewis Carroll (1865) [film adaptation: Clyde Geronimi and Wilfred Jackson, directors (1951)]

Sorry kids, this is one of those where you have to read the book. The Disney version is cute and all, but it leaves out all the hints and teases at the odd stuff that was floating through Carroll's brain. There is some serious social commentary hidden in this journey through an imaginary and quite insane world.

> *utopia* (chapter 2); *mediated reality* (chapter 11)

All Quiet on the Western Front
Erich Maria Remarque (1929)

This novel is part of the social, political, academic, and artistic reaction to World War I we talk about in chapter 12. Even though it sounds like this guy might be French, he was actually a German who moved to the United States and married a movie star. The idea behind this story—finding humanity in the enemy—is often imitated, though never with the finesse or impact of the original.

> *alliances* (chapter 3); *security dilemma* (chapter 3)

All the King's Men
Robert Penn Warren (1946)

After Hurricane Katrina, picking on Louisiana has gone out of style, but this book will

help students understand why the Bayou State has always been in the satiric crosshairs. If anything, the reality of the corruption and insanity is understated here, and students might wish to refer to *A Confederacy of Dunces* for a better insight into the raw comic material available in those swamps. Actually, *The Water Boy* isn't that far off either.

> *realism* (chapter 1); *institutions* (chapter 6); *presidency* (chapter 7); *Arrow's Theorem* (chapter 10)

All the President's Men
Alan Pakula, director (1976)

This is <u>the</u> film for understanding Watergate.

> *government* (chapter 3); *power* (chapter 3); *cockroach theory of politics* (chapter 11)

All Animal Farm
George Orwell (1945)

Some animals are more equal than others. There is no line that better captures the way that institutions and ideologies can be twisted to serve the interests of leadership.

> *institutions* (chapter 6)

Apocalypse Now
Francis Ford Coppola, director (1979)

Speaking of New Orleans, flying into the city is eerily similar to the opening scene of this Vietnam War movie. When the 737 drops down low over the swamp on approach, the

only thing that is missing is the "Flight of the Valkyries" blaring in the background. With all the refineries out by the airport, it even smells like napalm when you disembark.

alliances (chapter 3); *security dilemma* (chapter 3)

 Boston Legal
David E. Kelley, creator (2004–)

Denny Crane is William Shatner's best character, best role, best performance ever, and we are a couple of old geeks who love the original *Star Trek*. Not to be overlooked is the way that Denny Crane uses his supposedly failing mind to evade the restrictions of social and political structures—insanity as a source of power.

power (chapter 3); *law in action* (chapter 9)

Brave New World
Aldous Huxley (1932)

This is a must-read for any kind of examination of the modern take on utopian thought. Written during the hedonistic excesses of the economic boom that preceded the Great Depression, it makes some serious statements about the hollowness of the unrestrained pursuit of pleasure.

utopia (chapter 2)

 Brazil
Terry Gilliam, director (1985)

Warning: if you ever have the opportunity to see the four-hour director's cut of this film, pass. We are devoted fans of Gilliam, but this is one of those instances where some interference in the creative process by the studio executives saved the film and actually made it great. We seriously wish that someone had done the same with Peter Jackson's take on *King Kong*. Seriously, Peter, cut thirty minutes, and you would have the best movie in years. What? Oh, the plot of Brazil . . . uhm . . . well, the infallible bureaucracy makes a mistake, and a guy gets caught up in the chaos, sort of. Seriously, you just gotta trust us and watch it.

bureaucracy (chapter 7)

 Broadcast News
James L. Brooks, director (1987)

This is a pretty good one for getting a feel for the dynamic of the newsroom and how that might influence what does and does not end up on the TV during dinner.

dramatic imperative (chapter 11); *mediated reality* (chapter 11); *mutual exploitation model* (chapter 11)

 Bro'Town
The Naked Samoans, creators (2004–)

Good luck finding this in North America, and it really is too bad. It provides a great twist on the British-style, intellectual slapstick that made *Monty Python* such a hit, and it adds a touch of New Zealand's innocent, slightly naïve take on social responsibility to give it just that bit more than the laugh. One of its most interesting serious questions concerns the nature of satire in the relationship between minorities and dominant groups in a society. When a minority culture inserts itself into the mainstream through self-satire, does that help or hinder its acceptance as a meaningful part of the whole?

culture (chapter 13)

 A Bug's Life
James Lassiter, director (1998)

Call us naïve, but we suspect that if a kid ever actually encountered a bright blue ant that talked, hysteria would ensue. The grasshoppers are supposed to be bad, though the thought of Dennis Leary as a ladybug is actually the scary part. Kids are supposed to learn that they should team up with circus freaks to form a street gang.

> *alliances* (chapter 3); *collective action* (chapter 3); *security* (chapter 3)

🎥 *Caddyshack*
Harold Ramis, director (1980)

We have no real reason for including this movie in the textbook, other than it is the funniest movie that students might have never seen. Best golf movie ever.

> *cockroach theory of bureaucracy* (chapter 8)

📖 *Cannery Row*
John Steinbeck (1945)

This is one of those books that misses the target—not its target, our target. It is an excellent social and political commentary on life in hard times—a pretty good book even if it counts as literature—but it doesn't quite tell us enough about the collapse of the anchovy fishery to really drive the tragedy of the commons story home.

> *the tragedy of the commons* (chapter 3)

🎥 *Capricorn One*
Peter Hyams, director (1978)

This movie provides a classic example of what is meant by the term mediated reality. How do you really know what is and is not real if you haven't experienced it yourself?

> *mediated reality* (chapter 11)

📖 *Catch-22*
Joseph Heller (1985)

This is one of those rare stories where either the book or the movie works. The story attempts to capture the irrationality of war, but also can be interpreted in terms of power and the structure of society.

> *security dilemma* (chapter 3)

📖 *A Christmas Carol*
Charles Dickens (1843)

First, the Timmy in this story is not the Timmy from South Park. Second, maybe he should have been. This tale really could have used a bit of Cartman's eloquence and grace. Enough already—rampant unchecked capitalism is miserable—we get it.

> *laissez-faire capitalism* (chapter 5)

🎥 *A Christmas Story*
Bob Clark, director (1983)

The NRA was widely rumored to have bankrolled this seemingly charming tale of Christmas wishes. All Ralphie wants from the jolly fat man is a Red Ryder BB gun—but it seems everyone is saying no—and he has to deal with a bully who really needs shooting.

> *forceful control* (chapter 4); *preference falsification* (chapter 4); *safety valve* (chapter 4)

🎥 *A Clockwork Orange*
Stanley Kubrick, director (1971)

This is one seriously disturbing movie. From the choreographed rape scene to the brutal murders, it is supposed make us question where we draw the line between the needs of society and the rights of criminals, but the biggest questions it raises usually center around the exact formulation of the drugs Stanley must have been on when he made it.

> *personal nature of politics* (Introduction)

🎥 *Dick*
Andrew Fleming, director (1999)

This satiric version of the Watergate story that puts forth the novel idea that the scandal was all caused by the bubble-headed blondes that Nixon hired to walk the presidential dog should not be taken seriously—

unless of course, you are a die-hard Nixon supporter.

> *authority* (chapter 3); *government* (chapter 3); *hierarchy* (chapter 3)

The Dispossessed
Ursula K. Le Guin (1974)

This book might just be the best literary take on socialism ever. A must-read for anyone who thinks they might be either a socialist or a capitalist.

> *utopia (chapter 2); capitalism* (chapter 5); *socialism* (chapter 5)

Do the Right Thing
Spike Lee, director (1989)

Who would have thought delivering pizza could be this troublesome? Sal's pizzeria is the central location in Spike Lee's graphic portrayal of racial tension in Brooklyn, New York.

> *safety valve* (chapter 4)

Dr. Strangelove: Or How I Learned to Stop Worrying and Love the Bomb
Stanley Kubrick, director (1964)

Kubrick's twisted mind really works to perfection in this prototype of the "war as accident" story line, and it is unquestionably Peter Seller's best performance ever.

> *causes of war* (chapter 12)

Ender's series
Orson Scott Card (1977)

Originally appearing as a short story in the August 1977 issue of *Analog,* we leave it to the true geeks in the class to debate if the expansion into first a novel and then a series of novels was brilliant or tragic. The end of childhood and exploitation of innocence themes of the short story were powerful, but they get lost in the novel's and the series's focus on the nature of humanity, construction of the other, essence of souls, religion, and the meaning of life.

> *causes of war* (chapter 12); *culture* (chapter 13)

The FairlyOdd Parents
Butch Hartman, creator (2001–   )

Is there anyone better than Cosmo? We don't think so. This ranks right up there as one of the top cartoons of all time. Subversive, fun, twisted, but still innocent enough to let little kids watch—it is great.

> *utopia* (chapter 2)

Field of Dreams
Phil Alden Robinson, director (1989)

We say more than enough about this one in the text. Try reading chapter 2.

> *ideology* (chapter 2); *utopia* (chapter 2)

Fletch
Michael Ritchie, director (1985)

This is the best movie ever for one-liners. It seems that every line Chevy Chase has is a one-liner. We use its depiction of newsroom dynamics as an excuse for putting it in this textbook.

> *mediated reality* (chapter 11)

The Flintstones
Joseph Barbera and William Hanna, creators (1960–1966)

The modern Stone Age Drama with the Flintstones and their neighbors the Rubble clan. Fred and Wilma, Barney and Betty—all you needed was a bridge night. We were surprised that the kids didn't get their own series: "Pebbles and BamBam Got Married."

> *power* (chapter 3)

The Forever War
Joe Haldeman (1974)

Classic, award-winning science fiction novel. We reference it as a wrong example of the causes of war, but as the characters skip forward through time, and we see not only the way society changes but also the way normalcy changes, it has a lot to offer for that dreaded term paper about politics in fiction.

causes of war (chapter 12)

Forrest Gump
Robert Zemeckis, director (1994)

Stupid is as stupid does. This movie probably has the oddest spin-off of any feature film ever, the Bubba-Gump Shrimp Company restaurant. Today's students probably do not realize that one of the big talking points about the film was the way the special effects people managed to insert Forrest into real archival footage. Everyone was wondering if we would ever again know what was real.

government (chapter 3); *the other* (chapter 3); *politics* (chapter 3)

The Front
Martin Ritt, director (1976)

It is a question as to whether this or the original *Manchurian Candidate* is the best film about McCarthyism. Both tell us something extremely relevant in the post–9/11 era. Just replace communists with terrorists and the parallels are scary.

cold war (chapter 2); *government coercion* (chapter 2); *McCarthyism* (chapter 2)

Full Metal Jacket
Stanley Kubrick, director (1987)

This straight-up war flick really gives a solid kick to the "horribleness of being a soldier" story line.

alliances (chapter 3); *security dilemma* (chapter 3)

Gilligan's Island
Sherwood Schwartz, creator (1964–1967)

In the original *Lost*, seven men and women, including the hapless Gilligan, are stranded on an island after their boat is lost in a tropical storm. The real question is: If the professor can build a satellite receiving station out of coconuts and a car out of bamboo, why can't he just build a boat?

alliances (chapter 3); *anarchy* (chapter 3)

Gladiator
Ridley Scott, director (2000)

We're not sure if this is a great film or a horrible one. We suspect the latter. We suspect that too much cinematic spectacle and not enough meat in the story line will make it one of those films that vanishes from the collective consciousness by the end of the decade.

authority (chapter 3); *leadership* (chapter 3)

Great Expectations
Charles Dickens (1861)

In the grand tradition of British comedy, Dickens has to be the humorist we understand the least. Boy growing up to fall in love with a cruel woman and then lose everything. We just don't get the joke. Dark humor still needs to be funny. Try *Shaunn of the Dead* instead.

laissez-faire capitalism (chapter 5)

The Guns of Navarone
J. Lee Thompson, director (1961)

Great flick, but not much use in talking about the causes of war.

security dilemma (chapter 3)

A Hitchhiker's Guide to the Galaxy
Douglas Adams (1979)

This is the first book in a four or five novel trilogy that ruthlessly skewers government

and all things related to social propriety. Adams originally wrote this as a radio play, adapted it for television, and eventually packaged it into a book. It provides the perfect case study for the differences in story construction and the nature of comedy for these different mediums. Students should be aware that the movie sucked in comparison to the earlier versions, and we refuse to acknowledge its existence.

institutions (chapter 6)

Home Improvement
Matt Williams, Carmen Finestra, and David MacFadzean, creators (1991–1999)

Incompetent to the extreme, Tim Taylor is the host of a cable TV tool show. The plot of half the episodes can be summed up by the fact that he has his own coffee mug at the emergency room. This is one of those sitcoms that is actually good. The writing is good. The characters are good. The performances are good. And it has something of a soul to it, with Wilson and the family angle and everything. The reruns of this will be floating around for a very long time.

structures (chapter 6)

The Hunt for Red October
John McTiernan, director (1990)

Another great flick, but we use it as an example of how socialism and communism are misrepresented in terms of the cold war.

socialism (chapter 5)

It's A Wonderful Life
Frank Capra, director (1946)

Yeah, it's a classic. Whatever.

institutions (chapter 6); *structures* (chapter 6)

Jackass: The Movie
Jeff Tremaine, director (2002)

Take stupid people off the television and give them a movie deal. Whoever came up with this idea should really be shot—and as soon as we finish rounding up the reality TV people, Mr. Knoxville and company are our first priority.

politics (chapter 1)

Jerry Maguire
Cameron Crowe, director (1996)

Tom Cruise plays a sports agent who loses it all for being foolish enough to say something when he realizes that he actually believes in something. "You had me at, 'Hello' " is now officially the most over-satirized film line ever.

power (chapter 3)

The Jetsons
Joseph Barbera and Oscar Dufau, creators (1962–1988)

The theme music is supposed to be exactly the same as *The Flintstones,* but we're not sure if we believe that.

power (chapter 3)

Judge Joe Brown
Peter Brennan, creator (1998–   )

A bad version of Judge Judy, if that is possible.

civil law (chapter 9)

Judge Judy
Peter Brennan, creator (1996–   )

Bad. Worse than reality TV.

civil law (chapter 9)

L.A. Law
Steven Bochco and Terry Louise Fisher, creators (1986–1994)

This used to be the prime-time soap opera to watch. They never, ever let the lawyering part get in the way of the melodrama.

power (chapter 3); *dispute resolution* (chapter 9); *going rate* (chapter 9); *law in action* (chapter 9)

 ### The Lathe of Heaven
Ursula K. Le Guin (1971) [TV adaptation: David Loxton and Fred Barzyk, creators (1980)]

Forget the TV show, read the book. It isn't that long, and it is pretty good. Ask yourself questions about the power of social structures when you do. Actually, even though we mention this in terms of mediated reality in the text, it is probably a better example of the subjectivity of utopias. Wait, we do mention it in the utopia chapter. Somebody should have caught that. Why is there never an editor around when you need one?

utopia (chapter 2); *mediated reality* (chapter 11)

 ### Law and Order
Dick Wolf, creator (1990–   )

This must be the most ripped-off and spun-off TV series ever. It is also a fantasy. It is just not possible to have that long of a run of sexy female district attorneys and handsome male cops replacing the sexy and handsome ones who quit or die.

power (chapter 3); *common law* (chapter 9); *criminal law* (chapter 9); *going rate* (chapter 9); *original jurisdiction* (chapter 9)

 ### The Life of Brian
Terry Jones, director (1979)

Monty Python's second best film. It beats out *The Meaning of Life* by just a smidge. There actually is a fair bit of political story in here as the characters are caught up in a political struggle against the Roman Empire.

ideology (chapter 2)

 ### Logan's Run
Michael Anderson, director (1976)

This film is another one of those "be careful what you wish for" stories. Yes, everybody is young and beautiful, but that is because they are killed on their thirtieth birthday.

utopia (chapter 2); *bureaucracy* (chapter 7)

 ### Lord of the Flies
William Golding (1963)

Your high school English teacher probably told you this story was about the fragility of civilized society or about the animal in people and the descent into savagery. We say it is about the dynamics of anarchy. Who are you going to believe? Remember, your grade depends on your answer.

anarchy (chapter 3); *group identity* (chapter 3); *security* (chapter 3)

 ### Lost
Jeffrey Lieber, creator (2004–   )

How far can you twist and spindle a plot before it falls apart? Tune in for season three and see for yourself.

anarchy (chapter 3); *authority* (chapter 3)

 ### M*A*S*H
Robert Altman, creator (1972–1983)

This is possibly the best comedy/drama ever made. 'nuff said.

security dilemma (chapter 3)

 ### Mad Max 2: The Road Warrior
George Miller, director (1981)

Americans know this one as *The Road Warrior*, and most do not know it was a sequel. One of the best Aussie films ever made. We realize that isn't saying much, but it is a great flick, and the Aussie part should not be discounted too hastily. When Hollywood tried to make a *Mad Max 3*, they really stuffed it up. This is a seriously good story about anarchy and the search for security.

alliances (chapter 3); *anarchy* (chapter 3); *security dilemma* (chapter 3); *the tragedy of the commons* (chapter 3)

The Mary Tyler Moore Show
James L. Brooks and Allan Burns, creators (1970–1977)

This is another one of the newsroom television shows that have fallen out of favor—in fact it was the first one. It is also the one with the least to say about the dynamics of the newsroom and might be better used as an example of a feminist statement about the empowerment of women in a male-dominated society.

mediated reality (chapter 11)

The Matrix series
Andy and Larry Wachowski, directors (1999)

The Matrix films provide the object lesson that no matter how successful the first film was, some directors should not be given free rein on the sequels. The first movie is the perfect mediated reality, "how do you know what is real" kind of flick. The second two wallow so self indulgently in Christian, Greek, and even Egyptian mythology that there is little worth watching.

The Cave (chapter 2); *Plato* (chapter 2); *mediated reality* (chapter 11)

Monty Python and the Holy Grail
Terry Gilliam and Terry Jones, directors (1975)

This is the funniest film ever made, bar none—the best work by the best comedy team ever.

institutions (chapter 6)

Moon over Parador
Paul Mazursky, director (1988)

Little-known actor, Jack Noah, is working on location in the dictatorship of Parador at the time the dictator dies. He is made an offer he cannot refuse—run the country. One of those

pretty good films that tends to get lost in the mix and overlooked when it comes to scheduling old flicks on cable.

legitimacy (chapter 4); *revolution* (chapter 4)

The Mouse that Roared
Jack Arnold, director (1959)

A classic. Rent it and watch it.

world systems theory (chapter 12)

Mr. Smith Goes to Washington
Frank Capra, director (1939)

This actually could be a film about unnatural fetishes and obsessions. Monuments, monuments, monuments—enough already.

idealism (chapter 1); *institutions* (chapter 6); *bicameral legislature* (chapter 7); *filibuster* (chapter 7)

Mulan
Tony Bancroft and Barry Cook, directors (1998)

This is supposed to be a "girls can be heroes, too" kind of story, but that benevolently feminist moralizing just does not work, and not even Eddie Murphy can save this rather lame Disney film. If you want a Disney film with a strong female lead struggling successfully against a male-dominated society, try *Beauty and the Beast.*

the other (chapter 3)

Murphy Brown
Diane English, creator (1988–1998)

A comedy series about the newsroom. The dynamics of the news as a business are hidden beneath the comedic insanity of the quirky collection of characters, but it is there and surfaces now and again.

mediated reality (chapter 11)

Network
Sidney Lumet, director (1976)

This is probably the best film about the newsroom.

mediated reality (chapter 11)

 Nineteen Eighty-Four (1984)
George Orwell (1949) [film adaptation: Michael Radford, director (1984)]

Takes a light-hearted romp through the cheery little nightmare of life under the unblinking gaze of Big Brother. Government is everywhere, watching everything and everyone, and it is a crime to think the wrong thoughts.

cold war (chapter 2); *dystopia* (chapter 2); *utopia* (chapter 2); *atomization* (chapter 4); *government control of individuals* (chapter 4); *panopticon* (chapter 4); *peer policing* (chapter 4); *preference falsification* (chapter 4); *self-policing* (chapter 4); *bureaucracy* (chapter 7)

Nixon
Oliver Stone, director (1995)

This film got a lot of attention when it came out, but *All the President's Men* is probably a better film and is certainly a more accurate one.

politics (chapter 1); *hierarchy* (chapter 3); *power* (chapter 3)

Oliver Twist
Charles Dickens (1838)

Again, we don't get the joke. What is so funny about starving orphans and clouds of coal smoke so thick that they block the sun?

laissez-faire capitalism (chapter 5)

Once Were Warriors
Lee Tamahori, director (1994)

This movie depicts the struggle of trying to live when you are caught between a traditional society of warriors and the demands of a modern, Western European society. On the lighter side, the director was arrested, in drag, on a street corner.

cultural ownership (chapter 13); *political culture* (chapter 13)

The Paper
Ron Howard, director (1994)

This movie is a seriously good depiction of the business imperatives and structural dynamics of the newsroom.

mediated reality (chapter 11)

 Peanuts
Charles M. Schulz, creator

Snoopy—widely regarded as the most famous dog in history—and his owner Charlie Brown first appeared in print in 1950. This cartoon community continues to feature in print, television, and movies fifty-five years later.

security (chapter 3)

 The People's Court
Stu Billett, creator (1981–   )

How many synonyms for wretched are there in the thesaurus? Not enough.

civil law (chapter 9)

Popeye
E.C. Segar, director (1956–1963)

The original Popeye appeared in a 1933 cartoon, but made it onto television for a seven-year stint. The often graphically depicted brutal violence is argued to be one of the inspirations for the Itchy and Scratchy characters on *The Simpsons*.

security (chapter 3)

 **The Practice**
David E. Kelley, creator (1997–2004)

This show that came before *Boston Legal*, offers probably the best peek at the

unpleasant side of the law. Most of the drama was angst over the fact that these defence attorneys were far too committed to winning at all costs, and they were far better at it than they wanted to be. It lasted two years longer than it should have, but the Alan Shore character—who is now on *Boston Legal*—was brought in for part of the last season and made the extra forty episodes worthwhile.

> *power* (chapter 3); *common law* (chapter 9); *criminal law* (chapter 9)

 The Probability Broach
L. Neil Smith (1981)

Hidden gem, underappreciated—there are a lot of ways of describing this book. It uses that well-worn and often abused "parallel worlds" plot device, but it more than makes up for that by providing what may be the closest thing to a workable anarchic political environment that has yet been dreamt up.

> *utopia* (chapter 2); *anarchy* (chapter 3); *hierarchy* (chapter 3)

 Raiders of the Lost Ark
Steven Spielberg, director (1981)

Raiders is the quintessential action film, combining good visual effects with a story line that is more than strong enough to carry them. With the Nazis and World War II elements in the story line, there is probably a lot that could be said about the politics of war, power, and such, but we don't ever get around to that in the text.

> *mediated reality* (chapter 11)

 Red Mars
Kim Stanley Robinson (1992)

The *Red Mars, Green Mars, Blue Mars* series has a lot to offer for that paper you are being forced to write on the politics in a novel. Try environmentalism, socialism, self-determination,

terrorism, the role of technology in society, or the changing conceptualization of humanity, for a few themes.

> *anarchy* (chapter 3); *equality* (chapter 3)

 River Queen
Vincent Ward, director (2005)

Supposedly, this film was cursed. It did suffer from more than its share of production problems, but it is also a cinematic treat. *River Queen* won some awards, but none of the big ones. In addition to the cultural bit we use it for in chapter 13, it could also be used to discuss the politics of war, colonization, and race.

> *cultural ownership* (chapter 13); *political culture* (chapter 13)

 Roger and Me
Michael Moore, director (1989)

This is the documentary that thrust Michael Moore—who has sometimes been called the attack dog on the liberal side of the fence—into the limelight. Unabashedly political, this film would be interesting to talk about in the text box on politically effective protest. Michael is clearly protesting.

> *politics* (chapter 1)

 Saving Private Ryan
Steven Spielberg, director (1998)

Private Ryan is another "horrors of war" flick. In fact, the extended opening scene is probably the best "horrors of war" example there is, and if our description of World War I did not faze you, imagine, it was worse than Normandy.

> *group identity* (chapter 3)

 Secret Honor
Robert Altman, director (1984)

This film depicts a Nixon supporter's version of the Watergate scandal. The most telling point about it is that nobody remembers it, and it is almost impossible to find a copy of it. Did it really exist?

> *politics* (chapter 1); *power* (chapter 3); *presidency* (chapter 7)

Sex in the City
Darren Star, creator (1998–2004)

We suppose there might be something to say about the shock value of the naughty bits on screen, and there is the novelty of seeing a group of reasonably pretty women who obsess about sex as much as men do, but this has got to go in the category of shows that got very tiring very fast.

> *cognitive frameworks* (chapter 11)

The Simpsons
Matt Groening, creator (1989–   )

The longest running cartoon ever, maybe the longest running series ever—*The Simpsons* covers it all. From ecology to racism, pick a political topic and you can probably find an episode with something relevant to say.

> *politics* (chapter 1)

The SpongeBob SquarePants Movie
Stephen Hillenburg, director (2004)

You know, we really didn't want to refer to the movie. We were talking about the cartoon series when we mentioned SpongeBob. The movie really wasn't all that good. If you want to see the very best of SpongeBob, you have to see the imagination box episode.

> *power* (chapter 3); *laissez-faire capitalism* (chapter 5)

Star Trek
Gene Roddenberry, creator (1966–1969)

Despite all our self-deprecating jokes about being *Star Trek* geeks and all, this really was one of the most influential shows of the twentieth century. You could pick just about any theme in this book and find that one of the original *Star Trek* episodes has something to offer. The first show to put a black woman in a position of responsibility and command, it tackled the social issues of its time and pulled no punches.

> *utopia* (chapter 2); *federal system* (chapter 6)

Star Trek: Insurrection
Jonathan Frakes, director (1998)

While this may not be the best movie in the world, or even the best of the *Star Trek* movies, it does have an interesting take on the socialist commune as an idyllic utopia.

> *group identity* (chapter 3) *socialism* (chapter 5)

Star Wars
George Lucas, director (1977)

This is the movie to end all movies. A lot of people got caught up with the spectacle created with the special effects, but we would argue that it was the heroic story line—the humble farm boy following his heroic instinct and rescuing the princess—that made this movie such a phenomenon. The parallels with Christian religious beliefs were made obvious by the fact that Luke wears very Jesus-like clothes. The clash of the realist and the idealist hit all of the right chords with an American society that was in the depths of one of the worst economic and political times since the Great Depression.

> *idealism* (chapter 1); *realism* (chapter 1)

Star Wars, the other five episodes
George Lucas, director (1983–2005)

We can forgive George for not stopping with the first one, which was actually the fourth episode, and *Empire Strikes Back* and *Return of the Jedi* were both okay, except for the Ewoks.

But those three prequels were wretched. We didn't even watch the third one until it came out on cable. Seriously, George, legislative intrigue is pretty seriously boring. What made you think you could make it exciting?

> *idealism* (chapter 1); *realism* (chapter 1)

Survivor
Charlie Parsons, creator (2000–   )

Surprisingly, these are not the people to blame for the reality TV pandemic. The Norwegians—or maybe it was the Swedes—came up with the idea. Just to be safe, we should just forbid anyone north of Munich from ever making a TV show ever again

> *alliances* (chapter 3); *group identity* (chapter 3); *Arrow's Theorem* (chapter 10)

Team America: World Police
Trey Parker and Matt Stone, directors (2004)

This is a "love it or hate it" kind of movie. It either causes laughter that threatens bladder control or bores you to tears. We tend to like the more subversive and subtle parts of Trey and Matt's humor, like the way they turned the *South Park* movie into a satire of a Disney cartoon. This one was just too much crass "in your face" slapstick. The one funny part was the Film Actors Guild, but there just wasn't enough of that kind of fun in it.

> *socialism* (chapter 5)

To Kill a Mockingbird
Harper Lee (1960)

This is another one of those "must-read-even-though-it-counts-as-literature" kinds of books. There's plenty of discussion of it in the text.

> *politics* (chapter 1); *institutions* (chapter 6); *dispute resolution* (chapter 9); *law in action* (chapter 9); *law in books* (chapter 9); *natural law* (chapter 9); *positivist jurisprudence* (chapter 9)

Tora! Tora! Tora!
Richard Fleischer and Kinji Fukasaku, directors (1970)

This story of Pearl Harbor is not much use here as it doesn't really tell us a great deal about the politics surrounding war, but it may be the best of the World War II movies.

> *conceptual frameworks* (chapter 1); *security dilemma* (chapter 3)

A Tree Grows in Brooklyn
Betty Smith (1943) [film adaptation: Elia Kazan, director (1945)]

Ah, yes. Professors really like assigning this one, so beware and be warned. If you really like sucking up to the teacher, choose this book for your writing assignment. That said, for such a dreary story line filled with human misery, it is not that intolerable to read. The standard plot summary is that that the Nolans manage to enjoy life, despite . . . (insert unpleasantness of life here) . . . but something touchy-feely about family might be better.

> *idealism* (chapter 1); *realism* (chapter 1); *laissez-faire capitalism* (chapter 5)

12 Monkeys
Terry Gilliam, director (1995)

A disease has wiped mankind off the face of the earth, and only a handful of B-list actors are managing to survive in a soundstage that looks like a psychotic interior designer went nuts with chain-link fencing. Bruce Willis travels back in time to pull out his own teeth. Brad Pitt is all too convincing in the part of a raving lunatic, and the world still ends.

> *collective action* (chapter 3); *the tragedy of the commons* (chapter 3)

The Untouchables
Brian De Palma, director (1987)

A movie that uses the "Good cop versus bad mobster" theme. The gritty old realist teaches the idealist to cope with the reality of fighting crime in gangland Chicago.

idealism (chapter 1); *realism* (chapter 1)

Utopia
Thomas More (1515)

The original *Utopia* turns out to be a horrible and miserable place. The book is worth a read if only to drive home the point that utopias are subjective.

utopia (chapter 2)

Wag the Dog
Barry Levinson, director (1997)

This movie is an unconvincing attempt to tell a horror story about the mediated reality of politics. There are a lot of ways this could have been done well, but there are just too many holes in the idea that a president could create an entirely imaginary war. In the end, the viewer feels beaten about the head by the heavy-handed moralizing in the story.

legitimacy (chapter 4); *framing* (chapter 11); *mediated reality* (chapter 11); *spin* (chapter 11)

War Games
John Badham, director (1983)

Computer goes nuts and takes over the U.S. nuclear launch system in a classic example of the "war as accident" story line with a teenage kid saving the day.

causes of war (chapter 12)

The West Wing
Aaron Sorkin, creator (1999–2006)

One of the new, realistic political dramas, this series provided a reasonably not-outlandish depiction of what life in the White House might really be like. The drama is a bit overdone, and the sinisterness of the political confrontations is a bit over the top, but still, it's better than most.

politics (chapter 1); *institutions* (chapter 6); *presidency* (chapter 7)

Whale Rider
Niki Caro, director (2002)

One of the best examples of the cultural emphasis of the New Zealand film industry. There are numerous political themes that could be examined from the story, ranging from the clash of modern versus traditional cultures to the role of leadership. However, we recommend the *Bro'Town* satire of it where Jeff the Maori plays the Keisha Castle-Hughes part and has to save his Iwi from developers.

cultural ownership (chapter 13); *political culture* (chapter 13)

What About Bob?
Frank Oz, director (1991)

We had no good reason for including this in the book.

gridlock (chapter 8)

White Nights
Taylor Hackford, director (1985)

White Nights provides an excellent representation of the Soviets as the "Evil Empire" fictional depiction of socialism and communism. An emergency landing puts a former Russian Ballet star back in the hands of the big bad communists, and he has to dance or die. Okay, it's not quite that extreme, but they do hold him prisoner and just generally are not very nice to him, and it takes the sacrifice of a friend to help him escape back to freedom. Just remember that socialism is an economic term that is conceptually distinct from evil dictatorships.

socialism (chapter 5)

Why Not Me?
Al Franken (1999)

Franken pulls off this pseudo-autobiography

perfectly, and by portraying himself as an idiot rather than attacking the real idiots playing politics out there, it takes the partisan edge off. That makes it, perhaps, the funniest political satire ever written.

Arrow's Theorem (chapter 10)

WKRP in Cincinnati
Hugh Wilson, creator (1978–1982)

Another media as a business show with Les Nessman as the intrepid anchorman who pronounces Chihuahua—Chee-hooah-hooah.

mediated reality (chapter 11)

Woman on the Edge of Time
Marge Piercy (1976)

This is another one of those books that professors really like assigning. The story is littered with lots of complex ways to discuss power relationships and structural violence and to question the nature of reality. Basically, you are never sure if the woman committed to the asylum is insane or gifted as she struggles against the constraints the structures of society place upon her.

mediated reality (chapter 11)

X-Files
Chris Carter, creator (1993–2002)

Here is the ultimate alien conspiracy theory series. In addition to what it says about cognitive frameworks and the interpretation of incoming information, it could be used to discuss the role of secrecy in democratic governance, technology, and myth.

cognitive frameworks (chapter 11)

APPENDIX B

A Strategic Approach to Writing for the Classroom

James G. Van Belle | Douglas A. Van Belle

Most students are more than capable of writing a most excellent essay. Even if they have difficulties with the more mechanical skills of writing—spelling, grammar, and punctuation—they are usually still quite capable of constructing sentences and stringing them together to make coherent paragraphs. However, undergraduates almost universally abhor this seemingly simple task. More often than not the mere mention of a paper or essay exam in a syllabus is enough to start a terrified rush for the door. Even for the better students, a simple essay assignment may be a daunting, almost Herculean task. Why, if students are capable of writing these essays, does writing cause such a visceral reaction? And why do birds continue to fly south every fall when they could just land on the top of a southbound semi and ride I-95 to Florida?

Though there are probably several complex social and psychological processes that combine to cause both students and birds to behave irrationally, one of the biggest and most constant sources of the students' fear seems to stem from a more straightforward source, uncertainty over the content of an essay. There are several books and other types of guides that tell a student how to write an essay—formats, styles, citations, and such—but when it comes to what to put in those properly formatted sentences and paragraphs, the vast majority of students, even the studious and hard-working students, are clueless. A few have a natural knack for it, an intuitive feel for what a professor or a boss wants to see in there, but for most it is a shot in the dark and they all end up trying to hide it all behind the selection of a tasteful Book Antiqua font.

Combining the often-divergent insights derived from teaching introductory composition, teaching writing-intensive political science courses, and watching documentaries on bird migration, a lecture-style description of a strategic approach to writing is presented here. The primary objective is to provide students with something they can use to help focus and organize the content of a brief, report, or other type of essay. Obviously, every paper is going to be different, and it is impossible to tell a student what he or she should put in any specific essay. However, just as it is possible to teach a mechanic methods and techniques to more effectively use the tools of the trade to attain an end such as fixing a car, it is possible to outline a method students can use to more effectively construct an essay. By focusing on the effort to persuade the reader and adding a few other suggestions regarding the content of writing, students can make the whole process easier and more effective.

THE GOAL OF WRITING

Writing is a goal-oriented process, a means to an end, and it needs to be approached as such. In short, you are not just writing an essay, you are trying to accomplish something with your essay. Specifically, in writing an essay you are presenting an argument. You are trying to convince the reader of something. At the very least you should be trying to persuade a reasonable and open-minded reader that what you are arguing, what you are trying to say, the position you are trying defend, the opinion you are trying express, is reasonable. When you are writing for a boss, or judge, or banker, or client, you are not filling pages so you can get enough and stop typing, you are trying to convince them to sell this widget, to let my client go, to loan me this money, to follow this advice. When you are writing for a professor, you should also keep in mind that you are doing more than regurgitating the information that has been delivered to you throughout the course. Professors do not want brain vomit. They want you to use that information in a novel way. They want you to take what you have been given and form it into an argument that will convince your professor that you understand the material and its application. You have to use that material to convince your professor of two things: you know the topic well enough to be writing an essay about it, and that he/she/it should take your argument seriously.

How does this focus on convincing the reader of something translate into a strategy for writing an essay? Perhaps the simplest starting point is to use this goal as a point of reference throughout the writing process. When you are faced with the task of writing, ask yourself "what am I trying to convince my reader of?" Often this will help determine what material should go into an essay and how it should be organized.

For example, pretend you are sitting across the dinner table from your less-than-bright Uncle Larry. Everybody has that occasionally tolerated relative who occasionally shows up for a holiday meal here or there. Everyone has that uncle who is just a little slow on the uptake but does not let that get in the way of a good debate.

"Why do you have to go off to college? You don't need to go to college. I did just fine working at the gas station," Uncle Larry says.

You sit there, and for some unknown reason you feel compelled to explain to Larry why you went off to college. It is that effort at explanation that captures the essence of what you should be trying to do every time you write.

What do you do? You probably start with something along the lines of, "Going to college was the best thing for me to do."

A statement like this is more or less the topic sentence that everyone talks about when they try to teach you to write. Whether it is called a thesis, hypothesis, proposition, or something else, a topic sentence for an essay is nothing more than a simple statement of what you are trying to convince the reader to believe; in this example you are trying to convince Uncle Larry that going to college was a good thing. In a way, this statement or proposition is merely the simplest version of your argument you can make.

You know, of course, that Larry is going to challenge your assertion, so you need more support and examples to work with.

A crucial aspect of making an argument is to explain why your reader should believe your thesis. Describe the basic logic, the reasons why the reader should consider your argument to be reasonable. What reasons do you give to Larry to make him believe that going to college was the best thing for you to do? This can be thought of as the "because" portion of the argument, and a simple set of statements starting with "because" can be an easy way to get yourself used to thinking in this way as you write.

- Because — People who attend college, on average, make more money than people who do not.

- Because — People who go to college are more likely to find a job that provides full benefits such as health care, vacations, and retirement plans.

- Because — People who go to college tend to do less physically demanding work and are more likely to be healthier in their old age.

- Because — Going to college is the only way that I can get the job I want.

You have just laid out several reasons why Uncle Larry should agree with your assertion that going to college was a good choice. You have also just outlined your essay. In fact, you have almost written the first paragraph.

When you approach an essay for an exam or a short paper, you should employ this same strategy. You start out by saying, as clearly and simply as you can manage, this is what I want to convince you of. For an essay exam this can be as simple as "this is the best answer to the essay question." Don't be afraid to simply answer the question being posed. For example, a sociology exam that asks the question "Is the Internet good for society?" is begging for a straightforward answer. An effective response to this question could start by simply answering the question: The Internet is good for society. The writer then goes on to say that the reader should believe this answer because...and states what that reason is and adds a second reason, and a third reason, and possibly even a fourth reason.

That is your first paragraph. It clearly and blatantly states what you are arguing and why it should be accepted as reasonable. That first paragraph also outlines your essay. You can call it what you want, topic paragraph, introductory paragraph, or whatever, but that is all there is to it. Now, if you think about it, this is pretty much the same thing your high school English teacher taught you about an introduction to an essay, but what was probably missing in high school was the part about what goes in it. What is the logic behind a topic sentence, what is it supposed to accomplish? How can you write a topic sentence if you don't know what it is supposed to accomplish? How can you write that first paragraph if you don't know what you are trying to use it for? The first sentence of the first paragraph unambiguously lays out what you are arguing, then the remainder clearly states the logic so that the reader knows exactly what to expect from the rest of the essay. If this is done properly, a professor should be able to grade the entire essay just by reading the first paragraph. This emphasis on directness and clarity is one very important way in which this strategic approach might differ from the way composition is often taught.

When you are using writing as a tool for making an argument, subtlety is bad. Outside of literature, subtlety just doesn't work; it can't work. Why? Well, there is a practical reason. First, think about your professor. He/she/it is probably going to have to sit down and read at least twenty of these essays, more likely twice that many, and sometimes hundreds. What are the chances that anyone, robotic or biological, could sit down in front of all those essays and be able to tease out subtle details and understated nuances? Similarly, your boss isn't going to want to take the time to eek out subtle nuances from a strategy document. And do you really want to take the risk that he or she misses them? Be clear, be direct, and by all means state your argument early.

If the above constitutes your first paragraph, what comes in your next paragraph? Think of your next paragraph as your first "evidence" paragraph. What you do is you take this first reason, the first "because" statement, and give the reader the evidence. Give the details, and explain how this evidence demonstrates what you are trying to convince the reader of.

In your effort to convince Larry the first reason you gave him to explain why people should go to college was that they make more money. In your second paragraph you should tell him how much more money college graduates make. How do you know this? How quickly will that extra income make up for the costs of college and cover the costs of not working for the seven and a half years it takes you to graduate with your certificate in TV and VCR repair? Anticipate Larry's questions and critiques. Tell the reader the answers to unasked questions. Convince them that you have thought it through, give the details, and most importantly explain why it supports your argument. Explain why that evidence should make the reader believe.

You do this convincing with about one or two paragraphs for each one of the points you made in your first paragraph. Each "because" you offered in the introduction paragraph should have at least a paragraph worth of evidence and explanation. If you cannot fill a paragraph, perhaps you should revise your "because" statement to be slightly broader, or perhaps you should add something to it. If you cannot fit all of the explanation for the "because" statement into a couple of paragraphs, perhaps you should try to split it up or narrow it to make it a little more exclusive. Overall, you should probably have at least three "because" statements and three evidentiary paragraphs to support your argument. If you fall short, you might want to consider revising your argument to be a little broader, or try searching for some other evidence and other reasons it should be believed. Similarly, you should probably try to avoid going beyond five or six reasons, or seven or eight long evidentiary paragraphs that support your argument. If you have more than that, you might want to think about splitting up the argument, narrowing the focus, or using some form of larger organizational scheme like the one discussed near the end of this essay.

It seems simple, but that is almost it. That is really all there is to writing an essay. If you put together a first paragraph that lays out your argument with some specific reasons for the reader to consider it reasonable, then write a handful of evidentiary paragraphs, you are just a concluding paragraph away from finishing an essay that is about the right length for a one-hour, in-class, essay exam.

That leaves just one thing left to talk about. What should you do with your last paragraph? If asked, most students who think a great deal of their intellectual abilities will quickly say, "Restate your hypothesis like your composition teacher told you in high school."

Wrong. Absolutely not.

Your hypothesis is your topic sentence, the statement of what you are trying to convince the reader to accept as reasonable. If the reader gets to the last paragraph, if your professor gets to this last paragraph, and does not already know what you are trying to argue, you have pretty much failed. Actually, if your reader gets to the end of that first paragraph and does not know exactly what you are arguing and the logic you are offering to support your point, if he/she/it does not finish the first paragraph knowing exactly what is coming, you have not done your job. The reader should know your argument from the very first paragraph, often the very first sentence. It should be absolutely clear and unmistakable.

Instead of restating something the reader should already be quite aware of, you should instead remind yourself that everything in an essay must contribute to the effort to convince the reader. Don't waste space and don't waste the reader's time.

Does restating a hypothesis add anything for your reader?

Instead, what you should do is use that last paragraph to accomplish something. But what?

Well, here is where you have some options, and what you choose to do will depend a great deal upon what you arguing and who you are trying to convince. The last paragraph is where you can do some additional tailoring to fit the audience you are trying to convince. You could add little tidbits of evidence that don't require much if any explanation and don't fit in with your larger evidence paragraphs. This is particularly effective if you have something you know will strike a key with your readers.

For example: "And Larry, there is a party every night at college."

Larry will buy that. You would not use that to convince your mother, but for Uncle Larry, that might work.

Another thing that often works well is to use the last paragraph to demonstrate that you know both the strengths and the weaknesses of your argument, the scope and limitations.

For the going to college argument you also could acknowledge that college isn't for everyone. If we were making this argument to Uncle Larry we might use the example of a good friend from high school. He was more than capable of going to college, honor student, good SAT scores, and all that, but he was passionate about cars. Instead of going to college he decided to go to England for a couple years and work in a mechanic's shop. He came back and opened up a shop that repairs and restores British sports cars. For what he wanted to do, college wasn't the right choice. By showing Larry that you understand the limits of your argument, you demonstrate that you have thought through the entire argument, and your argument should be more convincing overall.

Keeping a constant and conscious focus on making an argument will almost certainly make your essays easier to write. Whenever you get blocked, whenever you have a question of what to put in, what to say, how to word something, just remind yourself to think of the argument, the effort to convince. In many cases just that focus can improve the quality of the essays. It will give you instant coherency because you are constantly organizing what you are writing around this goal of convincing the reader of something. This ties everything together because whenever you are not sure, whenever you have a question about how to handle something, you are constantly referring back to that goal of making an argument, convincing the reader of something.

LONGER ESSAYS

This strategy for developing the content of an essay, when combined with the structure outlined above gives you an essay that is about five to ten paragraphs long, just about the right size for an hour-long, in-class essay. What do you do if you need to write something bigger?

To write a longer essay you should still keep the focus on making an argument, keep the conviction that everything in the paper should be part of that effort to convince, and keep the basic strategy. All you really need to do differently is adjust the structure to something that can accommodate a lengthier, more complex argument. One of the best ways to do this is to nest several related, five- to ten-paragraph arguments within a similar structure that makes a larger argument.

Take a look at your evidence paragraphs; isn't your evidence paragraph really an argument? You are making an argument that explains how this evidence supports the overall point you are trying to make. Well, there is no reason that arguments regarding the evidence cannot be made in the essay form outlined above. In other words, look at the outline for the essay, then replace each evidence paragraph with an essay-length argument that makes a point supporting the overall argument, and suddenly you have a ten-page essay. Repeat that for each of those three essays, and you have a twenty-five-page paper, nest those within an even larger argument and you are approaching a dissertation. You have built a pyramid crafted out of these smaller essay chunks.

Don't believe us. Fair enough, most people don't until it is too late. Look at well-written research articles, and we bet that some form of this structure is exactly what you find.

You will discover something akin to the nested sets of essays described here. The research article is split up into small sections and each section has an argument that it is trying to convey information to the reader. A research article starts with an introductory section that states the question being researched and perhaps an argument regarding why this subject or approach to this subject is important. Then there is a section that presents a nested set of arguments regarding what other research is relevant, how it is relevant, why it is relevant, and how it relates to the question at hand. The next section is an argument that states how the author(s) decided to research the question and that section also probably tries to convince you that the chosen approach is reasonable. The next section goes into what is discovered and why you should consider it reliable. Finally the article concludes with an argument discussing why the finding is important or what implications it has for the question being addressed.

This research article is simply the nesting of small arguments within the context of a broader question. Nesting arguments like this has the added advantage that you can take this monster essay you have to write, such as a senior thesis, and break it down into a bunch of small, manageable parts that you can tackle one by one.

CONCLUSION

Using a strategic approach to the content of an essay can help many, if not most, students tackle writing more effectively, with less effort and better results. Though focusing on making an argument and organizing your essay as suggested above is effective, it is not a cure-all. Writing, translating your thoughts and ideas first into language and then into written form, is such a complex process that the only real way to learn to write better is by writing. This strategy, or any other help that might be offered for writing, can only be effective if applied, repeatedly.

Just write, then write some more. Your first assignment is to explain why migrating birds don't ride on the tops of semi-trucks.

NOTES

Chapter 1

1. *Star Wars,* directed by George Lucas (Lucasfilm Ltd., 1977).
2. *The Untouchables,* directed by Brian De Palma (Paramount Pictures, 1987).
3. *The Republic of Plato,* translated by Francis MacDonald Cornford (New York: Oxford University Press, 1981), 14–29.
4. George Orwell, *Nineteen Eighty-Four* (New York: Harcourt Brace, 1949).
5. William Golding, *Lord of the Flies* (1954; rpt. New York: Capricorn Books, 1959).
6. *Jacobellis v. Ohio,* 378 U.S. 184, 197 (1964), Stewart, J., concurring.
7. Harold D. Lasswell, *Politics: Who Gets What, When, How* (New York: Peter Smith, 1950).
8. David Easton, *The Political System* (New York: Knopf, 1964), 129–134.
9. See Sandra Guy, "McDonald's Issues Report on Social Responsibility," *Chicago Sun-Times,* April 17, 2002, 67; and Roger Cowe, "Rules of Engagement: Ethical Investment: A New Approach Will Help to Balance Financial and Social Demands, Says Roger Cowe," *Financial Times* (London), April 4, 2002, 20.
10. Matt Groening, *The Simpsons* (Fox Broadcasting Co., 1989).
11. *Roger & Me,* directed by Michael Moore (Warner Bros., 1989).
12. *The Politics of Aristotle,* edited by Ernest Barker (New York: Oxford University Press, 1981).
13. Aristotle, *Nicomachean Ethics,* translated by Terrence Irwin (Indianapolis: Hackett, 1985).
14. This is the approach of W. Phillips Shively's "little book," *The Craft of Political Research,* 4th ed. (Upper Saddle River, N.J.: Prentice Hall, 1998), which does a masterful job of introducing the basics of the political science research enterprise.
15. Earl Babbie, *The Practice of Social Research,* 10th ed. (Belmont, Calif.: Wadsworth, 2004).

Chapter 2

1. *Field of Dreams,* directed by Phil Alden Robinson (Universal Studios, 1989).
2. Thomas More, *Utopia* (Baltimore: Penguin Books, 1965).
3. Ursula Le Guin, *The Lathe of Heaven* (New York: Scribners, 1971).
4. *Logan's Run,* directed by Michael Anderson (MGM Studios, 1976).
5. Aldous Huxley, *Brave New World* (New York: Harper Collins, 1932).
6. George Orwell, *Nineteen Eighty-Four* (New York: Harcourt Brace, 1949).
7. William Golding, *Lord of the Flies* (1954; rpt. New York: Capricorn Books, 1959).
8. Neil L. Smith, *The Probability Broach* (New York: Del Rey Books, 1980); *Star Trek,* directed by Gene Roddenberry (NBC, 1969).
9. *The Front,* directed by Martin Ritt (Columbia Pictures, 1976).
10. Robert C. Tucker, ed., *The Marx-Engels Reader,* 2nd ed. (New York: Norton, 1978). See esp. pt. II, 203–465.
11. *The Republic of Plato,* translated by Francis MacDonald Cornford (New York: Oxford University Press, 1981).

12. Niccolò Machiavelli, *The Prince*, edited and translated by David Wootton (Indianapolis: Hackett, 1995), 48.
13. Ibid., 52.
14. Thomas Hobbes, *Leviathan* (New York: Penguin, 1985).
15. John Locke, *The Second Treatise of Government*, edited by J. W. Gough (Oxford: Blackwell, 1966).
16. Jean-Jacques Rousseau, *On the Social Contract*, translated by Donald A. Cress (Indianapolis: Hackett, 1987), 17.
17. Ibid., 24.
18. Ibid., 26.
19. Sun Tzu, *The Art of War*, translated with an introduction by Samuel B. Griffith (Oxford: Clarendon Press, 1963).
20. Kautilya, *The Arthashastra*, edited, rearranged, translated, and introduced by L. N. Rangarajan (New York: Penguin, 1992).
21. Karl Marx and Friedrich Engels, "Manifesto of the Communist Party," reprinted in Tucker, *Marx-Engels Reader*, 469–500.
22. Charles Dickens, *A Christmas Carol*, illustrated by Greg Hildebrandt (New York: Messner, 1983).
23. *Mr. Magoo's Christmas Carol*, directed by Abe Levitow (NBC, 1962).
24. Some, however, argue that the distinction between ideologies and theory is used to improperly denigrate ideologies. See Nancy S. Love, *Understanding Dogmas and Dreams: A Text*, 2nd ed. (Washington, D.C.: CQ Press, 2006), 9–11.
25. Adam Smith, *The Wealth of Nations*, edited by Edwin Cannan (New York: Collier, 1902).
26. *The Life of Brian*, directed by Terry Jones (Universal Studios, 1979).
27. Eduard Bernstein, *Evolutionary Socialism* (New York: Schocken Books, 1961).

Chapter 3

1. *A Bug's Life*, directed by John Lasseter and Andrew Stand (Pixar, 1998).
2. Brian L. Job, ed., *The Insecurity Dilemma: National Security of Third World States* (Boulder, Colo.: Lynne Rienner, 1992).
3. William Golding, *Lord of the Flies* (1954; rpt. New York: Capricorn Books, 1959).
4. *The Road Warrior*, directed by George Miller (MGM Studios, 1981).
5. *Lost*, created by J. J. Abrams, Damon Lindelof, and Jeffrey Lieber (ABC, 2004).
6. *Survivor*, created by Charlie Parsons (CBS, 2000).
7. Lewis Coser, *The Functions of Social Conflict* (New York: Free Press, 1956).

Chapter 4

1. *Moon over Parador*, directed by Paul Mazursky (Universal Pictures, 1988).
2. *Jerry McGuire*, directed by Cameron Crowe (Columbia/TriStar Pictures, 1996).
3. Michel Foucault, *Discipline and Punish* (New York: Random House, 1975).
4. *A Christmas Story*, directed by Bob Clark (Paramount Pictures, 1983).
5. Georg Simmel, *Conflict and the Web of Group Affiliations* (1908; rpt. Glencoe, Ill.: Free Press; 1964); Lewis Coser, *The Functions of Social Conflict* (Glencoe, Ill.: Free Press, 1956).
6. *Do the Right Thing*, directed by Spike Lee (Columbia Pictures, 1989).

Chapter 5

1. *A Tree Grows in Brooklyn*, directed by Elia Kazan (Twentieth-Century Fox, 1945).
2. *Robin Hood*, directed by Allan Dwan (United Artists, 1922).
3. For a good collection of edited Marx works, see Robert C. Tucker, ed., *The Marx-Engels Reader*, 2nd ed. (New York: Norton, 1978).

4. Adam Smith, *The Wealth of Nations* (New York: Everyman's Library, 1964), vol. I, 4–5.
5. Charles Dickens, *Great Expectations* (New York: Dodd, 1942); Charles Dickens, *Oliver Twist* (New York: Tom Doherty Associates, LLC, 1998).
6. Charles Dickens, *A Christmas Carol* (New York: Weathervane Books, 1972), 12–14.
7. Vladimir Lenin, *Imperialism, the Highest State of Capitalism* (New York: International Publishers, 1939).

Chapter 6

1. *Home Improvement,* created by Carmen Finestra, David McFadzean and Matt Williams (ABC, 1991).
2. James Madison, *Federalist No. 51,* 322, in Clinton Rossiter, ed., *The Federalist Papers,* (New York: New American Library of World Literature, 1961), 320–325.
3. Ibid.
4. *It's a Wonderful Life,* directed by Frank Capra (Liberty Films, 1946).
5. George Orwell, *Animal Farm* (New York: New American Library, 1996.)
6. Douglas Adams, *A Hitchhiker's Guide to the Galaxy* (New York: Ballantine, 1979).
7. Sidney Verba, "Comparative Political Culture," 513, in Lucian W. Pye and Sidney Verba, eds., *Political Culture and Political Development* (Princeton: Princeton University Press, 1965).
8. Ernest Barker, ed., *The Politics of Aristotle,* book IV, 1981–1982 (New York: Oxford University Press, 1981–1982), 154–202.
9. *Monty Python and the Holy Grail,* directed by Terry Gilliam and Terry Jones (Twickenham Film Studios, 1975).
10. *New State Ice Co. v. Liebmann,* 285 U.S. 262, 311 (1932) (Brandeis, J., dissenting)
11. For a good discussion of federalism, exit costs, and public choice, see James Eisenstein, Mark Kessler, Bruce A. Williams, and Jacqueline Vaughn Switzer, *The Play of Power: An Introduction to American Government* (New York: St. Martin's, 1996), 141–144.

Chapter 7

1. *The West Wing,* created by Aaron Sorkin (NBC, 1999).
2. *Mr. Smith Goes to Washington,* directed by Frank Capra (Columbia Pictures, 1939).
3. P. Parameswaran, "Filipinos Debate Shift to Parliamentary Rule," *Agence France Presse,* January 7, 2003.
4. BBC Monitoring International Reports, "Kyrgyz Leader Backs Strong Presidency as Constitutional Reform Gets under Way," *Lexis/Nexis,* September 4, 2002.
5. Gary W. Copeland and Samuel C. Patterson, *Parliaments in the Modern World: Changing Institutions* (Ann Arbor: The University of Michigan Press, 1994), 1.
6. For another look at legislative functions see Gerhard Loewenberg and Samuel C. Patterson, *Comparing Legislatures* (Boston: Little, Brown and Company, 1979).
7. Andrew Reding, " 'Baskin-Robbins' Voting; European Systems, with '31 Flavors,' Offer Citizens Better Representation," *Los Angeles Times,* July 6, 2003, 5M.
8. The Churchill Center's FAQs Quotes, www.winstonchurchill.org/i4a/pages/ index.cfm?pageid=435 (accessed May 15, 2002).
9. Max Weber, "On Bureaucracy," *From Max Weber* (New York: Oxford University Press, 1946).
10. Woodrow Wilson,"The Study of Administration," *Political Science Quarterly* 2 (June 1887): 197–222.
11. Frank J. Goodnow, *Politics and Administration* (New York: Macmillan, 1900).

Chapter 8

1. *Brazil,* directed by Terry Gilliam (Universal Pictures, 1985).
2. Robert Penn Warren, *All the King's Men* (Orlando: Harcourt, 1996).

3. Arthur M. Schlesinger Jr., *The Imperial Presidency* (Boston: Houghton Mifflin, 1973).
4. *What about Bob?* directed by Frank Oz (Touchstone Pictures, 1991).
5. *Survivor,* created by Mark Burnett (CBS, 2000).
6. For the U.S. case, see Roger H. Davidson and Walter J. Oleszek, *Congress & Its Members,* 10th ed. (Washington, D.C.: CQ Press, 2006).
7. Douglas Adams, *The Hitchhiker's Guide to the Galaxy* (New York: Pocket Books, 1985).
8. Anthony Downs, *Inside Bureaucracy* (Boston: Little, Brown, 1967).
9. *Caddyshack,* directed by Harold Ramis (Orion Pictures, 1980)
10. Jon Stewart, *The Daily Show with John Stewart Presents America (The Book): A Citizen's Guide to Democracy Inaction* (New York: Warner Books, 2004).

Chapter 9

1. *Law and Order,* created by Dick Wolf (NBC, 1990).
2. *The Practice,* created by David E. Kelley (ABC, 1997).
3. *Boston Legal,* created by David E. Kelley (ABC, 2004).
4. *Dragnet,* created by Jack Webb (NBC, 1967).
5. *Perry Mason,* executive produced by Gail Patrick Jackson (CBS, 1957).
6. *L.A. Law,* created by Steven Bochco and Terry Louise Fisher (NBC, 1986).
7. Harper Lee, *To Kill a Mockingbird* (New York: Warner Books, 1982).
8. Ibid., 75.
9. Ibid., 205.
10. Roscoe Pound, "Law in Books and Law in Action," *American Law Review* 42 (1910).
11. See Letter from James Madison to Thomas Jefferson (October 17, 1788). Last accessed from "Madison Jefferson Correspondence on a Bill of Rights" at http://1stam.umn.edu/main/historic/Jefferson%20Madison%20correspondence.htm, on June 4, 2006.
12. *Courts, Judges, & Politics: An Introduction to the Judicial Process,* 6th ed. (Boston: McGraw Hill, 2006), 44–46.
13. Harry P. Stumpf, *American Judicial Politics,* 2nd ed. (Upper Saddle River, N.J.: Prentice Hall, 1998), 5–17.
14. Islamic law is quite complex, and its different nations and sects have different means of interpretation and mechanisms for interpretation. See generally, Sami Zubaida, *Law and Power in the Islamic World* (London: I. B. Tauris & Company, 2005).
15. Prithi Yelaja and Robert Benzie, "McGuinty: No Sharia Law" *The Toronto Star,* September 12, 2005, A1.
16. Stumpf, *American Judicial Politics.*
17. *Rochin v. California,* 342 U.S. 165, 169 (1952).
18. Sir William Blackstone, *Commentaries on the Laws of England.* Last accessed on 6/4/2006 from the Avalon Project at the Yale Law School, www.yale.edu/lawweb/avalon/blackstone/blacksto.htm.
19. *Shelley v. Kraemer,* 334 U.S. 1 (1948).

Chapter 10

1. Al Franken, *Why Not Me? The Inside Story of the Making and the Unmaking of the Franken Presidency* (New York: Delacorte Press, 1999).
2. With apologies to *Mad Magazine.* www.ariekaplan.com/benandjerrys.htm.
3. Kenneth. J. Arrow, *Social Choice and Individual Values* (Yale University Press, 1963).
4. Barbara A. Serrano, "New initiative would set $30 fee for all vehicle licenses—Voters would also have to OK every tax increase," *Seattle Times,* May 8, 1999, p. B2.

5. Erkik Lacitis, "The man who has gone from rhymin' to Eyman," *Seattle Times,* March 6, 2003, p. F1.
6. Anthony Downs, *An Economic Theory of Democracy* (New York: Harper, 1957).
7. In 1946, the French sociologist Maurice Duverger demonstrated that "(1) a majority vote on one ballot is conducive to a two-party system; (2) proportional representation is conducive to a multiparty system; (3) a majority vote on two ballots is conducive to a multiparty system, inclined toward forming coalitions." *Party Politics and Pressure Groups* (New York: Thomas Y. Crowell, 1972), 23.
8. Joseph A. Schumpeter, *Capitalism, Socialism and Democracy* (New York: Harper and Row, 1976), 250.

Chapter 11

1. Lewis Carroll, *Alice in Wonderland* (New York: Norton, 1971).
2. *The Matrix,* directed by Andy Wachowski and Larry Wachowski (Warner Brothers, 1999).
3. Ursula Le Guin, *Lathe of Heaven* (New York: Scribners, 1971).
4. Marge Piercy, *Woman on the Edge of Time* (New York: Knopf, 1976).
5. *Wag the Dog,* directed by Barry Levinson (New Line Cinema, 1997).
6. *Capricorn One,* directed by Peter Hyams (Warner Brothers, 1978).
7. Earl Babbie, *The Practice of Social Research,* 10th ed. (Belmont, Calif.: Wadsworth, 2004).
8. Hugh Wilson, *WKRP in Cincinnati* (CBS, 1978).
9. Diane English, *Murphy Brown* (CBS, 1988).
10. James L. Brooks and Allan Burns, *Mary Tyler Moore* (CBS, 1970).
11. *Broadcast News,* directed by James L. Brooks (20th Century Fox, 1987).
12. *Network,* directed by Sidney Lumet (Metro-Goldwyn-Mayer, 1976).
13. *The Paper,* directed by Ron Howard (Imagine Entertainment, 1994).
14. *Fletch,* directed by Michael Ritchie (Universal Pictures, 1985).
15. *Raiders of the Lost Ark,* directed by Steven Spielberg (Lucasfilm Ltd, 1981).
16. Patricia Morrison, *Shortland Street* (TVNZ, 1992).
17. Richard M. Nixon, "The Checkers Speech." An audio portion and text of the speech was accessed on June 20, 2006, at www.historyplace.com/speeches/nixon-checkers.htm.

Chapter 12

1. *Mulan,* directed by Tony Bancroft and Barry Cook (Disney, 1998).
2. *Saving Private Ryan,* directed by Steven Spielberg (Amblin Entertainment, 1998).
3. *Full Metal Jacket,* directed by Stanley Kubrick (Warner Brothers, 1987).
4. Joseph Heller, *Catch-22* (New York: Dell, 1985).
5. Joseph Haldeman, *The Forever War* (New York: St. Martin's Press, 1974).
6. *Tora! Tora! Tora!* directed by Richard Fleischer and Kinji Fukasaku (20th Century Fox, 1970).
7. Erich Maria Remarque, *All Quiet on the Western Front* (Boston: Little, Brown, 1929).
8. *Apocalypse Now,* directed by Francis Ford Coppola (United Artists, 1979).
9. *M.A.S.H.* directed by Robert Altman (20th Century Fox, 1970).
10. *The Guns of Navarone,* directed by J. Lee Thompson (Columbia Pictures, 1961).
11. *Dr. Strangelove: Or How I Learned to Stop Worrying and Love the Bomb,* directed by Stanley Kubrick (Columbia Pictures, 1964).
12. *War Games,* directed by John Badham (Metro-Goldwyn-Mayer, 1983).
13. For example, Orson Scott Card, *Ender's War* (Garden City, N.Y.: Doubleday, 1986).
14. Ryszard Kapuscinski, *The Soccer War,* translated by William Brand (New York: Knopf, 1991).

15. *Mad Max*, directed by George Miller (American International Pictures, 1979).
16. *The Road Warrior*, directed by George Miller (Warner Brothers, 1981).
17. Lewis Coser, *The Functions of Social Conflict* (Glencoe, Ill.: Free Press, 1956).
18. Edward Hallett Carr, *The Twenty Years' Crisis, 1919–1939: An Introduction to the Study of International Relations* (London: Macmillan, 1949).
19. Hans J. Morgenthau, *Politics among Nations: The Struggle for War and Peace,* 5th ed. rev. (New York: Knopf, 1973).
20. A copy of Kant's essay can be found on Mount Holyoke College's International Relations Program's Web page at www.mtholyoke.edu/acad/intrel/ (last accessed June 8, 2006).
21. Johan Galtung, "A Structural Theory of Imperialism," in *Transnational Corporations and World Order: Readings in International Political Economy,* ed. George Modeliski (San Francisco: W. H. Freeman, 1979), 155–171.
22. John Steinbeck, *Cannery Row* (New York: Viking Press, 1945).
23. *12 Monkeys,* directed by Terry Gilliam (Universal Studios, 1995).
24. *The Mouse that Roared,* directed by Jack Arnold (Columbia Pictures, 1959).

Chapter 13

1. *Bro'Town*, created by the Naked Samoans (New Zealand: TV3, 2004).
2. Arthur E. Rowse, "Teary Testimony to Push America toward War," *San Francisco Chronicle*, October 18, 1992, 9.
3. *Whale Rider,* directed by Niki Caro (ApolloMedia, 2002).
4. *Once We Were Warriors,* directed by Lee Tamahori (Avalon Studios, 1994).

GLOSSARY

agency theory: Also called the principal-agent model, the basic premise is that bureaucracies are agents that act on behalf of the legislature—the principal or "client"—in a relationship similar to a business contract.

agents of political socialization: The sources from which a group learns the political culture, which can include schools, parents, the media, politicians, friends, and religious leaders.

agreement reality: Things that we believe are real even though we have never directly experienced them through our five senses.

alliances: An agreement between groups or individuals to join resources and abilities for a purpose that individually benefits the members of the alliance.

anarchists: Radical ideologues who long for a lack of authority or hierarchy because they believe that human beings are capable of peacefully intermingling and ordering society without broad, formalized governmental structures.

anarchy: The absence of any kind of overarching authority or hierarchy.

appellate jurisdiction: A higher court's authority to review the record from a trial court.

Aristotle: An ancient Greek philosopher and political theorist who categorized types of government and believed that people should work toward building the best government possible for their situation.

Arrow's Theorem: The idea that elections cannot be the perfect means of making decisions because the method by which the votes are tallied can significantly alter the outcome.

atomization: The deliberate isolation of people from each other in society to keep them from forming a group that could threaten a leader's hold on power.

authority: Where knowledge, natural ability, or experience makes it rational for people to choose to place themselves in a subordinate position to another individual or group.

balance of power: The way in which the distribution of power across the international system influences the pattern of alliances that tend to form in an anarchical environment.

bandwagoning: Opportunistic international alliances in which nations ally with the bully in order to carve out their own slices of the spoils.

bicameral legislature: A legislature with two houses.

bureaucracy: The position within the political administrative structure—the desk, not the person, that defines the role or function to be performed.

capitalism: An economic system based on the free market and individual competition for profits.

checks and balances: A system whereby each branch of government can limit the powers of the other branches.

civil law: The branch of law that typically deals with relations among private individuals and groups.

classic conservatism: A political ideology that maintains that unrestrained individual human reason cannot take the place of long-standing, traditional institutions.

classic liberalism: A political ideology that emphasizes the belief that people should be generally free from governmental constraints or interference.

cockroach theory of bureaucracy: The idea that bureaucracies serve the public as best as they can and hope to stay hidden from the media and well fed in the darker recesses of an anonymous bureaucratic government.

cockroach theory of politics: The idea that politicians do not want to be spotted anywhere where they might be stomped on; thus, when they see others caught by the media in a scandal they try to avoid getting noticed for a similar indiscretion.

cognitive frameworks: The set of instinctual and learned filters the human mind uses for sorting the mass of incoming information and selecting which bits it will recognize and pass on to the thinking parts of the brain.

cohabitation: Under the French political system, when the president is from one political party while a different political party controls the legislature.

collective action: Coordinated group action that is designed to achieve a common goal that individuals acting on their own could not otherwise obtain.

communism: A political ideology that advocates, via revolution, a classless, socialist society in which justice and fairness for the whole prevail over the interests of individuals.

conceptual frameworks: The personal experiences, preferences, and expectations that we all use to make sense of the world.

confederal system: A system where the local governmental units have all the real power.

constructivism: A theoretical perspective in international relations that holds as its fundamental claim that human beings construct the reality around them—the reality upon which decisions and choices are made—through language and communication.

criminal law: The branch of law that concerns relationships involving the government and its relationship with individuals and organizations.

cross-cutting cleavages: When a group contains many different points of conflict, thus allowing people to find many points of agreement and conflict within the group.

cultural ownership: The idea that something that is part of a group's shared identity can also be owned.

delegates: Representatives who attempt to do exactly what their constituents want.

democratic peace: The observation that liberal democratic political regimes do not fight one another.

democratic socialism: A political ideology that advocates for a socialist state through democratic means.

direct democracy: A political system in which all citizens gather together to share perspectives, debate, and actually vote on policies.

dispute resolution: The role of courts to peacefully settle disputes and keep order in society.

divided government: When one political party controls the presidency and another party controls either all or part of the legislature.

dramatic imperative: The need for commercial news outlets to focus on rare and unusual events that have a tremendous impact on people in order to draw an audience.

enlightened self-interest: The idea that people will restrain their self-interest in recognition of the need to preserve a common resource.

experiential reality: Things that we directly experience through our five senses.

fascism: A political ideology that argues for the supremacy and purity of one group of people or nationality in a society.

federal system: Systems where the final authority for at least some aspects of government are left to the local or subnational level.

feudalism: An economic system under which peasants raise crops and livestock on small plots within the landlord's estate and are obligated to give a substantial percentage of their production to the landlord in exchange for protection.

filibuster: A delaying tactic used by a senator or a group of senators—who indefinitely talk about the bill—to frustrate the proponents of the bill and ensure defeat of the measure.

first-past-the-post system: An electoral system where the candidate with the most votes wins regardless of whether that person has a majority of the votes cast; there is no run-off election.

foreign policy analysis: A theoretical perspective in international relations that holds that understanding how those decisions are made within the structure, process, and context of domestic politics is essential for understanding international politics.

framing: The use of a speech to provide a cognitive framework for understanding an issue, policy, or candidate to predispose people to interpret a myriad of facts and snippets in one way rather than another.

geographic representation: A legislature which is divided according to geography, in which people are represented by the area they live in.

gerrymandering: The process of intentionally drawing districts to gain a partisan advantage.

going rate: When judges, through past sentencing, set the context for plea bargaining as defense attorneys and prosecutors negotiate about what the appropriate penalty should be for an offense for which a plaintiff pleads guilty.

government: The creation of institutions or structures to provide the security that people continually need; the result of a group's need to institutionalize, or make permanent, its power.

gridlock: When the checks and balances within the presidential system work too well so that they not only prevent one institution from overwhelming the others, but also prevent anyone from doing much of anything.

group identity: The degree to which members identify with a group, and conversely, identify who is not part of that group, a process that affects the group's strength, cohesiveness, and survival.

hegemon: A dominant power, either an individual or, in the case of international politics, a country powerful enough to dominate all others.

hierarchy: A societal structure that elevates someone or some group to a position of authority over others.

Hobbes, Thomas: An English political theorist who believed that without government, life would be chaos.

humanist: An idealist who is interested in and motivated by concern for the broader human condition and the quality of people's lives.

idealism: A way of looking at the world where the focus is on what we would like to do; what we would like the world to be. Also refers to a theoretical perspective in international relations that stresses the quest for peace.

idealist period: The two decades between the world wars that were marked by the effort to envision and attain a perfectly peaceful world.

ideological representation: Representation in which people's belief is the main concern to leadership.

ideology: A body of work aimed at organizing and directing goal-oriented action.

immobilism: When, because of the complexity and fragility of a ruling coalition, it becomes nearly impossible to enact any kind of coherent policies out of fear that a coalition party will break away and force the government to collapse.

imperial presidency: The accumulation of tremendous power in the presidency at the expense of the other branches of government, especially the legislative branch.

initiatives: Questions that are put on the ballot by citizens, usually after some type of qualification process, for example, the collection of a significant number of signatures on a petition.

injunctive power: The power of courts to stop governments, individuals, or groups from acting.

inquisitorial system: In a civil law system, a prolonged pretrial investigative process.

institutions: The organizational structures through which political power is exercised.

iron triangle: The situation where the bureaucracy is captured and redirected to focus on the needs of an interest group rather than on the public interest or even its original mandate.

judicial review: The power to declare laws and government acts to be in violation of the nation's constitution or in some other way illegal under the structure of the country.

jurisprudence: A philosophy of law.

laissez-faire capitalism: An economic system allowing very little, if any, government involvement, interference, or regulation.

law in action: How laws are applied and enforced in the real world.

law in books: The laws as they are written.

League of Nations: An international institution created after World War I that attempted to bring nations together to peaceably resolve conflict in a form of collective security.

legitimacy: People's voluntary acceptance of their government and its exercise of authority.

Locke, John: An English philosopher and political theorist who believed that people hand over only a limited number of their rights to the government in exchange for protection of their person and property.

Machiavelli, Niccolò: An Italian political theorist often referred to as the father of the modern theoretical tradition known as realism.

majoritarianism: Rule by the majority.

Marx, Karl: A German economist, theorist, sociologist, and philosopher most notable for his works criticizing capitalism and advocating communism, a classless, collective socialist society.

means of production: The mechanisms for transforming labor into wealth.

median voter: The one voter in the center of the ideological spectrum.

mediated reality: Reality that comes to us through channels of information flow, primarily through the news media, and our understanding of how information is selected, sorted, and presented to us through the news media.

minority government: When the majority party does not share power with any other party, but relies on an agreement where another party will provide support, or will abstain from voting if there is ever a no-confidence vote.

multi-party systems: A system comprised of multiple, distinct, and officially recognized groups, otherwise known as political parties.

mutual exploitation model: The idea that the news media exploit elites by using them for cheap sources of news that they know will interest the public while, at the same time, the elites exploit the news media by using them to communicate with the public and present a public image that will help their political, economic, or social ambitions.

natural law: A type of jurisprudence that presumes that there is some higher law, which originates with God or nature, and that this higher law is discoverable by the use of reason.

original jurisdiction: A court's authority to be the first tribunal to hear a case.

"the other": Someone who is identified as an outsider and not part of the group, defined as a means of initiating conflict, and is therefore identified as the enemy.

panopticon: A social mechanism of control where people know that while they are not watched all the time, they may be watched at any time.

parliamentary system: A system in which there is a fusion of legislative and executive institutions.

peer policing: A system in which people police each other.

Plato: An ancient Greek philosopher and political theorist who believed that the best form of government was one where enlightened philosopher-kings should rule.

policy stability: When the social and economic environments within the country tend to be very consistent over time.

polis: The ancient Greek notion of a state or country.

political capital: An individual's or institution's reserve of power that can be called upon to achieve political goals.

political culture: The shared social context from which people make political choices.

political socialization: The process by which the group teaches the shared context to members of society.

political theory: A body of work aimed at developing knowledge about politics and political systems.

politico: A person active in party politics.

politics: Individual or combined actions of individuals, governments, and/or groups, that are aimed at getting what they want accomplished; when those actions have public consequences.

pork-barrel politics: Where representatives use their political office to bring federal money to their districts through projects and jobs.

positivist jurisprudence: A type of jurisprudence that views law as simply the command or will of the recognized sovereign authority of the state.

power: The ability to get something done.

preference falsification: When people hide the way they truly feel while publicly expressing what those in power want them to communicate.

presidency: An executive institution that includes all formal and informal powers; the offices, the staffs, and the historical precedents that define it.

presidential system: A system in which there is a separation between legislative and executive institutions.

prime minister: A member of parliament, who, as the leader of the winning party in the parliament, exercises some of the functions of a chief executive.

principal-agent model: Also called agency theory, the basic premise that bureaucracies are agents that act on behalf of the legislature—the principal or "client"—in a relationship similar to a business contract.

private law: Law that is concerned with the relations among private individuals and private organizations.

proportional representation: A system in which there is representation of all parties in a legislature in proportion to their popular vote.

public law: Law that concerns relationships involving the government and its relationship with individuals and organizations.

realism: A way of looking at the world where the focus is on what we are able to do; what is possible for the world to be. Also refers to a theoretical perspective in international relations that views international politics as a strategy game.

realist jurisprudence: A school of jurisprudence in which the key to understanding the judicial system is to understand the tremendous amount of discretion that is available to legal actors.

referenda: Questions that legislatures put on the ballot for people to vote on.

reform liberalism: A political ideology that argues that within a capitalist system, government should play a role in regulating the economy and removing major inequalities.

regime security: The leaders' ability to protect their hold on power.

republic: A government in which decisions are made by representatives of the citizens rather than by the citizens themselves. Also refers to a country without a monarch or an authoritarian leader.

revolutions: Mass uprisings focused on the goal of tearing down and replacing the current government.

Rousseau, Jean-Jacques: A French philosopher and political theorist who argued that society should be governed according to the general will rather than by a majority of people voting for their own interests.

safety valve: A mechanism that allows people to blow off steam in order to avoid larger conflict.

scientific method: A specific set of rules and processes for pursuing knowledge with observation, hypothesis-building, experimentation, and replication.

security: The ability to protect oneself and one's property.

self-policing: A social mechanism where only a few enforcers are needed to maintain control of the population because the fear of being punished keeps people in line.

separation of powers: A system designed so that no one branch of government can become too powerful over the others.

shadow government: A type of oversight or checking performed in a parliamentary system by those members of the minority party who would take the office if that party were to capture the majority.

shari'a: The system of Islamic law.

Smith, Adam: An English economist, whose *Wealth of Nations* argued that individual rational choices in a free market are the ideal way to foster efficient economic activity.

socialism: An economic system in which society controls the means of production.

socially responsible investing: The purchasing of stock in corporations or the acquiring of proxy votes from willing corporate stockholders by groups seeking to change or influence the direction of corporate policies.

sophist: One who in ancient Greece taught promising young men practical skills, such as rhetoric, so that they could be successful in public life; they did not focus on metaphysics or ethics.

spin: The use of a speech to provide a cognitive framework for understanding an issue, policy, or candidate to predispose people to interpret a myriad of facts and snippets in one way rather than another.

stag hunt: A commonly used parable that demonstrates how the interdependence of actions and choices affects collective efforts to attain a goal.

state security: The ability at the governmental level to protect borders and governmental structures from outside threats.

statutory interpretation: When courts must interpret what a law precisely means to maintain specificity.

structures: Basic elements that governments need in order to govern, which determine, enable, and limit how the particulars of the government take shape.

subcultures: Smaller cultures within the main political culture.

Sun Tzu: A Chinese political theorist whose *Art of War* is the oldest secular text still in existence.

tragedy of the commons: A problem that demonstrates how the rational choices of individuals collide with the needs or interests of the larger community.

two-party system: A system that favors moderate political parties that can create coalitions to gain sizeable amounts of voters.

tyranny of the majority: An unrestrained majority that bands together to rule a society with a ferocity and cruelty comparable to a dictator.

unicameral legislature: A legislature with one house.

unitary system: A system in which sovereignty and authority rest quite clearly with the national government.

unity government: When the two major parties, though in opposition, work together to achieve a higher national purpose.

utopia: An ideal world.

vote of no confidence: A parliamentary device by which the government can be dissolved by a simple majority vote of the legislature.

winner-take-all: An electoral system in which there is no proportional representation.

world systems theory: The idea that politics occurs within an economic structure defined by exploitative trade relationships, with corporate, class, and multinational entities defining the units of action.

INDEX

Page numbers followed by *n* indicate a reference to footnoted text.